Psychological Theories and Human Learning

SECOND EDITION

Psychological Theories and Human Learning

SECOND EDITION*

*Parts of which have been purloined from a 1972 book with the
pretentious title *Psychological Theories and Human Learning:
Kongor's Report*, written by Kongor himself
(or herself—we were never quite sure)

Guy R. Lefrancois

The University of Alberta

Brooks/Cole Publishing Company
Monterey, California

Brooks/Cole Publishing Company
A Division of Wadsworth, Inc.

Printed in the United States of America
10 9 8

Library of Congress Cataloging in Publication Data

Lefrançois, Guy R.
  Psychological theories and human learning.

  Rev. ed. of: Psychological theories and
human learning. 1972.
  Bibliography: p.
  Includes index.
  1. Learning, Psychology of.   I. Title.
LB1051.L567   1982   153.1'5   81-15511
ISBN 0-8185-0501-X   AACR2

Subject Editor: *C. Deborah Laughton*
Manuscript Editor: *William Waller*
Production Editor: *John Bergez*
Interior Design: *Angela Lee*
Cover Design: *Ron Grauer*
Technical Illustrations: *Tim Keenan*
Cartoons: *Tony Hall*
Typesetting: *Graphic Typesetting Service, Los Angeles*

Photos of Wilhelm Wundt (p. 21), Ivan Petrovich Pavlov (p. 24), B. F. Skinner (p. 46), and Jean
Piaget (p. 182) courtesy of The Bettman Archive, Inc. Photo of Edwin Guthrie (p. 30) courtesy of
the University of Washington. Photos of Edward Thorndike (p. 36) and Wolfgang Kohler (p. 142,
middle photo) courtesy of The Granger Collection, New York. Photo of John Broadus Watson (p.
27) courtesy of Culver Pictures, Inc. Photo of Clark Hull (p. 76) courtesy of the Yale University
Library. Photos of Kenneth Wartinbee Spence (p. 85) and Kurt Lewin (p. 148) courtesy of the
University of Iowa Archives. Photo of Donald Olding Hebb (p. 106) courtesy of McGin University
Archives, Montreal. Photo of Edward Chace Tolman (p. 134) by Dorothy Moore. Reproduced by
permission of the University Archivist, The Bancroft Library, University of California, Berkeley.
Photos of Kurt Koffka and Max Wertheimer (p. 142) courtesy of the Smith College Archives and
United Press International, Inc.

To pigs rampant, turkeys *glissant*,
and other noble but beleaguered creatures

An Explanation

Nobody has time to read prefaces anymore, but there are still a few who will stop and look at an explanation. Or a confession.

This is both.

I confess that I didn't write all of this book. Kongor (M-III 216,784,912, LVKX4) wrote the first edition. And now I have stolen pieces of it (including a piece of the title and a piece of the flag), added some of my own pieces, and talked a soft editor into publishing it as though it were entirely mine.

Let me explain. Kongor came here from Androneas (third solar system) in the spring of 1970. He was a behavioral scientist sent here by his superiors to discover the dominant life form and to compile a report on its behavior.* I was the first human he met. We became friends, and he left parts of the report with me when he was recalled. That became the first edition of this book.

Now, an entire decade later, much of what Kongor originally wrote is misleading, inaccurate, or irrelevant—hence this second edition. Kongor promised to come back when he left and also to sonarduct the remainder of the report back to Earth. (Ah, the books I could have written had he done so!) Evidently, aliens are not always true to their word. Can you blame me, then, for having purloined a few insignificant passages from what was really a very dull and pointless report in any case?

About the chapter openings. Some years ago I wrote a book on adolescents (1976; revised 1981). In the preface I wrote that the entire thing was a rather long letter to my grandmother and implied, perhaps a little strongly, that her opinions were not always very valid. In response to that preface and to another book (on children), Tony Hall produced the accompanying cartoons.

And my grandmother sent Pouf, the dog, after me.

She was upset.

*That Kongor was (is) male has never been clearly established, in spite of what my grandmother suspects following Kongor's disappearance during the dance that Saturday. Nor do we have any convincing reason to believe him/her female. And "it" is somehow too demeaning for him. Hence the male appellation.

I apologized later, although I'm sure my grandmother never understood the depth of my regret. Subsequently we became friends again. She now understands that I have the utmost respect for her. And I almost always let her read what I write before it's published. She always responds. Sometimes she's very loving; at other times she threatens to send the dog after me again (he's part wolf and part stupid). Often she writes me long letters telling me why she's so loving—or why, if it wasn't such a bother, she might feed me to the dog.

So, the chapters in this book open with excerpts from letters she wrote me after reading parts of my manuscript, or pieces of my replies, or pieces from other letters and other replies.

If you want to get to the meat (what a reprehensible image) of the book a little faster, you can ignore the chapter openings.

About the flag. It is really just a bit of a rag that Kongor planted near the beaver dam close to the southwest corner of the northwest quarter of Section 15, Township 48, Range 23, west of the 4th Meridian. It is made of synthetic fibers and boasts both a pig rampant and a turkey *glissant* on a field of flowers that look suspiciously like dandelions.

It's on the cover.

A Bit of a Preface

This book is a survey and interpretation of some of the important theoretical positions in the psychology of learning. It treats representative stimulus-response and cognitive theories; evaluates them systematically in accordance with important criteria presented in the first chapter; presents current research in artificial intelligence, memory, motivation, and social learning; and concludes with an overall summary and integration. The emphasis throughout is on clarity of presentation, relevance of topics, and maintenance of high interest. This emphasis on motivating the reader has led me to begin more gently than I end. Thus, the first chapters contain somewhat more humor (I hope) than the last; in addition, there is more explanation and illustration in the early chapters. The book is written primarily for students of human learning, teachers, counselors, social workers, industrial psychologists, nurses, social psychologists, doctors, lawyers, dentists, engineers, housewives, farmers, judges, fishermen, and all others—in that order.

Thank You
>   to my first-grade teacher and his wife,
>   to my cousin Sylvia,
>   to all my other cousins,
>   to all my other relatives,
>   to their friends,
>   and to everybody else, if there is anybody else,

and especially to the reviewers of this evening edition: Charles A. Buhler, Georgia Southwestern College; John H. Mueller, University of Missouri; Barry S. Markman, Wayne State University; Glen I. Nicholson, University of Arizona; Robert E. Prytula, Middle Tennessee State University; and Robert L. Williams, Gallandet College (Washington, D.C.).

Guy R. Lefrancois

Contents

Part 5 *A Last Word* 299

Psychological Theories and Human Learning

SECOND EDITION

PART 1

Preamble: Science and Theory

Dear Guy,

Okay. You want to know what I think of what you've done so far. Well, quite frankly, you haven't written enough for me to have much of an opinion.

Except for one thing. You made a mistake with the cover. It isn't respectful to have a pig on the cover of a serious book for university students and their professors—after all, those are smart and important people. You say it's a flag, but that's really no excuse. If I know you, you probably had some reason for asking for that cover, and you probably wouldn't admit it if I asked you. So I won't.

But a pig on the cover. That's going a little too far. And a turkey too! You know what's going to happen someday? Someday, you . . .

CHAPTER *1*

Theories and Learning

Learning

A variety of definitions have been offered for the term *learning.* The layperson's notion is most often that learning is the *acquisition of information.* If I tell you that a planet is 48 billion years old and you can then repeat that it is 48 billion years old, it could be inferred that learning has taken place. In this instance the nature of the information that you have acquired is obvious, but that is not always the case. Consider, for example, the experiment in which police recruits were presented with a different image for each eye—one neutral and the other depicting some form of violence (Toch & Schulte, 1961). Why is it that third-year trainees reported seeing significantly more violent pictures than did novices? Had the trainees learned? What had they learned? What specific information had they acquired? Obviously the term *learning* is more complex than the initial definition would suggest. The police-recruit illustration involves a change in perception or behavior that may have resulted from the acquisition of new information, although the specific information acquired is not clear. Nor did the learning simply manifest itself in the regurgitation of information; instead,

3

behavior changed. We need a second definition of learning—learning is a change in behavior or in perceptions.

When I first brought home a Volkswagen beetle, my dog reacted in a most peculiar and embarrassing fashion. As I drove around to the back of the house, the dog followed, her nose to the ground and her tail wagging in excitement. Whenever I stopped she would raise her paw, stretch her nose to within an inch of the hood emblem, raise her tail high in the air, and remain rigid until I moved again. This behavior continued for some weeks, much to the amusement of my neighbors, none of whom had ever been sympathetic to my valiant efforts to train this pathetically stupid dog.

Eventually the dog realized that the orange beetle was not a new species of game bird and abandoned her attempts to "point" it. This change in behavior can be construed as an example of learning.

Consider, in contrast, the case of the student who after taking LSD finds that the fire hydrants have become deranged turkeys and who runs madly down the street shouting "Help!" Here is a rather striking change in behavior, but to say that this change is an example of learning is to stretch the inclusiveness of the term beyond reasonable limits.

A somewhat more precise, although not entirely satisfactory, definition is that *learning comprises all relatively permanent changes in behavior that are due to experience*. Such changes include not only the acquisition of new information but also those modifications in behavior whose causes are unknown. The definition excludes changes due to maturation (genetically determined changes), artificial chemical changes such as those that can result from taking drugs, or temporary changes such as might result from fatigue.

Theory

Theory is a global term often employed to signify a particular way of looking at things, of explaining observations, or of solving problems. It is not uncommon to hear people saying "I have a theory about that," when all they really mean is that they are willing to guess the explanation for some phenomenon. Students who say they have a theory about the way professors deliver lectures are simply saying that they think they know why some lecturers behave in a certain manner.

Despite the widespread use of the word *theory*, it assumes a fearsome and threatening stature when placed in a scientific or quasi-scientific context. Students have so often been exposed to complex, jargon-laden attempts to "theorize" that the term *theory* has become almost synonymous with "incomprehensibility." Theories seem to occasion an avoidance reaction in students, whereas the terms *principles* and *laws* usually meet with less resistance. The irony of this situation is that *theory* is intended to be a parsimonious simplification of observations—it is the observations that are complex, not the theory. If the observations are simpler than the theory, then the theory should be scrapped.

A theory can be defined as a collection of related statements whose principal function is to summarize and explain observations (which are assumed to be facts). Some of these statements can be referred to as *laws*, and others as *principles*; the majority can qualify neither as laws nor as principles but can more appropriately be described as *beliefs*.

Laws are statements whose accuracy is beyond reasonable doubt. Physics, chemistry, astronomy, and other natural sciences are characterized by a number of great laws ($E = mc^2$, for example). These laws should not be confused with *truth*, however, since any law can be refuted given sufficient contrary evidence. By definition, truth should never be found to be untrue. Physical sciences do not deal with truth. Social sciences, including psychology, do not deal even with laws. They deal, instead, with principles and, perhaps more often, with beliefs.

Principles are statements that relate to some predictability in nature or, more pertinent for psychology, in behavior. Obviously, principles do not have the same scientific status as do laws, since they are almost always tentative and open to doubt. Although the predictability and uniformity for which psychology searches are virtually never certain enough to qualify its findings as laws, the term *law* is often employed interchangeably with *principle*.

Beliefs describe statements that are more private and more personal than are principles or laws. Beliefs, too, attempt to describe fact and, unfortunately, are often treated as though they had the greater universality of principles.

FUNCTIONS

The principles and beliefs that make up a psychological theory have a number of important functions. As mentioned earlier, one of these functions is to simplify and organize observations. If a theory is successful in so doing, it should also lead to prediction. A prediction based on a theory is labeled a *hypothesis.* If, as I have suggested (Lefrancois, 1980a), my grandmother's theory concerning why various types of manure are effective for different plant crops is correct, (if it is an accurate explanation of the relationships among some important observations), then her theory should allow her to hypothesize or predict with greater accuracy what will happen to her garden when she employs different fertilizers. In much the same way, the usefulness of a theory in psychology ultimately resides in how accurately it predicts. Thus, a theory that attempts to explain how humans learn should lead logically to suggestions for arranging experiences in such a way that learning will be maximized (or, alternately, will be prevented from occurring).

Quite apart from these practical considerations, theories also serve to suggest which facts (observations) are most important as well as which relationships among these facts are most important (Thomas, 1979). Since theorists may have dramatically different ideas about what is important, however, a large number of theories may emerge in the same area of investigation. And although these theories may be quite different, none will *necessarily* be totally incorrect, although their usefulness may vary a great deal.

CRITERIA

How, then, should a theory be judged? Thomas suggests five important criteria. First, a theory should reflect facts. And since facts do not always stand still in the social sciences, this criterion is particularly relevant for psychological theory. Second, a good theory should be clear and understandable. Third, as indicated earlier, it should be useful for predicting as well as for explaining. Equally important, a theory should be internally consistent rather than contradictory. And it should not be based on a large number of assumptions (beliefs accepted as fact but essentially not verifiable—see Table 1-1).

Psychological Theories and Science

It is commonly accepted that science is both a collection of information and a way of dealing with it or obtaining it. It is also popularly believed that a discipline is more or less scientific according to the validity of the information it claims as its own and the rigor with which it obtains that information. There is a common story intended to illustrate the precision and rigor with which psychologists approach their subject. It tells of a brilliant young investigator who conditioned a flea to respond to the command "Jump" and then experimented with variations of the procedure. Specifically, he wanted to discover the relationship between the removal of a flea's legs and its response to the command "Jump." At every step of the experiment he made careful and detailed notes in his lab book:

Table 1-1. Criteria of a good theory, together with a quick look at my grand-mother's fertilizer theory. This theory holds, in part, that horse manure stimulates potatoes and carrots, that chicken droppings invigorate cabbages, and that dried cow dung excites flowers.

Criteria	Grandmother's Theory
Does it reflect the facts?	Yes, if carrots, potatoes, and other plants behave as expected under specified conditions.
Is it clear and understandable?	Quite, except to the very stupid, who are seldom asked to judge theories.
Is it useful for predicting as well as explaining?	Very. We can predict in the spring what will happen in the fall. But will we be correct? Only if the theory fulfills the first criterion.
Is it internally consistent?	Unfortunately, no. The old lady has sometimes claimed that chicken droppings are better for potatoes than horse manure.
Is it based on many unverifiable assumptions?	No.

Time. 1:30.7

Procedure. The two hind legs of the flea were grasped securely between thumb and forefinger of the right hand. The flea was held gently in the left hand with the thumb of that hand underneath the abdomen. Both legs were removed simultaneously by means of a sharp pull. The flea was placed on the conditioning table at 1:32.8 in position 3-Y, facing north. The experimenter than said "Jump" in a normal tone.

Observation. The flea jumped.

The experimenter "delegged" the flea in three stages. After the first two pairs of legs were removed, it still jumped vigorously. After the last two legs had been pulled off, however, the flea remained quivering on the table even when the command was repeated. The last recorded observation was this:

Observation. When a flea has six legs removed, it becomes deaf.

This illustration suggests that the validity of conclusions does not always follow from careful experimental procedures, although it is certainly true that such procedures increase the likelihood that inferences will be accurate.

One of the most useful ways of looking at the meaning of the term *science* is to consider it as an attitude rather than as one of several bodies of knowledge or as a series of recipes for acquiring and systematizing knowledge. As an attitude, science insists on objectivity, precision, and replicability; it will accept as valid only those observations that have been collected in such a way that they can be repeated by others under similar circumstances.

THE SCIENTIFIC METHOD

This view of science as an attitude leads logically to certain prescribed methods for gathering information. These methods collectively make up what is often referred to as the scientific method.

The scientific method in psychology is similar to that employed in the natural sciences. The investigator first formulates a problem, often in the form of a hypothesis (prediction), and proceeds to gather data (observations) that will serve to substantiate or refute the prediction. Often, the data deal with two kinds of variable: dependent and independent. Independent variables are those conditions that are directly under the control of the experimenter; dependent variables are thought to be affected by the independent variables. For example, psychologists investigating the effect of sex (as a category, not an activity) on the learning of language skills can manipulate the sex of the groups used in the study. In other words, they can decide that one group will consist of males and another of females. The sex of these groups is an *independent* variable. The hypothesis predicts that achievement in the learning of language skills is *dependent* on sex. A test of the hypothesis can be obtained by comparing the achievement of the two groups.

This *design*, in which two groups that differ on one relevant independent variable are compared on a dependent variable, is one of the simplest and most common designs used in psychological experimentation. Many other experimental designs are possible. One possibility is to compare one group with itself in a before-and-after design. For example, a group of obese people can be given shock treatments in an attempt to reduce their weight, and they can be weighed before and after treatment. Another design is the comparison of a *control* group with an *experimental* group. The experimental group is subjected to some form of treatment; the control group is comparable to the experimental group in every way except that it is not subjected to any treatment. Final differences between the groups may be assumed to be due to the treatment. Numerous other more complex designs can also be devised (see Cook & Campbell, 1979).

LIMITS OF PSYCHOLOGICAL EXPERIMENTS

One of the principal limiting features of experimentation in psychology is that many of its observations do not constitute incontestable facts. It is a fact that apples fall when they become detached from a tree, and it follows that if a lazy Newton is sleeping directly under such a detached apple, it *will* hit him. Is it also a fact that 6-year-old North American children have a vocabulary of 3,000 words? Is it a fact that 3-year-old boys love their mothers whereas 4-year-olds love their fathers? Or are these observations "facts" only frequently or occasionally. In other words, the subject matter of psychology often represents no more than the most logical affirmations that can be made on the basis of the data available. Sometimes the affirmations are less than logical.*

A second limitation that makes psychological investigations less than completely scientific is the fact that the subject matter is confounded by the subject. Investigators have some difficulty disentangling themselves from the subject they propose to study. Pre-20th-century psychologists—such as James (1890) and Titchener (1898)—who were less concerned with the division between object and subject, were able to employ the relatively unscientific, but intuitively satisfying, tool of introspection. The technique involves subjectively analyzing one's own thought processes, feelings, and sensations and extrapolating from them to the behavior of others. Contemporary psychologists usually actively avoid this practice and are consequently forced to employ stratagems that are sometimes relatively inappropriate and wasteful, although highly objective. As an extreme example, consider the turkey-whiffing test (Lefrancois, 1982, p. 222).

Konorski (1967) has argued that the data of subjective experience should be as valid in the scientific investigation of human behavior as the more objective data which commonly form the basis of that science. He contends that in order to discover something as obvious as, for example, the fact that a connection is formed between the smell of turkey and the image of that noble bird, it is not necessary to assemble a group of hungry subjects. Probably, however, the volume of printed *research* depends on the use of objective rather than subjective data. Imagine the amount of prose that could result from a detailed analysis of the salivation of twenty hungry subjects who are allowed to catch a whiff of turkey from the laboratory kitchen. To this could be added a detailed examination of changes in subjects' pupil size, and a correlation of these changes with eyeball movements. The conclusion—20 pages, $4000, and 5 months later—might well be: "There is evidence to suggest that in some cases, perhaps, some degree of measurable change in pupil size results from turkey-whiffing. These changes are not correlated with either salivation or eye movements. There is also some tentative evidence that salivation increases as subjects undergo the turkey-whiffing test." The original question, interestingly, was whether or not a whiff of turkey would evoke an image of turkey. Subjective experience says clearly that if people have been exposed to turkey sufficiently often, its odor "reminds" them of it.

Psychological investigations are also limited by the amount of control that can be exercised over relevant variables. Two rats reared in identical cages and subjected to the same daily routines from birth may reasonably be assumed to have had highly comparable experiences. The same assumption cannot be made as confidently about two children who are raised in middle-class homes. Their parents, friends, siblings, and peers are all different. Thus, the concept of *control*

---

*It should not be inferred from this statement that physical facts are more "factual" than psychological facts. Indeed, in this relativistic and inexact world, "fact"—be it physical or psychological—is a statistical concept of varying probability. In both areas, fact implies agreement. The point is that while it is simple to observe an apple falling, it is less easy to ascertain the vocabulary of children or to measure their attachment to their mama.

in psychological experimentation should take into account relevant differences among subjects.

Consider the following illustration:

Problem. To determine the effect of age on problem-solving behavior.

Subjects. Two groups are selected from a private school for the study. One group comprises older subjects; the other group, younger children.

Hypothesis. Older subjects will perform significantly better on a problem-solving test.

Method. Subjects are administered the test, and results for the two groups are compared.

Results. The older group does significantly better.

Is the conclusion that age is related to problem-solving ability warranted? The answer is "yes," *providing that a number of other relevant variables have also been controlled.* If, for example, the older group is generally more intelligent, is all male or female, or has had previous training in problem solving, these variables could also account for the differences in test performance. It would then not be logical to conclude that age is the significant factor. One way to control for relevant variables is to match the groups on them. If all subjects are similarly intelligent, balanced by sex, and have no previous training, then the conclusion is more justifiable. However, since it is usually impossible to account for all relevant variables in psychological experimentation, the possibility that results may be confounded by uncontrolled factors remains a limiting feature.

Animals as Subjects.   For ethical and practical reasons, it is often necessary to make use of animals in the psychological laboratory as a means of approaching the study of human behavior. The degree to which conclusions derived from animal studies can validly be generalized to humans cannot be easily determined, for human behavior is ordinarily far more complex than the behavior of lower animal forms. In addition, despite the fact that the term is often avoided in psychology, we are assumed to possess a degree of *awareness* not possessed by a rat, for example. Nevertheless, it is often possible to generalize from animals to people. (See Bandura, 1967.)

Despite the disadvantages of using animals, it is often necessary. Our environments cannot be controlled as can that of a rat in a cage; we do not reproduce as rapidly as do most other animals, and certain important investigations involve procedures that would be unethical with human subjects (for example, in medical research).

Thus, while psychology attempts to be scientific, it is limited in that attempt by the nature of the subject with which it deals. Nevertheless, psychologists continue to make interesting and useful observations and are increasingly successful in organizing these observations into systematic interpretations of human behavior.

Learning Theory

Since learning is defined as changes in behavior that result from experience, the psychology of learning is concerned with observations of behavior and behavior change. Not surprisingly, the terms *learning theory* and *behavior theory* are essentially synonymous in psychological literature. Learning theories (or behavior theories) are attempts to systematize and organize what is known about learning. Often these theories include statements about the conditions under which learning will take place—they are essentially predictions that can be tested.

Learning theories have become increasingly complex as psychologists recognize that earlier positions are not inclusive enough to account for all the facts. It is important to note, however, that rarely are the early theories discarded completely; instead they are often incorporated into larger theoretical frameworks. But that story comes later.

The earliest learning theories that retain more than historical interest were the stimulus-response (S-R) theories. They were the attempts of the pioneers of 20th-century psychology to objectify the study of behavior. Stimuli (conditions that lead to behavior) and responses (actual behavior) are the *observable* aspects of behavior; hence, they are the objective variables that can be employed in developing a science of behavior. This early preoccupation with the observables of behavior gave rise to the behavioristic movement. *Behaviorism* is simply used to denote concern with stimuli and responses and with discovering the relationships between them. Behavioristic theories include those of Pavlov, Watson, Guthrie, and Thorndike (Chapter 2); Skinner (Chapter 3); Hull (Chapter 4); and Hebb (Chapter 6).

In addition to these S-R theories, there is a second major division of learning theory: *cognitivism.* Cognitive psychologists are typically interested in perception, decision making, information processing, and understanding. They include Tolman and the Gestaltists (Chapter 7), Bruner (Chapter 8), and Piaget (Chapter 9). Cognitive approaches are also highly apparent in current investigations of artificial intelligence (Chapter 10), memory and attention (Chapter 11), and motivation (Chapter 12).

Preview of the Text

This section presents short previews of each of the remaining 13 chapters of the text. They are offered as hors d'oeuvres. Like hors d'oeuvres, they may whet your appetite, satiate you completely if your appetite is extraordinarily tiny, or make you quite ill. You may choose to go directly to the entreé (there is no dessert).

CHAPTER 2. EARLY BEHAVIORISM: PAVLOV, WATSON, GUTHRIE, AND THORNDIKE

Thorndike once had the human urge to impress his friends with the intelligence of his dog. To this end he knelt with the dog at dinner one evening and proceeded to fill the air with the kind of barking sounds that might be expected of a particularly intelligent dog. The dog listened politely and then ate ferociously. The following evening Throndike repeated the procedure. He knelt and bayed, barked, howled, whined, and yipped with wild abandon. Again the dog listened attentively and then effectively demolished its supper. Thorndike was obviously trying to teach the dog to bark—not just in an ordinary way but in an *intelligent* manner—for its supper. This procedure is referred to as conditioning. It half worked. At the end of two weeks the dog still would not bark, but it absolutely refused to eat until Throndike had knelt and vocalized in canine fashion. Why?

CHAPTER 3. SKINNER AND OPERANT CONDITIONING

A bright psychologist once decided that he would show a rat how to eat. "Pshaw," his grandmother croaked, "rats already know how to eat." She was obviously not *au courant* (whatever that means). Her grandson explained to her that he intended to teach this rat how to eat properly, how to use a knife and fork, how to tuck in a napkin, how to sit at a table, and how to chew with its mouth closed. He also expected that the rat would eventually learn how to wipe its chops delicately with the napkin after a particularly mouth-watering chew.

The psychologist tried and almost succeeded. Unfortunately, both the rat and the grandmother died of old age before the learning program was completed. How was the rat trained?

CHAPTER 4. HULL AND SPENCE: INTERVENING VARIABLES

My colleagues complain that their classes often go to sleep when they present their magnificent lectures on Hull and Spence. They think that the students are bored, but perhaps most of them are simply suffering from symbol shock.

What does this mean: $_sE_R = {_sH_R} \times D \times V \times K$?

CHAPTER 5. TRADITIONAL BEHAVIORISM REEXAMINED

As a child I was hungry, and supermarkets were only a vague luxury in cities sometimes too far away to even be imagined. I killed for food.

We ate well: fish and all manner of wild fowl; venison and bear; and roots and berries, for we killed those too. But most especially, we ate rabbits. Dozens—no hundreds—every winter. Until the one night when the stew was too old, the milk rancid, or the rabbit diseased, and we all became violently ill shortly after dinner. From then on, rabbits gamboled about our evening bushes unmolested. And to this day I find it difficult even to write about rabbit stew, let alone eat it. Why?

CHAPTER 6. HEBB: A TRANSITION

A poverty-stricken graduate student in psychology was compelled by his increasing hunger to seek employment one summer. It was with some excitement that he accepted a position with the forestry division. His duties were simply to man a remote fire-lookout tower for 2 months. He was flown to the tower by helicopter and left alone in the peaceful grandeur of a world unblemished by people. From his vantage point atop the tower, he looked out over unbroken forest as far as the eye could see.

There he was—alone. It was quiet and peaceful, tranquil even. A man, the forest, and his soul. A soul can't talk—nor can a forest. And the radio died the second morning. There he was, alone. It *was* quiet.

Four days later the helicopter flew in with someone to repair the radio—but the student was gone. Three hundred miles of impenetrable forest and muskeg. He was never seen again.

Why? Not why was he never seen again, but why did he leave? He was not stupid.

CHAPTER 7. TOLMAN AND GESTALT PSYCHOLOGY

At the time that the First World War broke out, a young German found himself marooned on an island off the coast of West Africa, unable to return to his home because of the war. His name was Wolfgang Kohler; he was a psychologist. The name of the island was Tenerife; it was inhabited by numerous apes. During the next four years Kohler studied apes, and the apes studied him. Kohler reported his studies in a book entitled *The Mentality of Apes*. It is uncertain what the apes did with their observations.

What did Kohler discover?

CHAPTER 8. BRUNER AND CATEGORIES

If a woman sees a head with curly black hair and a handsome, bearded face smiling at her over a sea of foam in a blue bathtub, does she simply see a head with curly, black hair and a smiling face over a sea of foam in a blue bathtub? (The question is surely of more than passing academic interest.)

CHAPTER 9. PIAGET AND COGNITIVE DEVELOPMENT

An interesting game is often played by psychologists with their wise and ancient grandmothers. The grandmother is asked whether a child will solve the following problem correctly: Two equal balls of clay are shown to a 5-year-old; one of them is flattened; the child is then asked whether the balls still contain the same amount of clay. Much to the psychologist's delight, a grandmother will often make the wrong prediction, since most 5-year-old children will answer incorrectly. As a sort of *coup de grace*, the grandmother is then challenged to teach the child to answer correctly. She will probably not succeed. Why?

CHAPTER 10. ARTIFICIAL INTELLIGENCE

Can machines think?

CHAPTER 11. MEMORY AND ATTENTION

In a carefully guarded psychological laboratory of a large North American university, a small, bespectacled, shabbily dressed undergraduate student sits on a straight-backed kitchen chair. In front of her there is a dish filled with curled, grayish pieces of food. The student doesn't know what the food is, but when well salted and peppered it is quite palatable. She has not been fed for 24 hours and is now busily eating.

Prior to being given this meal, the student was presented with a simple problem in advanced calculus. Much to her embarrassment, she failed miserably. Now, after eating four dishes of the unnamed food, she is expected to be able to solve the problem. Why? And do you really believe this one?

CHAPTER 12. MOTIVATION

Three radical student leaders are cleverly coerced into volunteering for a psychological investigation. They later discover that they will be required to write an essay strongly advocating a pro-Establishment, nonradical point of view. None of them dares refuse for fear of incurring the wrath of the psychology instructor. One student is paid $50, the second is paid $10, and the third is presented with a crumpled $1 bill. The students are told that their essays are quite good and that the authorities would like to see them published. The money is ostensibly payment for this right of publication. The students agree to allow their work to be published. A day later a skilled interviewer casually uncovers how each of the subjects really feels about the Establishment. A grandmother would almost certainly predict that the student who was paid $50 dollars would be most likely to feel better about the Establishment—but the grandmother is wrong. Why? She isn't stupid.

CHAPTER 14. SOCIAL INFLUENCES

CHAPTER 15. INTEGRATION AND EVALUATION

The integration and evaluation should be the reader's own.

Summary of Chapter 1

This chapter has presented definitions of learning, theory, and learning theory. In addition, the role of science in developing theories of learning was discussed. A preview of the remaining 13 chapters of the text was also given.

1. Learning can be defined as changes in behavior that are due to experience.
2. Theories are systematic interpretations of phenomena intended to be a description of an approach to subject matter, a summary of knowledge about a subject, and an explanation of observations related to the subject.
3. Learning theories are attempts to systematize and organize what is known about human learning.
4. The traditional divisions in theories of learning are based on the primary concerns of different theorists. *Behaviorism* describes an approach that deals primarily with the observable aspects of human functioning; *cognitivism* refers to a preoccupation with such topics as perception, information processing, concept formation, awareness, and understanding.
5. Psychologists attempt to employ scientific methods for gathering, interpreting, and reporting data. The scientific character of psychology is limited, however, by the nature of the subject matter. Observations do not always constitute incontrovertible fact, nor can the investigators always isolate themselves from their subject.
6. The text consists of 13 more chapters but has no Chapter 13.

PART 2

Learning: Stimulus-Response Explanations

My Dear Grandmother,

Thank you for your kind comments. I'm sorry you don't like my idea for a cover. I assure you I have no hidden motives for suggesting it. I just happen to like chartreuse.* Besides, I have nothing against pigs or turkeys—or any other animal, for that matter.

I'm really sorry about your cat. I'm sure that when Robert threw it out of the boat he thought it had had enough experience swimming. I know he'd been training it in the slough behind his house most of last summer, and not once did the cat have any trouble at all getting to shore no matter how far we threw it in.

Anyway, I'm sure glad the cat made it back. But I'm really sorry that it has such a tremendous fear of water now that you think maybe it's going a little strange. We call that a phobia in psychology, and I'm sure one of the people here would be happy to cure it if you have enough money. I'd do it myself, but I'm pretty busy right now.

One more thing. You're wrong about Sylvia, and that's not why I put her name in my acknowledgments. And I'd appreciate it if you didn't . . .

*Maybe so, but there are some things we won't do, even for Lefrancois.— *Ed.*

CHAPTER *2*

Early Behaviorism: Pavlov, Watson, Guthrie, and Thorndike

Theories of Learning

Chapter 1 pointed out some distinctions between behaviorism and cognitivism. The real significance of these distinctions is that they permit a simple classification of explanations of human learning and thereby make it easier to understand, remember, and apply learning theories. I pointed out earlier that learning theory has progressed from simple, rather mechanistic approaches toward more complex orientations. However, the sequence is not perfectly chronological, for some of the more recent positions are often as behavioristic as they are cognitive. In addition, cognitive positions have not clearly demonstrated that they improve on the explanation, prediction, and control of human behavior.

Behaviorism focuses on the objective and observable components of human behavior—that is, the stimulus and response events that concerned Pavlov, Watson, Guthrie, Thorndike, and Skinner. Some behaviorists extend their sphere of interest to events that occur between stimuli and responses (Hull and Spence, for example). In some cases, discussion of the actual neurological units and their role in behavior is an integral part of the system (Hebb, for example).

The essential difference between the cognitive approach and the behavioristic approach is that the cognitivist is not concerned with stimulus and response events so much as with organizing, information processing, and decision making. This distinction is illustrated in Table 2-1. You should be warned, however, that behaviorism and cognitivism exist only as convenient labels for extremely complex theories. No one theory can be said to be a clear example of any one theoretical division; each has characteristics corresponding to other positions with ostensibly different orientations.

Origins of Learning Theory

Learning theory deals primarily with behavior change; it attempts to understand and explain changes in behavior as well as to predict them. When the observations, hypotheses, hunches, laws, principles, and guesses that have been made about human behavior are organized, they make up theories of behavior (and when they are not organized, they sometimes appear to be no more than old wives' tales or common sense).

Among the origins of contemporary psychological theory are early attempts by psychologists to explain behavior on the basis of instincts and emotion. Early psychologists—for example, William James and Edward Bradford Titchener—relied heavily on introspection (examining one's own feelings and motives and generalizing from these) as a means of formulating their positions. Ironically, probably the most profound and long-lasting effect of this early work stems from the strong negative reaction to it at the turn of this century, particularly in the United States.

Table 2-1. Major divisions in learning theory

	Symbolic representation	Variables of concern	Representative theorists
Stimulus-response theories (behaviorism)	S-R	Stimuli Responses Reinforcement	Pavlov Watson Thorndike Guthrie Skinner Hull Spence
A transition	O ╱ ╲ S R	Stimuli Responses Reinforcement Mediation	Hebb
Cognitive theories	O	Perception Organizing Information processing Decision making Problem solving Attention Memory	Tolman Gestaltists Bruner Piaget

WILHELM WUNDT (1832–1920)

Generally acknowledged as the founder of modern psychology, Wundt, the son of a Lutheran minister, obtained a medical degree at the age of 24 and subsequently became an instructor in physiology. His professional career was long: 17 years at Heidelberg University on the medical faculty, 1 year in Zurich as a professor of philosophy, and 42 years at Leipzig. He is described as a quiet, unassuming man who seldom left his laboratory and his home. He wrote almost constantly. Boring (1950) estimated that Wundt wrote an average of one published word every 2 minutes, day and night, for 68 years. His major textbook on psychology, unlike this one, appeared in three volumes in its first edition: 553, 680, and 796 pages of very complex German.

The establishment of a psychological laboratory in Leipzig, Germany, by Wilhelm Wundt in 1879 has been taken to mark the beginning of psychology as a science. Wundt and his followers—both in Europe and in North America—continued to deal with mentalistic concepts: consciousness, sensation, feeling, imagining, and perceiving. By the early 1900s an orientation toward behavior rather than thought had begun to appear in the United States. This movement, which later became known as behaviorism, has as its primary leader John B. Watson. The influence of behaviorism on contemporary psychological thought throughout the world has been remarkable.

Ivan P. Pavlov (1849–1936)
John B. Watson (1878–1958)

The term *behaviorism* coined by Watson (1913), has come to mean concern with the observable aspects of behavior. More precisely, behaviorism assumes that behavior comprises responses that can be observed and related to other observable events, such as conditions that precede and follow behavior. The ultimate goal of a behavioristic position is to derive laws to explain the relationships existing among antecedent conditions (stimuli), behavior (responses), and consequent conditions (reward, punishment, or neutral effects).

CLASSICAL CONDITIONING

Watson's (1930) explanation for learning was concerned with the antecedent conditions of behavior rather than its consequences. Much of his theorizing was based on the earlier work of the Russian physiologist Ivan Pavlov. In the course of his work with animals Pavlov had observed that some of the dogs in his laboratory began to salivate before they were fed. This behavior occurred only in dogs that had been in the laboratory for some time. In attempting to arrive at some scientific explanation for this phenomenon, Pavlov developed the model of *classical conditioning*—a model that was the basis for a large number of early theoretical formulations and continues to form an accepted part of contemporary psychological knowledge.

In his experiments, Pavlov demonstrated that not only could the sight of food eventually bring about salivation in his dogs, but almost any other distinctive

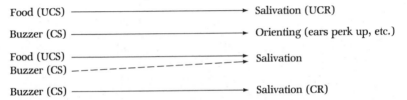

Figure 2-1. Classical conditioning. Food elicits salivation in a dog, but a buzzer does not. After successive pairings of food and buzzer, the buzzer begins to elicit salivation.

stimulus could have the same effect if paired with the presentation of food often enough. The food is referred to as the unconditioned stimulus (UCS); the initial salivation to the food is the unconditioned response (UCR). The UCS and UCR form an unlearned (reflexive) stimulus-response unit. If a buzzer is sounded every time food is presented to the dog, eventually the buzzer (now a conditioned stimulus, CS) will elicit the response of salivation (now a conditioned response, CR). An illustration of this procedure is given in Figures 2-1, 2-2, and 2-3.

This kind of learning is also referred to as learning through *stimulus substitution* since the conditioned stimulus, after being paired with the unconditioned stimulus frequently enough, can then be substituted for it. It will evoke a similar, but weaker, response. It is also referred to as *signal learning* since the conditioned stimulus serves as a signal for the occurrence of the unconditioned stimulus.

Figure 2-2. What Pavlov first noticed was that the sight of the handler alone was enough to cause many of his experimental dogs to salivate. Through further experiments, he reconstructed and validated the process that must have produced the effect.

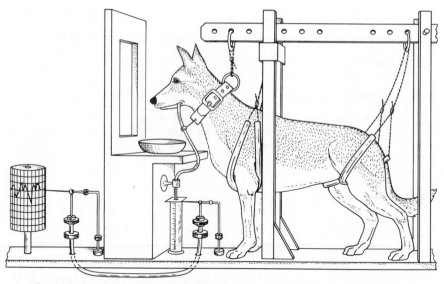

Figure 2-3. Pavlov's dogs were placed in a harness like this one. Food powder can be placed either in the dog's mouth or in the dish. Saliva is measured as it drops into a tube in the dog's mouth. The resulting movement of a tiny balancing mechanism in the tube is transmitted to a pen, whose movement in turn is recorded on a revolving drum. In the experiment illustrated here, the UCS (food) is paired with a CS (light shining in the window).

IVAN PETROVICH PAVLOV (1849–1936)
Pavlov was the son of a village priest in Russia. His early education was in a local seminary. From there he went to the University of St. Petersburg, specializing in animal physiology and in medicine. After he obtained his medical degree, he went to Germany, where he studied physiology and medicine for another 2 years. He then returned to St. Petersburg and worked as an assistant in a physiology laboratory until he was appointed professor of pharmacology and head of a physiology department at the age of 41. His work, for which he received a Nobel Prize in 1904, continued to deal almost exclusively with physiological topics, specifically with digestive processes. It wasn't until the age of 50 that he began to study classical conditioning, these studies lasting 30 years. To the end, however, he insisted that he was a physiologist and not a psychologist. In fact, he viewed psychology with considerable disdain, and he fined any of his laboratory assistants who used psychological rather than physiological terms (R. I. Watson, 1971).

It occurred to me some years ago that, if Pavlov could teach a dog to salivate in response to the sound of a buzzer or a bell, then another stimulus that was slightly more sophisticated, but perhaps not so highly distinctive, might have the same effect. The stimulus I selected was the word *salivate*. I took an attractive piece of moose meat (no artificial meat powder for this dog) and elicited a copious flow of saliva from a German short-haired pointer, all the while saying, clearly, distinctly, and authoritatively, "Salivate!" The training sessions took place in the seclusion of the garage. (Great steps in science are often taken in secluded garages.) Some days later, after repeated pairings of moose meat and the command "Salivate," I brought the dog into the house. There, in front of my grandmother, the first (and last) person ever to witness this event, the dog drooled and slobbered profusely on a new carpet as her ecstatic master shouted repeatedly "Salivate, salivate, yahoo! Salivate, yippee!!"

The appreciation of scientific demonstrations is not universal.

ACQUISITION

The ease with which a classically conditioned response is acquired is related to a number of factors. Not the least important is the distinctiveness of the conditioning stimulus. Buzzers and other tones have been particularly good conditioning stimuli in animal experimentation precisely because they can be highly distinctive stimuli.

Another important variable in classical conditioning concerns the particular temporal arrangement of the CS and the UCS (see Figure 2-4). A response is

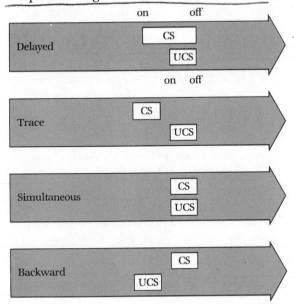

Figure 2-4.   The pairing sequences are shown here in the order of effectiveness. Acquisition of conditioning takes place most quickly in the "delayed" sequence, when the conditioned stimulus (for instance, the buzzer) is presented shortly before the unconditioned stimulus (food powder) and continues throughout the time the UCS is presented.

conditioned most rapidly when the conditioned stimulus is presented before the unconditioned stimulus and continues during presentation of the unconditioned stimulus. (This is termed delayed conditioning.) Also highly effective is trace conditioning, in which the conditioned stimulus just precedes the unconditioned stimulus.

Backward conditioning, in which the unconditioned stimulus is presented and *removed* before presentation of the conditioning stimulus, was long thought to be completely ineffective. And indeed, in most circumstances it is. That is, classical conditioning does not ordinarily occur when the conditioned stimulus follows the unconditioned stimulus. In a small number of highly specific experiments, however, investigators have succeeded in bringing about backward conditioning. In one experiment representative of these studies, Keith-Lucas and Guttman (1975) classically conditioned an avoidance response in rats by shocking them electrically (UCS) and subsequently placing a plastic hedgehog toy in their cages (CS). A significant number of rats responded with apparent fear when shown the plastic toy the following day, providing it had been placed in their cages within 10 seconds of the electric shock. Others, which had experienced a 40-second delay, showed little fear.

The significance of this study and of related studies is not so much that they establish that backward conditioning is possible but rather that they add to the growing evidence that some types of learning are far easier for certain organisms than are other types. As is shown in Chapter 5, we seem to be *prepared* to learn certain things (language, for example), and *contraprepared* to learn others. The discovery and elaboration of these *biological constraints* on learning constitute an important and growing area of psychological research and theorizing.

LITTLE ALBERT

Watson's emphasis on behaviorism, coupled with his reaction against mentalistic concepts, led him to abandon all nonobjective approaches to the explanation of human and animal behavior. For example, he considered emotional behavior to be simply another instance of classical conditioning. He assumed that individual differences are virtually nonexistent and that all people are born with a limited number of reflexes. Among these reflexes are such unlearned behaviors as the knee-jerk reflex as well as the emotional reactions of fear, love, and rage. These reflexive behaviors occur in response to certain specific stimuli, such as loud noises and sudden loss of support, which he believed led to fear reactions; stroking and fondling, which elicit love; and confinement in tight clothing, which was thought to evoke rage. According to Watson's theory, all later emotional reactions would be the result of classical conditioning involving these reflexive emotional responses.

JOHN BROADUS WATSON (1878–1958)

The founder of U.S. behaviorism, Watson was born in Greenville, South Carolina, in 1878. By his own admission, he was not a particularly good student (Murchison, 1936), although on one occasion he was the only person who passed a final Greek exam, an accomplishment that the attributed to having spent the previous afternoon cramming and drinking an entire quart of Coca-Cola syrup. He took his graduate training at the University of Chicago, working his way through school as a rat caretaker. After obtaining his degree he lectured at the University of Chicago. Several years later he was offered a full professorship at Johns Hopkins, where he remained until his wife apparently discovered his infidelities (with his assistant, Rosalie Rayner) and sued him for divorce. The ensuing front-page scandal led to his being fired from Johns Hopkins. From there he went to New York, married Miss Rayner, had two more children (he had already fathered two), and went to work for the J. Walter Thompson Company. His first assignment required that he go up and down the Mississippi River asking people what brand of rubber boots they wore, and he moved from there to virtually every department in the company until he became its vice-president. During this time he wrote popularized psychology articles for such magazines as Harper's, McCall's, Liberty, Collier's, *and* Cosmopolitan. *These activities, for which he was well paid, did little to endear him to his former colleagues, who spent some time and effort criticizing the articles. He never returned to academic life.*

In connection with his views on emotional development, Watson performed one of his most famous experiments (Watson & Rayner, 1920). The subject of this somewhat cruel experiment was "Little Albert," an 11-month-old boy. Watson conditioned fear of a white rat in Albert by making a loud noise whenever the rat was presented to the boy. Following seven pairings of rat and noise (a hammer hitting a steel bar), the mere sight of the white rat was sufficient to make Albert cower and attempt to crawl away, whimpering.

Clearly, then, it is possible to condition negative emotional reactions by repeatedly pairing a stimulus ordinarily associated with some negative emotion and another distinctive stimulus. By the same token, it is also possible to condition positive emotional reactions to neutral stimuli. It is highly probable, for example, that if the white rat had been paired with a dish of ice cream or a wet kiss, Little Albert might very soon have come to love white rats with some passion. Similarly, even after being conditioned to respond with fear to the presence of a white rat, it might still have been possible to condition a positive response to the rat—a procedure termed *counterconditioning,* which is illustrated in the next section on Edwin Guthrie. It seems clear from the original article that

Watson had intended to do just that (see Harris, 1979; Prytula, Oster, & Davis, 1977). Unfortunately, Albert was Watson's subject only because he happened to be in a hospital at the time. And, as luck would have it, he was released from the hospital the day before Watson was to have begun his counterconditioning procedures. That these procedures would probably have been successful was demonstrated 4 years later when Mary Cover Jones found a small boy, Peter, who had a profound fear of rabbits. She cured him of his fear through a classical conditioning procedure (Jones, 1974).

CLASSICAL CONDITIONING AND PEOPLE

Watson's early theorizing about emotional development has not stood the test of objective inquiry. Despite his attempts to deal only with objective variables, the fact remains that fear, rage, and love are emotional reactions that are difficult to identify in young children. A number of controlled studies have shown, for example, that babies left completely unclothed in temperature-regulated environments show as much rage as do babies wrapped in cumbersome clothing (Irwin & Weiss, 1934; Taylor, 1934).

It remains true, however, that many human behaviors are the result of classical conditioning: fear in response to the sound of a dentist's drill, although the *sound* of the drill has never hurt; depressing an automobile accelerator when the light turns green; salivating on seeing food (usually with more restraint than the German short-haired pointer); and countless other automatic responses that result from previous stimulus pairings.

Below are descriptions of two experimental procedures that can be used to demonstrate classical conditioning.

Illustration 1. Keller (1969) describes a procedure in which subjects are asked to dip their right hand in a pitcher of ice water. This immersion causes an immediate drop in the temperature of that hand and, interestingly, also causes a more easily measured drop in the temperature of the left hand. If the hand is dipped in the ice water at regular intervals (3 or 4 minutes) and each dip is preceded by a buzzer, after 20 or so pairings the buzzer alone will cause a measurable drop in hand temperature.

Illustration 2. Pavlov's work on conditioning has influenced many Soviet psychologists, who have conducted experiments involving the conditioning of responses not ordinarily under control of the organism. For example, blood-vessel constriction or dilation, which is brought about by the external application of cold or hot packs, can be conditioned to a bell or a buzzer. Urination can also be classically conditioned. If sufficient air is introduced into a person's bladder, it increases pressure inside the bladder and urination occurs. If the introduction of air is paired with a bell or buzzer, after a relatively small number of pairings the bell alone will elicit urination. This procedure appears to have important implications for toilet training children.

Watson's contribution to the understanding of human behavior is difficult to assess, largely because the behavioristic approach for which he was a strong spokesman continues to exert a profound influence on the direction of contemporary psychological thinking. Within the rather narrow perspective of psychological issues as they relate to learning theories, his contributions can be seen as an attempt to make the science more rigorous and more objective, the popularization of the notion that environmental experiences are potent forces in the shaping of behavior patterns, and the elaboration of a learning model (classical conditioning) that is adequate to explain at least some simple animal and human behaviors.

WATSON AND ENVIRONMENTALISM

A recurrent theme in psychological literature is the controversy over the nature/nurture question: are humans largely a product of genetic makeup, or are they molded and shaped mainly by environment? The chief spokesman for the nature position at the turn of this century was Francis Galton (1870), a cousin of Charles Darwin; the chief spokesman for the nurture camp was Watson (1930). Watson went so far as to say that, given a dozen healthy infants of any background and given complete freedom to bring them up in any environment that he chose, he would make of them anything that he wished. In other words, he assumed that all human differences result from learning.

The controversy surrounding this question is far from being completely resolved, although most psychologists readily admit that both heredity and environment are involved in the determination of many facets of human behavior and personality. As Anastasi (1958) put it, the important question may not be "how much" environment or heredity contributes but rather "how" each exercises its influence.

Edwin Guthrie (1886–1959)

Edwin Guthrie's approach to explaining human behavior was very similar to Watson's: both theorists were highly preoccupied with being objective, and both dealt with observable aspects of behavior. Their explanations for learning were also identical in many ways.

Probably the most important theoretical distinction between the two behaviorists is Guthrie's denial of Watson's notion that practice strengthens learning. Guthrie's denial was actually less a contradiction of Watson's position than an expression of a different way of interpreting learning.

EDWIN R. GUTHRIE (1886–1959)

Guthrie was born January 9, 1886, in Lincoln, Nebraska. It was also there, at the University of Nebraska, that he began his academic career, receiving an arts degree in 1907 and, 3 years later, a master's. Interestingly, his interests at that time lay in mathematics and philosophy rather than in psychology. His master's included a major in philosophy and a minor in mathematics—and an additional minor, almost as an afterthought, in a fledgling new discipline, psychology.

From the University of Nebraska Guthrie went to the University of Pennsylvania, where in 1912 he obtained a Ph.D. in philosophy. Most of the remainder of his 42-year academic career was spent at the University of Washington. His shift to psychology, which occurred in 1919, was largely influenced by the philosopher Singer, who believed that many philosophical problems could be reduced to problems of behavior. A contemporary of Watson's (he was only 8 years younger), Guthrie was also profoundly influenced by Watson's classical conditioning, an influence that is strongly reflected in his first text, published in 1921.

The most important of Guthrie's writings is his major book, The Psychology of Learning, *published in 1935 and revised in 1952. He was widely recognized during his academic career, served as dean of graduate studies at the University of Washington, and was honored by the American Psychological Association (of which he was president for a time).*

A LAW OF LEARNING

Guthrie's (1952) explanation for learning is summarized in his one major law, which states simply that the stimulus or the combination of stimuli that has led to a response will tend to lead to that response again if repeated. He went one step further to say that the full strength of the "bond" between a stimulus and a response is attained on the occasion of the first pairing and that it will be neither weakened nor strengthened by practice. In other words, when an organism does something on one occasion, it will tend to do exactly the same thing if the occasion repeats itself. In behavioristic terms, if a stimulus leads to a specific response now, it will lead to the same response in the future. The interpretation of this law together with its subsidiary is summarized in the declaration that Guthrie's theory is that of "one-shot learning"—a description often applied to it in all seriousness. In other words, complete learning occurs in one trial.

For Guthrie, learning was a process of acquiring S-R bonds (he referred to these as habits) through pairing behavior with stimuli. His position does not provide a clear answer for the question of why specific behaviors occur to begin with. The charge is made that his law of learning is obviously incorrect, since we often behave differently in the same situation. His answer appears to be both simple and plausible: if the responses to two stimuli are different, it is because the stimuli are not exactly identical—or it may be that through one of a number of procedures, an old habit has been replaced by a new one. The old one is not forgotten—it is merely replaced.

BREAKING HABITS

From a teaching point of view, Guthrie's suggestions about how one habit can be replaced with another are particularly relevant. He listed three techniques that can be effective in bringing about desirable responses in the place of undesirable ones. However, in order to be consistent with his theory, he maintained that in no case is the old response ever forgotten. It is merely replaced by a newer, more desirable response that is *incompatible* with the old one. Hence, only the newer response will take place in the future. The three techniques, described below, are labeled the *fatigue method*, the *threshold method*, and the *method of incompatible stimuli*.

The Fatigue Method. The fatigue technique, sometimes termed *flooding*, involves presenting the stimulus repeatedly in order to elicit continued repetition of the undesired response. Eventually the organism will become so fatigued that it can no longer perform the response; at that point a different response will be emitted, or the organism will do nothing. Doing nothing can also be interpreted as a kind of response—one that is probably incompatible with the undesirable response. It follows from Guthrie's theory of one-shot learning that as soon as the organism has emitted a response, that response, together with the stimulus (or combination of stimuli) that elicited it, will have been learned. This response, since it is the most *recent* reaction to that stimulus, will be repeated if the stimulus is presented again. In this way the original undesirable habit has been broken.

The Threshold Method. The threshold technique involves presenting the stimulus that forms part of the undesirable S-R unit (habit) but presenting it so faintly that it does not elicit the undesirable response. If it does not elicit the undesirable behavior, then it probably elicits another response; again it may simply be the response of not reacting in an undesirable fashion. The stimulus is then presented repeatedly over a succession of trials, but its intensity is increased each time. The degree of increase, however, is carefully kept sufficiently small that the undesirable response will never be elicited. By the time an intensity is reached that would initially have stimulated the undesirable behavior, a different habit has been formed.

The Method of Incompatible Stimuli. The final technique involves presenting the stimulus when the response cannot occur. If the undesirable reaction cannot occur, then, again, a different response takes its place and eventually replaces the old habit entirely.

All three of these techniques can be illustrated in the training of horses. (See Figure 2-5). A bucking horse, most people will readily admit, has a bad habit. Rigid behaviorists will go so far as to say that a bucking horse has an S-R unit

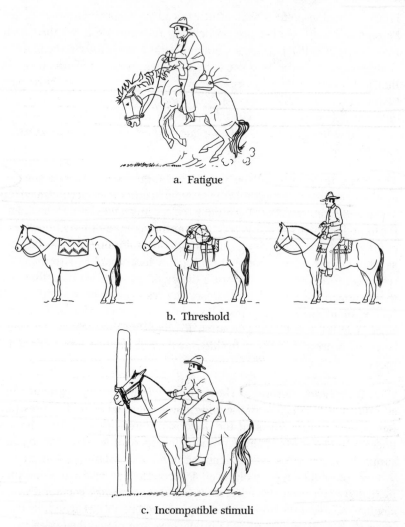

a. Fatigue

b. Threshold

c. Incompatible stimuli

Figure 2-5. Guthrie's three ways of breaking habits. In (a), the horse is "broken" in the traditional sense, being allowed to buck until fatigued. In (b), the horse is "gentled" by having progressively heavier weights placed on its back, beginning with a blanket and culminating with a saddle and rider. In (c), the horse is tied down so that it cannot buck when mounted.

that should probably be modified. The stimulus part of this unit is represented by the various objects that are put onto a horse's back, leading it to react in an asocial, and sometimes antisocial, manner. The response part of the S-R unit is represented by the asocial activity—the bucking response. Within the context of Guthrie's theory, any attempt to modify a horse's behavior will take the form of one or more of the three techniques he describes.

The common "rodeo" technique of breaking a horse is simply to throw a saddle on its back and to ride the living _____ out of it. When it gets sufficiently tired, it will stop responding in an undesirable way, and if the rider is still on its back, the horse may eventually begin to respond by standing, walking, or running. This change in response is an illustration of the application of Guthrie's fatigue technique.

The threshold method is also commonly used for breaking horses. It breaks as many horses as the rodeo technique but many fewer riders. This method involves "gentling" the horse—beginning by placing a light blanket on its back and increasing the weight (increasing the intensity of the stimulus) over successive trials. Given sufficient time and patience, a horse may be broken in this fashion.

The third technique, that of incompatible stimuli, is probably used less frequently with horses but can also be effective. It involves presenting the stimulus (saddle and rider on the horse's back) when the response cannot occur. The incompatible stimulus usually involves tying the horse to a post ("snubbing short") so that it cannot buck.

BREAKING HUMAN HABITS

Each of Guthrie's three techniques can be applied to people. Of course, it is quite unacceptable to break a child in the same manner that a horse would be broken. But, with due consideration for the *humanity* of the child, it is possible to remove certain bad habits that might be acquired even in the very best of homes. Consider, for example, a small boy who habitually responds to the sight of his grandfather with very intense fear, which he acquired because the old grandfather was the first individual to punish him with a short whip. (Of course, this illustration is fictitious.) In the manner of Jones and her subject, Peter, one can remove the boy's fear by having him eat something pleasant while the grandfather stands quietly in the distance. Over succeeding trials, grandpa can be invited to move a little closer each time but never close enough to bring about the old fear reaction (threshold method). Eventually the fear response will be replaced by a more desirable behavior..

Guthrie's threshold technique is highly similar to another approach popularized by Wolpe (1958), sometimes called *counterconditioning,* or *systematic desensitization.* This method has often been successfully employed with patients suffering from severe fears (phobias). In its simplest form, the technique

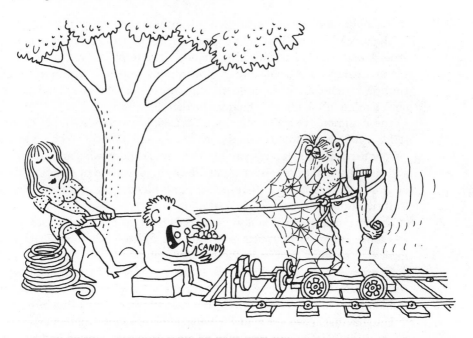

requires that the patient list all situations that are associated with the phobia. These are ranked hierarchically, beginning with the stimulus associated with the least amount of fear, progressing through other stimuli associated with increasing fear, and culminating with those associated with the most intense fear reaction. Following this first step, the therapist trains the patient in one or more of a variety of relaxation techniques. Therapy, which generally occurs over a number of sessions, then involves having the subject imagine or describe a situation low on the hierarchy of fear-producing stimuli. While this is happening, the patient is continually instructed to relax. The object of the procedure is to have the patient imagine fear-producing stimuli without anxiety. Care is taken to ensure that the stimuli being imagined remain *below the threshold* for fear—in other words, that they do not lead to the phobic reaction; this is the similarity to Guthrie's threshold method. In the end, if the therapy is successful, the undesirable fear reaction will have been replaced by a response that is essentially incompatible with it—a response of relaxation.

The fatigue method and the method of incompatible stimuli can also be used to correct a variety of behavior and emotional problems, a fact of which my Uncle Renault is still painfully aware. The story, only slightly distorted by time, is that his sweet tooth would have led him unerringly in the direction of juvenile criminality had it not been for my grandmother's cunning and resourcefulness. You see, my uncle, as devious as any other fledgling criminal, had become so successful at pilfering doughnuts, pies, cakes, and other assorted delights from my grandmother's kitchen that the poor lady was quite at her wit's end. She had by now realized that beating little Renault with her poplar cane wasn't likely to teach him anything other than to dislike poplar and to fear the old lady herself. And cleverly inserting vinegars, mustards, pickles, and other surprises in her pastries had done nothing but make him more cautious. Now, like a dog, he smelled everything before he ate it. But eat it he did, almost as fast as the old lady baked. And once more Renault would decline his supper, except perhaps for one or two small cookies or a wedge of pie if there was one left. There wasn't? Well, okay then, a little corn syrup and brown sugar, thank you.

It was about then that the old lady considered the method of incompatible stimuli. "Make a muzzle for him," she told Frank, my grandfather, "and he'll have to leave my baking alone." But the muzzle was never made; they both realized that Renault would learn little from wearing a muzzle, other than not to eat with a muzzle on.

As a last resort, Renault was exposed to the fatigue technique. One June day when the sun hung forever in the hot sky, my grandmother baked. Pies and cakes; creamy tortes and almond cookies; chocolate wafers and sugar doughnuts; lemon meringues and cherry cupcakes. And my Uncle Renault ate. Sitting on a straight-backed wooden chair, my grandfather encouraging him, he ate. Jubilantly at first. Then less gladly. Finally quite reluctantly, until he was certain he could eat no more. But even then he ate a little more, for he had no choice.

"Eat. You never have enough. You're going to sit there and eat everything."

Renault is reported not to have eaten everything. Even now he still turns slightly green at the thought of eating dessert.

Contiguity and Reinforcement

In learning theories that are based on conditioning, one of two different explanations for learning has typically been advanced, or more recently a combination of the two has been utilized. When my dog learned to salivate in response to the command "Salivate," why did the learning occur? The two alternative answers are contiguity or reinforcement. The first explanation maintains simply that an association was formed between the stimuli (the UCS, food; and the CS, "Salivate") because they were presented in contiguity (together, simultaneously, overlapping in time, or at least in close temporal proximity). This explanation is probably the most reasonable for this particular learning. The second alternative, reinforcement, is not a good explanation for the behavior of the pointer, however. This explanation maintains that learning occurs because of the consequences of the behavior—or, more specifically, because the behavior leads to pleasant consequences or the elimination of something unpleasant or both. The presentation of a pleasant stimulus or the removal of a noxious (unpleasant) one is a clear and accurate definition of what is meant by reinforcement.

Both Watson and Guthrie used contiguity to explain learning. Watson maintained that the simultaneous presentation of two stimuli would lead to the development of some sort of equivalence between them. For example, the bell becomes at least partly equivalent to food when it elicits a response similar to that elicited by the food. Guthrie maintained that a link is formed between a stimulus and a response because they are simultaneous (in contiguity). In order to maintain this position in view of the apparent time lag between the presentation of most stimuli and their responses, he posited the existence of minute responses that occur between an overt stimulus and a response. Thus, stimuli give rise to a series of responses which are somewhat similar to stimuli. For this reason the responses are called *movement-produced stimuli* (MPS). Each response in the chain overlaps with the next (temporally); therefore, through the mediation of these MPS, stimuli and responses are in contiguity.

Probably the major shortcoming of both these theoretical positions is that neither theorist paid much attention to the possible effects of the consequences of behavior on learning. Both were contiguity theorists—neither was a reinforcement theorist. It remained for Edward L. Thorndike to introduce the notion of reinforcement in psychological theory.

Edward L. Thorndike (1874–1949)

Thorndike's work is often given short coverage in psychology textbooks because aspects of his theorizing seem to have found a more popular spokesman in B. F. Skinner.

While Thorndike did not deny the relevance of much of the work of Watson and Guthrie, his final system relies heavily on the principle of reinforcement, which was essentially denied by them. The effects of recency, frequency, and contiguity were summarized in his *Law of Exercise* (Thorndike, 1913), which stated that bonds between stimuli and responses would be strengthened through being exercised frequently, recently, and "vigorously." This law plays a relatively minor role in his final system, but it had a tremendous influence on educational theory and practice in the early decades of this century. Briefly, belief in the effectiveness of "exercising" S-R bonds did a great deal to justify and encourage the repetitive, "drill" approaches to learning that became increasingly popular in the 1930s and 1940s.

EDWARD LEE THORNDIKE (1874–1949)

Like Pavlov, Thorndike was the son of a minister, a fact whose significance probably relates to the somewhat higher probability that the children of ministers and pastors would receive a higher education. Born the second child in his family, Edward was only one of three Thorndike brothers who later taught at Columbia University.

Thorndike studied at Wesleyan, Harvard, and Columbia. It was at the latter that, in 1898, he obtained a Ph.D. in psychology. His thesis, published that same year (Thorndike was then 24), dealt with animal intelligence. It attempted to establish, through experimentation, that animals (specifically cats) learn through a gradual process of trial and error that eventually leads to the "stamping-in" of the correct response. Much of his later career in psychology involved generalizing this observation to human learning and demonstrating how humans, too, do not learn through insight but through trial and error as a function of reward or punishment.

Thorndike wrote extensively. Much of this writing was in the form of articles dealing with an extremely wide range of topics, the bulk of which relate to education and psychology. He was widely honored, not only in North America but also in Europe.

BASIC NOTION OF LEARNING

For Thorndike, learning consists of the formation of bonds between stimuli and responses—bonds that take the form of neural connections. Consequently, the term *connectionism* has been applied to the theory. Learning involves the "stamping in" of S-R connections; forgetting involves "stamping out" connections. Both processes—stamping in and stamping out—are subject to a number of laws that explain learning and forgetting, the most important of which is the *Law of Effect* (Thorndike, 1913). Simply stated, the Law of Effect maintains that *responses just prior to a satisfying state of affairs are more likely to be repeated.* The converse also applies, although it is of considerably less importance in explaining learning: *responses just prior to an annoying state of affairs are more likely not to be repeated.* In other words, whether or not a response will be stamped in or stamped out is largely a function of the consequences of that response.

In order to objectify the interpretation of the Law of Effect, Thorndike found it necessary to define what *satisfiers* and *annoyers* are. A satisfying state of affairs is one that the animal (or person) either does nothing to avoid or attempts to maintain. An annoying state of affairs is one that the animal (person) does nothing to preserve or attempts to end.

The significance of the Law of Effect in the development of learning theory can hardly be overestimated. Bitterman (1969) described it as one of Thorndike's two great contributions to psychology. The other is his notion of intelligence, a notion that is essentially a denial of the belief that the human being is simply another animal that can reason. Instead, he maintained that intelligence can be defined solely in terms of greater or lesser ability to form connections. According to Bitterman (1960), this view has been widely and uncritically accepted until recently.

The Law of Effect is essentially one model of *instrumental learning.* An organism performs a response and establishes some connection between it and the stimulus preceding it if it is followed by satisfaction. The important aspect of this model from a theoretical point of view is that the connection is assumed to be formed between the stimulus and the response rather than between the reward and the response. As is made clear in succeeding chapters of this text, Hull accepted Thorndike's view and made it one of the central features of his system. Skinner, in contrast, adopted the current notion that the reward and the response become associated. Numerous animal studies have been performed in attempts to substantiate one or the other point of view (see, for example, Bitterman, 1967; Crespi, 1942; Hulse, 1958; Postman, 1962). Some of these were reviewed by Bitterman (1969), who, interestingly, concluded with the speculation that perhaps the Law of Effect is a "perfectly general law of learning" and that human psychology may well be at the beginning of its Thorndikean era rather than at the end.

SUBSIDIARY LAWS

Five additional laws also form part of Thorndike's explanation for learning:

1. **Multiple Response.** The first law states that in any given situation the organism will respond in a variety of ways if its first response does not lead immediately to a more satisfying state of affairs. In other words, it is through *trial and error* that an individual will attempt to solve problems.

Thorndike's most famous experiments are those that have been cited as an illustration of this principle. They typically involve a hungry cat in a cage that has been placed a short distance from a fragrant piece of fish. The cat can open the door leading out of the cage, and thereby acquire the fish, only if it pulls a looped string that hangs in the cage. The typical feline response to this situation is to pace up and down the cage, meowling and scratching at the walls. Eventually, the cat will accidentally pull the string and escape. Over succeeding trials, the amount of time required for the cat to escape becomes progressively shorter until it can finally open the door immediately on being placed in the cage. Thorndike interpreted this behavior as evidence that learning results from the slow process of stamping in a correct response, which was originally acquired through trial and error.

2. **Set, or Attitude.** The second law makes the observation that learning is partly a function of attitude, or set, set being defined as a predisposition to react in a given way. This law applies not only to satisfiers and annoyers but also to the nature of the responses that will be emitted by a person. There are culturally determined ways of dealing with a wide variety of problems. For example, many cultures find it generally acceptable to react to aggression with aggression; however, these cultures also have decreed that the outcome of physical aggression will be a satisfying state of affairs for the victor and an annoying state of affairs for the vanquished.

3. **Prepotency of Elements**. Thorndike suggested that it is possible for a learner to react to only the significant (prepotent) elements in a problem situation and be undistracted by irrelevant aspects of the situation. For example, recognizing that a figure is a square rather than a rectangle requires only that the subject respond to the relationship among the sides of the figure, and not to its color, placement, and so on. For this problem, stimuli associated with shape are *prepotent*; others are irrelevant.

4. **Response by Analogy.** The fourth principle recognizes the fact that a person placed in a novel situation may react with responses that they would employ for other situations with some identical elements. In other words, the *transfer* of responses from one situation to another will be based on the similarity of the two situations. This principle (Thorndike's theory of transfer) is sometimes referred to as the theory of *identical elements*. Response by analogy is well illustrated by the unfortunate child who ran after the skunk shrieking "Here kitty! Here kitty, kitty."

5. **Associative Shifting**. The last of the five subsidiary principles is closely related to stimulus substitution. It is simply an admission that it is possible to shift any response from one stimulus to another. Thorndike illustrated this process by training a cat to stand. Initially the cat stands because the experimenter holds up a piece of fish. Gradually the amount of fish is decreased until the cat stands even when no fish is presented.

SUMMARY OF THORNDIKE'S LEARNING THEORY

These five subsidiary laws, together with the two major laws that have been described (there is a third major law, the Law of Readiness, which is not of crucial importance to the system), present a relatively clear, although simplified, picture of Thorndike's views on learning. For him, learning consists of the formation of physiological bonds or connections between stimuli and responses. These bonds are stamped in through use or because of the satisfying nature of their consequences; conversely, they are weakened or stamped out through disuse or because the responses are associated with unpleasant states of affairs. In addition, humans arrive at appropriate responses largely through trial and error. They may also respond in given ways because of predetermined set, or attitude, perhaps determined by culture or by more immediate aspects of the situation. For example, a hungry person will respond to food in a different way from one who is not hungry. Some responses will be based on behavior learned in other somewhat similar situations (response by analogy), while others may have resulted from a conditioning procedure (associative shifting). In many cases, the person will engage in behavior only in response to the most important aspects of a situation (the most prepotent elements).

THORNDIKE'S CONTRIBUTION

Thorndike's most important contribution to the development of learning theory is probably the emphasis he placed on the consequences of behavior as determiners of what is learned and what is not. In addition, he was largely responsible for the introduction of animal studies as a means of verifying predictions made from theory. A third area in which Thorndike made significant contributions is the application of psychological principles, particularly in teaching. A large number of his writings were devoted specifically to pedagogical problems, sometimes in specific areas—arithmetic (Thorndike, 1922) Latin (Thorndike, 1923), and the psychology of interest (Thorndike, 1935).

A Brief Evaluation

Pavlov, Watson, Guthrie, and Thorndike. All S-R theorists, in that all were primarily concerned with discovering and explaining regularities that underlie relationships among stimuli and responses. Among the important regularities that these theorists discovered were those we now describe as classical *conditioning*, as well as certain important notions concerning the role of repetition and of reward and punishment in human and animal learning.

But were these good theories in terms of the criteria discussed in Chapter 1? Yes and no. First, how well do they reflect the facts? It is with respect to this first criterion that these theories are most easily faulted. Although they fit the facts reasonably well *as the facts were known then,* a great many observations had yet to be made—a great many experiments had not been conducted. In addition, the "facts" explained by these theories are those that the theorists in question deemed to be most in need of explanation, an observation that is true of virtually all psychological theories. Accordingly, these early behaviorists did relatively little to explain "higher" mental processes: language, thought, problem solving, perception, and so on.

With respect to the other criteria, the theories fare much better. Most tend to be clear and understandable; few are internally inconsistent; and their *behavioristic* insistence on objectivity generally meant that they would not be based on a great many unverifiable assumptions. And although the extent to which they explain (and consequently the extent to which they can be employed to predict behavior) is severely limited by the fact that they were typically based on incomplete data, their contributions to the subsequent development of learning theories can hardly be overestimated.

While these early behavioristic positions fall far short of their goal of explaining human learning, they provide some valuable insight into human and animal functioning. They should probably not be dismissed on the basis of their failure to explain symbolic functioning or so-called "higher" mental processes—as could easily be done—but should, instead, be looked at in the light of their contribution to the development of a science that has never been adequate to explain all, or even most, human behavior but that explains more behavior, more clearly, with each succeeding theoretical contribution. And the apparently minor contributions of these men are much more significant when viewed as the beginning of the development of this science.

Summary of Chapter 2

This chapter has presented an introduction to the study of theories of learning. These theories have been described as systematic attempts to explain and predict changes in human behavior. Several related theoretical positions have been described: Pavlov's and Watson's theories of classical conditioning. Guthrie's one-shot-learning theory, and Thorndike's trial-and-error position. All three illustrate the behavioristic preoccupation with the objectification of the science of psychology, and all (as is made evident in succeeding chapters) contributed to the development of more recent formulations.

1. Learning is defined as behavior change that is due to experience. This is a "behavioristic" definition of learning. It is meant to include attitudinal changes, since behavior includes not only overt acts but also covert ones. This definition of learning does not include the effects of maturation and neurological change on behavior, nor does it account for the effects of drugs or fatigue.

2. Behaviorism is the movement in psychology whose followers are primarily concerned with ("behaving") rather than with "thinking," "feeling," or "knowing." Learning theorists who are more concerned with "knowing," or cognition, and less with observable behavior are sometimes referred to as cognitivists.

3. Watson was the originator of the behavioristic movement in North American psychology. His position was a carefully objective reaction to an earlier, more mentalistic psychological orientation. He based much of his theory on the work of the Russian physiologist Pavlov.

4. Classical conditioning is the process of acquiring new behavior through the repeated pairing of stimuli. The usual illustration of this phenomenon is Pavlov's dog, who learned to salivate in response to the sound of a buzzer after the buzzer and food had been presented to the dog simultaneously over a number of conditioning trials.

5. The ease with which a classically conditioned response is acquired depends in part on the distinctiveness of the conditioning stimulus as well as on the temporal arrangement of the UCS and the CS. The best arrangement is where the UCS just follows the CS (termed delayed conditioning); conditioning is impossible in the arrangement termed "backward" (where the UCS precedes the CS) except for very specific behaviors that the organism seems to be "prepared" to learn.

6. The model of classical conditioning is particularly useful for explaining the learning of emotional responses in people. Reactions of fear, love, hate, and so on can often be traced, particularly in young children, to experiences where previously neutral stimuli are associated with emotion-producing stimuli. It is probably through such a procedure that most humans come to dislike the sound of a dentist's drill.

7. Watson was a strong believer in the power of the environment in determining people's behavior. Probably the most often quoted statement attributed to Watson is his claim that he would be able to make anything he wished out of a dozen healthy infants if he were given a free hand in determining their environments.

8. Guthrie's explanation of learning is referred to as a one-shot-learning theory based on contiguity. He maintained that whatever response follows a stimulus will be likely to follow that stimulus again when it is repeated. In addition, the strength of the bond between the stimulus and the response is thought to be fixed after the first pairing.

9. The notion that stimuli and responses occur in temporal contiguity was made plausible by Guthrie through his statement that external stimuli give rise to movement-produced stimuli (MPS). MPS are really responses that serve as stimuli for other responses in the chain of response events that is maintained between the presentation of a stimulus and the occurrence of a response.

10. Guthrie suggested that there are three ways of breaking habits. These methods are based on the notion that habits are really never forgotten but can nonetheless be replaced. The three methods involve repeated presentation of a stimulus (fatigue method), presenting the stimulus so faintly that a response is not elicited (threshold method), and presenting the stimulus when the response cannot occur (method of incompatible stimuli).

11. The two alternative explanations for the formation of relationships between stimuli (S-S), between responses (R-R), or between stimuli and responses (S-R) are contiguity and reinforcement. The contiguity explanation maintains that the co-occurrence of the events in question is sufficient; the reinforcement position takes into consideration the notion that pleasant consequences of behavior will have a facilitating effect on learning, whereas unpleasant consequences will be detrimental. Watson and Guthrie were contiguity theorists. Thorndike was not.

12. Thorndike described learning as involving the formation of bonds between neural events corresponding to stimuli and responses. Learning involves stamping in bonds; forgetting involves stamping out bonds.

13. Thorndike's major contribution is his Law of Effect, which specifies that the "effect" of a response will be instrumental in determining whether it

will be stamped in or out. He believed that pleasure is much more effective in stamping in responses than pain is in stamping them out.

14. Five subsidiary laws also form part of Thorndike's system. The most important is the law of multiple response, which states that the learning of an appropriate response is achieved through trial and error. In addition to this law, Thorndike had others that state that behavior is generalizable (response by analogy), that culture and attitude affect behavior, that people are selective in responding (prepotency of elements), and that stimulus substitution (classical conditioning) occurs.

15. Among Thorndike's most important contributions are his emphasis on the importance of the consequences of behavior (reward and punishment), popularization of the use of animals in psychological research, and a determined attempt to apply psychological principles to real problems, particularly in the area of education.

16. Although it is true that early behavioristic positions present a somewhat mechanistic view of human behavior and although they do little to explain "higher" mental processes, they contributed a great deal to the subsequent development of psychological theories that relate to human learning.

Dear Dr. Lefrancois,

As a devoted former, current, and future user of your text Of Children, I, as well as many of my students have become more than mildly interested in your relationship to your grandmother(s). She has made the text in writing, in pictures (shoveling theories), and even in the glossary. For those students bent on denouncing you as a chauvinist, and for those who admire your sense of humor, I would like to be able to tell my next class what defense/explanation you offer for memorializing your grandmother in the pages of your book. Does she know of, approve, condemn your comments, and does she still send you a card on your birthday?

Sincerely,
John R. Haig
Assistant Professor, Psychology
Philadelphia College of Textiles and Science*

*The letter is reproduced with the permission of John R. Haig.

CHAPTER *3*

Skinner and Operant Conditioning

Skinner's Theoretical Orientation

It may appear to be a contradiction to state at the outset that Skinner's theoretical orientation is antitheoretical, but the statement is only superficially contradictory. Skinner's views on theorizing are summarized in his declaration that theory, while it can be amusing to its creators, will be of little practical value (Skinner, 1961). His system is not intended to state in principles and laws what is known about behavior but simply to describe the observations he has made. Interestingly enough, it is precisely because Skinner's work has taken a clearly objective, descriptive form and not a more inferential, speculative one that his most basic work remains relatively free from sound invalidating criticism. The main critics are those who interpret Skinner's system as implying that principles of operant conditioning can eventually be used to explain and control *all* human behavior. However, their criticism is aimed more at the application of the system than at the system itself.

BURRHUS FREDERIC SKINNER (1904–   )
B. F. Skinner, like many of psychology's pioneers, did not enter graduate school with the intention of becoming a psychologist. Instead, he studied biology, but in the course of his studies he was exposed to the writings of Watson and Pavlov, and these profoundly influenced his career. In 1931 he obtained his Ph.D. in psychology from Harvard and spent the next 5 years doing research before beginning a career as lecturer, researcher, and writer. Chief among his early works was his 1938 book, The Behavior of Organisms, which laid the groundwork for operant-conditioning principles. A novel, Walden Two (1948), did much to popularize his conception of an ideal society, based on scientific principles of human behavior and engineered in such a way that positive rather than aversive techniques of control would predominate. He was soon recognized as the leading proponent of the behavioristic position—a position that has not had universal acceptance and that he has had to defend on numerous occasions. A recent book, Beyond Freedom and Dignity (1971), presents a highly readable exposition and defense of Skinner's beliefs.*

For the sake of simplicity, Skinner's observations can be divided into those concerned with independent variables (factors that can be directly manipulated experimentally) and those concerned with dependent variables (variables not manipulated by the experimenter that are thought to be affected by the independent variables). In addition, he is very much interested in discovering the specific relationships between dependent and independent variables, with the explicit goal of increasing and refining control over dependent variables. The essential elements of the system, viewed in terms of dependent and independent variables, are summarized in Table 3-1.

Table 3-1. Skinner's system

Independent variables	Dependent variables
Type of reinforcement	Acquisition rate
Schedules of	Rate of responding
reinforcement	Extinction rate

The central question that Skinner's system is intended to answer is how do the independent variables—reinforcement types and schedules—affect learning?

Two Types of Learning

In his attempts to explain learning, Skinner had available to him the explanation that had already been advanced by Pavlov and elaborated by people like Watson and Guthrie. It appeared to him, however, that classical conditioning explained only a very limited variety of human and animal behavior. Specifically, he maintained that these earlier theoretical formulations could be used to explain the acquisition of behaviors *only* where the initial response could be elicited by a known stimulus. The learning that would then occur would result from pairing this stimulus with another over a number of trials.

While Skinner accepted this model as accurate for explaining some behavior, he declared that many of the responses that people manifest do not result from obvious stimuli. He further maintained that, in any case, the stimuli, observable or not, are often not central to an accurate and useful explanation of learning. Responses elicited by a stimulus are labeled *respondents*; those responses simply emitted by an organism are labeled *operants.* In other words, in respondent behavior the organism reacts *to* the environment, while in operant behavior it acts *on* the environment. Classical conditioning can be employed to explain learning based on respondent behavior. Skinner called this type of learning *Type S* conditioning. He advanced a different model to explain learning based on operant behavior: the model of operant or instrumental conditioning, also referred to as *Type R* conditioning. The distinctions between these two forms of learning are detailed in Table 3-2.

Table 3-2. Classical and operant conditioning

Classical	Operant
Deals with respondents that are elicited as responses to stimuli	Deals with operants that are emitted as instrumental acts
Type S (stimuli)	Type R (reinforcement)
Pavlov	*Skinner*

A. *Operant conditioning*

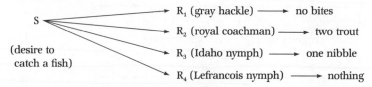

How I learned to use a royal coachman fly

B. *Classical conditioning*

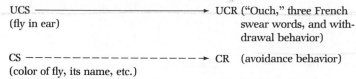

How I learned to avoid a Lefrancois nymph

Figure 3-1.   Two types of conditioning

It was Skinner's (1938) contention that most significant behaviors people engage in are operant. Walking to school, writing a letter or a textbook, answering a question, smiling at a stranger, fondling a rat, fishing, shoveling snow, skiing, and reading are all examples of operant behavior. While it could be argued that there are known and observable stimuli that readily and reliably lead to some of these behaviors, the real point is that the stimuli that can lead to these responses are not central in the learning that takes place.

Stated very simply, the model of operant conditioning says that when a response—regardless of the conditions that might or might not have led to its emission—is followed by a reinforcer, the result will be an increase in the probability that this response will occur again under similar circumstances. Further, the model states that the reinforcer, together with the circumstances surrounding its administration, is a stimulus that can come to have control over that response through repeated presentation. A simplified presentation of a model of operant conditioning and of classical conditioning is presented in Figure 3-1.

Essentially any behavior that is acquired as a result of reinforcement can be interpreted as an illustration of operant conditioning. Figure 3-1 shows one example—a fly fisherman who becomes conditioned to using a certain type of fly because he has been reinforced for using it in the past.

The extent of the applicability of this model to human behavior will be made more evident as we proceed to a discussion of the variables involved.

Reinforcement

Skinner's explanation of learning through operant conditioning is based on the somewhat hedonistic notion that we tend to behave in such a way as to increase pleasure and decrease pain. However, subjective terms like *pain* and *pleasure* do not have an important role in a position so clearly and explicitly objective as Skinner's. Accordingly, reinforcement is defined in a rather operational, if somewhat circular, manner. Reinforcement includes *any and all stimuli that increase the probability of a response's occurring or that maintain a certain level of responding*. Therefore, reinforcement is *not* necessarily a pleasant stimulus in any universal sense. A stimulus that is reinforcing for one situation is not necessarily reinforcing in another; in addition, what is reinforcing for one person is not necessarily reinforcing for another.

To illustrate these comments, let us consider, on the one hand, Henry, a buck-toothed, freckle-faced, lovable little school child of 10. Henry took a spelling test, for which he studied very hard, using a number of mnemonic devices. For example, in order to remember how to spell "separate" he talked himself into remembering that there is "a rat" in "separate." He gets his results back—95%. This knowledge of results serves as a reinforcer; it increases the probability that the response of studying hard and using mnemonics will occur again.

Consider, on the other hand, Agnes. Agnes is a bright little girl. She always gets 100% in spelling. This time she has studied differently—she has used the same mnemonic device Henry used. Unlike Henry, however, she became confused on the test and thought there was "erat" in separate. She also received a grade of 95%. However, this same stimulus is not a reinforcer for Agnes and will probably have the opposite effect on her behavior.

TYPES OF REINFORCEMENT

Skinner distinguishes between two types of reinforcement: positive and negative. A *positive reinforcer* is a stimulus that, when *added* to a situation, increases the probability of the response's occurring again in similar circumstances. A *negative reinforcer* is a stimulus that, when *taken away* from a situation, increases the probability of a response's occurring. It is important to note that the effect of both positive and negative reinforcers is to *increase* the probability of a response's occurring. It is also important to note that the effect of the stimulus on a response—not the nature of the stimulus itself—determines whether or not it is a reinforcer.

PUNISHMENT

Punishment, like reinforcement, is also defined in terms of its effects. In this case, however, the effect is not a strengthening of the behavior but rather a suppression of it. The same considerations need to be applied to punishment that were applied to reinforcement. That is, some stimuli may be punishing in some circumstances but not in others; some stimuli may be punishing for some people but not for others.

PUNISHMENT AND NEGATIVE REINFORCEMENT

An error in definition prevalent in textbooks of psychology and educational psychology is the confounding of punishment with negative reinforcement. It is very common to read such declarations as "punishment is a negative reinforcer" immediately following definitions specifying that reinforcement, whether positive or negative, increases the probability of a response's occurring while punishment does not. How, then, can punishment be a negative reinforcer?

Table 3-3. Reinforcement and punishment

	Pleasant stimulus	*Noxious stimulus*
Added to a situation after a response	Positive reinforcement (1)	Punishment (2)
Taken away from a situation after a response	Punishment (3)	Negative reinforcement (4)

The confusion can easily be clarified by reference to Table 3-3, which shows the four possibilities involved in presenting or removing pleasant or unpleasant stimuli. The effects of each of these four activities define positive (1) and negative (4) reinforcement on the one hand and the two types of punishment (2 and 3) on the other. Each possibility is illustrated below with a rat and then with a person.

RAT ILLUSTRATION

Skinner has made extensive use of rats in investigating the effects of types and schedules of reinforcement on learning. Typically the apparatus used consists of what is known as a Skinner box, a cagelike structure that can be equipped with a lever, a light, a food tray, a food-releasing mechanism, and perhaps an electric grid through the floor (see Figure 3-2). The object of a typical experiment might be to condition a rat to press the lever whenever it is placed in the cage. A number of experimental variations can be employed to illustrate punishment and reinforcement.

Positive Reinforcement (1).* If, when the rat depresses the lever, the food mechanism releases a pellet of food into the tray, the effect may be an increase

*The numbers refer to Table 3-3.

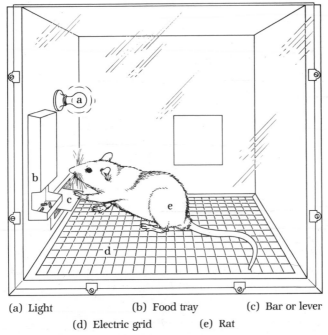

(a) Light   (b) Food tray   (c) Bar or lever
(d) Electric grid   (e) Rat

Figure 3-2.   A Skinner box

in the probability that bar-pressing behavior will occur. In this case, the food is a positive reinforcer.

Punishment (2). If the rat, which must stand on the electric grid when it depresses the bar, is given a mild shock every time it does so, it will probably attempt to avoid the bar in the future. The shock is, in this case, one type of punishment, and may lead to avoidance, or escape learning.

Punishment (3). If the rat, while in the process of eating, stops to lick its chops and a sadistic experimenter takes away its food, the probability of the rat's licking its chops again will decrease. Perhaps if the experimenter continues to remove the food every time the rat licks its chops, the rat may eventually cease licking them altogether. A rat with slovenly table manners is a rarity well worthy of psychological investigation. In any case, this would be an example of punishment as well.

Negative Reinforcement (4). If the current is on continuously in the grid but is turned off every time the rat presses the lever, the rat will probably eventually learn to depress the lever immediately on entering the cage. The electric current is, in this case, a negative reinforcer.

PEOPLE ILLUSTRATION

The following examples of punishment and reinforcement are based on observations of human behavior. The subject was my 3-year-old son. His experiences for one day included the following:

Positive Reinforcement (1).   Early in the morning the boy offered to kiss his father, claiming that he had "dreamed up" a few kisses. Both parents lavished verbal praise on him for this touching filial behavior. The praise, assuming that its effect was to increase the probability of the reoccurrence of the kissing response, is a positive reinforcer.

Punishment (2).   Some time later, the same young hero kicked his sister in the posterior. The sound blow dealt him by his sister probably illustrates the first type of punishment. He is perhaps, though not necessarily, less likely to kick her again in similar circumstances.

Punishment (3).   At lunchtime, he was given a handful of jelly beans after his dessert. He promptly ate one, licked another and rubbed it on the wall, and hurled a third one at his sister. His mother's taking the candies from him is another illustration of punishment that might, again, decrease the probability of his throwing jelly beans or otherwise mistreating them.

Negative Reinforcement (4).   For a more serious misdemeanor, the boy was isolated in his bedroom and made to stay there until he stopped crying, which he eventually did. Allowing him to leave the room as a consequence of stopping crying is an example of negative reinforcement. Theoretically, this might lead to his stopping crying earlier next time; it might also decrease the probability of the same misdemeanor's occurring again, since the situation involves punishment as well as negative reinforcement. That is, insofar as isolating the child in his bedroom might involve both the withdrawal of a pleasant stimulus (preventing him from being where he is or from doing what he is doing) as well as the presentation of an unpleasant stimulus (if isolation is unpleasant), two types of punishment and negative reinforcement are illustrated.

SOURCES OF REINFORCEMENT

In addition to distinguishing between positive and negative reinforcement, Skinner describes two sources of reinforcement—primary and generalized. *Primary reinforcement* includes stimuli that are reinforcing without any learning having taken place. Examples of primary reinforcers are stimuli such as food, water, and sex, which satisfy basic, unlearned needs (primary needs). *Generalized reinforcement* (sometimes called secondary reinforcement) includes stimuli that are not reinforcing to begin with but become reinforcing as a result of being paired with a primary reinforcer or with other reinforcers. The light in the Skinner box is sometimes used as a secondary reinforcer. Over a succession of trials, it is turned on every time the animal is fed (given a primary reinforcer). Eventually the animal will respond simply in order to have the light go on. At this point, the light has acquired secondary reinforcing properties.

For humans, generalized reinforcement includes a multitude of stimuli that come to be generally reinforcing for a wide range of behaviors. Many of these are culturally determined. For example, prestige, social status, power, wealth, fame, strength, and intelligence are all culturally prized attributes. The external symbols of these attributes constitute generalized reinforcers that are extremely powerful in determining human behavior.

Extinction and Forgetting

Forgetting is a topic of considerable interest to teachers, since it is one of the most common activities of students. In fact, one could perhaps describe the process of teaching as an attempt to bring the rate of learning somewhere above the rate of forgetting. One could arrive at an index of a teacher's effectiveness by computing the difference between these two rates.

In the context of Skinner's system, the terms *extinction* and *forgetting* are not identical. Extinction is often, although not always, the result of an experimental or contrived process, whereas forgetting is the result of a natural process. Extinction occurs when an animal or person who has been reinforced for engaging in a behavior ceases to be reinforced; the outcome will be a relatively rapid cessation of the behavior in question. Forgetting, on the other hand, is a much slower process that also results in the cessation of a response but not as a function of withdrawal of reinforcement. According to Skinner, forgetting occurs simply as a result of the passage of time with no repetition of the behavior during this time.*

*There are, of course, other important explanations of forgetting. See Chapter 11 for a more detailed discussion of memory.

It is quite simple to condition a pigeon to peck at a colored disk. If food is used as the reinforcer for this response and this reinforcement is suddenly withdrawn completely, the pigeon will in all likelihood continue to peck at the disk sporadically for some time. However, in a relatively short time it will cease pecking entirely, at which point extinction will have occurred.

Not infrequently, a behavior that has been extinguished through withdrawal of reinforcement will reappear without any further conditioning; this phenomenon is referred to as *spontaneous recovery*. The second extinction period will almost invariably be much shorter than the first.

Assume that the pigeon that has been conditioned to peck at a disk is taken out of the cage and not allowed to return to it for a very long period of time. If it does not peck at the disk when it is reintroduced into the cage, one can say that forgetting has occurred. Skinner reported the case of at least one pigeon that had still not forgotten the disk-pecking response after 6 years. He also reported one instance of a pigeon that emitted 10,000 pecks prior to extinction.

Schedules of Reinforcement in Experiments

Skinner's observations and experiments are largely directed toward elaborating and clarifying the effect of such variables as types and schedules of reinforcement on measures of learning. These measures include extinction rate, acquisition rate, and rate of responding.

Probably the most easily manipulated and most effective variable in operant conditioning is the way rewards are administered. In a carefully controlled laboratory situation, experimenters can determine precisely what reinforcements will be used and how and when they will be used. In other words, experimenters are in complete control of schedules of reinforcement.

Basically, there are two choices: every desired response can be reinforced—that is, reinforcement can be *continuous*; or reinforcement can be *intermittent*.

(see Figure 3-3). If reinforcement is continuous, on the one hand, there are no further choices to make. Every trial (correct response) will be rewarded in the same fashion. (Note: It is entirely possible, however, to use a combination of continuous and intermittent reinforcement schedules. This type of arrangement is sometimes referred to as a combined schedule.) On the other hand, if experimenters employ an intermittent (sometimes called partial) schedule of reinforcement, they can make one of two further choices. The intermittent schedule can be based on a proportion of trials or on a time interval. That is, experimenters can decide to give reinforcement intermittently but in accordance with a predetermined pattern based on time or on trials. They might, for example, decide that the ratio of reinforced to nonreinforced responses will be 1:5, in which case they will reinforce one out of five correct responses. This schedule is a *ratio* schedule of reinforcement. On the other hand, they might decide to reinforce the animal once every 5 minutes, providing it emits at least one correct response prior to reinforcement. This alternative is an *interval* schedule of reinforcement.

The experimenters would further have to decide whether the reinforcement would be administered in a fixed or in a random (variable) manner. A fixed schedule is one in which the experimenter predetermines the time or the trial

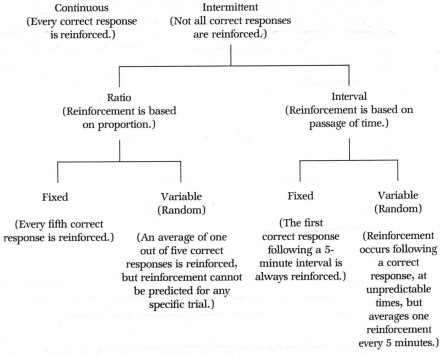

Figure 3-3. Schedules of reinforcement

of reinforcement. For example, in the case of a fixed-ratio schedule, reinforcement might occur on every fifth trial. Fixed-interval reinforcement might occur, for example, at the very beginning of each 5-minute interval but only immediately after a correct response.

The second alternative would be to administer reinforcement at random. The same ratio or interval could be used, but the reinforcement would not always occur at the same time or on the same trial. A random ratio schedule of reinforcement based on a one-reinforcement-to-five-trial proportion might involve reinforcing the first 4 trials, not reinforcing the next 16, reinforcing numbers 17 and 18, and so on. After 100 trials, 20 reinforcers would have been administered.

In short, the major schedules of reinforcements investigated by Skinner and his followers include continuous reinforcement on the one hand and fixed-ratio, variable-ratio, fixed-interval, and variable-interval reinforcement on the other. Any combination of these schedules is also possible.

EFFECTS OF DIFFERENT SCHEDULES

The real significance of schedules of reinforcement is not limited to the possible combinations and sequences of schedules or to the number of experimental designs that can be generated by this type of discussion. For practical purposes the effects of these schedules on learning are much more crucial.

Effects on Acquisition.   It is generally correct to state that initial learning is more rapid if every correct response is reinforced. Initial learning appears to be haphazard, difficult, and slow if any of the intermittent schedules of reinforcement are utilized. In training rats to press levers or pigeons to peck disks, Skinner typically deprives the animal of food for 24 or more hours (sometimes reducing weight to 80% of normal) in order to increase *drive*. Initial training usually begins with "magazine training." Here the animal is trained to eat from the food tray and, consequently, learns to recognize the noise made by the food mechanism and to associate it with the imminent presentation of food. After magazine training all correct responses, and sometimes even responses that merely approximate the desired behavior, are reinforced.

Effects on Extinction.   While one measure of learning is the rate at which an animal acquires a new response, another is the rate at which this response becomes extinguished after the withdrawal of reinforcement. Interestingly, while a continuous schedule of reinforcement results in a faster rate of learning than does an intermittent schedule, it also leads to more rapid extinction after withdrawal. Further, the fixed schedules of reinforcement, while they have shorter acquisition times associated with them than variable schedules, also lead to more rapid extinction than the variable schedules. Probably the best training combination for an animal is a continuous schedule initially, followed by a variable-ratio schedule. (Note: The ratio may also be varied over training sessions, with a decreasing ratio of reinforced to nonreinforced trials usually leading to even longer extinction periods.)

Effects on Rate of Responding. A third measure of learning is the rate of responding, which is a dependent variable remarkably sensitive to schedules of reinforcement. A rather interesting observation concerning the relationship between a schedule of reinforcement and the rate of responding can be made. It appears that, in general, an animal behaves as one would predict it would behave if it is valid to assume that the animal develops expectations and has some time sense. For example, under variable schedules of reinforcement, when the animal is less likely to develop an expectation of receiving a reward at a given time, rate of responding will be uniformly high and relatively unvarying. If the variable schedule is a ratio schedule rather than an interval one, rate of responding will be higher. Under a fixed-interval schedule of reinforcement, the rate of responding drops dramatically immediately after reinforcement and often ceases altogether. Just prior to the next reinforcement, however, the animal again responds at a high rate (see Figure 3-4).

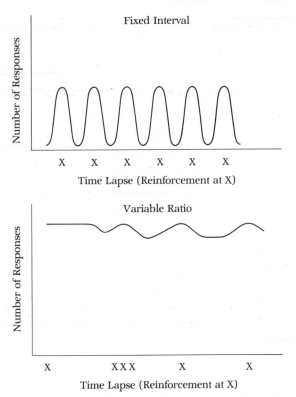

Figure 3-4. Idealized representation of the effects of two schedules of reinforcement on rate of responding

Schedules of Reinforcement in Everyday Life

In order to examine the nature of the schedules of reinforcement that affect people's daily lives, it is necessary first of all to determine what is reinforcing for people. Commonly accepted reinforcing stimuli are money, praise, satisfaction, and food. Two of these stimuli appear to be on fixed-interval schedules: money and food. For a large number of people, money arrives regularly (at fixed intervals) in the form of a paycheck, and food is taken routinely in the form of meals. For both of these rather important reinforcers, however, there are usually no immediate, simple operants that will predictably result in their presentation. The operants involved in acquiring money have become so complex and so remote from the actual source of reinforcement that it has become difficult to see the relationship between the two. The confusion is further compounded by the fact that the reinforcers themselves are inextricably bound together. That is, money allows one to buy food and, in some cases, praise as well. In addition, the acquisition of money sometimes appears to be a source of satisfaction in itself.

While it may be true that the relationship between behavior and reinforcement is not always simple or obvious, this fact does not necessarily invalidate the notion that a great many human behaviors are affected by reinforcers and their scheduling. Indeed, in many cases, the person whose behavior is affected remains completely unaware of the relationship between his behavior and its consequences. It is relatively simple, in fact, to illustrate through a variety of examples how behavior is controlled and modified by reinforcements.

Illustration 1.   A fisherman has fished in the same stream for 22 years. Every time he goes fishing he catches at least four fish (continuous reinforcement). Now, at the beginning of this pollution-conscious decade, he suddenly ceases to catch fish (withdrawal of reinforcement). After four fruitless trips to the stream, he stops going altogether (rapid extinction following continuous reinforcement).

Illustration 2.   Another man has also fished in the same stream for 22 years. Sometimes he catches fish and sometimes he doesn't. On occasion he doesn't catch a single fish for an entire season. He has occasionally caught as many as 18 trout in one day (intermittent reinforcement). Now he ceases to catch fish (withdrawal of reinforcement). At the end of the decade, he might still be frequenting the same stream (slow extinction following intermittent reinforcement).

Illustration 3.   A young child is given her first rattle. A cruel but clever psychologist has removed its innards. The child holds the rattle up, looks at it, shakes it, bites it, strikes her knee with it, drops it, and forgets it. (The unreinforced response of shaking the rattle is not strengthened.)

Illustration 4. The same young child is given a rattle that has been kept away from all psychologists. She looks at it, shakes it, looks at it again, and then proceeds to shake it vigorously for some time (the sound of the rattle serves as a reinforcer and strengthens the operant that causes it).

Shaping

Shaping—one of Skinner's procedures that has received a great deal of attention—is employed to train animals to perform acts that are not ordinarily in their repertoire. (The discussion of operant conditioning presented so far in this chapter has considered only instances of behavior where the operants in question were available to the animal.) It is entirely possible that, if one waited long enough beside a Skinner box, the rat in the box would eventually accidentally depress the lever in the course of exploring the environment. This operant could then be slowly conditioned through the use of reinforcement.

However, if the experimenter wanted to train a rat to go to corner *A* of the cage, pick up a marble in that corner, carry it to corner *B*, drop it there, return to the center of the cage, lie down, roll over, get up, return to corner *B*, pick up the marble again, and carry it to corner *C*, the rat would probably die of old age before it emitted the operant.

Nevertheless, it is possible, through *shaping*, to teach a rat to engage in behaviors that are very impressive, if not as complex as the behavior described above. Shaping is sometimes referred to as the method of *successive approximations*, or as a method involving the *differential reinforcement of successive approximations* (Skinner, 1951). An experimenter using the technique of shaping reinforces every behavior that takes the animal closer to the final response,

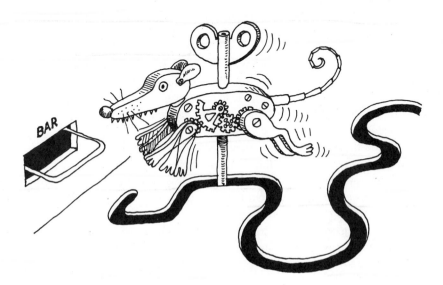

instead of waiting for the final desired response to be emitted. Even a behavior as superficially simple as bar pressing or disk pecking is usually brought about through shaping. The experimenter begins by reinforcing the rat every time it turns toward the bar. Later, only movements that bring it closer to the bar are reinforced. After the rat has learned to approach the bar, it is not reinforced again until it touches it. Eventually its behavior will have been so *shaped* that it will readily press the bar when put in the cage.

Most animal trainers employ techniques that amount to shaping procedures. Thus are parrots trained to walk on tightropes, parachute, play tunes, and ride bicycles; porpoises to jump incredible heights with military precision in predetermined order; bears to play guitars, dance, roll somersaults, and clap hands; chickens to play ball; and horses to count.

One critical requirement for the successful use of shaping procedures is that the environment be controlled. For example, the Skinner box is constructed so that the rat cannot perform very many responses other than those the experimenter wishes to reinforce. Similarly, a professional animal trainer would not attempt to condition a dog when the dog is chasing a rabbit but would first confine the dog and secure its attention. In other words, the environment is arranged to facilitate the appearance of the desired response.

SHAPING AND PEOPLE

Many more human behaviors are probably acquired through shaping than people are aware of. For example, in the course of learning any task involving muscular coordination, a large number of inappropriate or ineffective responses are abandoned, while appropriate (and, consequently, reinforced) responses become more firmly established.

The verbal behavior of people is also susceptible to the effects of reinforcement (Skinner, 1957), a phenomenon that Greenspoon (1955) illustrated experimentally through a technique referred to as *verbal conditioning.* In this study, the experimenter simply interviewed subjects and asked them to say words. The subjects, who had no idea what words were required, began to verbalize. Each time they said a plural noun, the experimenter reinforced them by saying "mm-hm." Over the course of the training session the incidence of plural nouns increased significantly.

While this type of experimental procedure may, at first glance, appear to be somewhat remote from the realities of everyday life, on closer examination it becomes evident that people engage in many behaviors that are examples of the effects of verbal conditioning. For example, a high-pressure, door-to-door salesperson often gets customers to commit themselves by employing a verbal-conditioning technique. First, the salesperson suggests that the customers are intelligent. Then the salesperson proceeds to reinforce all declarations of intelligence made spontaneously by the customers. Eventually they will have admitted either that they are so intelligent that they cannot pass up such a good deal or that, being so intelligent, they are sufficiently concerned for their children to purchase an encyclopedia.

Verbal fluency (sometimes called verbosity) can sometimes be turned on or off by a skillful listener who reinforces a speaker or withdraws reinforcement through subtle facial expressions and gestures. A rather striking, although sometimes boring, illustration of the power of reinforcement in conversation can easily be provided by almost anyone. The procedure involves simply making the decision that your next conversation will be with someone who will talk only about herself. It is quite likely that by making only a minimum number of comments but by expressing great interest in certain personal expressions, you can easily control the substance of your conversation.

On several occasions, I have attempted to demonstrate for a class the power of reinforcement in shaping the verbal behavior of subjects. Below are descriptions of two such attempts. In neither case did the demonstration work as planned, but in both instances the outcomes were illustrative of equally striking phenomena.

Demonstration 1.   The first demonstration was intended to be a simple replication of the Greenspoon experiment with a number of important variations. The subject was asked to sit in front of a rather large senior undergraduate psychology class of which he was a member. The students had previously had the Greenspoon experiment explained to them and had been instructed to reinforce all plural nouns by paying attention, nodding occasionally but not too obviously, and smiling from time to time. They were asked to appear less interested when the subject said words that were not plural nouns. One member of the class surreptitiously recorded the number of plural nouns emitted during each 2-minute interval of the session.

A number of factors detracted from the experiment and were probably responsible for the fact that it did not work as planned. It appeared that not all members of the class immediately recognized plural nouns. In addition, the subject, being a psychology student, was somewhat suspicious and perhaps overly tense. In any case, the number of plural nouns did not increase significantly over a 20-minute period. What did happen, however, was a clear illustration of verbal conditioning. It appeared (this was verified through an interview afterward) that the subject had, on the previous Saturday night, gone to a country dance and imbibed somewhat too freely. He had then challenged some of the local citizens to display their pugilistic skills for him. As a result he had spent the better part of that night in the local jail.

As this brave subject sat in front of his fellow students the following Monday morning, looking at them through bleary eyes, it was inevitable that he should, in the process of free association, say such sequences of words as "Saturday night, drunk, fight, yippee, . . . police, jail . . . ." The mood of the class was such that each of these words occasioned titters and suppressed laughter. But the subject was a "ham"—knowing his audience, he repeated some of his words again, sprinkling an odd neutral word here and there. In the end the class laughed openly every time he said a Saturday-night-related word, and the number of such words increased dramatically as the session progressed. The subject's behavior was indeed shaped by the reaction of his audience.

Demonstration 2. A second classroom demonstration was attempted with two other classes consisting entirely of teachers who had returned to the university for a 6-week summer course. The attempt in these demonstrations was an even bolder one, for the experiment involved trying to change people's attitudes through reinforcement. Two experimental sessions were undertaken—one with each of the two classes. The procedure was to have four persons volunteer as panelists for a discussion of the merits of physical punishment in schools. It was assumed that the topic was sufficiently controversial to be suitable for a good two-sided debate. The panelists were given 5 minutes in which to consult one another and organize their thoughts; none was asked to be for or against punishment. However, the entire class in the first demonstration was instructed to reinforce all statements supporting the use of physical punishment in the schools. They were allowed to participate in the discussion but were asked to make only pro-punishment statements. The intention was to increase pro-punishment statements on the part of the panelists, both through the effects of reinforcement and perhaps through the effects of group pressure as well.

In the second class, the procedure followed was identical except that statements condemning physical punishment were reinforced.

The results of both of these demonstrations are rather striking. In neither case was there an increase in the number of reinforced statements given by panelists during the experimental session. It appeared that panelists solidified their views whether or not they were reinforced. One plausible explanation for this behavior is that the panelists probably anticipated receiving reinforcement from the professor for putting up a good argument. It was also clear, after the fact, that panelists saw themselves as debaters and, as such, would have been violating implicit rules had they changed their minds.

What did change, however, were the attitudes of the entire classes. After each session, students were asked to indicate what they really believed about physical punishment. In the first session, students were overwhelmingly in favor of it; in the second, they were equally overwhelmingly opposed to it.

While shaping was probably not involved in this attitude change, perhaps reinforcement was, since every time someone *in the class* made a good point, he or she would be very strongly reinforced by the entire class. Despite the fact that students knew what was going on, the praise of fellow students could easily have affected their behavior.

Fading, Generalization, and Discrimination

Shaping is one technique employed in training animals to perform complex behaviors. Another is *fading.*

Reese (1966) described a procedure whereby a pigeon is taught to "read" two words: *peck* and *turn.* It is assumed that the pigeon has learned to read if it responds appropriately to either of these words.

This type of training presents some special problems. While it is relatively simple to train a pigeon either to peck or to turn using a shaping procedure, the bird will then immediately *generalize* the learned response to the other word. For example, if the pigeon is taught to peck in response to the word *peck*, it will also peck in response to the word *turn.* If, however, the two stimuli are made highly different so that the pigeon can easily *discriminate* between the two, it can be taught to respond appropriately to each stimulus through *shaping.* For example, the word *turn* might be printed in large black letters and the word *peck* in small red letters. Pigeons have excellent color vision. Over successive trials, after the pigeon has learned to peck and to turn as instructed, the differences between the stimuli are *faded* out: the large black letters become smaller, and the small red letters become both darker and larger, until finally each word is black and the letters are of uniform size. The pigeon can now *discriminate* between the two.

Generalization and discrimination are of considerable importance in human learning. Generalization involves engaging in previously learned behaviors in response to new situations that resemble those in which the behaviors were first learned. One example is obviously that of a pigeon turning in response to the word *peck* before it has learned to discriminate between *turn* and *peck.* Examples of generalization in human behavior are infinite. Any 5-minute segment of behavior in the life of a normal person is likely to be replete with instances of old behaviors being generalized to new situations. New cars are driven in ways similar to those employed in driving old ones; someone who hits a stranger accidentally may apologize; when faced with the problem of adding 27 kangaroos and 28 zebras, a farmer reasons that 27 kangaroos and 28 zebras are as many animals as 27 pigs and 28 horses; people assume that objects fall from mountaintops as they do from treetops; strangers shake hands when introduced; and so on. All of these behaviors can be interpreted as examples of responses to new situations that are based on previous learning; all are examples of generalization. It is precisely because not all, or even most, situations to which a person must react in a lifetime can be covered in schools or in other learning situations that generalization is of such crucial importance. Hence, teaching for generalization (which is really teaching for transfer) is one of the primary functions of schools.

Discrimination is a process that is complementary to generalization in that it involves making distinctions between similar situations in order to respond appropriately to each. The pigeon's learning to respond to the two highly similar

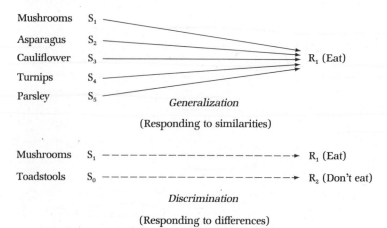

Figure 3-5.   Discrimination and generalization

situations involved in the presentation of the words *peck* and *turn* is an example of discrimination.

Discrimination learning is probably as important for human behavior, particularly in learning socially appropriate behavior, as is generalization. Children must learn to discriminate at relatively early ages which responses are appropriate to which situations. For example, it is permissible to kiss one's parents but not strangers; sisters should not be punched, but neighborhood bullies can be; it is sinful to make noises in quiet churches but permissible to make the same noises in quiet houses; and so on. Accordingly, socially appropriate adult behavior is very much a function of having learned to discriminate between similar situations calling for different types of behavior.

The processes of discrimination and generalization are illustrated in Figure 3-5.

In the first case, the appropriate response is to eat any of the five vegetables; in other words, a generalization of the eating response is appropriate. In the second case, it is necessary to discriminate between two stimuli. Generalization here is inappropriate.

Superstitious Behavior

Earlier in this chapter a fixed-interval schedule of reinforcement was defined as the administration of rewards based on a time interval but occurring only *immediately after a correct response*. A *superstitious* schedule—so called because it might explain some superstition in humans and animals—is a slight variation of a fixed-interval schedule of reinforcement.

A superstitious schedule of reinforcement is a fixed-interval schedule without the provision that reinforcement will occur only after a correct response. In other words, the reinforcement will be given at a specified time regardless of the behavior being engaged in at the time. It follows from the law of operant conditioning that any behavior just prior to reinforcement is strengthened. Whether or not the behavior is related to the reinforcement in a causal manner is of no consequence. It seems that for both humans and other animals, temporal contiguity alone is sufficient to establish a relationship between reinforcement and behavior.

Numerous examples of superstitious behavior in animals are cited in the literature. In fact, it appears that in most conditioning sequences there are behaviors that accidentally precede reinforcement and temporarily become part of the animal's repertoire. For example, a rat that has just learned to depress a lever may do so with its head always to the right or with its left leg dangling. Both actions are examples of superstitious behavior.

Skinner (1951) reports conditioning six out of eight pigeons using a superstitious schedule of reinforcement. Whatever the birds happened to be doing at the time of reinforcement tended to be learned. One bird turned clockwise prior to each reinforcement. Another tossed its head toward a corner, and two others developed an unnatural pendulum motion of the head and body.

There is no better place to observe superstitious behavior associated with thinking than in a crowded examination room at the end of a semester. Some people scratch their heads; others frown; some move their lips, hands, legs, or feet; some chew their hair, and others engage in a variety of behaviors not causally related to clear thinking. One year I observed a student repeatedly crossing her eyes and looking at her nose as she attempted a multiple-choice test. She passed the test.

How much of our behavior is superstitious? That is, how much is related to rewards or punishment that, in effect, are not caused by our behaviors? And how much of our behavior can be accounted for by its actual positive or negative consequences?

The debate continues.

Positive and Aversive Control

Although there is much to be said for the use of positive methods to control behavior, these are not always possible or effective. Unfortunately, as Skinner (1971) notes repeatedly, we make extensive use of *aversive* control when positive control would be far more humane and probably more effective as well. He writes, for example, that our major social institutions operate to a large extent through aversive control. These methods are sorely evident in schools, where reprimands, detention, low grades, and threats of punishment are too often a more salient fact of a student's daily life than are praise, the granting of favors, the promise of high marks, or the possibility of other important reinforcement.

POSITIVE CONTROL IN SCHOOLS

It is possible to draw an analogy between a classroom and a Skinner box. On the one hand, teachers are experimenters; that is, they administer rewards and punishments. Students, on the other hand, are analogous to Skinnerian rats. As experimenters, teachers can profit from knowing that reinforcement is effective in bringing about changes in behavior, that schedules of reinforcement can be varied to good advantage, that punishment is not very effective for learning, and that some reinforcers are more powerful than others. They can profit from greater knowledge about *sources* of reinforcement. For example, Bijou and Sturges (1959) classified reinforcers in five categories: consumables (such as candy); manipulatables (like toys); visual and auditory stimuli (for example, a bell signal that means "good work"); social stimuli (like praise); and tokens (such as disks that can be exchanged for other reinforcers). To this list can be added the Premack Principle (Premack, 1965), which states that behavior that occurs frequently and naturally (and that must therefore be pleasant) can be used to reinforce less frequent behavior. For example, children who read a great deal but dislike arithmetic could be told that they will be allowed to read if they do an arithmetic assignment. Each of these classes of reinforcers can be employed effectively by a teacher. Indeed, there are numerous illustrations of their use in psychological literature, particularly in investigations of what is termed *behavior modification.* Briefly, this label describes the systematic application of principles of learning. These principles are typically behavioristic; indeed, most are based directly on operant conditioning. Behavior modification is employed extensively in schools, hospitals, and other institutions, and is described and illustrated in Chapter 14.

AVERSIVE CONTROL

There are two types of aversive (or negative) control described by Skinner: punishment and negative reinforcement. Earlier, I was careful to point out that these are fundamentally different from each other. Whereas negative reinforcement increases the probability that a response will occur again, punishment is intended to have an opposite effect.

Punishment: Against. Few topics in child rearing and education have received more attention than punishment. It is interesting that much of this attention results from the prevalence of punishment rather than from its effectiveness. Since Thorndike's (1932) early work, it has generally been accepted that punishment is much less effective in eliminating undesirable responses than reinforcement is in bringing about desirable ones.

From a learning-theory point of view, a number of practical and theoretical objections to the use of punishment can be raised. First, the likelihood that punishment will lead to appropriate behavior is often remote. Essentially punishment serves to draw attention to undesirable behavior but does little to indicate what the desirable behavior should be. Second, punishment does not eliminate behavior but usually only suppresses it. What is affected is the rate of responding. The advantage that nonreinforcement has over punishment is that, theoretically, it leads to the extinction of the unreinforced behavior.

Third, punishment can lead to emotional states that will probably not be associated with love or happiness or any other pleasant feeling. These negative emotional states may, through contiguity, become associated with the punisher rather than with the undesirable behavior.

A fourth, more general objection to punishment is that it often does not work. Sears, Maccoby, and Lewin (1957) cite evidence to show that mothers who punish children for toilet accidents are more likely to have children who wet their beds, and parents who punish aggression are more likely to have children who are aggressive.

Punishment: For. Our most passionate objections to the use of punishment apply primarily to physical punishment. The same objections are not nearly as pertinent with respect to several other forms of punishment, some of which are quite common in schools and homes. Among these are the so-called "time-out" procedures, in which children are removed from a situation where they might expect reinforcement and placed in another situation where they are less likely to be reinforced. Children who are removed from a classroom in response to some misbehavior are being punished not by the administration of an unpleasant stimulus (unless, of course, they are sent to the principal's office or given detention), but rather by being removed from what is assumed to be a reinforcing environment.

Other common punishments include the use of reprimands, most of which are verbal, but a number of which might be nonverbal (a negative shake of the head or frown, for example). A series of studies in classroom situations (O'Leary et al., 1974; O'Leary & Becker, 1968) found that the most effective verbal reprimands are those described as "soft." Soft reprimands are those given in such a way that only the child involved can hear them. In those classes in which teachers employed "loud" reprimands, there was a significantly higher incidence of disruptive behavior. In this connection, it is also worth noting that praise, a highly effective reinforcer in the classroom, is far more effective if it is "loud." In brief, in most cases reprimands should be soft, and reinforcement should be more public.

The case for the use of punishment is based on a number of observations. First, although reinforcement, imitation, and reasoning might all be highly effective in bringing about and maintaining desirable behavior, there are numerous instances when they do not appear to be sufficient. As Ausubel (1957) notes, it is not always possible for a child to determine what is undesirable by generalizing in reverse from what has been identified as desirable. Nor, of course, is the child always going to be immediately convinced through gentle persuasion of the undesirability of certain behaviors. If Johnny persists in throwing the cat in the bathtub even after being told that the poor thing cannot swim, punishment might be in order. And although psychologists have long noted that punishment does not appear to be very effective in eliminating undesirable behaviors, there is considerable evidence that it might be very effective in at least suppressing these behaviors (see, for example, Parke, 1974). In fact, the argument that punishment does not lead to the extinction of the behavior in question is really irrelevant. If Johnny now stops throwing the unfortunate cat in the bathtub, we would not dare believe that he has quite forgotten how to do so—but we might hope that he would refrain from doing so in the future.

Like reinforcement, punishment appears to be most effective when it immediately follows behavior. However, this observation is far more valid for other animals than it is for humans, presumably because our ability to symbolize allows us to form associations between behavior and its consequences even when these are separated by significant expanses of time. In addition, punishment appears to be most effective when administered by a warm and loving parent (or other adult). And there is no evidence that the affection that exists between parent and child is damaged or reduced as a result of the judicious use of punishment (Walters & Grusec, 1977).

Negative Reinforcement. One final distinction needs to be made here. It involves the difference between negative and positive reinforcement, both of which lead to an increase in the probability of a response's occurring, but each of which is likely to have different effects. As I note elsewhere (Lefrancois, 1982), a rat can be trained to jump a stool by being fed every time it does so (positive reinforcement). It can also be trained to jump onto the same stool by being given an electric shock when it does not do so. In the end it may jump onto the stool equally hastily no matter how it has been trained, but there is little doubt that the positively reinforced rat will display considerably more enthusiasm for stool-jumping than will its aversively trained colleague. There is a fundamental difference between learning an *approach response*, as is generally the case with positive reinforcement, and *escape*, or *avoidance, learning*, which frequently results from negative reinforcement. And much like the rat that has learned to jump onto a stool to escape an electric shock, students who are attentive and studious because of aversive control (negative reinforcement or punishment) cannot be expected to like school as much as those who are attentive and studious because of positive reinforcement. Perhaps the same is true of those who go to church to avoid hellfire.

It is worth noting that our environments provide us constantly with a variety of aversive stimuli that appear to be extremely effective in shaping our behaviors. Stoves that are hot, insects that bite, mushrooms that poison—all of these quickly lead to important learning. If they didn't, our species probably would not have survived this many generations. Although we should recognize the importance of emphasizing positive rather than aversive control, we should not too glibly dismiss the latter.

Skinner's Position in Retrospect

Skinner stands out in the history of psychological thinking as one of its great system builders. Although behaviorism was originated and defined by Watson and although many other theorists have contributed significantly to its development, it is Skinner's name that is most frequently brought to mind when one thinks of behavioristic psychology.

Probably his greatest contribution to the understanding of human behavior is his description of the effects of reinforcement on responding. In addition, Skinner has attempted to relate these findings not only to individuals but also to social groups (see, for example, *Science and Human Behavior*, 1953). Since the inception of Skinner's work, numerous theorists have incorporated large portions of his system into their own positions.

One of the tangible applications of Skinner's work has taken the form of programmed instruction, a teaching technique premised specifically on principles of operant conditioning. Essentially, a program consists of a series of related statements (frames) that require students to emit responses (operants) and attempt to reinforce them by telling them that they have answered correctly. An example of a teaching program of the Skinnerian type (called linear) is found at the end of Chapter 6 in this text. A second highly visible application of Skinnerian principles is, as was mentioned earlier, behavior modification.

With respect to the criteria for good theories described in Chapter 1, Skinner's system fares relatively well. Skinner himself has been highly reluctant to generalize far beyond his data, preferring to limit his system to the actual observations he made. Accordingly, the system reflects the facts relatively well. The argument must be made, however, that he does not consider all the facts. For example, he does not concern himself very much with symbolic processes or with other topics that are of primary interest to contemporary cognitive theorists (decision making, problem solving, perception, and so on). And his attempts to explain language in terms of reinforcement theory are rather inadequate. Also, there is a range of findings relating to certain behaviors that are either very difficult or very easy to condition that cannot easily be explained by this theory. These findings are discussed in Chapter 5.

However, the system does explain certain kinds of learning remarkably well; it is clear and understandable; and it is characterized by a high degree of internal consistency. This is primarily because it makes use of a relatively small number of key concepts, which are clearly defined in operational terms. And although it is not based on a *large* number of unverifiable assumptions, like all other psychological theories it stems from a handful of fundamental assumptions. The most important of these, and also perhaps the most controversial, address such central questions as whether or not we are free. Skinner assumes not. Like all assumptions, this one is unverifiable.

If, indeed, most significant human behaviors are operant, the importance of Skinner's observations can hardly be overestimated. There is some argument, however, about the extent to which behavior is controlled by reinforcement contingencies. Much of this argument centers on our inability to decide whether we possess free will or whether freedom is merely an illusion. Is behavior entirely determined by its consequences or the unconscious anticipation thereof? Is Skinner correct when he asserts that "autonomous man is a device used to explain what we cannot explain in any other way" (1971, p. 200)? Or are we captains of our own ships, in charge of our moment-to-moment behaviors if not our larger destinies?

Skinner's estimate of the human condition has come under severe critical attack from a number of quarters. Most notably, humanistically oriented psychologists have often been appalled at Skinner's apparent assault on human freedom and dignity. A fundamental Skinnerian position seems, on the surface, totally incompatible with a concern for human worth and individuality.

In the end, we are what we are. As Skinner notes, (1971, p. 215), a theory does not change what it is a theory about. "Man remains what he has always been."

Have we always been free? Or never?

The question is yours.

Summary of Chapter 3

This chapter has presented an account of the work of B. F. Skinner. The principles of operant conditioning were discussed and related to animal and human behavior.

1. Skinner observed and described the relationship between independent variables (reinforcement types and schedules) and dependent variables (rate of acquisition, rate of responding, and extinction rate). He did little theorizing in the form of deriving laws from his observations and basing inferences on these laws.

2. Skinner identified two major types of learning: that involving stimulus-elicited responses (respondents) and that involving emitted instrumental acts (operants). A classical-conditioning model (Type S) explains respondent learning; an operant-conditioning model (Type R) explains operant learning. Skinner's system deals almost exclusively with operant learning.

3. One of the most important variables in the Skinnerian system is *reinforcement*. A reinforcer is a stimulus that increases the probability of a response's occurring. It can be positive (effective through its presentation) or negative (effective through its removal). A negative reinforcer is not the same thing as punishment. Punishment does not increase the probability of a response's occurring.

4. Reinforcement can be primary or generalized. That is, it can satisfy basic needs (such as food), or it can become reinforcing through association with other reinforcers (money).

5. Reinforcement involves presenting a pleasant stimulus following behavior (positive reinforcement) or removing an unpleasant stimulus (negative reinforcement). Punishment involves removing a pleasant stimulus following behavior or presenting an unpleasant stimulus, also following behavior.

6. *Extinction* is the elimination of a behavior through the withdrawal of reinforcement. *Forgetting* is the elimination of behavior through the passage of time. Extinction is a relatively rapid process, whereas forgetting occurs more slowly.

7. *Scheduling of reinforcement* refers to the manner in which an organism receives reinforcement. Two broad categories of schedules exist: continuous and intermittent. Intermittent schedules of reinforcement can be based on proportion of trials (ratio) or on time lapse (interval). Both ratio- and interval-based schedules can be either fixed (unvarying) or random (variable).

8. Continuous schedules of reinforcement typically lead to rapid acquisition and also rapid extinction. Intermittent schedules have longer extinction

times associated with them but are less efficient for early training. As one would predict, rate of responding is typically based on the expectations of reward an animal or person is likely to develop during training. High rates of responding usually occur where reinforcement is dependent on the number of responses emitted. Varying rates occur for a fixed-interval schedule with high response rates preceding reinforcement and a virtual cessation of responding just after reinforcement.

9. *Shaping*, or the differential reinforcement of successive approximations, is a technique used to bring about novel behavior in animals. It involves reinforcing responses that move in the desired direction until the final response has been conditioned.

10. *Verbal conditioning* is a procedure employed to condition people to emit predetermined verbal responses. It is often used, consciously and unconsciously, in controlling conversations. The technique simply involves reinforcing, often through nonverbal signs of approval, certain verbal behaviors in the subject.

11. *Fading* is sometimes employed to bring about discrimination learning. When an animal is to be trained to make different responses to two highly similar stimuli, the differences between the stimuli can be exaggerated for the initial training. As learning becomes more established, the differences are faded out until the animal can respond differentially to the two original stimuli.

12. *Generalization* and *discrimination* are of considerable importance for learning. The former involves transferring one response to other stimuli; the latter involves making different responses for highly similar stimuli.

13. *Superstitious behavior* is incidental behavior that becomes learned when it is present at the time of reinforcement. It has no real relationship to reinforcement but is engaged in as though it had.

14. *Punishment*, while prevalent, is not always successful. It is argued that punishment does not tell the offender what to do but merely what not to do. In addition, it may have some undesirable emotional side effects. But it does often lead to the temporary suppression of a behavior and might provide an opportunity for learning a more desirable response.

15. The most valid objections to punishment apply primarily to physical punishment. Other forms (reprimands and time-out for example) are often necessary and effective. The emphasis should always be on methods of positive rather than aversive control, however.

16. Two important practical applications of Skinnerian principles are found in programmed instruction and in behavior modification.

17. Skinner's system fares quite well with respect to the important criteria for good theories. It explains and predicts certain behaviors remarkably

well, is internally consistent and clear, and reflects some facts well. However, it does not explain all facts (observations) equally well, and it is based on a fundamental and controversial assumption concerning human freedom.

Dear Guy,

You thank me for my "kind comments" in your last letter. That's what I mean about some of the things you write. You often use expressions without even thinking about what they mean, because if you had read my letter carefully, you would see that I wasn't very kind. In fact, maybe I went just a little bit too far about Sylvia, because, after all, she's married now and she has a family to think about. And a husband too.

But I have more important things to talk to you about right now. Remember that letter you brought me from that professor in Philadelphia? August, I think it was, because I was working around the garden when you came over. You wanted me to write him a letter or something. Well, I'm a little bit embarrassed to say this, but I can't find his letter. Maybe you could come over and look for it sometime if you're not too busy. You haven't been here for quite a while now, you know, and I'm sure you'd like to see how the cat is doing on that mega-vitamin therapy stuff.

So far, I'd say your book is coming along not too badly, except you should try harder to be more serious instead of every once in a while being a little bit wacko (that's your word, not mine). But you really are doing much better than you used to, and if you continue to practice writing books, I'm sure some day you'll write a really good one . . .

CHAPTER *4*

Hull and Spence: Intervening Variables

Clark L. Hull (1884–1952)

Hull was among the most ambitious of the behavior theorists. The final system he developed is of such complexity and scope that only a brief glimpse of it can be given here. A complete account of the system is found in Hull's own books (1943, 1951, 1952). Summaries are provided in numerous psychology textbooks.

The development of the system consisted essentially of the elaboration of 17 postulates (Hull, 1943), which were meant to be statements descriptive of human behavior. From these postulates, 133 specific theorems and numerous corollaries were derived (Hull, 1952). A third book describing the application of this system to behavior in social interactions was to be written. Unfortunately, Hull died shortly after finishing the second book, and the third was never begun.

CLARK L. HULL (1884–1952)

Hull was born in Akron, New York, on the 24th of May, 1884, but spent most of his boyhood in rural Michigan. He is reported to have been in poor health throughout much of his childhood, was laid low by poliomyelitis for a lengthy period during his early college years, and had extremely poor eyesight. Nevertheless, at the tender age of 17 he spent an entire year teaching in a one-room school in Michigan before continuing his education at the University of Michigan. His initial aspiration was to become a mining engineer, but for some reason he switched to psychology and went on to the University of Wisconsin, where he obtained a Ph.D. in 1918.

Hull's early interests were highly varied. They included systematic investigations of the effect of tobacco on intellectual functioning, of human and animal aptitudes, of thinking machines (robots), and of hypnosis (to which he devoted a full 10 years of study and research). In 1929 he went to Yale, where he became a research professor and where, with a number of ardent disciples, he generated the monumental system that, in extremely simplified form, makes up the bulk of this chapter. Following his first major descriptions of this system in Principles *of Behavior, published in 1943, he rapidly became the most frequently cited psychologist in the United States. A final revision of this book was published just after his death in 1952.*

NATURE OF THE SYSTEM

Hull's explicitly behavioristic system is marked by all of the behaviorist's concerns for objectivity, precision, and rigor. It is referred to as a hypothetico-deductive system in recognition of his attempt to derive hypotheses—in the form of theorems and corollaries—from the postulates he had advanced. However, his work went much further, for he was not content simply to derive theorems but also attempted to verify them in laboratory situations. As one can see from an examination of the system, this was a monumental task—consequently, Hull was only partially successful.

True to the behavioristic approach, Hull looked at human behavior in terms of stimuli and responses. However, he dealt with them in considerably more detail than had most of his contemporaries. For Hull, stimuli consist of a large number of conditions that affect the organism but that might or might not lead to behavior; he referred to these antecedent conditions as input variables. Accordingly, responses are described in terms of a number of variables referred to as output variables. A number of his postulates are devoted to explaining the nature of input and output variables as well as the relationships that exist between the two. A third set of behavior variables, which forms a central part of Hull's system, is referred to as intervening variables.

Hull's interest in intervening variables is a significant departure from the preoccupations of those S-R theorists we have considered earlier: Pavlov, Watson, Guthrie, Thorndike, and Skinner. It is for this reason that Hull is sometimes described as a neobehaviorist rather than simply as a behaviorist.

Hull was greatly impressed by Pavlov's work on reflexive behavior and classical conditioning. This Pavlovian influence is reflected in part by the fact that the cornerstone of Hull's system is his belief that all behavior consists of S-R connections. The central concept in behavior is that of *habit*, and a habit is an S-R connection, or a collection of such connections termed a *habit-family hierarchy*. Another source of profound influence on Hull was the work of Thorndike, particularly his Law of Effect. The influence of reward on learning became the main explanatory notion in the final system.

SUMMARY OF HULL'S SYSTEM

It may appear somewhat presumptuous to begin this discussion with a summary. However, in this case the summary is as much an outline of the following pages as it is a recapitulation of their content.

The system is replete with symbols and mathematical terms and values. While the mathematical terms are not essential to this discussion, the symbols simplify the presentation of the theory—although they do impose some strain on memory. On several occasions, I have had to take special precautions to prevent "symbol shock" from occurring in undergraduate classes being exposed to Hull's

Symbol shock

theory for the first time. These precautions consist largely of indelicate stories (told in a delicate manner so as not to offend) interspersed with good Hullian terminology. Symptoms of symbol shock include lower respiration rate, some lowering of body temperature, a change in EEG pattern from beta to alpha waves, and closed eyelids. On occasion, some sufferers make strange noises through their mouths. These students are probably in more extreme states of shock.

Figure 4-1 is a summary, in symbolic form, of the major variables in Hull's system.

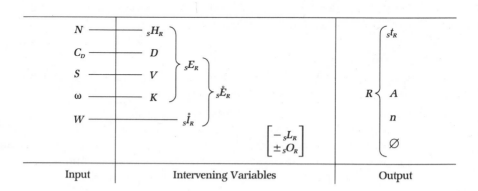

| Input | Intervening Variables | Output |

Input variables
N = number of prior reinforcements
C_D = drive condition
S = stimulus intensity
ω = amount of reward (weight)
W = work involved in responding

Intervening variables
$_sH_R$ = habit strength
D = drive
V = stimulus-intensity dynamism
K = incentive motivation
$_sE_R$ = reaction potential
$_s\mathring{I}_R$ = aggregate inhibitory potential
$_s\mathring{E}_R$ = net reaction potential
$_sL_R$ = reaction threshold
$_sO_R$ = oscillation of reaction potential

Output variables
R = the occurrence of a response, measured in terms of $_st_R$, A, and n
$_st_R$ = response latency
A = response amplitude
n = number of nonreinforced trials to extinction
$\emptyset$ = no response (not used as a symbol by Hull)

Figure 4-1. The Hullian system. *(Adapted from Hilgard and Bower, 1966, p. 164, by permission of the publisher, Appleton-Century-Crofts.)*

The presentation of Hull's system in this highly symbolic form may make it appear much more difficult to understand than it really is. While it is extremely complex in scope and detail, its most fundamental ideas are quite straightforward.

The first point to be made is that the model in Figure 4-1 is much simpler to understand when interpreted not as a general description of human behavior but only as the representation of one specific behavior for one person at a given time. Understanding how the system works in this connection makes it easier to interpret it in a wider sense.

Hull was primarily concerned with developing a system that would enable him to predict a person's behavior, given knowledge about the stimulus. One of the real difficulties in the application of this system to behavior is that a great deal of knowledge about the subject's past experiences is necessary, since a stimulus is a complex product of preceding events. Nevertheless, this stimulus complex becomes a predictor in the system; the output, or response, variables are predicted. In different terms, the stimulus variables are independent variables, and the response variables are dependent variables. When one examines Figure 4-1, it becomes clear that complete knowledge of input requires knowing how many times in the past the S-R bond in question has been reinforced (N). This variable, combined with knowledge about the physical intensity of the stimulus (S); the drive conditions of the organism (C_D); the reward attached to responding (ω); and the amount of work required in responding (W) would theoretically allow prediction of the output variables.

INTERVENING VARIABLES

While the input and output variables are the only directly observable and measurable events described in the system, the intervening variables are probably more crucial for understanding what Hull's theory is really about. These variables have direct links with the external variables in that they intervene between stimulus events and response events in such a way as to determine whether or not a response will occur for a stimulus. However, it is important to note that the power of intervening variables in determining responses is, theoretically, completely determined and controlled by input variables. Thus, the intervening variables are nothing more than explanations of observed S-R relationships. For each stimulus variable there is a specific corresponding intervening variable, which can be interpreted as the effect that an input variable (a feature of the environment) has on an individual. Viewed in this way, intervening variables are relatively easy to interpret. Each variable is described in turn in the following section.

1. $_SH_R$. The most important intervening variable, habit strength, is a behavioristic concept defined in terms of the strength of the bond between a specific stimulus and response. For Hull, habit strength was determined largely by the number of previous pairings of a stimulus with a response, provided that rein- forcement occurred on every trial. It is here that Thorndike's influence on Hull is most evident. Unlike contiguity theorists, both Thorndike and Hull maintained that the strength of a habit (of an S-R bond) is a function of reinforcement rather than simply of repetition.

Hull introduced specific numerical functions to illustrate the precise relation- ship between number of reinforced S-R pairings and habit strength (these are of much more academic than practical interest). While at first glance it might appear that habit strength would be most influential in determining behavior, such an assumption is not accurate. In effect, it appears that habit strength is but one of a number of variables that affect behavior.

2. D. Because of its connection with reinforcement, drive is a central concept in Hull's learning theory. He saw learning as the process of responses becoming connected with stimuli when they lead to a reduction in drive or, more precisely, when they lead to the removal or reduction in number or intensity of stimuli associated with drive. Drive can be primary or secondary (as can reinforcement, since it involves reducing drive). Primary drives are those associated with tissue needs; secondary drives are conditioned to primary drives through contiguity. Drive, as an intervening variable, corresponds to the input variable *drive con- dition*, which is defined in terms of number of hours of deprivation. Hull iden- tified two components of drive: the *drive proper* increases as a direct function of the length of deprivation, and the *inanition component* is recognition of the fact that drive decreases if deprivation (starvation) lasts too long.

Drive assumes three central functions in Hull's theory. (1) It provides for reinforcement, without which learning would not occur; (2) it activates habit strength—meaning that, without drive, behavior will not take place even if there is a strong previously established habit $_sH_R$—and (3) drive stimuli become attached to specific behaviors through learning. Were it not for this distinctive- ness of drive stimuli, the behavior engaged in might be totally inappropriate; people might drink when they were hungry, eat when they were cold, or cover up when thirsty. . . . Essentially, it is this distinctiveness of drive stimuli that determines whether a response will be reinforcing. As we note later, subsequent research has established that learning can occur, even in animals, in the absence of drive (when drive is defined in terms of deprivation). This observation does not necessarily invalidate Hull's system, although it does point to some of its inadequacies.

3. V. Stimulus-intensity dynamism is the label applied to the intervening var- iable that corresponds to the input variable *S*, or stimulus intensity. It is assumed that increasing the physical intensity of a stimulus increases the probability of a response's occurring. This effect is manifested in stimulus-intensity dynamism, which interacts in a multiplicative fashion with habit strength and drive to determine the probability of a response.

4. K. The symbol K in Hull's system stands for two things: *Spence* and *incentive motivation*. Hull chose to honor his prize pupil by selecting the first letter of his name, Kenneth, as a symbol for incentive motivation.

Incentive motivation, which is determined by amount of reward (ω as an input variable), was added to Hull's system as a function of some important experiments reported by Crespi (1942). These experiments made it apparent that drive (D) alone could not account for motivation. In Crespi's experiment, three groups of rats received different amounts of reward (food pellets) for running to a goal box. The fact that the rats that received the greatest reward ran faster than those that received less is quite compatible with Hull's original notion that drive is reduced *more* by greater reward, hence leading to a stronger habit. In a related study, however, Crespi also found that when these three groups of rats were subsequently all given the same amount of reward, those that had previously had the least amount now ran fastest, whereas those who had received the greatest amount reduced their speed the most. Accordingly, Hull now had to modify his system to take into account the fact that previous reinforcements are also effective in determining behavior. Their effects, described by Hull as involving incentive motivation, interact with other intervening variables (including drive) to determine the probability that a response will occur.

These four intervening variables ($_sH_R$, D, V, and K) make up the first and most important term in the equation employed by Hull in determining what he called reaction potential ($_sE_R$): $_sE_R = {_sH_R} \times D \times V \times K$. It is interesting and revealing to note that, since reaction potential is a multiplicative function of these variables, if the value for any of them is zero, reaction potential will also be zero. In other words, in the absence of drive, it makes no difference how intense the stimulation, how great the reward, or how strong the habit, the response will not occur; in the absence of the appropriate stimulus at sufficient intensity, R will not occur; in the absence of reward, there will be no response, and in the absence of a previously learned habit, there will also be no response. Consider the case of a person sitting at a table on which is set a variety of appetizing dishes. If that person has just eaten, not a single dish may be touched, despite the fact that the stimulus, the reward, and the habit are all very strong. In this case, drive would be too low. By way of further illustration, consider the other possibilities: no food ($K = 0$); the person is blind and cannot smell ($V = 0$); or the person has not learned to eat ($_sH_R = 0$). In no case will the response occur.

It is also important to note that the probability of responding ($_sE_R$) is a multiplicative function of drive, habit strength, and so on. What this means is that identical changes in one of these variables will have different absolute effects, depending on the values of the other variables. Doubling drive, for example, will make a greater difference if habit strength ($_sH_R$) is already large than if it is small. Put another way, increasing the motivation of a professional golfer should have more effect than increasing that of a rank amateur.

5. $_sE_R$. The fifth intervening variable is not tied as directly to input variables as it is to other intervening variables or to output variables. Reaction potential, sometimes called excitatory potential, is a measure of the potential that a stimulus has for eliciting a specific response. This potential will depend on how many times the stimulus has been paired with the response and reinforcement, how intense it is, how great the reward, and how strong the drive. In other words, $_sE_R = {}_sH_R \times D \times V \times K!$

The significance of the magnitude of reaction potential in this system is that a minimum amount of potential is required before behavior will take place. Increasing reaction potential will be reflected in shorter response latency ($_st_R$), more response amplitude (A), and longer extinction time (n).

~~BULLSHIT~~*PSHAW*

6. $_s\overset{\circ}{E}_R$. The use of two symbols denoting reaction potential might appear to be somewhat confusing. Actually, Hull used three symbols for reaction potential, the third one being based on the potential for responding that is carried over (generalized) from related behaviors. This second symbol refers to net reaction potential, so called because it is the reaction potential that results from summing the generalized potential with the ordinary reaction potential that results from drive, habit strength, stimulus intensity dynamism, and incentive motivation (and then subtracting inhibitory potential, $_s\overset{\circ}{I}_R$).

7. $_s\overset{\circ}{I}_R$. Aggregate inhibitory potential (reactive inhibition) results from two input variables: the amount of work involved in responding (W) and any habits of not responding that might have been acquired by the organism. The assumption is that those responses requiring a high expenditure of physical energy are less likely to be engaged in. With continued repetition of a response, this inhibitory potential summates. Its effect is to lower the net reaction potential until eventually the response no longer occurs. Inhibitory potential dissipates quickly, so that the response might reoccur very soon.

8. $_s\overset{\circ}{L}_R$. The reaction threshold is the magnitude that net reaction potential must exceed before a response will occur (if $_s\overset{\circ}{E}_R > {}_sL_R$, a response, R, occurs; if $_s\overset{\circ}{E}_R < {}_sL_R$, no response, Ø, occurs).

---

*The indelicate expression (delicately crossed out) is not intended as a description of content but simply as an antidote to the "symbol shock" that might, by now, have overcome an assiduous reader.

9. $_sO_R$. Behavioral oscillation is the variable that accounts for the fact that, given relatively complete information about input variables, predictions are not always accurate. Guthrie's answer for this problem was simply that the stimulus situation has changed. Hull's answer was that reaction potential is not exactly fixed, that it varies around a central value. This variation he labeled behavioral oscillation ($_sO_R$).

OUTPUT VARIABLES

The response variables of concern to Hull include the time lapse between the presentation of the stimulus and the appearance of the response (response latency, $_st_R$), the amplitude of the response in a physical sense (A), and the number of unreinforced responses that would occur before extinction (n). Hull postulated that response latency would decrease with increasing reaction potential, whereas both resistance to extinction and amplitude of response would increase.

Two additional symbols standing simply for the occurrence of a response (R) or its nonoccurrence (Ø) have been included in Figure 4-1. A summary of the contents of that figure can be given as follows:

$$\text{if } [_s\mathring{E}_R = (_sH_R \times D \times V \times K) - _s\mathring{I}_R > _sL_R], \text{ then } R.$$

This expression reads: if net reaction potential—which is the product of habit strength, drive, stimulus-intensity dynamism, and incentive motivation—minus aggregate inhibitory potential is greater than the threshold, a response will occur.

Two additional concepts arrived at by Hull in the course of deriving theorems and their corollaries are of particular importance here: habit-family hierarchies and fractional antedating goal reactions. Both represent significant departures from theoretical formulations that had preceded Hull, and both are relevant for the development of cognitive positions.

FRACTIONAL ANTEDATING GOAL REACTIONS

It will be recalled that the major explanation for learning advanced by Hull is a reinforcement explanation. More specifically, he maintained that reinforcement consists of drive reduction. The ordinary way of reducing a drive is to attain a goal, or to make a *goal reaction*. Goal reactions, as described by Hull, are often consummatory responses, as in the case of food. A fractional antedating goal response (r_G, read "little rG") is a response made by an organism prior to the actual goal reaction. Such responses include the variety of reactions to environmental stimuli that the organism might make. In the case of a rat that has run through a maze and is approaching food, antedating goal reactions might include licking its chops, sniffing, and turning a last corner, as well as seeing and smelling the maze. These antedating responses are important in that they serve as stimuli (s_G, read "little sG") that maintain behavior toward a goal. In this sense they serve the same purpose as Guthrie's movement-produced stimuli (MPS), but unlike the MPS, r_G-s_G are linked with reinforcement and therefore became rewarding. They are also related to what Hull termed *habit-family hierarchies*.

THE HABIT-FAMILY HIERARCHY

In the course of acquiring habits (S-R bonds), an individual will learn a number of different responses for the same stimulus; in many cases, each response will lead to the same goal. These alternative responses constitute a *habit family* arranged in hierarchical order. They are referred to as a *family* because they are assumed to be integrated by common *fractional antedating goal reactions* and as a *hierarchy* because there is a preferential ordering based largely on previous reinforcements. In other words, one alternative will usually be preferred over another because it has been rewarded more often in the past; the reaction potential ($_sE_R$) associated with it will therefore be higher.

Both concepts—antedating goal reactions and habit-family hierarchy—are employed in somewhat different form by Osgood in his description of *meaning* as involving "associative hierarchies" of mediating r_M-s_M processes (Osgood, 1957). Like r_G-s_G's, r_M-s_M's are "intervening" responses that relate to frequency of previous S-R pairings. Figure 4-2 presents an illustration of an associative hierarchy.

The introduction of these concepts represents one of Hull's major contributions. Another important contribution from a theoretical point of view is his influence on the design of a wide variety of psychological experiments. This influence has resulted largely from his insistence on precision, rigor, and quantification, as well as his emphasis on logical consistency. This last characteristic of his system most sets Hull apart from other learning theorists. It remains true, however, that his system has failed where he most wanted it to succeed: behavior remains largely unpredictable. His failure has discouraged others from attempt-

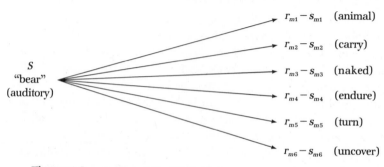

$r_{m1} - s_{m1}$ (animal)

$r_{m2} - s_{m2}$ (carry)

$r_{m3} - s_{m3}$ (naked)

$r_{m4} - s_{m4}$ (endure)

$r_{m5} - s_{m5}$ (turn)

$r_{m6} - s_{m6}$ (uncover)

S
"bear"
(auditory)

Figure 4-2.   An associative hierarchy

ing the development of such formal and inclusive systems. Instead, smaller systems dealing with a limited number of aspects of learning are typically advanced.

Kenneth Spence (1907–1967)

The Hullian tradition was continued in the writings of Kenneth Spence, who is considered to have been Hull's major follower. Indeed, it is widely accepted that, had Hull lived, the further development of his system might well have progressed along lines followed by Spence, as summarized in his two major books (1956, 1960). Spence continued the development of Hullian behaviorism, with a number of important variations from Hull's original system, which are discussed briefly below.

KENNETH WARTINBEE SPENCE (1907–1967)

Among the many well-known psychologists who were students and admirers of Hull (including Dollard, Miller, Mowrer, and Gibson), probably none followed more closely in the footsteps of his teacher than Spence. Indeed, his most notable contributions to psychology can be summarized in terms of the ways in which he expanded and modified Hull's system, particularly after Hull's death in 1952.

Spence was born in Chicago on May 6, 1907, but his family moved to Montreal before he started school. It was there that Spence grew up and there, at McGill University, that he did his undergraduate work. Like so many other psychologists of his era, he too had no intention of being a psychologist when he first went to college. Instead, he majored in physical education. It was not until he went to Yale that he began to study psychology under Hull, receiving a master's degree in 1930 and, 3 years later, a Ph.D. in psychology. And although he spent the rest of his academic career at the University of Iowa (26 years) and at the University of Texas (3 years), Hull's influence was to remain with him for all those years.

HULL AND SPENCE

While the systems of both Spence and Hull are dedicated to the development of elaborate and formal deductive theories, there is a marked difference in the restraint each exercised in the development of his work. Whereas Hull was willing to derive theorems, postulates, and corollaries, leaving to others a great deal of the work of experimentally verifying these statements about behavior, Spence was less willing to commit himself to this approach. One manifestation of his caution is inherent in the intended scopes of the two positions. Hull, on the one hand, had clearly wanted his system to be sufficient to account for most of the behavior of higher animals and of humans. Interestingly, the experimental work incorporated in his system dealt largely with studies of animal behavior or of the conditioned eye blink in people. Spence, on the other hand, explicitly limited the generality of his system to those situations analogous to the experiments from which he derived his conclusions.

In addition to these rather general distinctions between the theories of Spence and Hull, a number of very specific and very basic changes were made by Spence. Indeed, he was careful to point out these points of distinction between his system and Hull's. The most important of these departures are discussed below.

First, Spence did not accept Hull's concept of need reduction in relation to reinforcement. Hull had maintained that drive stimuli (S_D) give rise to conditions of drive in the organism (C_D) and that the original stimuli are associated with needs. The reinforcement of behavior was assumed to involve the satisfaction of the need and the consequent elimination of the drive condition. Spence's interpretation differed in that he did not give reinforcement any role in the formation of habits. Habit strength was no longer defined in terms of the number of times a response had been paired with a stimulus *and reinforced* but was assumed to be a function solely of the frequency of pairings. Second, Spence saw the reinforcement itself as a result of fractional antedating goal responses ($r_G\text{-}s_G$). The fractional responses define incentive motivation (K) in the Spence system. In other words, reinforcement affects K (incentive motivation) but does not alter habit strength ($_sH_R$ in Hull's system; H in Spence's).

A second distinction between the two systems is Spence's substitution of an additive function for a multiplicative one in the major formula. Hull defined reaction, or excitatory, potential as a multiplicative function of drive, habit strength, and incentive motivation (in addition to a number of other variables of lesser importance). That is, $_sE_R = {_sH_R} \times D \times K \dots$. Spence, on the other hand, defined excitatory potential (E) as a function of the product of habit strength (H) times drive *plus* incentive motivation. In other words, $E = H(D + K)$. The practical difference between these two formulations is that in Hull's expression, if any of the values are at zero, excitatory potential must also be at zero, as illustrated earlier in this chapter by the person sitting at a banquet table. The point made there was that if $H = 0$ (that is, the person does not know how to eat) and so on, behavior would not take place. Spence's reformulation of this equation makes it possible for either D or K to be zero without completely eliminating the possibility of a response. This change obviously takes into account the possibility that where a habit is particularly strong, behavior may take place in the absence of drive or incentive.

Despite these distinctions between Spence and Hull, the points of similarity probably have greater theoretical importance. Both systems are essentially hypothetico-deductive, and both attempt to develop relatively precise formulas for the explanation and prediction of behavior—although, admittedly, Spence's system strives for less precision than does Hull's. In addition, Spence makes use of the same kind of symbolism as does Hull and deals essentially with the same problems of human behavior. His contribution, like Hull's, will only be determined in the wisdom of later years. Early indications are that the Hull-Spence tradition has been a powerful force in shaping the direction of empirical behaviorism in the latter part of psychology's brief history.

So What?

Abstract and apparently remote theoretical systems such as that advanced by Hull and Spence are sometimes met with indifference or skepticism. Yet there are at least two important reasons for studying this theory. One is that understanding the system contributes greatly to an understanding of later theoretical developments. Another is that the system is such an overwhelming example of theory building (or attempted theory building) that it deserves to be studied simply for that reason.

With respect to the criteria that we have been employing to evaluate psychological theories, the Hull-Spence formulations present some difficulties. To begin with, we cannot easily assert that they reflect the facts, even as they were known at the time, since much of this theorizing is speculative. Hull's system consists largely of what are termed "logical constructs." These are entities that are inferred—that follow logically from that which is observed but that cannot themselves be observed. Thus, reaction potential, aggregate inhibitory potential, behavioral oscillation, incentive motivation, and the raft of other related "intervening" variables cannot be shown to be "facts." This does not mean that they are invalid or that inferred entities have no place in psychological theorizing. Quite the contrary. Logical constructs, like other theoretical "truths," should be judged in terms of their usefulness.

So. Are the Hull-Spence intervening variables useful? Clearly, within the system itself they are immensely useful, providing a compelling logic. That they contribute to explanations of human behavior, that they lead to more accurate predictions than would otherwise be the case, that they are clear and understandable, and that they are based on few unverifiable assumptions is not nearly so apparent. Ironically, then, in spite of the impressive logic and mathematics that are fundamental to the Hull-Spence system, the theory does not fare particularly well with respect to our criteria.

Summary of Chapter 4

This chapter has presented an introduction to the formal theories of Hull and his follower, Spence.

1. Hull's analysis of behavior is a highly formalized attempt to account for behavior in terms of the precise relationships thought to exist between input, intervening, and output variables.
2. A summary of the major Hullian variables and the relationships that exist between them is given by the equation $_sE_R = {_sH_R} \times D \times V \times K$. It reads:

reaction potential is the product of habit strength, drive, stimulus-intensity dynamism, and incentive motivation.

3. Two Hullian concepts that are of special significance in the development of learning theories are *fractional antedating goal response* (r_G-s_G) and *habit-family hierarchies*. The former is a behavior that precedes the reaching of a goal but becomes associated with the goal through conditioning and hence acquires reinforcing properties. Habit families are hierarchical arrangements of habits that are related by virtue of the fact that they have common goals.

4. Spence continued the Hullian tradition by attempting to modify and complete Hull's system. It is not unusual to encounter references to the "Hull-Spence" system.

5. Among the major differences between the theories advanced by Hull and Spence are Spence's rejection of drive reduction as a definition of reinforcement, his redefinition of K in terms of r_G-s_G, and his introduction of an additive function in the major formula.

6. In spite of the impressive mathematics and logic of the Hull-Spence system, it does not fare well with respect to several criteria of good theories. Not only is it based on a number of unverifiable assumptions, but it does not always explain clearly or lead easily to useful predictions. Nevertheless, its contribution to the further development of learning theories is vast.

Dear Grandmother,

   I'm sorry you weren't home when I went over the other day. The lock on the shed was broken before I got there, so I'm surprised that there didn't seem to be anything missing. It must have been a burglar or one of the neighbor's kids. I really don't know why Robert told you he thought I broke it, because you know that if it hadn't been broken before, I would just have gone home.

   Anyway, I found that letter you had lost, right there in the shed under one of your bags of fertilizer. You must have seen it when you got home, because I slipped it through the mail slot on your door. I hope you find time to answer it.

   I'm glad you think my book is coming along not too badly. I've been taking your advice and trying to be serious most of the time, and sometimes it works. You're probably right that people don't care to be amused when they're reading and studying important things.

   By the way, mom says you think I shot Pouf with the pellet gun again, so I have to defend myself. I hate to say it, but I think Robert was the one who did it, because he borrowed my gun when I left your place that day.

   I hope it hasn't made Pouf any meaner to be shot in the rump like that.

   One more thing, grandma. I don't know just how to say this, but I'm going to have a hard time making ends meet this month. So I was wondering if you . . .

CHAPTER 5

Traditional Behaviorism Reexamined

Traditional Behaviorism

Behavioristic theories described in the early part of this text are of two general kinds: those that deal with behaviors resulting directly from stimulation and those dealing with behaviors that are simply emitted by the organism. Skinner refers to these two classes of behaviors as respondent (where the behavior occurs in *response* to stimulation) and operant (where the behavior does not stem as obviously from stimulation).

Traditional behavioristic theories offer two different sets of explanations relating to respondent and to operant learning: classical conditioning on the one hand, and what is sometimes referred to as the Law of Effect, on the other (Herrnstein, 1977).

In their simplest form the laws of classical conditioning assert that when a neutral stimulus is accompanied or slightly preceded by an effective stimulus sufficiently often, the neutral stimulus will eventually acquire some of the properties formerly associated only with the effective stimulus. Thus a dog eventually comes to salivate in response to a tone (previously neutral stimulus) after the tone has been paired a number of times with food (effective stimulus). The apparent equivalence of neutral (conditioned) and effective (unconditioned) stimuli following classical conditioning led Pavlov to describe this procedure as one of *stimulus substitution.*

The Law of Effect also in its simplest form, maintains that a behavior that is followed by a reinforcing state of affairs will tend to be repeated; one that is not followed by reinforcement will tend to be eliminated from the organism's repertoire. In other words, behaviors that have been repeatedly reinforced become highly probable; behaviors that have not been reinforced (or that have been punished) become increasingly improbable. Furthermore, the discriminable aspects of the situations in which behaviors have been reinforced (or not reinforced) come to exercise a degree of control over the occurrence or nonoccurrence of the behavior. Thus, a dog that is reinforced for rolling over whenever its master says "Roll over" may eventually discriminate between the commands "Roll over" and "Fetch my slippers." At this point these verbal commands will have acquired stimulus control over the behaviors in question.

That my own miserable hound never performed these rather simple and impressive behaviors publicly, while never ceasing to amaze me in private, is relevant here. She had learned not only to discriminate between these two verbal commands but also to discriminate between private and public situations. That she delighted in embarrassing me is not relevant.

Operant Conditioning and Autonomic Responses

Early investigations of classical and operant conditioning led quickly to the observation that the types of behavior being explained by each were fundamentally different. Most theorists *assumed* that autonomic (reflexive) behaviors such as salivation or eye blinking could not be brought under stimulus control through operant conditioning, although they responded very well to classical conditioning procedures. By the same token, it was also assumed that operants became more or less probable solely as a function of reinforcement contingencies and not as a function of contiguity.

These assumptions were incorrect. Salivation *can* be conditioned using operant procedures. And so can control of heart rate, blood pressure, kidney functioning, and a host of other autonomic functions that we do not ordinarily control consciously. Neal Miller (1969) was among the first to demonstrate some of these phenomena when he conditioned increases or decreases of heart rate in rats in response to a combination of a light and tone. In this experiment rats were administered curare, a skeletal muscle paralyzer, in order to ensure that what was being learned by the rats was not some combination of muscular movements that affects heart rate but rather actual control of autonomic functioning. And although subsequent attempts to replicate this and related experiments were not always successful (see Miller & Dworkin, 1974), more recent experimental refinements have now established that any number of autonomic responses can be brought under stimulus control through operant rather than classical conditioning (see, for example, Dworkin & Miller, 1977).

BIOFEEDBACK

One of the important applications of this finding has taken the form of *biofeedback*. Biofeedback refers to information an organism receives about its own functioning. Although we are ordinarily unconscious of most aspects of our physiological functions (heart and respiration rates, blood pressure, electrical activity in the brain), there is a wide range of monitoring devices that can simply and accurately provide us with information about these functions. The use of these devices in an attempt to bring about some degree of control over autonomic functioning defines biofeedback as it is currently being studied and applied in psychology.

In a typical biofeedback experiment, for example, subjects are connected to a device that records brain waves (popularly called an alpha recorder). It is constructed in such a way that a tone or some other distinctive stimulus will be activated whenever the subject produces the right type or frequency of waves (Knowlis & Kamiya, 1970, for example). Subjects are simply instructed to try to activate the tone as often as possible. Experimental results suggest that subjects can often learn very quickly to exercise considerable control over brain-wave functioning. The results are typically explained by an operant-conditioning paradigm; the tone (or light or other distinctive stimulus) serves as a reinforcer and the behaviors involved in controlling the autonomic response are the operants. Practical applications of biofeedback include attempts to alleviate migraine headaches, to reduce blood pressure and heart rate, and to reduce stress (see, for example, Stern & Ray, 1977; Stoyva, Kamiya, Barber, Miller, & Shapiro, 1979).

In a thorough review of biofeedback research, Miller (1978) cautions that early biofeedback experiments have not always been replicated. In particular, some recent studies have questioned the contention that the results of biofeedback can be explained in terms of the subject's having learned to control autonomic functions (Hardt & Kamiya, 1976). In some cases it is possible for subjects to learn a motor response that affects the instrumentation in the same way as an appropriate change in autonomic functioning might. Certain alpha recorders, for example, can be made to respond to changes in eye movement. In these cases, it is perhaps more likely that subjects learned to control eye movement (albeit unconsciously) rather than brain activity. In the same way, changes in heart rate can be brought about by skeletal contractions of the lower chest and of the diaphragm or sometimes by controlling pressure in the thoracic cavity (Anand & Chhina, 1961). Similarly, changes in blood pressure can sometimes be brought about through a combination of muscular movements or through changes in breathing (Levenson, 1976).

These observations do not invalidate the practical applications of biofeedback, although they should make researchers and practitioners somewhat more cautious about interpreting the results of these applications. Miller (1978) suggests that there is a need to conduct controlled experimentation and to compare biofeedback with other forms of therapy but that the wholesale application of biofeedback therapy at this point would be premature.

Operant versus Classical Conditioning

Biofeedback research, as well as research on the conditioning of autonomic responses in rats, leads to the conclusion that classical and operant conditioning are not distinct in terms of the classes of behaviors for which each is appropriate. In brief, it has now been demonstrated that autonomic responses, once thought to be solely the domain of classical conditioning procedures, can be brought under stimulus control through operant conditioning.

In what way, then, are classical and operant conditioning distinct? Staddon and Simmelhag (1971) suggest that they really are not very different at all, particularly when the reinforcer in an operant-conditioning model is viewed as a stimulus whose function is simply to ensure that some behavior occurs. The food pellet in the Skinner box, together with a light or other discriminative stimulus, simply ensures that bar pressing will occur. One can argue that learning then occurs because of temporal contiguity between reinforcement, light, and bar pressing (as well as between bar pressing and whatever other stimulation is peculiar to being in this Skinner box at this time). In much the same way, whatever learning occurs in a biofeedback situation can be explained in terms of temporal contiguity between a tone or light and the behavior that gives rise to the appearance of the tone or light. And to say that the light or tone is reinforcing really adds very little to our understanding of human or animal behavior.

It is important to note, however, that none of this means that reinforcement (and punishment too, for that matter) is of no consequence. We know too clearly (and too intuitively) that this is far from the case. Within the context of our conditioning models, reinforcement plays the fundamental role of assuring that there will be a behavior and that it will be repeated often enough to eventually be associated with some stimulus.

In conclusion, classical and operant conditioning are not nearly so distinct as was once thought. Thus, they can both be employed to explain very similar types of learning; and the explanations for each are also highly similar. Nevertheless, each is still typically associated with different circumstances (reinforcement, on the one hand, and contiguity, on the other); each has very distinct roots in the history of psychology; and each has contributed in different ways to the attempted resolution of problems of human and animal learning.

Generality of Conditioning Models

How many of these "problems" of human and animal learning have our conditioning theories resolved? Early theorists were highly optimistic with respect to the expected generality of their theorizing. They had little doubt that, if they could take a response as arbitrary as bar pressing in a rat and bring it under the precise control of specific environmental conditions, it would also be possible to take virtually any operant of which an organism is capable and bring it, too, under precise stimulus control. Similarly, even as it was clearly possible to condition salivation in dogs, eye blinking in adults, and sucking in infants, it should be possible to condition virtually any other reflexive behavior to any distinctive stimulus.

Not so. For some obscure reason, it is virtually impossible to condition the knee-jerk reflex or pupil dilation in humans. Not a very damaging observation for conditioning theory, surely.

Perhaps not. But there were many other observations that presented problems for traditional conditioning theories and that cried out for explanation far more urgently than did the recalcitrant knee-jerk reflex.

INSTINCTIVE DRIFT

In the early 1950s two of Skinner's students, encouraged by the remarkable success that experimenters had enjoyed in shaping the behavior of animals, decided to commercialize this process. These students, a man and wife by the name of Breland, proposed to train a number of animals to perform stunts sufficiently amusing that audiences might pay to see them. Through the "differential reinforcement of successive approximations" (more simply, through shaping), they taught a raccoon to pick up a coin and deposit it in a tin box; a chicken to pull a rubber loop releasing a capsule that then slid down a chute to where the chicken could peck it out of the cage; and a pig to pick up large wooden "nickels" and deposit these in a "piggy" bank. Operant-conditioning procedures worked exquisitely; all the animals learned their required behaviors.

But not for long. In Breland's words (Breland & Breland, 1951, 1961), each animal eventually began to "misbehave." The pig took longer and longer to bring its wooden nickel to the bank and deposit it, although it clearly knew that reinforcement was contingent on doing so. Instead, it spent increasingly long periods of time tossing the coins in the air, pushing them around with its nose, rooting around in the dirt with them, and otherwise behaving as might any

other uneducated pig on the trail of the elusive truffle. The Brelands reported that in the end the pig was taking so long to deposit the wooden nickels that it was in imminent danger of starvation.

The raccoon fared no better. It too began to take longer and longer in bringing the coins to the metal box and seemed progressively more reluctant to let go of them. Indeed, it often refused to do so, much preferring instead to dip them in the box, bring them out immediately, and rub them (almost gleefully, it seemed) between its paws.

And the chicken, not to be left out, became so engrossed in pecking at the capsule that it seemed to quite forget what was expected of it.

Subsequently, researchers have uncovered an increasing number of situations in which animals initially learn a behavior quickly and well but eventually begin to resort to other behaviors, the nature of which is highly revealing. It is surely no accident that the pig rooted, the raccoon "washed" its coin, or the chicken pecked. These are, after all, what pigs, raccoons, and chickens do with respect to food. What is being observed in these situations was described by the Brelands as an apparent "drifting" toward genetically related behaviors, a phenomenon now described as *instinctive drift*.

In general terms, instinctive drift results where there is competition between a genetically based behavior and a learned response. It appears that, with repeated exposure to a situation characterized by this kind of competition, organisms tend to revert to the more genetically based behavior. The problem that this poses for traditional behavioristic theory is implicit in the observation that not all behaviors can be conditioned and maintained through the careful arrangement of response consequences, a fact that I have known for some time. Was it instinctive drift that led my prize hunting hound to chew up a brace of fine mallards last fall, in spite of the fact that she will ordinarily turn her nose in utter disdain at the very thought of raw meat? Indeed, lately she will only nibble politely when presented with any meat dish—unless, of course, it has been cooked in an expensive Burgundy or a very dry Chablis.

AUTOSHAPING

Instinctive drift is only one of a number of related phenomena that present problems for traditional operant- and classical-conditioning explanations of behavior; another is *autoshaping.* If a pigeon is reinforced at intervals regardless of what it is doing at the time, the end result might be what Skinner has described as superstitious behavior. If, however, a response key or disk is illuminated for a few seconds just before the appearance of food, the pigeon will quickly learn to peck at the key or disk. That this behavior occurs and is learned in spite of the fact that the pigeon's pecking bears no causal relationship to the appearance of food has led to the use of the term *autoshaping* to describe the learning involved. The strength of an autoshaped response is dramatically illustrated in an experiment by Williams and Williams (1969). Pigeons were initially taught, through an autoshaping procedure, to peck at a light, but response consequences were then altered so that pecking would prevent reinforcement from occurring. In spite of this, the pigeons continued to peck at the light.

Instinctive drift and autoshaping have in common that both deal with responses that are highly probable in the animals concerned. Even as rooting and "washing" are genetically based, food-related behaviors in pigs and raccoons, so is pecking a highly probable, food-related response in pigeons. And that a pigeon should continue to peck at a lighted disk even when doing so means that it will not be reinforced presents some embarrassment for those traditional behaviorists who would prefer to believe that reinforcement should have general and predictable results on all behaviors.

ADJUNCTIVE BEHAVIOR

There is yet a third class of behaviors that presents difficulties for behavioristic explanations of learning. This class includes behaviors that often *follow* reinforcement in certain circumstances (Falk, 1967, 1969, 1970). Rats that are given unlimited access to water sometimes drink excessively (termed *polydipsia*); others that have access to nonfood materials such as wood shavings or paper sometimes become compulsive eaters of these materials (termed *pica*). On some occasions, the compulsion to engage in these behaviors is so powerful that rats will engage frantically in specific operants in order to do so. Rats already well bloated with water will energetically depress a lever just to be given one more sip of water; others whose adjunctive behavior involves "running wheels" will also perform a range of operants in exchange for an opportunity to run a little more.

Two observations are important with respect to adjunctive behaviors. First, these behaviors are not initially learned as a function of reinforcement but typically occur following reinforcement. There are other specific responses that frequently occur prior to reinforcement but are also unrelated to reinforcement. These behaviors, termed *interim* behaviors, often become learned in much the same way as adjunctive behaviors. Staddon and Simmelhag (1971), among the first to draw attention to them, noted that the superstitious behaviors that Skinner described are typically interim behaviors that have become learned.

The second important observation with respect to adjunctive behaviors is that the responses in question are frequently not the types that reinforcement theory would predict. That a bloated rat would continue to drink excessively, or that a well-fed rat would perform activities in order to be allowed to eat shavings and paper present strong contradictions to behavior theory. And unlike instinctive drift and autoshaping, both of which are manifestations of powerful hereditary tendencies, polydipsia and pica are not easily explained by reference to genetics.

TASTE AVERSIONS

More easily explained in genetic terms is a host of intriguing studies involving the learning of taste aversions in animals (Garcia, Ervin, & Koelling, 1966; Rozin & Kalat, 1971). It is both remarkable and of tremendous biological significance that animals that have been poisoned but not killed frequently display a marked aversion for the related food after a single learning trial. For example, rats that are exposed to radiation *after* eating and that subsequently become quite ill will avoid the food they ate prior to radiation. This effect has been found as long as 32 days after a single pairing of food and radiation (Garcia et al., 1966). As noted in Chapter 3, backward classical conditioning has always proven difficult if not impossible. Yet taste aversion can be learned following a single trial, and can be extremely powerful, even when there is a significant delay between the conditioning stimulus (food in this case) and the unconditioned stimulus (radiation).

Taste-aversion studies present a second set of problems for classical-conditioning theory. If a rat is fed a solution of lithium chloride (which makes it quite ill), it will subsequently avoid all food substances that smell of lithium chloride. And if the cage in which the rat is fed the lithium chloride is sprayed with perfume, the rat will develop an aversion to the perfume as well and will later eat significantly less in other cages that have been sprayed with the perfume (Garcia & Koelling, 1966). This observation appears reasonable in light of what is known about contiguity and classical conditioning. But when the same experiment is carried out with a light, beeper, or other distinctive sight or sound instead of a perfume, the rat does not later display avoidance behavior with respect to these stimuli, a finding that is directly contrary to what classical-conditioning theory would surely predict.

The same point is made even more dramatically in studies of cross-species aversion learning. Wilcoxon, Dragoin, & Kral (1971) produced taste aversion in rats and in quail by feeding them blue-colored flavored water and later injecting them with an illness-inducing drug. Both the rats and the quail developed a marked aversion to liquids characterized by the flavor in question. In addition, the quail developed a strong aversion to blue-colored liquids, but the rats did not.

The most plausible explanation for these findings is simply that quail have excellent color vision and probably rely to a considerable extent on visual cues to sort what is edible from what is not. In contrast, rats (like most other mammals) depend primarily on olfactory rather than visual cues. It therefore makes biological sense that rats should make immediate use of smell cues in learning about foods that should be avoided, even as it makes biological sense for quail to employ visual cues in the same kind of learning.

Biological Constraints

A great many of the situations described in the preceding pages of this chapter are striking examples of what have recently been labeled *biological constraints* (Hinde & Stevenson-Hinde, 1973; Seligman, 1975; Seligman & Hager, 1972). In its simplest sense, a biological constraint can be defined as a genetic predisposition that makes certain kinds of learning highly probable and easy and other kinds improbable and sometimes impossible. The most obvious general principle of a biological constraint is that it will favor behaviors that have a history of genetic survival value and that it will discourage those detrimental to survival. In Seligman's terms, organisms are *prepared* for certain kinds of learning and *contraprepared* for others. A rat when faced with danger is prepared to flee, fight, freeze, or perhaps to become frantic. Teaching it to do any of these through the use of noxious stimulation (an electric shock, for example) is a simple matter. But teaching it to engage in a behavior that is opposed to any of these is, in fact, virtually impossible. Thus, teaching a rat to depress a lever in order to escape an electric shock is almost impossible (Bolles, 1970).

Biological constraints (or genetic predispositions) are clearly involved in the reversion of pigs to rooting and chickens to pecking in the instinctive-drift experiments. Similarly, there are biological constraints at play in autoshaped behaviors. And perhaps nowhere are biological influences on learning more dramatically in evidence than in the single-trial taste-aversion studies.

It is perhaps less obvious but no less true that a great deal of human learning is also profoundly influenced by genetic factors. There is increasing evidence that we are genetically prepared to acquire language (Chomsky, 1972), perhaps in much the same way as goslings are genetically programmed to acquire a "following" response given appropriate stimulation at the right time in their development.

Sociobiology

That we are also biologically predisposed to engage in certain social behaviors rather than others is the single most important assumption of a budding new discipline, sociobiology. In a massive treatise one of its principal spokesmen, Edward O. Wilson, defines sociobiology as "the systematic study of the biological basis of all social behavior" (1975, p. 4).

Sociobiology is based directly on evolutionary theory and draws illustrations liberally from ethology (the study of the behavior of nonhuman animals). Among its most fundamental beliefs are those relating to the pervasiveness and importance of genetic tendencies that have survived evolutionary processes. Underlying these genetic tendencies is the single most important law of evolution—namely, that processes of natural selection favor the survival of the fittest. It is important to note, however, that fitness in an evolutionary sense does *not* refer to the likelihood that a specific individual of a species will survive but to the likelihood that genetic material itself will survive. Trivers (1971, 1974), Wilson (1976), and other sociobiologists have been at pains to point out that the quest for survival is far more meaningful at the group level than at the level of the individual. What is important, says Wilson, is "the maximum average survival and fertility of the group as a whole" (1975, p. 107). The life of a single individual of a group is important in an evolutionary sense only to the extent that it increases the probability that the genetic material characteristic of this group will survive and reproduce. Thus it is that a honeybee will sting intruders even though doing so means that it will die (Sakagami & Akahira, 1960). In much the same way, some species of termites explode themselves when danger threatens, and the explosion serves as a warning to other termites which can now save themselves (Wilson, 1975). These instances of selflessness (termed altruistic behavior) had long presented a puzzle for those who interpreted the law of survival of the fittest as meaning that every single individual does its utmost to survive, come hell, high water, or other catastrophes.

Generalizing from observations such as these, sociobiologists have argued that altruism among humans is a genetically based characteristic, ordained by years of successful evolution (see for example, Hamilton, 1970, 1971, 1972). In its purest form, an altruistic act is one that presents some sacrifice to the doer but that results in a *net* genetic advantage to the species. A blackbird that noisily signals the approach of a hawk may well be detected and eaten, but in the grand scheme of things that is a small price to pay for the eventual survival of all the other blackbirds.

Carrying the argument to its extreme, sociobiology predicts that the extent to which an individual will be willing to undergo personal sacrifice will not only

[handwritten marginal notes: "...tic or Love bond?" "...us about for an adopted child?"]

be a function of the net genetic advantage that results for the species but will also be directly related to the degree of genetic relatedness between the doer of the good deed and those who benefit most directly. Thus, one might hesitate to save a total stranger if the probability of losing one's life in the process were high. Net genetic advantage would be virtually zero. By the same token, one should scarcely hesitate to sacrifice one's life to save many others; net genetic advantage is high. It also follows that I will undergo considerably more risk and sacrifice to save my son than to save a stranger, since we have a great deal more in common genetically.

In much the same manner, sociobiology suggests tentative explanations for a great range of human social behaviors, including aggression, sexual mores, maternal emotion, and so on. Not surprisingly, these explanations have met with a great deal of resistance (see, for example, Eckland, 1977, Wade, 1976; "Why You Do," 1977). Sociologists, in particular, have reacted highly negatively to the suggestion that a great deal of human social behavior is genetically ordained. And a number of others have been taken somewhat aback at what is sometimes interpreted as excessive generalization from a handful of evidence, a great deal of which relates more directly to nonhuman animals than to humans.

In Retrospect

This chapter is entitled "Traditional Behaviorism Reexamined." It began with a summary of traditional behaviorism and stopped to look at the extent to which its two principal models, classical conditioning and operant conditioning, were distinct. From there it went to an examination of the generality of these models for explaining problems of animal and human learning. And it catalogued a number of observations that have presented problems for traditional behavioristic explanations. Chief among these are instinctive drift, autoshaping, adjunctive behaviors, and various other manifestations of biological influences.

Among the most important observations made in the chapter are these two: (1) Operant and classical conditioning are not totally distinct, either in terms of the types of behavior each explains or in terms of the explanations themselves. (2) Tendencies that appear to be genetically based sometimes compel (or at least urge) organisms to do certain things (or not to do certain things). At least on occasion they appear to be more powerful than the influences of operant or classical conditioning.

THE REEXAMINATION

How damaging are the foregoing observations for traditional behaviorism? There is no simple answer. The possibility that operant and classical conditioning are not nearly so distinct as they were once thought to be might well serve to simplify rather than to complicate or confuse. Certainly, if we can do away with superfluous explanation, then we should by all means do so. It remains true, nevertheless, that the procedures employed in classical and operant conditioning are still sufficiently distinct that there is some advantage in treating them as distinct in practice (if not in theory).

The discovery of the fact that traditional behavioristic explanations are not as general as had once been hoped is a far more optimistic than a pessimistic finding, even for the staunchest of behaviorists. In fact, most of what has been discovered to date in this respect can be reduced to the observation that biological constraints exercise a fundamental and highly important role in learning. The implication of this observation for behavioristic theorists is simply that a great deal more attention needs to be paid to these biological constraints. Having accepted this, it is likely that ethology, sociobiology, and findings from anthropology, biology, and related fields will be allowed a far greater contribution in the study of human behavior than has historically been the case.

It should be noted that the findings reviewed in this chapter do little to invalidate the fundamental tenets of behavioristic theory. At most, they indicate that biology may be more potent than learning in certain circumstances. We should bear in mind, however, that in most instances there is little conflict between biological predispositions and environmental pressures. Indeed, it almost goes without saying that the ability to learn is genetically based. In short, not only are we *prepared* (or *contraprepared*) to learn certain things; we are prepared simply *to learn*. How we do so is the continuing subject of this document.

Summary of Chapter 5

This chapter has presented a definition and review of traditional behaviorism. It looked at the extent to which classical and operant conditioning are distinct and general. And it described a number of situations where behaviors occurred that could not easily be predicted or explained on the basis of behavioristic theory. Many of these behaviors are more easily explained in terms of biological predispositions.

1. Behavioristic theory describes two kinds of behavior (respondent and operant) and two sets of laws for explaining them (classical and operant conditioning).
2. Early behaviorism assumed that classical conditioning was primarily useful for explaining learning involving autonomic behaviors (reflexes, for example) and that operant conditioning did not apply to these behaviors. Subsequent research has shown this to be incorrect.
3. Biofeedback defines information that organisms receive about their biological functioning. Biofeedback research attempts to modify people's physiological functioning by providing them with information about it.
4. Biofeedback techniques are sometimes employed in therapy, particularly for relieving stress, headaches, and a variety of other complaints. According to Miller, the field is still in a relatively primitive stage of development.
5. Early behaviorists assumed that if an arbitrary response such as bar press-

ing could easily be conditioned, virtually any other response could also be conditioned. They were not entirely correct.

6. Animals that are taught complex behaviors and reinforced with food will sometimes revert to a more instinctual behavior even if doing so means that they will no longer be reinforced. This phenomenon is termed instinctive drift.

7. Many organisms appear to be predisposed to performing certain behaviors and will often learn these behaviors even in situations in which the behavior interferes with reinforcement. This phenomenon, known as autoshaping, is illustrated by a pigeon that learns to peck at a key that is always lighted just prior to reinforcement, even though pecking at the key has nothing to do with the delivery of a reward.

8. Adjunctive behaviors, and interim behaviors describe specific responses that are often emitted and learned by animals but that occur either before (interim behaviors) the rewarded behavior or after it (adjunctive behaviors). These behaviors are not causally related to reinforcement but are nevertheless learned. Adjunctive behaviors such as polydipsia (excessive drinking) or pica (eating of nonfood materials) appear to be reinforcing for the animal.

9. Taste-aversion learning can be induced in a single trial involving delayed backward conditioning, a phenomenon that has obvious importance as a biological survival mechanism. It is well illustrated by the fact that those of us who have suffered the malaise of food poisoning frequently find ourselves unable to eat the dish that has poisoned us, even months later.

10. Biological constraints are genetic predispositions that make certain kinds of learning difficult and sometimes impossible (what Seligman describes as contrapreparedness); by the same token we are biologically predisposed toward certain kinds of learning (Seligman's preparedness). Biological predispositions probably underly instinctual drift, autoshaping, and taste-aversion learning.

11. Sociobiology is defined as the systematic study of the biological basis of social behavior. It is premised on the assumption that there are genetic explanations for a great deal of animal and human social behavior. These explanations are based heavily on evolutionary theory.

12. Many of the findings described in this chapter have occasionally been interpreted as presenting serious problems for traditional behavioristic theory. In fact, while they establish that behavioristic explanations are not nearly so general as was once hoped, they provide an extremely useful rapprochement between the biological and the social sciences. It may well be that biology, ethology, anthropology, sociology, and related disciplines will make an even greater contribution to psychology than has historically been the case.

Dear Guy,

    I found the letter, all right.* You might have had the good sense to clean it off a wee bit before slipping it through the door. As it was, I had to spray the hall with pine scent three or four times before the cat would walk through.

    About that letter. When I said maybe I'd answer it for you, I thought it would be just a friendly letter (I guess you don't get too many of those, the way you handle your finances, ha ha). Anyway, there's no way I'm going to answer that kind of letter. I have far more important things to do.

    I'm happy to say that Pouf seems to have recovered quite well from being shot that time, although I don't think he was shot in the rump at all. I think it was more on his back. He was never mean, like you said, so how could he be meaner? One thing, since he was shot, he doesn't seem to want to chase cars at all anymore, so Robert is thinking of trying to get a car instead of his bicycle so Pouf won't chase him. He still says he didn't shoot him, but you guys don't always tell the whole truth, do you?

    About what you asked for again in your last letter, I again have to say no. Not that I can't, you understand, but I think it's about time you started looking after that kind of thing for yourself.

    About your book . . .

---

*The letter in question is reproduced at the beginning of Chapter 3.

CHAPTER *6*

Hebb:
A Transition

D. O. Hebb (1904–)

D. O. Hebb has developed a position based heavily on physiological and neurological fact and hypothesis. Although he has at times been classified as a behaviorist (Chaplin & Krawiec, 1960), he makes extensive use of mediational constructs and deals considerably with "higher" mental processes. He describes his system as a pseudobehavioristic one (Hebb, 1960) and admits that his preoccupation is chiefly explaining thought processes and perception, which are topics not often within the scope of rigidly behavioristic positions. He cautions, however, against viewing his writings as constituting a theory; rather, he lays claim only to having advanced a *proposal* for a theory. His proposal is, to begin with, concerned with *higher mental processes*, a familiar term in contemporary psychological theorizing, though far from familiar among the more rigid behaviorists.

DONALD OLDING HEBB (1904–   )

Hebb was born in the small town of Chester, Nova Scotia, on July 22, 1904. It was in this region that he spent his childhood, eventually going to Dalhousie University in Nova Scotia. He was reportedly not an outstanding student as an undergraduate, earning only a very mediocre grade-point average. He received his B.A. in 1925. From Dalhousie he went to the University of Chicago, where he obtained an M.A., and later to Harvard, where at the age of 32 he was granted a Ph.D.

Since then he has held numerous academic positions and a number of other professional positions. These have included appointments at Harvard, at the Montreal Neurological Institute, and at Queen's University in Kingston, Ontario; a stint as editor of the Bulletin of the Canadian Psychological Association; *a research position with the Yerkes Primate Laboratory; the presidencies of both the Canadian Psychological Association and the American Psychological Association; and professor of psychology at McGill University in Montreal.*

Hebb's many honors include the Warren Medal (presented by the Society of Experimental Psychologists), which was also won by Hull and by Spence; a distinguished scientific contribution award (also won by Piaget); and a large number of honorary degrees. His publications include many important papers and two major books: The Organization of Behavior *(published in 1949), and* A Textbook of Psychology, *the third edition of which was published in 1972.*

Higher Mental Processes

When a woman comes face to face with her first saber-toothed tiger, as she inevitably must, she will turn immediately and run as though the very devil were after her. When the same woman comes to a stream with the intention of crossing it and finds that the stone she had laid there for that purpose is gone, she will stop; perhaps she will sit on the bank with her chin in her hands. Later she may decide to get another stone to replace the first.

In addition to the obvious lack of similarity between a person running from a sabertooth and one sitting on a river bank, there is a fundamental distinction to be made between these two behaviors. The first behavior can be interpreted in terms of the now familiar S-R model: the tiger serves as the stimulus; running is the response. The second behavior could perhaps also be considered within an S-R framework: the missing stone is the stimulus, and the act of leaving to get a replacement is a response. The problem with this last interpretation, however, is that there might be a delay of several minutes or even hours between the presentation of the stimulus and the response. Because of this delay, the S-R model is less than adequate.

The central question here is: what occurs during the lapse of time between a stimulus and a response? It is probable that something related to the stimulus and response must be occurring at least part of the time, since the eventual behavior is made in response to the stimulus that was present much earlier. One phrase used to describe what goes on between the stimulus and response is *higher mental processes*—in layperson's terms *thinking,* or thought processes. In Hebbian terms, this phrase refers to the occurrence of "processes which, themselves independent of immediate sensory input, collaborate with that input to determine which of the various possible responses will be made, and when" (Hebb, 1958, p. 101). In other words, higher mental processes are activities that mediate responses; in a neobehavioristic sense, they are mediating processes.

Because Hebb's theory (or proposal for a theory) is largely neurologically based, a brief account of human neurological functioning should be given first. This account is based largely on Hebb's summary of this process (1966, 1972).

The Conceptual Nervous System

The human nervous system consists of billions of cells called *neurons* (approximately 12.5 billion). Most of these are located in the brain (some 10 billion) and in the spinal cord, which together make up the central nervous system (CNS). The remainder are found throughout the body in the form of complex neural pathways and branches. A neuron is an elongated cell whose function is to transmit impulses in the form of electrical and chemical changes. Neurons form the link between receptors (for example, sense organs) and effectors (muscle systems) and thereby assure that the responses made by an organism will be related to the stimulation it receives. Bundles of neurons form nerves, composing the nervous system.

The simplest unit in the nervous system is, then, the neuron. While it can vary considerably in size and shape, it is microscopic. Neurons are composed of a *cell body*; the *axon*, which is an elongated part sometimes having many branches; and hairlike protrusions from the cell body, called *dendrites*. The space between the axon ends and the dendrites of an adjacent neuron is called a *synapse*, or synaptic space (see Figure 6-1). Transmission of impulses in a neuron is from the cell body outward along the axon and across the synaptic space between the axon end of one cell and the dendrites of the next. The receiving extensions of the neurons are the dendrites, while the transmitting ends are the axons. It is believed that repeated transmission of impulses between two cells leads to permanent facilitation of transmission between these cells. This facilitative property of neurons is central to Hebb's explanation of learning.

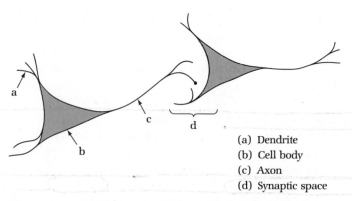

(a) Dendrite
(b) Cell body
(c) Axon
(d) Synaptic space

Figure 6-1.   Idealized representation of two neurons

The transmission of a neural impulse involves both electrical and chemical changes in cells. The exact nature of these changes is complex and not highly relevant here. What is important, however, is that cells can activate one another in sequence, that they can be activated by stimulation, and that they can transmit impulses that cause glands to secrete or muscles to contract. In addition, it is suspected that cells do not always fire only in sequence but that frequently one cell in a sequence can reactivate another that has fired previously, providing some time has elapsed. Neurons are incapable of firing in immediate succession. That is, once a neuron has fired, it undergoes a short period (approximately one millisecond), termed an *absolute refractory period*, during which it cannot be reactivated. This is followed by a longer interval (perhaps 1/10th of a second), termed a *relative refractory period*, during which intense stimulation is required for activation. After this the cell returns to its normal (resting) state.

When a cell is reactivated, it may cause the firing of the cell that reactivated it. In this case, it may be activated again (see Figure 6-2). The resulting circular pattern of firing is called a *reverberatory loop*. It is highly probable that series of such closed circuits can activate one another to form assemblies including thousands of neurons. These hypothetical assemblies are labeled *cell assemblies*.

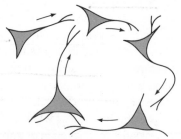

Figure 6-2.   A reverberatory loop

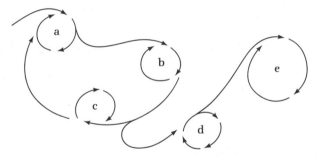

Figure 6-3. Schematic representation of a phase sequence: *a, b, c, d,* and *e* can be thought of as cell assemblies, each of which includes several reverberatory loops. A phase sequence is equivalent to a concept or a percept and may consist of activity in a large number of related neurons (Figure 6-2).

The activation of a number of related cell assemblies can also result in the formation of a third hypothetical structure—the *phase sequence* (see Figure 6-3). These units—the reverberatory loop, the cell assembly, and the phase sequence—play important roles in Hebb's proposal for a theory of learning.

From a physiological point of view, each cell assembly corresponds to what Hebb refers to as "relatively simple sensory input." Hence, the recognition of even very simple objects will involve the activation of a large number of such cell assemblies or phase sequences. The role assigned to these units in Hebb's explanation of higher mental processes is discussed in the following section. You might now want to turn to the Appendix to this chapter, which contains a 64-frame linear program by H. C. Fricker on Hebb's theory.

Learning

This brief introduction to the anatomy and functioning of the human nervous system is essential to an understanding of Hebb's explanation of learning processes. It is important to keep in mind, however, that the neurological units discussed in this and in the previous section are largely hypothetical. While behavioral and anatomical evidence would suggest that entities like cell assemblies and phase sequences probably exist, there remains the possibility that this interpretation is not an accurate one.* Nevertheless, it provides a relatively parsimonious and useful account of human behavior.

In Hebb's theory, as in most other accounts of learning, two properties of the human organism play a central role: reactivity and plasticity. *Reactivity* refers

*Jerzy Konorski (1967) advanced an alternative hypothesis: that the representation of perceptions does not take the form of *assemblies* of *cells* but of single units referred to as *gnostic units*. In addition he renamed the *association* area of the cortex the *gnostic* area. His position is somewhat similar to Hebb's in many respects, although it is much more detailed in its application to various types of learning.

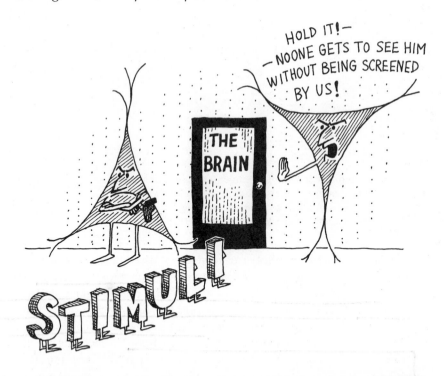

to the capacity of the organism to react to external stimuli. *Plasticity* is the property of the organism that allows it to change as a function of repeated stimulation. A simple demonstration can be used to illustrate these two properties. The procedure involves placing a subject 2 or 3 feet in front of the experimenter. The experimenter then, without warning, kicks the subject squarely and soundly in the seat of the pants. The subject's immediate behavior is an example of *reactivity*. The subject's subsequent refusal to repeat the experiment is an example of *plasticity*.

Within behavioristic positions, reactivity is interpreted as involving the emission of responses while plasticity is manifested when behavior is modified. The interpretation of these events in Hebbian theory takes the form of an attempt to account for behavior in terms of neurological events. For Hebb, plasticity and reactivity are properties of the CNS that account for behavior, rather than being properties of behavior.

MEDIATING PROCESSES

One of Hebb's primary concerns is to explain higher mental processes, or thought. In an attempt to arrive at some understanding of these processes, he offers a basic hypothesis and makes a number of assumptions. The previous section lays the groundwork for interpreting these assumptions, since they deal with the physiology of the nervous system.

The first and most basic hypothesis, which has already been described, is simply that mediation, or thinking, consists of "activity in a group of neurons, arranged as a set of closed pathways which will be referred to as a *cell assembly*, or of a series of such activities, which will be referred to as a *phase sequence*" (Hebb, 1958, p. 103). In addition, Hebb (1966) makes a number of assumptions about the formation of the *cell assembly*.

Assumption 1. A cell assembly (or mediating process) is established as the result of the repeated firing of cells. It arises as a function of the repetition of a particular kind of sensory event. In other words, the repeated presentation of a specific stimulus will tend to reactivate the same assemblies each time, serving to facilitate transmission of impulses across the synaptic spaces between the neurons involved. Hence, repetition has a facilitating effect on further neural activity. Behavioral evidence of this effect is provided by the fact that it is considerably easier to multiply two numbers if they have been multiplied many times previously. Or, more simply, it is easier to recognize a simple object if it has been presented frequently than if it is being seen for the second time. This property of neural transmission defines in part what is meant by *plasticity* of the conceptual nervous system.

Assumption 2. If two cell assemblies are repeatedly active at the same time, an association between the two will tend to form. In other words, if cell assembly *A* is always (or often) active when *B* is active, the two will tend to become associated neurologically. That is, the firing of cell assembly *A* may lead to firing in *B* and vice versa. The result will be the formation of *phase sequences.*

A closer examination of the implications of this assumption reveals that it can serve as an explanation for conditioning through contiguity. If cell assembly *A* corresponds to one specific sensory event and *B* does also, and if, further, *A* and *B* *do* represent the components of thought (mediation), then the establishment of a relationship between *A* and *B* simply means that presentation of the event associated with *A* may *remind* one of the event associated with *B*. There is considerable intuitive evidence that this process does indeed occur. For example, if a man is always seen with a cigar, then it is highly probable that anything that reminds one of the man will also bring the cigar to mind. The smell of wood smoke makes a person think of fire; lilacs go with spring; fish mean water or restaurants; the letter *q* in a word means *u* is next; and motherhood is a good thing.

Thus, the first purpose of this assumption is to explain learning by contiguity. A second achievement of the assumption is to explain the perception of objects when incomplete sensory data are available. The lines in Figure 6-4 are almost always perceived as a triangle, although they really are not. (This phenomenon is sometimes referred to as *closure* in Gestalt psychology—see Chapter 7). For the sake of simplicity, the cell assemblies associated with triangularity can be

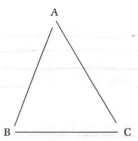

Figure 6-4.   Perception with incomplete data

said to include units representing each of the corners A, B, and C of the triangle, as well as each of the sides. Because these features of triangles have been present in contiguity many times, associations have been formed between the cell assemblies that represent them. It is now sufficient to present only limited sensory input (that is, only three sides of a triangle but no corners) in order to evoke activity in the entire sequence of assemblies corresponding to "triangle."

Assumption 3. An assembly that is active at the same time as an efferent pathway (a neural pathway leading outward from the CNS) will tend to form an association with it. This assumption, like assumption 2, allows Hebb to explain the formation of associations between events that are in temporal contiguity. Activity in an efferent pathway may result in some sort of motor activity. Hence, the associations that are explained by this assumption involve behavioral events and mediation—in other words, thought and behavior. Again there is ample evidence that such associations are very much a part of human learning. Particular sights, sounds, or smells, for example, become associated with a specific motor activity, so that engaging in the activity recalls the sensory impression. The reverse is also true. Activity in assemblies that have often been active during some motor response would tend to elicit the same response. This interpretation is obviously a simple neurologically based explanation for the Pavlovian model of classical conditioning. The assemblies relating to the sounding of a buzzer are always present at the time of salivation and are eventually sufficient to elicit salivation.

Assumption 4. Each assembly corresponds to relatively simple sensory input. This property of the cell assembly makes it necessary to involve large groups of such assemblies in explaining the perception of even relatively simple physical objects.

SUMMARY OF ASSUMPTIONS

The four assumptions described above can be summarized by describing what *learning* and *thinking* appear to be for Hebb, since the assumptions are made in order to enable Hebb to make those descriptions. Essentially, the term *think-*

ing is equivalent to *mediation.* Mediation consists of activity in assemblies of neurons, and the nature of the mediation (or of the thought) is determined by the specific assemblies involved. Hebb contends that it is clearly the activated area of the cortex that determines the subjective experience of the organism and not the nature of the neural activity itself. For example, it is possible to stimulate the optic nerve electrically or by using pressure. In either case, the effect is the same: the subject sees light (Hebb, 1966, p. 267). On the other hand, the activation of specific receptors will always affect the same area of the cortex (and presumably the same cell assemblies). Hence, it is possible to "feel" the same reaction for the same stimulation on different occasions. If this were not true, of course, human awareness, as it is now known, would not exist.

The acquisition of learned mediating processes results from the repetition of the same sensory event leading to the formation of associated assemblies. Thus, learning consists of the "permanent facilitation" of conduction among neural units. Essentially, a phase sequence is a neurological unit where the transmission of impulses has become so easy that the activation of one part of the sequence is sufficient to activate the entire organization. In Hebb's earlier writings (1949), he maintained that activity, once begun, is almost autonomous—that is, almost self-sustaining—but in the light of subsequent physiological discoveries, he has revised this notion (Hebb, 1958, 1966). He now considers the system semiautonomous, taking into account that some degree of external stimulation is necessary for continued cortical functioning.

Hebb's neurologically based explanation for learning accounts for the formation of stimulus and response associations in terms of connections that are formed between their corresponding neurological counterparts (active cell assemblies or phase sequences). Assumptions 2 and 3 deal with this type of learning. Higher processes involved in learning (insightful problem solving, for example) are assumed to involve the combination of phase sequences (sometimes through chance) in higher-order organizational units—supraordinate phase sequences. Again, these sequences are hypothetical constructs and not necessarily "real." Two additional concepts—*set* and *attention*—are discussed by Hebb, both as evidence of mediation and as illustrations of significant phenomena in human functioning.

SET AND ATTENTION

When a starter at a race tells the contestants that he or she will fire the pistol a few seconds after saying "On your mark" and that they can then proceed to run like scared rabbits over the dirty cinders, he is attempting to establish *set.* If he succeeds, the contestants will sprint forward when the pistol sounds. (It would be interesting to see what the effect on the starter would be if all contestants had agreed beforehand to relax when the pistol was fired.)

A superficial and incorrect behavioristic interpretation of this situation might be that the sound of the pistol was the stimulus that led to the response of running. On the other hand, consider what might have happened if the starter had said, "I'm going to fire this pistol to see if my blanks are any good. Just relax." If he then fired the pistol and no one ran, it would be quite obvious that the pistol alone was not the stimulus that led to the running response but that the initial instructions were also involved. In other words the "set" given to the contestants, *together with* the stimulus, is responsible for the behavior.

Consider, further, what would happen if a celebrity strolled along the track just prior to the sounding of the gun. Would *GSR* (galvanic skin response) increase? Would blood pressure and heart rate go up? Would temperature jump? Probably not. If, on the other hand, these same contestants had already finished the race and were lounging around recuperating when the celebrity walked by, the phase sequences activated might be quite different. These two examples are illustrations of the effect of *attention* on behavior. Set refers to selectivity among responses; attention refers to selectivity among input. both characteristics are assumed to be largely a function of the preactivation of specific cell assemblies. When racers are told to get ready to run, they are "set" to respond by running when they hear a bang. When they are "attending" to the imminent sound, they are less likely to attend to other distracting stimuli.

Both these characteristics of human behavior are particularly relevant for teachers. Set is intimately involved in choosing appropriate responses, attention is essential for learning, and each is obviously affected by the other. In addition, both attention and set are closely related to arousal, a concept that is central to Hebb's theory of motivation.

Motivation

Not only is arousal a key concept in Hebb's theory of motivation, but it is also central to his learning theory. Actually, it is misleading to speak of learning and motivation as different theories for two reasons: first, Hebb does not pretend to advance a theory for either learning or motivation but only a proposal for a theory; second, for Hebb learning and motivation are "different" only as they relate to different questions but not because different answers are proposed for them. In fact, the same arousal concepts are pertinent for both. It is simpler and clearer, however, to treat the topics in separate sections.

Hebb (1972) makes an important distinction between the two functions of a stimulus: the cue function and the arousal function. Briefly, the cue function is the message function; it tells the organism how to feel, think, or react. The arousal function is defined by the general activating, or arousing, effect of stimuli. The cue, or message, of a stimulus will, within the context of Hebb's theory, involve the activation of the specific assemblies corresponding to the stimulation. The arousal function, however, will involve a larger number of cell assemblies. This preactivation is thought to be effected through the reticular formation and is also considered to be essential for the cue to have its effect. It is in this sense that arousal is so intimately involved in learning, since learning is concerned with the cue component of stimulation.

Hebb's theory of motivation is known as a single-drive theory. The drive is defined in terms of generalized arousal, with arousal referring to the degree of alertness, or vigilance, of an organism. Arousal level is a function of the nature of the stimulation being reacted to, and it varies from very low (sleep or drowsiness) to very high (anxiety or panic). Hebb makes the assumption that there is an optimal level of arousal, above and below which behavior will not be maximally effective. He also makes the related assumption that humans behave so as to maintain arousal at or near the optimal level. This assumption implies that there is a *need* for maintaining a moderate level of arousal. Indeed, this assumed need is the reason arousal theories are referred to as *drive* theories (see Chapter 12). The question of whether there is a *need* for arousal has been indirectly examined through an investigation of the effects of prolonged reductions in arousal on the behavior of humans.

THE NEED FOR STIMULATION

The original experiments in a sequence of related investigations in this area were conducted at McGill University under the direction of Hebb. His collaborators, Bexton, Heron, and Scott, reported the results of the initial studies in 1954 and 1956. (Since then numerous investigators have replicated their early findings. See, for example, Schultz, 1965, or Zubek, 1969.)

The first experiment (see Heron, 1957), referred to as a sensory-deprivation or perceptual-isolation* study, employed a group of male college students who had volunteered for an experiment where they would not be asked to *do* anything and for which they would be paid $20 a day. In actuality, not only were they not asked to do anything, but they were not allowed to do anything. Instead, they were made to lie on cots, getting up only to use the toilet or to eat. Meals were served to subjects as they sat on the edge of their bed. Each cot was isolated in a soundproof cubicle, and subjects wore translucent visors that did not allow them to see but permitted diffuse light to enter. Over their ears they wore U-shaped foam pillows that were designed to prevent hearing. As a further precaution against the perception of sounds, air-conditioning equipment hummed ceaselessly and monotonously. Subjects wore cotton gloves and had cardboard cuffs that extended over their fingertips in order to discourage tactile sensation. In short, the experimenters attempted to ensure that a minimum of sensory stimulation would be experienced by the subjects for as long as they wished to remain in isolation. Interestingly, none of the subjects wished to remain for more than 2 days. In some later experiments where conditions of deprivation

*Zubek (1969) distinguished between sensory and perceptual deprivation. The former is assumed to involve conditions of darkness or silence, whereas the latter indicates an unvarying stimulus field, such as in the Hebb experiments.

were more severe (for example, complete darkness, no sound, body immersed in water to simulate weightlessness), subjects often did not last more than a few hours (see, for example, Barnard, 1962; Lilly, 1972; Shurley, 1966).

Since the chief source of cortical activation (arousal) is sensation, perceptual deprivation should result in a lowering of arousal. This assumption has been confirmed through EEG ratings of subjects before, during, and after isolation (Heron, 1957; Zubek & Wilgosh, 1963). After prolonged isolation, it is not uncommon for the cortical activity of subjects who are awake to approximate that of normal *sleep.*

Among the effects of sensory deprivation is impairment in perceptual and cognitive functioning as evidenced in later performance on simple numerical or visual tasks (Heron, 1957). In addition, subjects often become irritable, easily amused or annoyed, and almost childish in their reaction to limited contact with experimenters. For example, they often attempt desperately to engage the experimenter in conversation, acting in much the same way a child does when trying to gain the attention of a preoccupied parent.

Another striking finding of sensory-deprivation studies is that subjects frequently report experiencing illusions of various kinds—in some cases, hallucinations—after prolonged isolation. Numerous studies have since investigated the conditions under which hallucinations are most likely to occur (see, for example, Zuckerman, cited in Zubek, 1969). One general conclusion that can be derived from these studies is that hallucinations *do* in fact result from sensory deprivation but are somewhat infrequent and markedly affected by the subject's pre-isolation attitudes or set.

These studies of sensory deprivation tend to add further support to arousal-based explanations of human behavior. There seems to be little question that behavior is more nearly optimal under conditions of moderate arousal. In addition, it appears that humans do endeavor to maintain arousal at that level. For example, subjects in isolation often talk to themselves, whistle, recite poetry, or attempt to draw the experimenters into conversation. Such behavior led Schultz (1965) to hypothesize that the need for arousal is really a need for stimulation. In this connection he proposed a *sensoristatic* model of behavior — a kind of homeostatic model in which *sensation* is the dependent variable. Quite simply, the Schultz sensoristatic model is based on the contention that individuals seek sensory variation. Thus, this model is in effect, if not in terminology, identical to an arousal model.

Hebb's explanation of motivation is premised on the assumption that arousal is a central variable in human learning and behavior. It is similar to the motivational positions adopted by Bruner (Chapter 14) among others.

Hebb in Perspective

It should be clear by now that Hebb's theorizing represents a significant departure from the more traditional S-R theories that we have considered earlier. Indeed, his major preoccupations have been with internal neurological events, few of which are nearly as objective as the stimuli and responses that interested Watson and Skinner. And his goal has been less to explain the formation of relationships between stimuli and responses than to account for higher mental processes. Interestingly, his neurological speculating lends itself remarkably well to explaining learning through contiguity. Thus, classical conditioning in Hebbian terms is simply a matter of related cell assemblies having been simultaneously active often enough that the activation of one is sufficient to activate the other.

Subsequent chapters dealing with the more cognitive theorists also reveal that Hebb's theorizing sometimes lends itself well to an explanation of thought processes. This is particularly evident with respect to Bruner's theories. It is in this sense that Hebb's ideas serve as a liaison between traditional behaviorism and more cognitive orientations.

An Evaluation

As we noted at the very outset, Hebb's theorizing is based to a considerable extent on speculation concerning the nature of neurological events. It also bears repeating that he does not view his writings as constituting a theory but rather as a proposal for one. Nevertheless, his ideas represent a coherent and systematic attempt to explain important observations and can be treated as a theory.

Viewed in terms of the criteria we have been employing, Hebb's theory can be described as reflecting some facts rather well. Thus, it is highly compatible with what is known about neurological functioning. But, as we have noted earlier, it also goes some distance beyond what is known. We have no way of knowing at present whether, in this respect, it violates what is real. But in defense of the system, it bears repeating that the logical constructs represented by such inventions as cell assemblies have an important explanatory function. And at this point, the theory should not be judged in terms of its "truthfulness" but in terms of the extent that predictions based on the theory agree with actual observations and the extent to which the theory provides a clear and useful explanation of observations. Indeed, no psychological theory need be blessed with "truthfulness." Science would not recognize it in any case. What science insists on is objectivity, replicability, consistency, and usefulness. And this last, usefulness, is sometimes better judged by history than by science.

Summary of Chapter 6

This chapter has presented a description of D. O. Hebb's explanation for human behavior. A short program detailing Hebb's notions regarding neurological functioning follows. In addition, sensory-deprivation studies were discussed in relation to arousal theory.

1. Hebb has advanced a model based largely on neurological and physiological knowledge and hypotheses.

2. The human nervous system is made up of cells called *neurons*, which consist of a *cell body*, receiving extensions called *dendrites*, and an elongated part called an *axon*. Transmission among neurons is from axon ends across the *synaptic* space, which is the separation between the axon end and the dendrites of an adjacent cell.

3. Hebb attempts to explain *higher mental processes* in terms of activity in neural assemblies. He reasons that this activity must take the form of reverberatory loops, which are neurons arranged in such a way that they can keep reactivating one another.

4. Arrangements of related cell assemblies are called *phase sequences*. Both cell assemblies and phase sequences are hypothetical constructs employed to explain learning. Mediation (thinking) is defined in terms of activity in cell assemblies or phase sequences.

5. Hebb makes a number of important assumptions. First, he suggests that cell assemblies result from the repeated presentation of similar stimulus patterns and therefore the repeated activation of the same neurons. The second assumption is that, if two assemblies are often active at the same time, they will tend to form associations with each other. This last assumption can be used to explain conditioning.

6. A third assumption made by Hebb is that motor activity will become associated with the assemblies that are often active with it. This assumption explains the formation of motor habits. A fourth assumption is that each cell assembly corresponds to relatively simple sensory data.

7. *Set* and *attention* are central processes in learning and perception. Set refers to selectivity among responses, whereas attention refers to selectivity among input.

8. Hebb's *theory of motivation* is based on a concept of arousal. It centers on the assumption that there is an optimum level of arousal for maximally effective behavior and that people will behave so as to maintain that level.

9. Studies of *sensory deprivation* tend to support the contention that there is a need in humans for a variety of sensory stimulation.

Appendix to Chapter 6

(The following is a revision of an unpublished program written by H. C. Fricker. Used with permission.)

D. O. HEBB'S NEUROLOGICAL THEORY

Objectives. When you have completed this program you should be able to do the following:

1. Define:
   a. central nervous system

    b. neuron
    c. dendrite
    d. axon
    e. synapse
    f. synaptic knob
 2. Explain:
    a. the formation of a cell assembly
    b. the formation of a phase sequence
    c. mediation
    d. reverberation

Directions. The following is a 63-frame program. Most of the frames have one blank. On the right are the correct responses for each of the blanks. Fold a sheet of paper or make a strip of cardboard to cover these responses. With the correct answers covered, begin by reading the first frame. *WRITE* your response in the book or on a separate sheet of paper. As you move to each successive frame, lower the paper or cardboard so as to check your answer. The program can be completed easily at one sitting. You may wish to measure your learning by taking the short test at the end. If you make many errors, the program is not a good one. If you make no errors, you are very intelligent. Good luck.

 1. The brain and spinal cord are together called the "Central Nervous System" because of their function as a "switchboard" or "telephone exchange" between the receptors and effectors of the body. The basic element of the central nervous system is the NEURON. The C.N.S. contains billions of these _____ .

 2. The central nervous system consists of a network of neurons in the brain and spinal cord. The basic element of the C.N.S. is the _____ .

    neurons

 3. "C.N.S." is an abbreviation for <u>central</u> _____ _____ .

    neuron

 4. Impulses are transmitted over this vast system in the form of chemical changes and tiny electrical charges moving from one neuron or group of neurons to the next. In this way, "signals" picked up by the sense organs pass to the brain, and "instructions" are sent to the muscles of the body. This intricate system is known as the C_____ N_____ S_____ .

    nervous system

5. Neurons vary widely in shape, but basically each consists of a cell body with several hairlike extensions through which electrical-chemical impulses are received and passed on to other neurons. Above is a sketch of a _____ .

   central nervous system

6. The impulses that pass through the C.N.S. are in the form of tiny _____ charges.

   neuron

7. The senses receive millions of stimuli every waking hour (somewhat fewer during sleep). Most of these are of insufficient strength to set up impulses in the neurons associated with them. Of those that do, only the strongest reach the brain and are acted upon. This is one way in which the C.N.S. "mediates," or modifies, the S-R process. Of all the impulses received by the senses, what proportion reach the brain? _____ (all, most, few, none)

   electrochemical (electric)

8. "Mediation" refers to any resistance or interruption or modification to the passage of an impulse through the C.N.S. Suppose you are about to swear, but the presence of certain people plus your past experience lead you to choose a different word. This is an example of m _____ .

   few

9. You could not possibly respond to every detail of everything you see, hear, feel, etc. Hence, only the most intense impulses pass through the C.N.S.; the others are stopped, or _____ .

   mediation

10. If you have an urge to scratch your nose (not now, silly!), you may assume that the itch stimulus was a relatively persistent one, such that an impulse traveled the neuron path to your brain, where it excited a response path terminating in the muscles of your arm and hand. The C.N.S. provided a neuron path from the *stimulus* of the itch to the _____ of scratching.

    mediated (or similar word)

11. The receiving extensions of neurons are called   *response*
    DENDRITES. Say the word. Write the word:
    _____ .

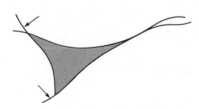

12. Dendrites receive impulses from the senses or from   *dendrites*
    other neurons and pass them into the cell body. Im-
    pulses enter the neuron via the _____ .

13. Dendrites are the extensions through which neurons   *dendrite(s)*
    _____(receive, pass on) impulses.

14. There may be one, two, or more dendrites on the neu-   *receive*
    ron. If these lie close enough to other neurons, and the
    other neurons contain a sufficiently strong electrical
    charge, an impulse will pass between. Receiving exten-
    sions of neurons are called _____ .

15. Each time an impulse passes from neuron *A* to neuron   *dendrites*
    B, it becomes easier to repeat in the future. This is the
    learning process, as we shall see later. Therefore,
    let's do it once more: when you think of the receiv-
    ing extensions of neurons, you think of the name
    _____ .

16. An extension of the neuron through which impulses are   *dendrites*

passed on to a following neuron is called an AXON. Say
and write the word: _____ .

17. The dendrites of one neuron receive impulses from the   *axon*
    _____ of another.

18. A neuron consists of a cell body and hairlike extensions   *axon(s)*
    called _____ s and _____ s .

19. The end of the axon may or may not touch the dendrite   *dendrites*
    of another neuron. The point of contact or near contact   *axons*
    is known as a SYNAPSE, and the impulse must jump
    this point in order to excite the next neuron. Dendrites
    and axons meet at a s_____ .

20. A weak impulse may be unable to jump the _____   *synapse*
    to the next neuron.

21. As successive impulses discharge across a synapse, a   *synapse*
    change takes place. Transmission becomes easier. The
    more frequent the transmission, the greater the ease

with which impulses pass. In this way, learning takes place. In a learned S-R sequence, impulses pass easily from a_____ to d_____ across the s_____.

22. Sometimes a synapse occurs directly between an axon and the cell body of the following neuron. Such an arrangement bypasses the _____ .

axon
dendrite
synapse

23. If a stimulating impulse entering the C.N.S. fails to produce the usual response, the S-R sequence has been interfered with. The interference is known as med_____ .

dendrite

24. Sometimes the mediation is due to other distracting stimuli. In this case, the distracting stimuli would be referred to as _____ing stimuli.

mediation

25. a

mediating

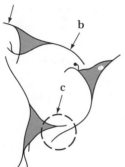

Fill in the labels for the preceding diagram.

(a) _____

(b) _____

(c) _____

26. We will now discuss the "cell assembly." As the name implies, the cell assembly is an association of neurons. You know now how one neuron "fires," or excites, another and how an impulse passes along a chain of neurons. Consider what happens when one of the later neurons lies near enough to fire one of the early ones. Voilà! Le ring around Rosie, no? This *assembly* of neural *cells* is called a _____ _____ .

dendrite
axon
synapse

27. The brain contains millions of cell assemblies, each associated with a particular basic stimulus. Cell assemblies are built up very slowly as learning takes place. Simple learning can be described in terms of the formation of _____ _____ s .

cell assembly

28. A cell assembly is a circuit containing, perhaps, thousands of neurons. The whole circuit is excited in response to a particular basic _____ .

cell assemblies

29. Each perceptibly different sense stimulus is represented in the brain by a cell assembly. You have one for each of the many different colors and probably thousands for the sounds you know. The more discriminating you are regarding colors, the more _____ _____ s you have associated with color.

stimulus

30. An accomplished musician has many very finely developed _____ _____ associated with _____ .

cell assemblies

31. Electric charges travel around the cell assembly, jumping from the axon of one neuron to the dendrite of the next. This gap, which is jumped by the electric charge, is called a _____ .

cell assemblies
sound (music)

32. Cell assemblies must not be thought of as independent of one another. Indeed there exists a vast network of crossconnections, and the firing of one cell assembly is likely to set off many more. In this way, the smell of cooking can elicit visions, tastes, even feelings in the mouth and stomach. A cell assembly is fired by an _____ charge passing through it.

synapse

33. If the sketch below brings to mind "triangle," it is because the cell assemblies associated with the separate lines fire enough other cell assemblies to complete the triangle in your mind. The cell assemblies together are known as a PHASE SEQUENCE. A phase sequence is a group of associated _____ _____ s .

electric

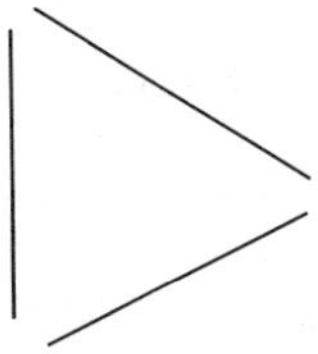

34. A group of associated cell assemblies is known as a ph_____ _____ .

cell assemblies

35. There may be a dozen cell assemblies associated with the mental concept of a simple shape. Such a collection of cell assemblies is called a _____ _____ .

phase sequence

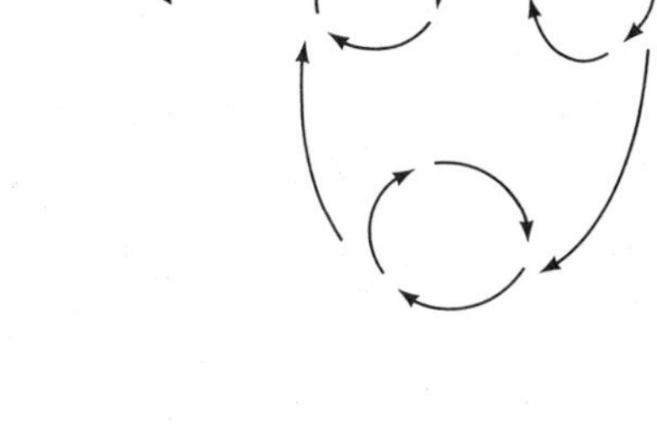

36. A collection of associated neurons is called a _____   *phase sequence*
    _____ ; a collection of associated cell
    assemblies is called a _____ _____ .

37. A phase sequence is a collection of associated   *cell assembly*
    _____ _____s; a cell assembly is a   *phase sequence*
    collection of associated _____ .

38. Every time you see a complete rectangle, all your cell   *cell assemblies*
    assemblies associated with rectangularity are fired   *neurons*
    together, and crossconnections are established among
    them. Then when some of them are fired by a visual
    stimulus like that below, the others are fired also. The
    abstract concept of rectangularity exists in the brain as
    a _____ _____ .

39. Do you remember the term used for the point of contact   *phase sequence*
    or near contact between neurons? _____ .

40. Even phase sequences are not independent of one   *synapse*
    another. Crossconnections exist, and this accounts for
    flexibility in thinking. Problem solving would be im-
    possible without the transfer of impulses among
    _____ _____ .

41. Cell assemblies and phase sequences are *reverberating*   *phase sequences*
    circuits. For some time after the stimulus stops, energy
    travels round and round the circuit. As long as the
    circuit reverberates, it can mediate other incoming
    stimuli. Mediation refers to any interruption or change
    in the connection between a stimulus and a
    _____ .

42. A neural circuit that remains active after the stimulus   *response*
    stops is said to re_____ate .

43. As long as a circuit reverberates, it can have a   *reverberate*
    _____ing effect on incoming stimuli.

44. A neural circuit that remains active after the stimulus   *mediating*
    stops is said to _____ .

45. You are told to "add the following numbers." This   *reverberate*
instruction activates its reverberating circuit, which is
then ready to mediate the stimuli that follow. Then
come the stimuli:

"5"

3

Your response is correct because of the mediating effect
of a _____ ing circuit.

46. Visualize, if you will, the phase sequences that spring   *reverberating*
to attention in your mind as you hear:

"Spell the following words."
"I don't want to scare you, but . . . "
"Did you hear what happened to Charlie?"
"We will now discuss sex."

Instructions and remarks such as these activate appropriate _____ circuits in your brain.

47. These reverberating circuits then stand ready to   *reverberating*
_____ incoming material.

48. A short review, now, before going on. C.N.S. stands for   *mediate*
_____ _____ _____ .

49. The basic element of the C.N.S. is the neuron. It consists   *central nervous*
of a cell body, with extensions called _____ s   *system*
and _____ s .

50. Dendrites and axons meet at what is called a   *dendrites*
_____ .   *axons*

51. A "closed circuit" of neurons is called a _____   *synapse*
_____ , which is activated by a particular
basic _____ .

52. A group of cell assemblies associated with a sim-   *cell assembly*
ple mental concept is called a _____   *stimulus*
_____ .

53. When a neural circuit remains active after the stimulus   *phase sequence*
stops, it is said to _____ .

54. Such reverberating circuits can have _____   *reverberate*
effects on incoming stimuli.

55. What, then, is the learning process, according to Hebb's   *mediating*
theory? Several stimuli are received together for the first
time while the C.N.S. is in a state of AROUSAL (alerted,
excited, ready). This means that there is a background
of impulses passing around the system. As a result, several chance firings are made between neurons, and
learning has started.
When the C.N.S. is excited, alerted, or "at attention," it
is said to be in a state of _____ .

56. With frequent repetition, cell assemblies and phase   *arousal*
sequences are formed, and *connections* among this
group of stimuli are learned. Learning is, then, the
building up of neural _____ s .

57. If a particular response is made each time these stimuli   *connections*
are received, it too is learned. For instance, connections
are made between the stimuli "add," "two," and "five"
and the response "seven." Two requirements for learning are a state of _____ and frequent
_____ .

58. A background of impulses passing around in the C.N.S.,   *arousal*
which is essential to the formation of new neural con-   *repetition*
nections, is known as a state of _____ .

59. The learning process is essentially the formation and   *arousal*
strengthening of neural _____ s .

60. Once connections have been made, drill serves to build   *connections*
up synaptic knobs, which improves connections.   *(circuits)*
Thus, drill is an aid to learning. This applies, of
course, to physical as well as mental learning. "Practice makes perfect" because it improves neural
_____ s .

61. The Hebb theory logically supports the principle of   *connections*
distributed practice. Can you see why? What hap-   *(circuits)*

pens within a neural circuit when the external stimuli stop? That's right, the circuit continues to

_____ .

62. If learning continues in a reverberating circuit, consider   *reverberate*
another principle; that of incubation in creative thinking. The creative thinker finds it effective to go through all the known information regarding a problem, consider all the known avenues of solution—then go to sleep or otherwise relax. Thus, the external stimuli are cut off, and a great many circuits are reverberating. Can you see how a solution often comes unexpectedly in this way? Think about it in the light of what you have learned.

63. Finally, bear in mind that Hebb's theory is just that—a theory. It is logical and reasonable and offers an interesting explanation of many things that cannot as yet be proven. But it is important to teachers as a theory of learning in that it suggests practical methods of teaching—which work. Put the theory into practice yourself. Sit back right now and let *your* neural circuits reverberate to reinforce what you have learned from this program.

SHORT TEST FOR HEBB LINEAR PROGRAM

True-False

1. The brain and spinal cord are together called the central nervous system.
2. The receiving end of a neuron is called the axon.
3. Hairlike extensions which protrude from the cell body of a neuron are called synapses.
4. Phase sequences are made up of groups of cell assemblies.
5. Arousal is necessary for the formation of connections between cell assemblies.

Complete:

6. Cell assemblies consist of many _____ .

7. The reactivation of a nerve cell by one which it had previously been instrumental in firing forms a(n) _____ _____ .

8. The transmission of impulses in the C.N.S. is in the form of

_____ _____ .

9. The elongated extension of a nerve cell is called a(n) _____ .

10. Facilitation of neural transmission is assumed to be caused by

_____ _____ .

(The answers to this test are provided below).

ANSWERS TO REVIEW TEST FOR HEBB LINEAR PROGRAM

1. true
2. false
3. false
4. true
5. true
6. neurons, or nerve cells
7. reverberatory loop
8. electrochemical impulses
9. axon
10. repeated transmission or firing

PART 3

Learning: Cognitive Explanations

Dear Dr. Haig:

On August 20th, this year, you wrote to inquire about my dear grandmother and her reaction to the comments that I have occasionally made about her in the pages of Of Children. I thought it fitting to have the old lady respond to your questions directly, and I immediately took your letter to her. At the time she was rather busily engaged in harvesting turnips and potatoes and in replenishing her soil with the particular fertilizers she finds so effective for invigorating cabbages and exciting flowers. Unfortunately, your letter was inadvertently misplaced under a bag of fertilizer she gets from Tremblay's horses, where it remained until yesterday. And although it no longer smells as sweet as it surely did when it first left the Philadelphia College of Textiles and Science, it is still legible—yellowed somewhat, but quite clearly legible.

I am saddened to have to report that my grandmother quite adamantly refuses to respond directly to your innocent inquiries. She has spent a good deal of her later years actively avoiding fame—and has, I might add, been eminently successful, although local notoriety has overwhelmed her for some time.

At any rate, this wise and notorious old lady has directed me to inform you that she has more important things to do than to approve or condemn my opinions or my references to her opinions. I suspect, however, that had she been talking directly to you rather than to me, she might have admitted that she is a tiny bit flattered at the attention that I have given her and that others sometimes give her as a result of her appearances in my writing.

In my own defense, I would like to add that I am not a very good chauvinist. I am so bad as a chauvinist, in fact, that I have now abandoned most of my efforts in that direction. As a result I spend considerably less time attempting to expose the stupidity of those so gifted, and I am much more easily persuaded of the intellectual excellence of those who invent theories such as my grandmother's. And that, of course, is my explanation/defense for including references to the old lady in what might otherwise be much purer psychology.

I trust this does not answer any of your questions.

Yours,

Guy R. Lefrancois

CHAPTER 7

Tolman and Gestalt Psychology

Traditional Behaviorism

The traditional behaviorism described in the early chapters of this book has a number of distinguishing characteristics common to most of its separate theories. First, and perhaps most obviously, early behavioristic positions came about largely as a reaction to the more mentalistic approaches that had previously characterized psychology. In contrast to these approaches, behaviorism sought to be impeccably objective. Accordingly, its most devoted theorists concentrated almost entirely on those aspects of behavior that could readily be observed and measured: stimuli and responses. The science of behavior became a question of discovering precise relationships among stimuli and responses. And theorists such as Hebb and Hull, who felt compelled to speak of intervening, or mediating, variables, were careful to link them as directly as possible to observable events. For them, intervening variables were far more than simply helpful abstractions; they were actual neurological events or processes that science might in time discover.

A second important characteristic of traditional behavioristic theories is that they sought to explain behavior by analyzing it at a *molecular* or elemental level. In other words, theorists were far more interested in specific responses and in sequences of individual responses than they were in more global and perhaps less easily managed behaviors. This approach, termed *reductionism*, is most evident in classical conditioning but is also characteristic of operant theories.

A third fundamental characteristic of traditional behaviorism is that it makes few assumptions about the objectives or purposes of behavior except insofar as these can be related directly to specific needs or drives. A strict behavioristic interpretation of a behavior does not raise any questions concerning the *intentions* of the actor; nor does it make any allowances for *wanting* or *willing*. It simply looks for relationships between response consequences and behavior, or it searches for an understanding of the ways in which temporal contiguity of stimuli, responses, and response consequences are important in determining behavior.

A strong negative reaction to traditional behaviorism took the form of *cognitivism*, a movement that had its roots in German Gestalt psychology. These roots are discussed in the later pages of this chapter.

A somewhat milder reaction to traditional behaviorism had its roots in the United States and is particularly well represented in the writings of Edward Tolman. Although Tolman's system was developed after Gestalt psychology, it is considered first in this chapter because it represents an important link between behaviorism and cognitivism.

EDWARD CHACE TOLMAN (1886–1959)
Tolman was born into a Quaker family in Newton,
Massachusetts, on April 14, 1886 (also the year of Guthrie's birth).
He attended the Massachusetts Institute of Technology, from which
he received a B.S. in electrochemistry in 1911. From there he went
to Harvard, where he obtained his M.A. in 1912 and his Ph.D. in
1915. Both of these degrees were in psychology.
Tolman began his teaching at Northwestern University, from which he was
released 3 years later, ostensibly for lack of teaching competence but more likely
because of his Quaker-based pacifist convictions at a time of war. From there

he went to the University of California at Berkeley, where he spent most of the remainder of his academic career. Finally, though, he was compelled to leave there as well—this time after refusing to take a controversial loyalty oath spawned by the McCarthy purges. As a result, in 1950 he accepted teaching positions at the University of Chicago and at Harvard. As a member of the American Civil Liberties Union he was instrumental in bringing about the granting of certain elements of academic freedom. One of the results of this effort was that he returned to Berkeley in 1953.

Tolman, who like Skinner, Hebb, and Guthrie served as president of the American Psychological Association, was often accused of not being as serious and single-minded as he might have been with respect to the development of his theories. Indeed, his writings are filled with whimsy and anecdotes. And perhaps his tongue was at least partly in his cheek when he dedicated one of his most important books to Mus norvegicus albinus *(the white Norway mouse, although it is generally believed that he meant the white Norway rat). (Sahakian, 1981; Woodworth & Sheehan, 1964.)*

Purposive Behaviorism

One of the most fundamental differences between Tolman's position and other behavioristic positions is implicit in the title of this section, taken from the title of one of Tolman's books (1967). The behaviorism that Tolman invented and described is *purposive*—the actor, be it human or rat, is assumed to have a purpose. Indeed, in spite of his very definite behavioristic inclinations, Tolman insisted that *all* behavior is purposive. By this he meant that behavior is directed toward some goal by *cognitions* rather than simply being the result of S-R connections.

SUPPORTING RESEARCH

What evidence is there that a rat, for example, directs its behavior *as if* it had certain purposes? And why should we believe that the direction, if it exists, is not simply a manifestation of learned S-R connections but is a result of cognitions?

There are a number of intriguing studies, most of which have been conducted with rats, that bear directly on these questions. Perhaps best known among them is Tolman and Honzik's *blocked-path* study (1930). The study involved releasing a rat in a maze with several alternative routes to the goal and allowing it to run in this maze until it had learned it. The next step was to introduce barriers in some of the paths and observe the rat's reaction. An approximate representation of the original Tolman and Honzik maze is given in Figure 7-1. The paths vary in length from the shortest, most direct route (1) to the longest (3). The rat that becomes completely familiar with the maze can be expected to develop preferences for paths, 1, 2, and 3, in that order. This expectation was

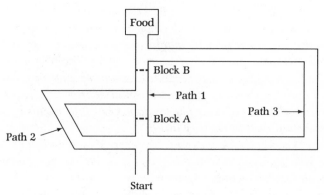

Figure 7-1.

confirmed by the observation that hungry rats almost invariably selected Path 1, thereby indicating a preference for it. When Path 1 was blocked at *A*, however, the rat usually selected Path 2 (approximately 93% of the time). This reaction followed from S-R explanations of behavior; the next observation did not. When Path 1 is blocked at *B*, S-R theorists might still predict that the rat would select Path 2, since the entrance to it is not blocked, and it is second in preference. Obviously, however, the block on Path 1 at *B* also serves as a barrier for Path 2, thus leaving Path 3 as the only alternative that still leads to the goal. The *cognitive* argument is that if the rat selects Path 3 rather than Path 2, it is because it has developed some sort of cognitive map of the maze. This knowledge of the structure of the maze would then allow the rat to arrive at an insightful solution to the problem. Amazingly, 14 out of the 15 rats involved in the original experiment selected Path 3.

Tolman's argument, based on experiments such as these, is that learning involves the development of *cognitive maps*, these being internal representations of relationships between goals and behaviors as well as knowledge of the environment where the goals are to be found. The organism develops a series of expectations with respect to behavior. These expectations can be described in terms of what Tolman labels *sign-significate* relationships, where a sign is simply a stimulus and a significate is the expectation of reward that results from learning.

Even nonhuman animals behave as though they had expectations. Tolman reports a study in which a monkey has been taught to locate and turn over a cup in order to obtain a banana. When lettuce is substituted for the banana, the monkey becomes agitated and continues to search. In other words, the monkey behaves as though it had expected to find a banana under the cup. Its agitation and continued search would be ill-explained by more traditional behavioristic explanations.

Among the many other studies that lend support to Tolman's theorizing are several that illustrate "place" as opposed to "response" learning, as well as several that illustrate "latent" learning. These terms are explained and illustrated in the following experiments.

In a classic experiment Tolman, Ritchie, and Kalish (1946) trained rats to run across an open, circular area and into a alley that, after several right-angle turns, eventually led to a goal box. In the next part of the experiment, the alley leading to the goal box was blocked and 18 new alleys were made available to the rat (see Figure 7-2). Which alley is the rat most likely to choose? Behavioristic theory would predict that rats will be most likely to enter alleys closest to the original, these being most similar (generalization). In fact, however, far more rats chose the alley that went in the approximate direction of the original goal box. It appears that what these rats had learned was not a series of connected responses, duly reinforced and stamped in, but a *place*. In other words, they had developed a cognitive map of the area, together with expectancies relating to this place. And it is these expectancies, tied as they are to the cognitive map, that direct the rat's behavior.

A second experiment that makes much the same point in a dramatic way was reported by Macfarlane (1930). It again involved rats that were taught to find a goal box in a maze, but these animals had to *swim* through the maze. Strict behaviorist interpretations of this phenomenon would maintain that the specific (molecular) responses involved in swimming are chained together, reinforced, and eventually learned as a complete sequence. These same interpretations would also have to predict that if the maze were drained so that the swimming response was completely ineffectual, the rats would have to learn the maze all

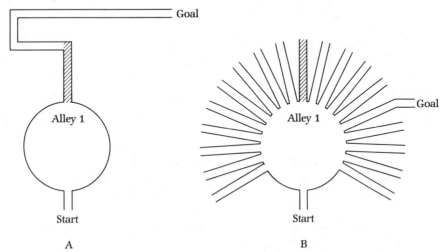

Figure 7-2. "Place" or "direction" learning in rats. In the Tolman, Ritchie, and Kalish (1946) study, rats learned a simple maze with an indirect path to the goal. In the second part of the experiment, the position of the goal and of the starting area remain the same, but the original path is blocked and 18 new paths are available.

over again. In fact, however, when the maze was dried out, rats ran to the goal box without hesitation and with no more errors than they had been making while swimming. Again, the evidence strongly suggests that there is more to learning mazes than the simple acquisition of stimulus-response or response-reward connections—a point that is made again in a final illustrative experiment.

In this study, Buxton (1940) allowed rats to spend several nights in large mazes but did not feed them. Strict behaviorists would surely predict that these rats would learn very little as a result of their exposure to the mazes. They would be more than a little amazed to find that at least half the rats learned the correct path from start to goal box without reinforcement. Buxton ascertained this by feeding the rat briefly in the goal box and then placing it immediately in the start box. The result? Half the rats ran to the goal box without a single error. It appears that rats are capable of developing cognitive maps even in the absence of a food reward. This learning, because it is delayed, is sometimes called *latent*.

SUMMARY OF TOLMAN'S POSITION

Several important principles are fundamental to an understanding of Tolman's system. The first, and most important, is his belief that all behavior is purposive. By this, Tolman meant that all behavior is guided by cognitions, or expectancies, that are themselves related to goals. In its simplest sense, a cognition is what develops following experience with stimuli and rewards. It is important to note that a cognition is an abstraction—a theoretical invention. Tolman did not believe, as did Hull and Hebb, for example, that intervening variables are "real" (though admittedly undiscovered and somewhat speculative) neurological things or events.

A second important principle of Tolman's system relates to his emphasis on the *molar* rather than the *molecular* aspects of behavior. By this is meant that Tolman did not reduce behavior to its smallest units (the reductionism of strict behaviorism) but dealt instead with large units of behavior that are unified in the sense that they are governed by a single purpose. It is this purpose, this search for goals, that directs behavior, not the reward itself. Put another way, the connections that explain behavior in Tolman's system do not involve links between reinforcement and responses or between stimuli and responses, but links between stimuli and expectancies. And the expectancies themselves develop as a function of exposure to situations in which reinforcement is possible.

A third fundamental principle in this system relates to the role of reinforcement in learning. As noted above, the connections that explain behavior in Tolman's system do not involve links between reinforcement and responses or between stimuli and responses, but links between stimuli and expectancies. Because expectancies develop in situations in which reinforcement is possible,

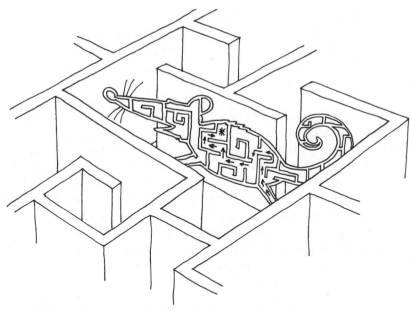

Tolman: Learning involves the development of cognitive maps.

the role of the reinforcement is primarily one of confirming expectancies. The more often an expectancy is confirmed, the more likely it is that the stimuli (signs) associated with it will become linked with the relevant significate (expectancy).

A final principle in Tolman's system concerns what is learned, and it is therefore implicit in the preceding three principles. In effect, what is learned is not a specific behavior in response to a stimulus or reward but a cognition—an item of knowledge concerning physical space and the possibilities of reward therein. More specifically, what is learned is a sign-significate relationship—knowledge of a link between stimuli and expectancies of acquiring a goal.

From Behaviorism to Cognitivism

Tolman's principal contribution to the development of psychological theory lies not so much in advances in knowledge and prediction made possible by his work as in the fact that it represents a transition from a strict behavioristic interpretation to a more cognitive approach. It would be far from accurate, however, to convey the impression that psychology went from the mentalistic concepts of the early instrospectionists to the rigid interpretations of the behaviorists and finally to a more enlightened cognitivism. In fact, cognitivism is approximately as old as behaviorism. Indeed, Gestalt psychology, one of the earliest forms of cognitive theory, developed at about the same time as early behaviorism. It is nevertheless true that North American psychology went from a period when Watsonian and Thorndikian behaviorism were supreme both in theory and in practice to a later period when interest turned increasingly to cognitive topics but behaviorism continued to flourish.

Cognitivism

Largely because of its concern with perception, awareness, and insight, Gestalt* psychology is considered to be the forerunner of contemporary cognitive psychology. Cognitivism is an orientation in psychology characterized by a relative lack of concern with stimuli and responses. Indeed, there is a tendency on the part of cognitivists to reject much of behaviorism on the grounds that it is overly mechanistic, incomplete, and unsuitable for explaining higher mental processes. In place of what they consider to be overly simplistic notions of human behavior, the cognitivists have substituted concepts that can be relatively complex and not always clear. Their primary preoccupations are with such subjects as perception, problem solving through insight, decision making, information processing, and understanding. In all of these processes, *awareness* (or cognition) plays a central role. Despite this focus on awareness, it is not at all unusual for cognitive psychologists to base some of their theorizing on observations of the behavior of lower animals. In this connection, Bertrand Russell made the interesting observation that American and German rats must be basically different. He is quoted as having said:

> Animals studied by Americans rush about frantically, with an incredible display of hustle and pep, and at last achieve the desired result by chance. Animals observed by Germans sit still and think, and at last evolve the solution out of their inner consciousness [cited in Commons & Fagin, 1954, p. 28].

Russell was obviously referring to the fact that American psychology was then largely dominated by the trial-and-error behaviorism of E. L. Thorndike, whereas the German school was more oriented toward insightful problem solving in a Gestaltist tradition. That rats do indeed sometimes behave as their investigators expect them to, *because* they are expected to act in that manner, has been demonstrated by Rosenthal and Fode (1963). Sixty ordinary laboratory rats were divided among 12 graduate students in an experimental-psychology class. Students in this class had previously learned that some strains of rats are *maze-bright* while others are *maze-dull*, according to their genetic background. They also knew that maze-bright rats were so called because they did, in fact, tend to learn mazes more easily than their dull cousins. For the experiment in question, half the students were told that their rats were bright; the other half were informed that theirs were dull. All students were asked to train their rats to run a simple maze. Each rat was allowed ten trials every day for 5 days. Results of the study indicated that the rats whose handlers expected them to be bright significantly outperformed the "dull" group. In addition, they were per-

Gestalt is a German word that means *whole* or *configuration*.

ceived as being "brighter, more pleasant, and more likeable." A similar experiment with rats (Rosenthal & Lawson, 1964), performed over a longer period and involving much more complex learning, yielded highly comparable results. This finding should not be taken to mean that all rat studies invariably lead to the desired results. They do so with probably no greater frequency than do studies involving humans (see Rosenthal & Jacobsen, 1968).

There are two important points in the preceding discussion. The first is that expectancies can affect experimental results. The second is that experimenters sometimes design experiments that cannot easily lead to observations directly contradictory to their initial beliefs. Perhaps Thorndike's cats *had* to solve their problems through trial and error, whereas the same approach *could not* work for Kohler's apes!

The remaining portion of this chapter consists of a description of Gestalt psychology in general terms and a discussion of Lewin's variation of a Gestalt approach. His position can be interpreted as representing a transition between a cognitivism that is largely perception-oriented and the contemporary cognitive approaches of such theorists as Bruner, Ausubel, and Weiner.

Gestalt Psychology

At the time that the First World War broke out, a young German found himself marooned on an island off the coast of Africa, unable to return to his home because of the war. His name was Wolfgang Kohler; he was a psychologist. The name of the island was Tenerife; it was inhabited by numerous apes. During the 4 years that Kohler spent on Tenerife he studied the apes. He reported his studies in a book entitled *The Mentality of the Apes* (1927).

Two types of studies employed by Kohler have been of particular interest, both involving the problem-solving behavior of apes in cages and leading to identical observations. The difference between the two lies in the nature of the problems to be solved—"stick" problems in the first study, "box" problems in the second. The problems required the ape to reach a bunch of bananas that was either hanging beyond reach overhead or was outside the cage, also beyond reach. In the first situation, the ape had to move a box underneath the bananas or pile boxes one on top of the other in order to reach the reward. In the second, it was necessary to reach outside the cage with a long stick, or, in some cases, to assemble two sticks in order to reach far enough.

According to Kohler, the most outstanding characteristic of the problem-solving behavior of apes is that they employ *insight* rather than trial and error. Indeed, even when they do attempt a variety of approaches, these do not ordinarily lead to the solution of the problem. The solution most often comes when the ape is sitting or lying down, perhaps contemplating the problem but not actively involved in trying to solve it. When the behavior of the ape seems to involve trial and error and when successive attempts appear to lead to a correct solution, Kohler assumes that each trial is the result of a small insight.

Kohler's studies of apes led him to the conclusion that not only are they capable of solving the banana problem, but their approach to problems is essentially the same as people's in that they use *insight*. Insight has since become the cornerstone of Gestalt psychology. It is ordinarily defined as *the sudden perception of relationships among elements of a problem situation*. Three terms in this definition are particularly crucial, since they serve as key words in Gestalt psychology—*insight, perception*, and *problem solving*. The basic question asked by Gestaltists is how people solve problems; the simplified answer is that they solve problems through insight that involves perception of relationships. Not surprisingly, one way of summarizing Gestalt psychology is to describe it in terms of laws of perception. These laws were developed and elaborated largely by the three men who are considered to be the founders of the Gestalt movement: Wertheimer (1959), Koffka (1922, 1925, 1935), and Kohler (1927, 1959). Of these three, Koffka and Kohler were the two most responsible for popularizing the movement through their writings; however, Wertheimer was the acknowledged leader. His book appeared posthumously (1945) and is concerned less with a discussion of Gestalt theory in general than with the application of the theory to education. It is interesting that the movement found much less support among psychologists, who were largely educated in a behaviorist tradition, than among educators, who claimed to have known all along that humans solve problems through insight rather than through trial and error.

KURT KOFFKA
(1886–1941)
WOLFGANG KOHLER
(1887–1967)
MAX WERTHEIMER
(1880–1943)

The ideas and theories of Koffka, Kohler, and Wertheimer are almost inseparable, as are their lives. All were graduates of the University of Berlin (they became known as the Berlin Group), all had training in philosophy and psychology, and all eventually emigrated to the United States.

Wertheimer, half a dozen years older than Kohler and Koffka, was born in Prague on the 15th of April 1880. His initial studies were in the field of law in Prague. Later he went to Berlin, where he studied philosophy and psychology and obtained his Ph.D. in 1904. His many interests included writing poetry and composing symphonies.

Acknowledged as the intellectual leader of Gestalt psychology, Wertheimer did far less to popularize the movement than did Kohler and Koffka, writing little but designing a number of important experiments and elaborating Gestalt principles in his lectures. It is reported that the idea for one of his most important experiments occurred to him at the very beginning of his career when he was on a train, vacationing. There he began to puzzle over the fact that lights that flash sequentially give the illusion of movement. Subsequent investigations of this "phi phenomenon," involved both Kohler and Koffka as his assistants and led eventually to the elaboration of Gestalt psychology.

In 1933 Wertheimer emigrated to the United States, where he remained until his death in 1943.

Kohler was born in Reval, Estonia, on the 21st of January, 1887. He obtained his Ph.D. from the University of Berlin in 1909 and subsequently, along with Koffka, worked with Wertheimer at Frankfurt.

In 1913 the Prussian Academy of Science invited him to spend time on the island of Tenerife in the Canary chain off the coast of Africa. There he was to be director of the anthropoid station. Six months after his arrival on Tenerife war broke out, and he was unable to leave. In the end he spent 4 years on the island studying the behavior of apes (and of chickens too). The results of his investigations were published in an important book entitled The Mentality of the Apes *(1917), which was revised in 1927.*

From Tenerife he went back to Berlin, where he remained until 1935. Kohler published extensively during this time, becoming one of the most important spokesmen for the Gestalt movement. Conflict with the Nazi regime forced him to leave Germany permanently in 1935. He went to the United States, where he had already spent considerable time lecturing and where he stayed until his death in 1967. He continued to write important books in the United States. He was awarded the Distinguished Scientific Contribution Award by the American Psychological Association and, as had Skinner, Guthrie, Tolman, and Hebb, served as president of that association.

Koffka was born in Berlin on March 18, 1886, went to the university there, and obtained his Ph.D. in psychology in 1909. He had earlier studied science and philosophy in Edinburgh. From Berlin he went to Frankfurt where he was associated with Wertheimer and Koffka and where he began the extensive writings that later became very influential in popularizing Gestalt psychology. He was the most prolific writer of the Berlin group, publishing a large number of important and sometimes difficult books.

Like Kohler and Wertheimer, he spent some time lecturing in the United States before moving there permanently in 1927. There he lectured at Smith College and continued to write until his death in 1941. (Boring, 1950; Sahakian, 1970; Schultz, 1969; Woodworth & Sheehan, 1964).

LAWS OF PERCEPTION

The first and most basic argument advanced by Gestaltists against procedures that emphasize the *analysis* of behavior is that behavior cannot be understood in terms of its parts. The classical cliché that has become the trademark of the Gestalt approach is "The whole is greater than the sum of its parts"—a statement that, as interpreted by Gestaltists, is demonstrably true. Gestalt psychology does not deny that the whole is composed of parts, nor does it deny that the parts can be discovered through analysis. But it does contradict the notion that the whole can be understood through analysis. An example commonly cited to support this contention is the *phi phenomenon*, labeled by Wertheimer, which is simply the observation that two or more lights flashing alternately or in sequence are not perceived simply as flashing lights but rather as *moving* lights. This phenomenon of apparent motion explains how people perceive neon signs or motion pictures.

Additional evidence that the perception of wholes (of gestalts) is different from the perception of parts is provided by numerous daily events. When listening to music, the overall perception is not of isolated notes but rather of bars or passages. If this were not so, the order of notes and the intervals of time during which they are held, as well as the spaces of time between them, would not be so important. In addition, it is readily obvious that any physical object derives its identity not only from the parts it comprises but more from the manner in which these parts are combined. An object as simple as an apple is no longer simply an apple after it has been attacked by a blender; nor is a car still a car after it has been completely dismantled.

The first concern of the Gestaltist was, then, to discover the laws governing the perception of wholes. These laws were first described by Koffka (1935) and are summarized briefly here. It should be pointed out that the laws are primarily perceptual and are discussed here as such. At the same time, it should be kept in mind that Gestalt psychologists see no discontinuity between perception and thinking and that they therefore consider these laws to be applicable to both.

There is one overriding principle—*Pragnanz* (meaning "good form"), which states that there is a tendency for whatever is perceived to take the best form possible. The exact nature of that form for all perceptual experience is governed by four additional principles discussed below.

Principle of Closure.   Closure is the act of completing a pattern, or gestalt. In terms of visual perception, closure usually involves incomplete figures of various forms (see Figure 7-3), which we tend to perceive as complete forms. The same phenomenon is readily apparent in perception of a melody with missing notes or of incomplete words like p*ych*l*gy. Although the term *closure* was originally employed only with perceptual problems, it has come to be used by non-Gestalt psychologists in a variety of situations, retaining much of its original meaning but also acquiring some broader significance. For example, it is not uncommon to speak of achieving closure when referring to solving a problem, understanding a concept, or simply completing a task.

Principle of Continuity.   Perceptual phenomena tend to be perceived as continuous. For example, a line that is started as a curved line (see Figure 7-4) tends to be perceived as continuing in a curving fashion.

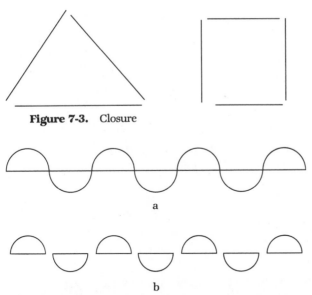

Figure 7-3. Closure

Figure 7-4. Continuity. The lines in (a) tend to be perceived as a straight line running through a curved one, not as a set of semicircles as in (b).

Principle of Similarity. This principle holds that objects that are similar tend to be perceived as related. For example, a person who hears two melodies at the same time recognizes each as a separate melody rather than hearing both as one. In Figure 7-5, there appear to be four rows of identical letters rather than ten columns of different letters.

a a a a a a a a a a
g g g g g g g g g g
c c c c c c c c c c
x x x x x x x x x x

Figure 7-5. Similarity

Principle of Proximity. Objects or perceptual elements tend to be grouped in terms of their proximity. Figure 7-6(a), for example shows four sets of curved lines, whereas Figure 7-6(b) is perceived as three faces.

These four principles, along with several others, were developed by Wertheimer and later applied by Koffka to thinking as well as to perception. The applications are not always clear and are sometimes less than convincing. It is argued, for example, that the Kohler ape achieved insight perhaps because of the proximity of the stick and bananas or of the box and the bananas. The objection can be raised that obviously there are numerous other objects (such as the bars of the cage) that are closer to the goal object than either boxes or sticks. These should form a gestalt with the bananas sooner than the solution objects.

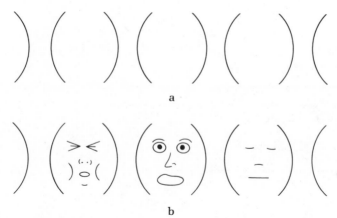

Figure 7-6. Proximity

LEARNING AND MEMORY

Since the Gestaltists were not concerned with such molecular aspects of learning and behavior as stimuli and responses, their explanations of learning and memory are considerably more global and nonspecific than those of the behaviorists. In general, the Gestalt view considers learning to result in the formation of memory traces. The exact nature of these traces is left unspecified, but a number of their characteristics are detailed. The most important characteristic is that learned material, like any perceptual information, tends to achieve the best structure possible (Pragnanz) in terms of the laws of perceptual organization just discussed. Hence, what is remembered is not always what was learned or perceived but is often a better *gestalt* than the original. Wulf (1938) described three organizational tendencies of memory, which he labeled *leveling,* *sharpening,* and *normalizing.*

Leveling is defined as the tendency toward symmetry or toward a toning down of the peculiarities of a perceptual pattern. Figure 7-7 presents a hypothetical illustration of leveling. It is assumed by Gestaltists (Koffka, for example) that the process of leveling is also applicable to cognitive material that is less perceptual.

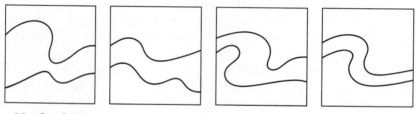

Stimulus object   Successive reproductions

Figure 7-7. Leveling

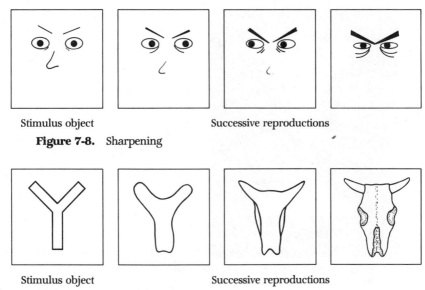

Stimulus object   Successive reproductions

Figure 7-8.   Sharpening

Stimulus object   Successive reproductions

Figure 7-9.   Normalizing

Sharpening is the act of emphasizing the distinctiveness of a pattern. It appears to be one of the characteristics of human memory that the qualities that most clearly give an object identity tend to be exaggerated in the reproduction of that object. Figure 7-8 is an illustration of this phenomenon.

Normalizing occurs when the reproduced object is modified in terms of preexisting memory traces. This modification usually tends toward making the remembered object more like what it appears to be—that is, to *normalize* it. A hypothetical illustration of normalizing is presented in Figure 7-9.

Kurt Lewin (1890–1947)

One of the men who worked with Wertheimer at the inception of the Gestalt movement departed significantly from the Gestaltists' traditional emphasis on perception, learning, and memory. He was Kurt Lewin (1935, 1936, 1947). His major concerns were personality, motivation, and social psychology, but he still retained much of the orientation of his colleagues.

The concept *field* plays a central role in Lewin's system, a concept that has a Gestaltic origin. Initially it was taken to mean the environment as perceived by an organism. That is, for the Gestaltists, a field consists of the object or objects that are being perceived (*figure*) and the background, or environment, that surrounds them (*ground*). Ordinarily the relationship between figure and ground is unambiguous—the figure is perceived, and the ground is simply its surroundings. On occasion, however, figure and ground alternate, so that one moment's perception is exchanged for a different perception the next. The inter-

Figure 7-10.   Figure-ground alternation

esting point is that we seem to be unable to perceive both figure and ground at the same time. The drawing in Figure 7-10, for example, is perceived either as a vase or as two faces in confrontation—not as both at once.

KURT LEWIN (1890–1947)

Lewin was born in Mogilno, Germany, on September 9, 1890. His early studies concentrated in mathematics and physics, both of which later influenced his psychological theorizing. In 1914, just in the wake of Koffka and Kohler, he obtained his Ph.D. in psychology from the University of Berlin. He remained there for the next few years, publishing extensively and conducting experiments on motivation, primarily with adults. It was while at Berlin that he began to develop his field theory. Like Wertheimer, Koffka, and Kohler, he eventually left Germany, moving permanently to the United States in 1935. In effect, he had already left Germany 3 years earlier and had spent a year teaching at Stanford and two at Cornell. English translations of his earlier works had been widely read in the United States by then, so Lewin was already a well-known psychologist.

From 1935 to 1944 Lewin taught at the State University of Iowa, where he was professor of child psychology and where he conducted extensive research on the behavior of groups of children in democratic and autocratic environments. In 1944 he was invited to lead a new research center on group dynamics at the Massachusetts Institute of Technology. Lewin's close association with contemporary "growth" groups can be traced back to this research center. At the age of 57, only 3 years after taking over this center, Lewin died. (Boring, 1950; Woodworth & Sheehan, 1964.)

The term *field* has a slightly different connotation in Lewin's system. Instead of indicating simply the perceptual environment, it also includes cognitive meaning. A field is defined by Lewin as not only, or even primarily, the figure and ground components of the physical environment but also the beliefs, feelings, goals, and alternatives of an individual. In other words, Lewin deals with a cognitive *and* a perceptual field—hence, the label *cognitive-field psychology*, which is often applied to his system.

LIFE SPACE

Instead of referring simply to an individual's field, Lewin employed the term *life space* to mean the world as it relates to a particular individual. Hence, a life space is a composite of all that is immediately relevant for the behavior of the individual. It includes not only motives, goals, means to goals, and impediments to these means but also the individual person. The physical environment, even though it may not be of immediate relevance for behavior, is also included in life space. A diagrammatic representation of a life space is presented in Figure 7-11. At the center of the space is the person, surrounded by the psychological environment, which includes all factors that are of direct relevance for immediate behavior. In addition, life space includes the more remote physical environment, labeled *foreign hull* by Lewin.

Lewin's primary goal was to arrive at some representation of a behaving individual that would permit the prediction of that individual's behavior. That representation is essentially his concept of life space.

Characteristics of Life Space. Life space is a central, and relatively complex, variable in Lewin's system. It can be described in terms of a number of characteristics.

A life space is relativistic in that it is defined in terms of the environment as it is perceived by the individual and not necessarily as it actually exists. A woman who believes that household dust becomes lethal after people undergo prolonged exposure has lethal household dust in her life space. In order to understand her

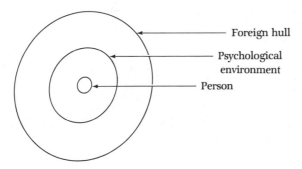

Figure 7-11. Life space

behavior in certain situations, it is necessary to know that this woman's life space contains a large corner devoted to poisonous dust.

Second, life space can be diagrammed in terms of areas representing the goals or aspirations of the individual at any given moment. In order to make such diagrams meaningful, Lewin employed a concept of *topological* space as opposed to ordinary geometry. The chief characteristic of topological representations is that the areas subsumed by them are irrelevant; only the relative positions of spaces are meaningful. Figure 7-12, for example, depicts the hypothetical life space of an imaginary student. The space contains the person, who is presently a student, and the four alternatives that he sees as being available to him.

Figure 7-12.   A student's life space

His ultimate goal is to make money. In Lewinian terminology, the goal, money, has high positive *valence*. The term *valence* indicates the attractiveness of various areas in the life space (indicated in the figure by plus signs). The four alternatives open to this student are stealing money, going into his father's chicken-sexing business, drifting down the California coast, or teaching school. The representation of his life space indicates that drifting down the coast is the most attractive of these alternatives (three plus signs). However, the likelihood of making a great deal of money while living in the lap of idealistic poverty on a beach somewhere is somewhat remote, as represented by the thickness of the wall that separates the "money" and "drifting" regions. In Lewinian terminology this wall is referred to as a *barrier*.

This student's life space also shows that teaching is more attractive (has higher valence) than going into business but that the barrier between making a great deal of money and teaching is even greater than that between drifting and making money. The easiest way of making money is obviously by stealing. This activity, however, has negative valence, as indicated by the minus sign in that region of the life space.

Since Lewin's system is intended to provide some basis for making predictions about an individual's behavior, the concept of a life space that comprises goals, ways of achieving goals, valences of alternatives, and the barriers impeding the attainment of goals should be of some value—at least theoretically. Obviously a great deal of information is required about the student and his present life space before meaningful predictions can be made.

A third characteristic of life space is that it constantly varies as the person's goals change or as alternatives change. A diagram of a life space is only a two-dimensional representation. It is possible to conceive of the space itself as being three dimensional, in which case any number of slices can be cut. While each will be highly similar in that the "person" and major goals will be the same, there might also be pronounced differences in the alternatives to achieving these goals.

VECTORS AND CONFLICTS

In attempting to diagram the motivated behavior of individuals, Lewin not only employed a topological representation of life space but also borrowed the concept *vectors* from physics. A vector is an arrow that is used to indicate the direction and strength of a force. Accordingly, in Lewin's system vectors are employed to show the direction toward which behavior tends as well as the strength of the force that is exerted. Figure 7-13 shows two vectors, one of which indicates a tendency to engage in navel contemplation and the other, a weaker tendency to work. The arrow indicates the direction of force, while the length of the vector represents its strength.

Figure 7-13.

Consideration of vectors as indicators of motivational forces leads simply and conveniently to a depiction of the three possible behavior conflicts that can beset humans. The first, referred to as an *approach-approach conflict*, occurs when the individual is drawn toward two incompatible goals at the same time. Consider, for example, the case of the woman who is offered a promotion from chicken counter to chicken sexer and who, on the same day, is invited by her brother to join him as assistant manager of a 14-bird turkey ranch. Both positions are very attractive; indeed, they are equally attractive. That aspiring young executive has an approach-approach conflict.

Numerous less facetious examples of this type of conflict can be seen in everyday life. The reader is invited to think of some.

Consider next the case of the obese fellow who likes chocolate sundaes garnished with "just a dash" of whipped cream. His problem is of another type. He is simultaneously drawn toward sundaes and pulled in the opposite direction by his desire to slim down. His is an *approach-avoidance conflict*.

The third conflict situation, the *avoidance-avoidance conflict*, is clearly illustrated by the suffering woman who has a toothache but passionately fears dentists. If she avoids the dentist, she must retain the toothache; yet if she is to avoid the toothache, she must suffer the dentist. Hers is the classical damned-if-you-do, damned-if-you-don't double bind of the avoidance-avoidance conflict.

The bulk of Lewin's theorizing is contained in his book *Principles of Topological Psychology* (1936). A great deal of this work is more relevant to personality theory and social psychology than to learning theory and is therefore not reviewed here. His concepts of life space and its vectors, valences, and barriers can be a useful way of describing behavior a posteriori. However, they are of relatively limited value for predicting behavior, largely because few guidelines are provided for arriving at an accurate description of vectors and valences prior to a behavior taking place. Since life space is defined in terms of how the individual views the immediate environment and since no one else can view it in exactly that manner, no one else can come close to describing it accurately. However, since life space also includes some factors that are unknown to the individual but that nevertheless exert a powerful influence on behavior, the individual, too, cannot always describe life space accurately. Consider, for example, the man who honestly believes that he likes delivering public addresses. His description of his own life space would probably place a high valence on speaking in public. It is not uncommon, however, to find people of this type who always seem to have some excuse for not accepting invitations to display their rhetorical skills. Since life space is determined by how people act rather than by how they say they will act, their personal description of their life space is not necessarily valid.

Lewin's Influence on Contemporary Psychology

The most widespread effect of Lewin's work on contemporary psychological theory and practice is probably to be found in the phenomena variously labeled T-groups, encounter groups, sensitivity training, human-relations laboratories, or, more generally, "growth" groups. These are training or therapeutic sessions involving groups of people who, through various communication exercises, perceptual activities, role-playing games, and other interpersonal activities, attempt to achieve a greater awareness of themselves and of one another. Although Lewin was not directly responsible for the inception of the growth-group movement, a large number of his ideas lend themselves particularly well to a theoretical foundation for it. For example, the Lewinian notion that the educational process consists of "unfreezing, restructuring, and refreezing" one's field is ostensibly illustrated in a T-group session where individuals are encouraged to break down interpersonal barriers (unfreeze) in order to develop new concepts of self (restructure). Similarly, the barriers that are assumed to exist between people are often described in terms of "psychological distance" between cognitive fields (Lewin, 1951).

Even more fundamental to the growth-group movement is the basic notion that each individual reacts to the world in a unique manner and that in order to understand individuals it is necessary to begin from that unique point of view. This notion, frequently labeled *phenomenology*, is not only the essence of Lewin's theory but is also the basis of the current emphasis on client-centered therapy (Rogers, 1951), as well as other humanistic movements.

A second, related manifestation of the influence of Lewin's theory is the humanistic movement in psychology—a movement characterized by its concern with human individuality and the development of human potential. The term *self-actualization* is ordinarily employed to describe this self-fulfillment. Like the advocates of growth groups, humanistic psychologists are typically phenomenological. It is in this orientation that both are particularly indebted to the earlier theorizing of Kurt Lewin.

A Review

Traditional behavioristic theories are highly objective, deal with the molecular aspects of behavior, make no assumptions about such mental conditions as might be implied by "intention," and seek to discover precise relationships among stimuli, responses, and the consequences of behavior. As we have seen in earlier chapters, most behavioristic theories reflect known facts adequately, are relatively clear and understandable, tend to be internally consistent, and are usually based on a small number of unverifiable assumptions. We have also seen that these theories are generally inadequate for explaining more complex aspects of human functioning such as language, problem solving, and other "thinking" processes; nor have they been entirely sufficient for explaining a number of simpler behaviors for which genetic tendencies run counter to the experimenter's intentions.

One of the important reactions to this type of behavioristic theory can be found in what are termed *cognitive* theories. These theories have generally rejected an examination of stimuli and responses in favor of an exploration of more-mentalistic processes. Their early beginnings are illustrated in Tolman's purposive behaviorism, which is essentially a transition between purely behavioristic concerns and a more cognitive orientation, and in the Gestalt psychologists. The principle common characteristics of these approaches are that they are concerned with more molar aspects of behavior and that they recognize the importance of goals and of intention in directing behavior.

An Evaluation

Traditional behavioristic theories have often been criticized on the grounds that they are too mechanistic, too superficial, and too simplistic. Their failure to take into account the possibility that human behavior is heavily influenced by intention and by other symbolic processes presents a rather strong contradiction to our intuitive notions of what it is like to be human. In this respect, cognitive theories are more closely aligned with our private beliefs. And it is perhaps for this reason that we might be tempted to conclude that cognitive theories reflect the facts better than do behavioristic theories. In reality, however, while they may reflect some facts rather well, they are based on a number of assumptions that are not easily verified. Perhaps even more damaging, they lend themselves very poorly to prediction—largely because they deal with global and imprecise concepts.

As noted earlier, one of the chief contributions of these early cognitive theories relates to their application in counseling and therapy. Perhaps even more important, it is theories such as these that were at least partly responsible for subsequent developments in both cognitive and behavioristic theory. In a real sense, Gestalt psychology served as a basis for contemporary cognitive theory, even as Tolman provided a transition from early behaviorism to contemporary cognitivism.

Summary of Chapter 7

This chapter has presented an account of Tolman's purposive behaviorism as well as of Gestalt psychology and Lewin's field psychology. Tolman's system serves as an important transition from strict behaviorism to cognitivism; Gestalt psychology can be viewed as the root of much contemporary cognitive theorizing.

1. Traditional behaviorism seeks to be impeccably objective, analyzes behavior at a molecular level, and makes no assumptions about any intentions the actor might have.
2. Cognitivism represents a strong reaction against traditional behaviorism; Tolman's purposive behaviorism represents a somewhat milder reaction.
3. Among Tolman's most important beliefs are the following: all behavior is purposive; behavior should be analyzed at the molar rather than the molecular level; learning involves developing expectancies as a function of exposure to situations in which reinforcement is possible (sign-significate relationships); expectancies can be described as cognitions, or cognitive maps.
4. Gestalt psychology can be viewed as an introduction to *cognitivism*. Cognitive approaches to learning are characterized by a preoccupation with such topics as understanding, information processing, decision making, and problem solving.
5. The primary beliefs of the Gestaltists can be summarized in two statements: the whole is greater than the sum of its parts; people solve problems through insight. The first gives voice to the belief that the analysis of a subject (or object) into its parts is not likely to lead to knowledge of that subject. The second is a rejection of the role of trial and error in solving problems.

6. Wertheimer, Kohler, and Koffka were the founders of the Gestalt school. As a system, it has been identified largely in relation to its studies of perception and its formulation of such laws of perceptual organization as *closure, similarity, continuity,* and *proximity.* The application of these laws to learning has not received wide acceptance.

7. Gestalt studies of memory have led to the observation that structural changes in information over time involve the processes of leveling (making symmetrical), *sharpening* (heightening distinctiveness), and *normalizing* (rendering more like the object should appear).

8. *Cognitive-field psychology* is characterized by a concern with people as they are affected by their immediate environment (field). Kurt Lewin's system is a good example of this approach.

9. Lewin described the behaving individual in terms of a *life space* (field) that comprises person, goals, available paths to these goals, and the attractiveness of the goals, as well as the barriers that impede progress toward them. Life space is defined in terms of the individual's *own perception* of the environment.

10. The notion of conflicts as involving incompatible approach and avoidance tendencies is represented by Lewin in terms of *vectors* that indicate both the direction and strength of a tendency to behave.

11. The value of Lewin's system is restricted by the amount of information that it is necessary to obtain about an individual before meaningful predictions about behavior can be made. It is nevertheless of considerable value in understanding and explaining behavior, particularly a posteriori, and has particular relevance for teaching.

12. The influence of Lewin's work on contemporary psychological theory and practice is manifested in the growth-group movement as well as in humanistic psychology.

13. While behavioristic positions have often been criticized as being too mechanistic and too simplistic to account for a great deal of human behavior, cognitive positions are often too global and too imprecise to lend themselves easily to prediction. Their contribution to the subsequent development of psychological theory is considerable, however.

My Very Dearest Grandmother,

Thank you so very much for the birthday gift. Boy, did my bank account ever need it. I think you're absolutely right that you can't take it with you. Besides, you wouldn't even need to bother with a will if you wanted to give it all away beforehand. Do away with a lot of taxes too. If you want, I have a friend who's a lawyer, and he could fix it up for you. Cheap.

I'm sorry you haven't had time to get through the first chapter of my book yet. I'm sure you'd find that things get a lot more interesting further on, but at the rate you're going, it will take you four years to read it all (heh, heh, just joking). I don't think it's fair to decide yet whether you like it or not, so I wish you wouldn't be quite as critical as you were at the end of your last letter. I can take it, mind you. You know I've been criticized before by some pretty important people.

By the way, I came by to see you the other day and Pouf almost broke his chain trying to get at me. It's my opinion that he might have some kind of mental disorder. He's getting pretty old. I've talked about it with one of the people up here who knows a lot about craziness because he's that way himself, and he thinks old dogs often become deranged. It would be no reflection on you and how well you brought Pouf up if you had to have him hospitalized. I could look after the details for you if you like.

Thanks again so very, very, very, much for the birthday gift. Incidentally, it was not me . . .

CHAPTER *8*

Bruner and Categories

Literal Descriptions and Metaphors

For years, physical scientists were convinced that the end result of their many investigations would be a complete, accurate, and absolutely *literal* description of the physical world and how it functions. In 1910 there seemed to be little reason to suspect that science might someday discover something about the world that could only be described in terms of "black holes," "quarks," "anti-matter," and other metaphors. Indeed, even in the 1980s many scientists still do not suspect that there might be something not quite literal about their knowledge.

159

And so it was, and sometimes continues to be, in psychology. During the first half of this century, a period dominated largely by an intolerant behaviorism, psychologists searched valiantly for a *literal* description of psychological functioning. As we have seen, they searched for that description in the observable aspects of behavior and thought they had found it among the stimulus-response laws they discovered and the intervening variables they invented. There is little doubt that Hull's intervening variables were intended to describe a literal state of affairs, even if it had not been entirely discovered yet. And so, too, with Hebb.

But Tolman began to present a somewhat different picture—a picture that he first glimpsed in the imagination of the white Norway rat, for it seemed to Tolman that even the rat learns more than S-R connections. It develops representations of the world—cognitive maps of what is out there and notions that somehow connect what is out there with alternative behaviors. These notions he called "expectancies."

In a very real sense, Tolman's "expectancies" are representations of the world. But they are not the literal representations that traditional behaviorists seek. They are *metaphors*.

Cognitive psychology deals with metaphors. It attempts to explain the most important features of human functioning in terms of *mental structures* that are representative, but not descriptive, and in terms of the *functions* that must be involved in constructing and utilizing these structures. Thus, it deals with memory in terms of the functions that are involved in learning and in remembering, as well as in terms of the *hypothetical* structures that correspond to (or represent) whatever it is that is learned. The short-term and long-term memories of which contemporary researchers speak are, in effect, metaphorical structures. By this is meant that they do not need to exist as identifiable neurological material but simply represent what might be (see Chapter 11).

The Content of Contemporary Cognitive Psychology

Cognitive psychology is identified not only by the fact that it is metaphorical but also by its principal areas of interest. These can be generally described as including all of the so-called *higher mental functions*. The most important of these deal with perception (how physical energies are translated into meaningful experiences), memory, language, thinking, problem solving, and decision making.

The single most important common characteristic of the topics listed above is that each, at least within a cognitive framework, presupposes mental representation (sometimes termed mental imagery). Accordingly, the most important theory building in the recent development of cognitive psychology has taken the form of metaphors relating to the nature of mental representation and to the processes involved in constructing and using these representations. Unfortunately, there have not been a large number of notable attempts to build systematic and inclusive cognitive theories although there are a handful of well-known and important endeavors. As will become clear in later chapters, the emphasis in the last several decades has been on intensive research in specific areas, rather than on the construction of systems that would be sufficiently general to encompass a great diversity of observations.

Among the important contributions to the development of contemporary cognitive psychology is that made by Jerome Bruner and elaborated in the remainder of this chapter. Jean Piaget's developmental system is another outstanding illustration of a cognitive orientation, and it is discussed in the next chapter. Subsequent chapters deal with specific areas where current research is primarily cognitive: artificial intelligence, memory and attention, and motivation.

Bruner's Theory: An Overview

In a classic article, Bruner (1964) compares the development of a child to the evolution of the human race. In the beginning (or perhaps some considerable time later) humans were far from the fastest, the fiercest, or the strongest of the predators. Indeed, there is little reason to suppose that the fabled saber-tooth tiger or some other awesome beast might not have been entirely successful in controlling human population had it not been for the fact that the human proved, in the end, to be more intelligent than all who preyed on human flesh. So intelligent was this creature that it eventually took the course of evolution in its own hands. This it did, Bruner informs us, through three waves of remarkable inventions. These inventions served three different functions. First, humans succeeded in developing devices that could amplify their motor capacities. These included simple machines (levers, pulleys, inclined planes, perhaps even the legendary wheel) and combinations of machines to make weapons (knives, arrows and spears, hatchets). Thus, by amplifying their motor capacities, humans became stronger and less vulnerable.

Centuries later, a second group of inventions appeared and again dramatically altered the pattern of human evolution. These inventions amplified not motor capacities but sensory capacities. They are extremely recent in human history and include the telescope, radio, television, and all of the other instruments that allow us to see, hear, feel, and *sense* things we would not otherwise sense.

The final group of human inventions includes those that amplify what Bruner terms our *ratiocinative* (intellectual) capacities. These are our symbol systems and our theories; they include our computer languages and systems. We are only at the threshold of this last major development and cannot yet easily determine what the impact of these inventions will be.

How does the development of the child compare to this glimpse of evolution? Bruner suggests that the representational systems that children employ as they develop closely parallel the history of human inventions. Thus, at the earliest ages, children represent objects in terms of their immediate sensation of them.

In Bruner's words, things get "represented in the muscles." This representation, termed "enactive," corresponds to the period in human evolution when the emphasis was on the amplification of motor capacities.

Early in development, children progress from a strictly motoric, or enactive, representation to what Bruner calls "iconic" representation. An icon is an image. Accordingly, iconic representation involves the use of "mental images" that stand for certain objects or events. This type of representation corresponds to the period during which human inventions were directed at the amplification of sensory capacities.

The most advanced form of representation available to the child is "symbolic," a type of representation that parallels the development of inventions that amplify intellectual capacities. The fundamental difference between a symbol and an icon is that the icon bears a literal resemblance to its referent, whereas the symbol does not. A symbol is completely arbitrary: a 2 does not look like a collection of two objects any more than the word *turkey* looks like that much maligned bird. Yet you and I have absolutely no difficulty in understanding what we mean by either of these or, indeed, by most of the thousands of other symbols in this text.

Although enactive, iconic, and symbolic representation develop sequentially, they do not replace one another. As adults, we continue to represent both enactively and iconically as well as symbolically. Thus, we "know" how to ride a bicycle, stroke a cue ball, or execute a golf shot not primarily in symbols or in images but in our bodies; in contrast, we recognize faces not in *activity* or even in symbols but in images.

In summary, as adults we have at least three distinct modes for representing not only the effects of sensory experiences but also our thoughts. How we build up and utilize these representations is one of the principal concerns of Bruner's theory, a theory that can be described as a theory of *categorizing*. All of human cognitive activity involves categories, Bruner informs us. The central question is, surely, what is a category? How is it formed? Of what value is it? Answers to these questions provide an account of Bruner's theory of learning (and of perception and motivation too, for that matter).

Categories

If a man sees a head with long blond hair and an attractive face smiling at him over a sea of foam in a pink bathtub, does he simply see a head with long blond hair and a smiling face over a sea of foam in a pink bathtub?* (The question is surely of more than passing academic interest.) Literally, yes, that is all he *sees*, but he probably goes much beyond the simple information given to him by his

---

*The observations that follow would have been just as appropriate had it been a woman looking at a head with curly black hair and a beard smiling at her over a sea of suds in a blue bathtub. It wasn't. I know.

senses. He imagines that this must be a girl—that she probably has two arms, two legs, toenails, and so on. Yet he cannot immediately perceive all these qualities, so he must go beyond the information given. First, he decides that this *is* a girl; second, he makes inferences about this girl on the basis of what is known about *all* girls. According to Bruner, inferences are made possible through using categories—in this case, the category *girl*. The category *girl* is a *concept*, in the sense that any representation of *related things* is a concept; it is also a percept, in the sense that a *physical thing* when apprehended through the senses is a percept.

CATEGORIES AS RULES

Another way of looking at *category* is to define it as though it were a rule for *classifying things as being equal*. This is a very logical definition, since concepts and percepts—which are achieved through categorizing—are collections of *things* that are in some way equivalent. To state it quite simply, the concept *book* is a category; a category is a rule; the category *book* is the rule that allows an individual to recognize an object as a book. In fact, this category is a collection of rules, among which may be the following. To be a book a thing must:

1. have pages
2. have a cover
3. contain writing
4. have a title.

Categories, as rules, obviously say something about the characteristics that objects must possess before they can be classified in a given way. Characteristics of objects are referred to as *attributes*. Bruner defines attributes as "some discriminable feature of an object or event which is susceptible of distinguishable variation from event to event" (1966, p. 26). Attributes are therefore properties of objects that are not possessed by all objects. They are further distinguished by whether or not they play a role in the act of categorizing. Those attributes that define an object are called *criterial*. Those that do not are *irrelevant*. Femaleness is probably a criterial attribute for the category *girl*; color of hair is irrelevant.

Categorizing is defined by Bruner as follows: "To categorize is to render discriminably different things equivalent, to group the objects and events and people around us into classes, and to respond to them in terms of their class membership rather than in terms of their uniqueness" (Bruner, Goodnow, & Austin, 1956, p. 1).

Categories are rules that specify four things about the objects being reacted to; they are described below in terms of the category *car*. (1) First, a category is defined in terms of certain specific characteristics that are referred to as *criterial attributes*. For the category *car* such attributes would include the presence of a motor, running gear, and control devices. (2) A category not only specifies the attributes that are criterial but also indicates *the manner in which they are to be combined*. If, for example, all parts of a car were disassembled and placed in plastic garbage bags, it is unlikely that anyone would treat the result as though it were equivalent to a car. The rule for *car* says that the parts must be assembled in a prescribed fashion. (3) A category *assigns weight to various properties*. A car might continue to be classed as a car even if it had no bumpers and no windows—perhaps even if it had no wheels. But if it had no motor and no body, it might be categorized as something else, for these properties are more necessary for membership in the category. (4) A category sets *acceptance limits on attributes*. Attributes are susceptible to variation from event to event. Such attributes as color, for example, can vary tremendously. A rule for a category such as *car* that specifies that a car has four wheels might set the limits of variation at zero. Thus, anything with three wheels or less, or five wheels or more, would not be a car.

In summary, we interact with the environment in terms of categories, or classification systems that allow us to treat different events or objects as though they were equivalent. Incoming information is therefore organized in terms of preexisting categories or causes the formation of new ones. In either case, the end product of the processing will be a decision about the identity of the stimulus input as well as a number of implicit inferences about the object or event associated with the input. It is Bruner's contention that *all* our interaction with the world must involve classifying input in relation to categories that already exist. In his own words, completely novel experiences are "doomed to be a gem serene, locked in the silence of private experience" (Bruner, 1957b, p. 125). In short, we can probably not perceive *totally* new stimulus input; or, if we can, we cannot communicate it.

DECISION MAKING

Not only is all information processed through an act of categorization, but all decisions also involve classifying. First, to identify an object is to make a decision about whether it belongs in a given category. Second, once an object is placed in a category and therefore identified, there is inherent in the category a decision about how the object should be reacted to. For example, the almost unconscious recognition that a traffic light is red is, in Bruner's terms, the result of interpreting the input in question as though it were an example of events belonging to the category *red light*. Implicit in this act of categorizing is the decision not to walk across the street.

A second aspect of decision making involves the selection of strategies for attaining concepts. These are discussed in a later section of this chapter.

It is never quite clear in Bruner's system how decision making differs from simple information processing or whether processing input from the environment (perception) is different from organizing information in the mind (conceptualization). Bruner states, in fact, that he sees no reason to believe that the processes underlying perception are any different from those involved in conceptualization (1966, p. 9). He treats thinking (1957a) and perception (1957b) in different writings, however. It should be remembered, nevertheless, that the following discussion of perception also applies to the more "central" processes.

PERCEPTION

The processes underlying perceptual activity have already been touched on in the previous section in the form of a more general discussion of the act of categorizing. Perception really does not involve anything more complicated than identification. The perceptual process itself, in a general sense, is the act of translating sensory data into awareness, knowledge, feeling, or whatever. Where the process ceases to be perceptual and becomes conceptual is a moot question.

Bruner describes two features of perception: it is "categorical" and it is "varyingly veridical." *Categorical* means that categorization is involved in perception; that is clear from the previous discussion. *Varyingly veridical* means that what we think we perceive somehow predicts, with varying accuracy, what the actual object is really like. To perceive is to categorize; to place an object in a category is to make predictions about properties that it *must* have but that are not now perceptible. Take a very simple example. A white circular object, ¼ inch in diameter and 3 inches long, is held up in front of a class. One of the students who is awake is asked what the white object is. "Chalk, sir," she says. She is a bright psychology student. Implicit in her perception of this object is her knowledge that if the instructor were to hold it with one end pressed lightly on a chalkboard and move it, it would leave particles of itself behind. This is a property of the object that she cannot now perceive but that she can predict because her category for chalk, in which she has placed this object, includes the attribute "capability of leaving particles of itself behind on a chalkboard when pressed to it lightly and moved across it." She is a precise, bright psychology student. Her prediction will probably, but not necessarily, be correct. It is varyingly veridical.

Veridicality of perception will depend on a number of factors, which Bruner describes as follows: "Adequate perceptual representation involves the learning of appropriate categories, the learning of cues useful in placing objects appropriately in such systems of categories, and learning of what objects are likely to occur in the environment" (1957b, p. 229).

Bruner describes four sequential steps involved in categorizing. The first is *primitive categorization*. At this point, the stimulus event is no more than an "object" or a sound. The object is isolated and attended to in this stage. The second step is labeled *cue search* and involves looking for the presence or absence of those attributes that are likely to be useful in identifying the object. This search leads to an initial categorization, after which additional *confirming* cues may be sought. This third stage is labeled *confirmation check*. The fourth stage, *confirmation completion*, is marked by a termination of cue searching. Additional cues, especially if they are not congruent with initial identification, are not likely to be reacted to. This sequence is marked by initial openness, then selectivity, and finally closedness to sensory input.

Perceptual Readiness.   The accuracy with which stimulus events are categorized is as much a function of perceptual readiness as it is of simply having the appropriate category. *Perceptual readiness* refers to the accessibility of a category, where accessibility is defined in terms of the stimulus input that is required for identification to occur. The more accessible the category, the less input is required, the wider the range of input that will be accepted, and the more likely that less accessible, but perhaps better-fitting, categories will be masked.

Obviously, then, the accessibility of an appropriate category plays a central role in the accurateness (veridicality) of perception. Two factors are assumed to determine category accessibility: the expectancies of the individual and the individual's needs. Thus, if you need to eat, you are likely to recognize a restaurant. Similarly, you immediately identify a person you expect to see. In both these cases, little input is required for identification. By the same token, the possibility of making a mistake is high. That is, if the category in question is very highly accessible (you expect to see *that* person *there*), other categories will be masked (you won't realize that it is another person there).

CODING SYSTEMS

A concept central to Bruner's explanation of thought processes is *coding systems*. It is probably evident that his notion of category is not sufficient to explain much more than the simple recognition of sensory input. Going beyond the immediate sense data involves more than simply making inferences on the basis of the category into which the input has been classified. More important, it involves making inferences on the basis of related categories. For example, the inference that a new pearlike object (called a korug) is edible is made not simply because the korug is pearlike and pears are edible, but also because the korug is orangelike and oranges are edible. (As a point of information, a korug might be a blue fruit resulting from crossing a pear tree with an orange tree and painting the graft blue). In fact, the korug is identified and predictions are made about it on the basis of a wide variety of related categories. These related categories are referred to as a *coding system* (see Figure 8-1).

One of the most important characteristics of coding systems is that they are hierarchical arrangements of related categories, such that the topmost category in the system is more generic (general) than all the categories below it. In other

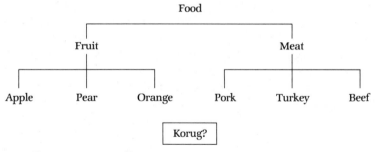

Food

Fruit　　　　　　　　　　Meat

Apple　　Pear　　Orange　　Pork　　Turkey　　Beef

Korug?

Figure 8-1. A coding system

words, as one moves up from the specific instances that define related categories, each subsequent concept (or category) is freer of specifics. According to Bruner, the nonspecificity of coding systems is central in determining their role in retention and in transfer. Essentially, Bruner's contention is that in order to remember a specific it is usually sufficient to recall the coding system of which it is a member. The details of the specific instance can then be recreated. The transfer value of coding systems is implicit in the notion that a generic code is really a way of relating objects and making inferences about them. There is obviously a significant amount of transfer involved in the decision that appropriate behavior toward a korug involves eating it.

Bruner describes four conditions that are assumed to affect the acquisition of generic codes—set, need state, mastery of specifics, and diversity of training.

Set.   Set refers to an individual's predisposition to react in a given way. It is generally recognized that predispositions can directly affect *perception*, responding, and learning. Specifically, Bruner contends that through instructions or previous learning a student can be made to proceed as though new subject matter were related to other learning and were organizable in terms of an underlying structure. Obviously a *set* (attitude) of this nature is more conducive to the acquisition of generic codes than one premised on the assumption that the new learning is unstructured and unrelated to previous learning.

Need State.   Bruner's ideas on motivation are virtually identical to Hebb's. His reference to need state can therefore be interpreted as a reference to arousal level, where arousal is defined as a drive related to the generalized need of individuals to maintain arousal at a moderate level. In the same way that learning or behavior is assumed to be maximally effective under conditions of moderate arousal, so the acquisition of generic codes is believed to be facilitated by arousal that is neither too high nor too low. In support of this inference, Bruner (1957a) cites an experiment in maze-alternation transfer performed with two groups of rats. The rats in one group had not been fed for 36 hours and were therefore presumably under conditions of high drive; the rats in the other group had been fed recently and could therefore be expected to be at lower levels of drive. In both cases, rats had previously learned to run a simple alternating maze (that is, one where the correct turns alternate, right-left-right-left and so on). A test of transfer of learning took the form of placing the rats in the opposite maze (left-right instead of right-left). In this situation, those rats that had been fed most recently outperformed their hungrier counterparts. It is not immediately clear, however, that this experiment can be generalized to human behavior. It appears that there may be some differences between a hungry rat and a highly aroused human. In addition, the transfer of maze learning does not seem to be directly analogous to generic learning in humans. Nevertheless, Bruner's notions about the effect of arousal level on learning are consistent with those of many other theorists (see Chapter 12).

Mastery of Specifics.   It can probably be accepted as self-evident that the formation of generic codes will be influenced by the extent to which the learner has mastered the information specific to the instances that are to be coded. For example, a korug would not easily be organized into a coding system along with other fruits unless at least *some* of the specific attributes of fruits (their edibility, the fact that they grow, and so on) were well known. It would follow that knowing *more* about its specifics would enhance the codability of an event or object.

Diversity of Training.   The fourth factor that is assumed to affect the acquisition of generic codes is closely related to *mastery of specifics*. Bruner's contention is that the wider the range of situations in which something is experienced, the more easily it will be related to other events. This contention can also be accepted as axiomatic, particularly because categories and codes are established on the basis of similarities and differences among events. Obviously, diversity of training may serve to highlight what is common among events as well as to point out what is unique to each.

Concept Attainment

Bruner's experimental work in the formation of concepts presents a significant contribution to this important area of cognitive psychology. Among other things, his is the first systematic attempt to examine the belief that we form concepts by generating and testing hypotheses concerning the attributes of the concepts in question.

Bruner makes a distinction between the *formation* of concepts and their *attainment*. To *form* a concept is to arrive at the notion that some objects belong together while others do not. To *attain* a concept is to discover the attributes that may be useful in distinguishing between members of a class and nonmembers of the same class. For example, when we learn that there are edible mushrooms but that there are also inedible mushrooms, we may be said to have *formed* the concept of edible versus nonedible mushrooms. This concept formation does not mean, however, that we can now go out into a field and bring back only those mushrooms that are clearly edible. When we have learned precisely what the differences between edible and inedible mushrooms are, we are said to have *attained* the concept. It is Bruner's opinion that the process of forming concepts is active until around the age of 15, after which there is a prevalence of concept attainment.

Types of Concepts. There are three types of concepts, distinguished by the relationship between the criterial attributes that define them. *Conjunctive* concepts are defined by the joint presence of two or more attribute values. For example, a pen is an object that can be held in the hand *and* that can be used to write. *Both* of these conditions *must* be met if the object is to be a pen—therefore, the concept of *pen* is conjunctive.

A *disjunctive* concept, in contrast, is defined *either* by the joint presence of two or more attributes *or* by the presence of any one of the relevant attributes. For example, a psychotic human may have delusions of grandeur and an intense fear of persecution as well as a mania for stealing, or the person may simply have the delusions, or the phobia, or the mania. This is a disjunctive concept.

The third variety of concept is referred to as *relational*. It is defined by a specified relationship between attribute values. A rectangle, for example, not only has four sides, but two sides must also be equal in length and longer than the other two, which must also be equal in length. *Rectangle* is a relational concept.

STRATEGIES FOR CONCEPT ATTAINMENT

Bruner's work on concept attainment is premised on several assumptions, one of which is that we form concepts to simplify the environment and to know how to react to it. Indeed, the formation of concepts is tantamount to the establishment of categories. A second assumption is that, in order to reduce cognitive strain as well as to ensure that concepts are attained quickly and accurately, we adopt certain *strategies*. These strategies take the form of regularities, or patterns, in the sequence of decisions that are made in determining whether objects belong to given classes.

In order to investigate these strategies, Bruner and his associates (1956) developed a series of cards, each of which could be used as an example of either a conjunctive, disjunctive, or relational concept. The 81 cards developed for this purpose included all the possible variations of four attributes, each with three values (see Figure 8-2).

In the experiments, subjects were told what a concept is and were given illustrations of disjunctive or conjunctive concepts, depending on the specific study. A card with two borders and three red circles may, for example, be an example of several conjunctive concepts. One conjunctive concept is *red circles*; thus, all other cards also having red circles are examples of the same concept. If the concept *red circles* were disjunctive, any card that had either red figures on it or circles of any color would illustrate the same concept, since disjunction indicates an *either/or* element. Conjunction, on the other hand, is defined in terms of *and* rather than *either/or*.

The experimental procedure was to have the subject try to discover (to attain) the concept the experimenter had in mind. In order to make the problem simpler the experimenter told the subject how many values were included in the concept (usually two) and whether the concept was conjunctive or disjunctive.

One group of strategies for the attainment of conjunctive concepts is discussed here as illustration. It is referred to as *selection* strategies, since the subject is first presented with all 81 cards, shown one example of the concept, and then allowed to *select* the card he or she wants tested next. After each test, the experimenter tells the subject that the card selected is or is not an example of

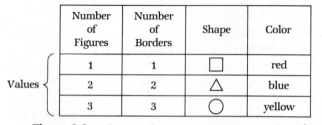
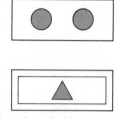

Number of Figures	Number of Borders	Shape	Color
1	1	□	red
2	2	△	blue
3	3	○	yellow

Values {

Figure 8-2. An experiment on concept strategies. The chart lists the four attributes and three values that, in all possible combinations, made up the 81-card deck used in the experiment. Two sample cards are also shown.

the concept. The object of the "game" is twofold: to arrive at the correct concept and to do it in the least number of trials possible. Four decision sequences have been identified as selection strategies for the attainment of conjunctive concepts.

Simultaneous Scanning.   The first strategy involves generating all possible tenable hypotheses on the basis of the first example (positive instance) of the concept and using each successive selection to eliminate all untenable hypotheses. For example, if the experimenter presents the subject with a card with two borders and three red circles on it, it would give rise to 15 tenable hypotheses (these are all two-valued conjunctive concepts) such as two borders and three figures, three circles, three red figures, red circles, two borders and red figures, two borders and circles, and so on. Unfortunately, the human mind is not ordinarily sufficient to consider so many hypotheses simultaneously. The strategy is theoretically possible but virtually nonexistent in practice.

Successive Scanning.   This second strategy imposes much less cognitive strain, since it is essentially a "trial-and-error" approach. It involves making a hypothesis ("Oh, oh . . . maybe the concept is red circles.") and choosing a card to test the hypothesis directly. If the original guess is not confirmed ("Darn it, I was wrong!"), a second hypothesis is made ("Maybe it's red squares."). The concept may sometimes be arrived at very quickly, *by chance*, with this procedure—it may also *never* be attained.

Conservative Focusing.   For several reasons the third strategy is the most logical one to employ. It imposes relatively little strain on memory or on inferential capacity, and it also assures that the concept will be attained. A subject employing this strategy begins by accepting the first positive instance as the complete hypothesis. For example, the concept is red circles *(RO)* and the first card has two borders and three red circles *(2B3RO)*. The subject has as hypothesis *2B3RO*. The person then selects a second card, which varies from the original in only one value—for example, two borders and two red circles. The experimenter confirms that this card is still an example of the concept. It follows, then, that the number of figures is irrelevant. The remaining hypothesis is *2BRO*. The next selection changes one more value—the color. The card chosen has two borders and three green circles. Since the instance is now negative, color *was* relevant. The subject now knows that red is part of the concept. If the next choice eliminates number of borders or confirms shape (which it will if only one value is changed), the subject will have attained the concept (see Figure 8-3).

Focus Gambling.   A slight variation of *conservative focusing* involves varying more than one value at a time—in other words, *gambling*. If two values are changed and the card remains positive, progress is accelerated. If, however, the

1. Card is presented as an example of the concept:

2. Temporary hypothesis is formed—the concept is two
borders and three red circles.

(2B3RO)

3. Card is chosen that changes one value: (1B3RO)

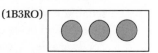

4. Choice is positive: number of borders is irrelevant— (2B2BO)
hypothesis becomes 3RO. Second card is chosen that
changes one of the remaining values:

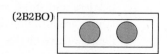

5. Number was not relevant, since card is still an example (2B3RS)
of the concept. Next choice changes one of the remaining
values—shape of figures:

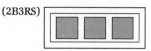

6. Choice is negative. Therefore, shape was relevant.
Concept is:

red circles

Figure 8-3. Decision sequence in attaining the concept *red circle* by using a
conservative focusing strategy.

instance becomes negative, the subject learns little, since either or both of the
changed values could be criterial.

Other series of experiments, whose results are not reviewed here, have dealt
with the attainment of disjunctive concepts and with the attainment of concepts
through *reception* strategies—that is, when the experimenter presents subjects
with each successive card rather than allowing them to select the next one
themselves.

STRATEGIES IN REAL LIFE

The results of Bruner's work on concept attainment are difficult to generalize
to nonexperimental situations, for we are not often presented with systematic
examples from which to select our experiences. Nor is there usually an authority
immediately available to say that "yes," this is an example of true love or "no,"
that is not an example of true love. (And indeed, discovering what true love is
appears to be a concept-attainment task of considerable importance.) A second
difficulty is that Bruner employed adult subjects in his experiments; but simpler
versions of the problems presented to children have not always led to the identification of the same strategies (Olson, 1963). A third problem is that even
adult subjects often employed no identifiable strategies. Difficult approaches

(such as successive scanning) were never employed by any subject and therefore remain "ideal" strategies (the terminology employed by Bruner).

Despite the preceding cautions, some of this work may be related to various aspects of human behavior. For example, the acquisition of inductive and deductive reasoning processes in children may involve the learning of strategies similar to those investigated by Bruner—particularly since the teaching process in schools frequently involves the presentation of related examples together with information about their class memberships. Although teachers and curriculum materials are seldom as systematic and rigorous as experimental procedures, they can occasionally be patterned after these procedures.

Summary of Bruner's Learning Theory

Bruner's theory of learning maintains that people interpret the world largely in terms of the similarities and differences that are detected among objects and events. Similar objects are reacted to as though they were equal; this similarity is recognized through the placement of stimulus input into *categories*.

Categories can be compared to the cell assemblies and phase sequences of Hebb's theory. They are essentially classifications of objects in terms of properties that are redundant for that type of object. Hence, they are based on associations developed largely through frequency or redundancy. For example, if the first people to arrive from Mars all have warts, eventually *wart* will become a criterial attribute for the category *Martian*. In Hebbian terms, the cell assemblies activated by warts will become associated with others activated by Martians.

In Bruner's system, the major organizational variable is called a *coding* system—a hierarchical arrangement of related categories, with each level of the hierarchy becoming more general, less defined by specifics, and more inclusive. The final, or most general, category in a coding system is defined in such a way as to include all of the more specific examples that lead to its formation. The act of categorizing is assumed to be involved in information processing (at both perceptual and conceptual levels) and decision making.

Recent Research

As noted at the very beginning of this chapter, one of the most important tasks undertaken by cognitive psychologists is to arrive at some understanding of the processes by which we develop cognitive representations. The point was also made that the explanation typically makes use of metaphors—that it is not an attempt at a literal description of the way things actually are. The metaphor most central to Bruner's theorizing is that represented by the terms *categories* and *coding systems*.

Bruner's description of categories and of the processes involved in categorizing continues to play an important role in contemporary cognitive research. For example, in a comprehensive review of recent research on categorization, Mervis and Rosch (1981) present this definition: "A category exists whenever two or more distinguishable objects or events are treated equivalently" (p. 89). This definition is essentially identical to that first advanced by Bruner a quarter of a century earlier. Mervis and Rosch then go on to assert that "categorization may be considered one of the most basic functions of living creatures" (p. 89).

Since the advent of Bruner's theory of categorization, research has focused on a search for the rules (hypotheses) subjects employ and on an attempt to specify more clearly the nature of categories as well as of attributes (see, for example, Bourne, Dominowski, & Loftus, 1979). Mervis and Rosch (1981) summarize conclusions and directions in this research as follows.

One of the recent trends has been an attempt to analyze categories in terms of their generality. Contrary to what we might suppose, children do not begin by learning the most specific concept and progressing from there to the most general. Instead, they typically begin by learning concepts of intermediate generality and then learn those that are more specific. Later they develop more supraordinate categories (coding systems, in Bruner's terms). For example, a child does not begin by learning the concept *German shepherd*, a highly specific category, but learns instead the concept *dog*. Eventually concepts such as *poodle*, *German shepherd*, and others at a similar level of specificity will be learned. Later, the child will be ready to understand the related generic concept *mammal*.

A second observation resulting from this research points to the fact that those items or events that are included in the same category are not all equivalent, even though they may be reacted to *as though* they were equivalent. Thus, although a large range of stimulus input will be interpreted as being *blue* (that is, as belonging to the category corresponding to blueness), some of that input will be interpreted as being *more* blue and some *less*. Similarly, some colors will be more green, others more black, some lighter, some darker; and yet under appropriate circumstances all will be reacted to as though they were blue. In the same way, those individuals who fit into our categories for *thin* or *fat* are not all equally thin or fat. It follows, then, that category boundaries are not always well defined, in addition to being somewhat arbitrary. In other words, not only might you and I not agree perfectly with respect to the attributes that are criterial for membership in our *fat* and *thin* categories, but, when pressed, we would be forced to recognize that our own personal categories for these qualities have somewhat fuzzy boundaries.

Research in categorization has also led to a third important observation relating to the nature of the information employed in categorization. At a superficial level, for example, we might assume that the perception of physical objects requires no more than some knowledge of their *physical* properties together with the availability of an appropriate category. Put another way, it might seem that the attributes we employ in simple perceptual recognition involve little more than the matching of sensations with appropriate categories. Thus, to recognize someone as belonging to my category *thin* or *fat*, I should need to do no more than "sense" thinness or fatness, probably through my visual sense although perhaps through palpation as well. In fact, however, "fatness" and "thinness" cannot be sensed directly. These are abstractions. Thus, even at the most elementary level of perceptual recognition, abstraction is often involved. At a less elementary level, Mervis and Rosch (1981) make the observation that abstraction is involved in virtually all models of categorization.

In summary, recent research in categorization suggests that categories vary in terms of generality, and that the most specific categories are not learned first but that categories at an intermediate level of generality are simplest for a child; items or events included in the same category are not equivalent even as the attribute values that are employed as criteria for inclusion in the same category are not necessary equivalent; finally, sensation and memory alone are not sufficient for an adequate explanation of categorization: abstraction is always involved.

Evaluation

The evaluation of a cognitive position such as Bruner's presents an interesting difficulty. Whereas traditional behavioristic positions attempt to describe a state of affairs in an exact and literal manner and can therefore be judged in terms of how accurate the description appears to be, cognitive theories such as Bruner's do not attempt a literal description. Accordingly, the theory cannot be judged in the same manner as can behavioristic positions. What is being judged is not a description but a metaphor; it is not an account of things or events that are assumed to actually exist but an abstraction that merely represents (symbolizes).

So we cannot say that Bruner's theory of categorizing reflects facts or that it does not. But we can tentatively say that it is a metaphor that does not do great obvious violence to what we intuitively suspect about human functioning. More than that, it appears to be relatively clear and understandable and internally consistent, both of which are important criteria of a scientific theory.

Perhaps the most important question that needs to be asked of any of our psychological theories concerns their usefulness in predicting and explaining. The behavioristic theories are sometimes highly useful in predicting specific behaviors where the relationships between stimuli, responses, and response consequences are clear and agree with our theoretical understanding of how these things should be. In other words, these theories are useful for explaining behaviors that are clear illustrations of operant or classical conditioning. They are not nearly so useful for explaining the so-called higher mental processes.

In contrast, cognitive theories such as Bruner's are not at all useful for explaining specific behaviors of the kind most easily explained by behavioristic positions. But they are of some value in explaining and perhaps sometimes in predicting preceptual processes, decision making, and the use of cognitive strategies. A decision concerning their ultimate usefulness awaits further investigation.

A Note on Educational Implications

Bruner has been particularly concerned with elucidating some of the educational implications of his work (Bruner, 1961a, 1961b, 1966). His emphasis on the formation of coding systems, together with his belief that the systems facilitate transfer, enhance retention, and increase problem-solving ability and motivation, has led him to advocate a discovery-oriented approach in the schools. This emphasis is premised in part on his belief that the formation of generic coding systems requires the *discovery* of relationships. Accordingly, he advocates the use of techniques by which children are encouraged to discover facts and relationships for themselves. For this purpose Bruner stresses that some form of *spiral* curriculum is probably the best. A spiral curriculum is one that redevelops the same topics at succeeding age or grade levels as well as at different levels of difficulty. For example, in early grades learners are exposed to the simplest concepts in a particular area; at succeeding grade levels they are reexposed to the same area but at progressively more advanced conceptual levels.

Not all educators or theorists are as enthusiastic as Bruner about the use of discovery methods in schools (see, for example, Ausubel, 1968; Ausubel & Robinson, 1969). Accordingly, a relatively mild controversy pitting discovery teaching against more didactic approaches (sometimes called reception learning) has been going on in educational circles for a number of decades. Research that has attempted to examine the relative merits of these two approaches is equivocal (see Lefrancois, 1982), a fact that need not be of any great concern. Teachers do not need to use discovery techniques *or* reception approaches; they can employ both.

Summary of Chapter 8

This chapter has presented an introduction to an area of current research emphasis: cognitive theory. Jerome Bruner's cognitive theory was presented in some detail as an example of this approach. It can be described as a theory of categorization, that being the metaphor employed by Bruner to represent cognitive representation.

1. Traditional behavioristic positions attempted to describe an actual state of affairs in a literal manner; cognitive psychologists present metaphors that are essentially "as if" rather than literal descriptions.
2. Cognitivism is concerned primarily with explaining those higher mental processes not easily explained using an S-R paradigm. Cognitive psychologists have therefore been interested in such topics as perception, information processing, decision making, and knowing. Each of these presupposes some form of mental representation.
3. Bruner compares the development of the child to the evolution of the human race. In the same way that humanity went from inventions that

amplify motor capacities to those that amplify the senses and finally to those that amplify ratiocinative capacities, the child progresses from enactive to iconic and finally to symbolic representation.

4. Bruner uses the term *categorizing* to describe both perceptual and conceptual activity.

5. To categorize is to place stimulus input into classes on the basis of similarities among input. A *category* can be thought of as a rule for classifying things as being equal. As a rule, it specifies the attributes (qualities) that objects must possess before they can be incorporated into a given category.

6. *Information processing* and *decision making* both involve categorization. An object is identified when it is placed in a category—a process that has implicit in it the possibility of "going beyond the information given." It involves making predictions about events or objects on the basis of their category membership.

7. Accurate perception not only is a function of having appropriate categories and knowing what attributes are criterial for membership in these categories, but it also depends on the *accessibility* of the appropriate category. Another term for category accessibility is *perceptual readiness*.

8. *Category accessibility* is a function of expectations and needs. The more accessible a category, the less input required for perception, the wider the range of input that will be accepted, and the more likely that other categories (perhaps better fitting) will be less available.

9. *Coding systems* are arrangements of related categories in hierarchical order. Higher-level categories are said to be more *generic* in that they subsume more examples and are freer of specifics (less defined by small details).

10. Four conditions are assumed to affect the acquisition of generic coding systems: set (predisposition to react), need state (immediate requirements), mastery of specifics (extent of previous related knowledge), and diversity of training (the number of different situations in which something is experienced).

11. To form a concept is to arrive at a notion that some things belong together and others do not (that is, some things are high-bush cranberries and some things are not); to attain a concept is to discover what attributes are criterial for membership in a given category (that is, to discover what it is that identifies high-bush cranberries and distinguishes them from other berries such as low-bush cranberries and pin cherries.)

12. Bruner describes three types of concepts: conjunctive (defined by the joint presence of two or more attribute values); disjunctive (defined by the joint presence of relevant attributes *or* by the presence of any of them singly or in other combinations); and relational (defined by a specified relationship between or among attribute values).

13. Much of Bruner's important experimental work has investigated strategies that subjects employ in attaining concepts. These include simultaneous scanning (generating all hypotheses—impractical and impossible for most subjects); successive scanning (trial and error—uneconomical); conservative focusing (accepting first instance as complete hypothesis and varying one attribute value at a time—economical and effective); and focus gambling (riskier than conservative focusing—sometimes faster payoff, sometimes slower).

14. Recent research on categorization is based in large part on Bruner's initial formulations. Among the findings from this research are the following: categories vary in terms of generality, but the most specific category (Guernsey cow) is *not* learned before a more general category (*cow*); items and events included in the same category, as well as the values that are employed in determining category membership, are not necessarily equivalent; and abstraction is always involved in categorization.

15. Bruner is a strong advocate of discovery-oriented teaching methods.

Guy,

How can somebody who's supposed to be as intelligent as you seriously think that a 10-year-old dog is an old dog? Besides, I've known an awful lot of dogs in my life, and I've never seen a single one go wacko. As for Pouf's trying to break his chain to get at you, I know you must be joking. If he's trying to get at you it's because he wants to lick your face and be friendly. He's never bitten anyone in his life except Mr. Garvie that one time. And maybe Luke, but I'm sure he asked for it. There was never any proof that he was the one who got loose in that mail carriers' convention three years ago.

About that birthday gift. This is a little bit embarrassing, but I'm sure you'll understand. I was paying my power bill and I guess I must have gotten the envelopes confused, because the power company just sent me back your birthday card. I'd like you to send me back their bill and the money I had with it, if you don't mind, and I'll go ahead and send you your birthday card. Better late than never. And I'll slip in a couple of dollars so you can buy yourself something.

As for that lawyer friend of yours, I don't need him at all. I'm going to take it all with me (ha ha). Besides, maybe someday you'll write a better book and you'll finally be able to trade in that old car. Or you should think about getting a better paying job. At your age, I don't think you should have to ask your dad and me for . . .

CHAPTER *9*

Piaget and Cognitive Development

A Developmental Cognitive Position

Jean Piaget's system is *cognitive*. Not only does it pay little attention to stimuli and responses, but its primary concern is describing the nature of mental representation. Unlike a number of other cognitive positions, however, Piagetian theory attempts to do far more than simply describe cognitive representation as it exists in older children or in adults: it is a *developmental* cognitive position. Accordingly, one of Piaget's most important contributions is inherent in his attempt to describe the processes by which children gain a progressively more adultlike understanding of their environment and of themselves. In brief, Piagetian theory presents an account of human cognitive development.

Like other contemporary cognitive positions, Piaget's system looks at perception, concept formation, decision making, and so on. But these topics are only a few of its many interests. Indeed, as Chaplin and Krawiec (1960) put it, "Jean Piaget is a 'school' unto himself" (p. 295). His writings deal with almost all facets of human conceptual functioning: language (1926); reality (1929); morality (1932); causality (1930); time (1946); intelligence (1950); play, dreams, and imitation (1951); and consciousness (1976), to name but a few. Throughout the development of this unified theoretical position, Piaget's closest associate and constant collaborator was Barbel Inhelder.

JEAN PIAGET (1896–1980)

Jean Piaget was born in Neuchatel, Switzerland, in 1896. He did not begin his formal work until some time later, although there are indications that he was a precocious child. At the age of 10 he published his first "scholarly" paper—a one-page note on a partly albino sparrow he had found. This early writing was an intimation of the wealth of published material he was to produce later. His first interests were primarily in the area of natural science, particularly in biology. Accordingly, his doctorate was obtained in this area with a dissertation on mollusks; he received his Ph.D. at the age of 22. By the time he was 30, he had already published two dozen papers, most of them dealing with mollusks and related topics.

After receiving his doctorate, Piaget spent a year wandering through Europe, uncertain about what he would do and where he would do it. During this year he worked in a psychoanalytic clinic (Bleuler's), in a psychological laboratory (that of Wreschner and Lipps) and eventually in Binet's laboratory, then under the direction of Simon. One of Piaget's duties while in the Binet laboratory was to administer Burt's reasoning tests to young children in order to standardize the items. This period probably marks the beginning of his abiding interest in the thought processes of children. It was at about this time also that he was presented with his first child. This event enabled him to make the detailed observations of breast-feeding (more specifically, of sucking behavior) that are incorporated in the origins of his theory.

Piaget subsequently published several dozen books and hundreds of articles. The bulk of his work is to be found in Archives de Psychologie *(of which he was co-editor), in French and untranslated. Increasingly, however, his writings are being translated and summarized in response to the tremendous interest in his work that has taken hold in North America since the early 1960s. When Piaget died in 1980, he was still publishing and doing research at an amazing pace.*

Theoretical Orientation

Consistent with his early training in biology, Piaget asked questions about human development borrowed directly from the concerns of the zoologist. Biologists are chiefly concerned with two questions: In what phylogenetic order can species be classified? and Which properties of organisms allow them to survive? The basic elements of Piaget's theory can be summarized as answers to these two questions as applied to human ontogeny rather than to phylogeny.* The questions can be formulated as follows (Lefrancois, 1982):

1. What characteristics of children enable them to adapt to their environment?
2. What is the simplest, most accurate, and most useful way of classifying or ordering child development?

Piaget's answers for these two questions are discussed after the presentation of a 38-frame linear program. The program is intended to enhance your comprehension of the material that follows, material that might otherwise be somewhat difficult given the newness of Piaget's terminology. The objective of the program is to clarify some of this jargon. After working through it, you should be able to define and give examples of the following:

1. adaptation
2. functioning
3. assimilation
4. accommodation
5. invariants
6. structure
7. schema
8. content

Piaget's Theory: A Program

(*The following program is adapted from Lefrancois, 1982, and is used by permission.*)

---

*Ontogeny refers to the development of one individual from birth (or conception) to death; phylogeny refers to the evolution of a species through various forms—for example, in simplistic terms, from monkey to human.

DIRECTIONS

Fold a sheet of paper or use a strip of cardboard to cover the answers, which are given in the right-hand margin. With the answers covered, read frame 1 and write your answer in the blank provided. Move the paper down so as to check your answer before proceeding to frame 2.

1. Jean Piaget has developed a theory that deals with human adaptation. It is a developmental theory of human _____ .

2. As children learn to cope with their environment and to deal effectively with it, they can be said to be _____to it.

adaptation

3. Adaptation therefore involves interacting with the environment. The process of adaptation is one of organism/ environment _____ .

adapting

4. One of the central features of Piaget's developmental theory is that it attempts to explain _____ through interaction.

interaction

5. Interaction takes place through the interplay of two complementary processes: one involves reacting to the environment in terms of a previously learned response. This process is called assimilation. Assimilation involves a pre_____ learned response.

adaptation

6. Whenever children use an object for some activity that they have already learned, they are said to be *assimilating* that object to their previous learning. For example, when children suck a pacifier, they are _____the pacifier to the activity of sucking.

previously

7. A girl is given a paper doll. She looks at it curiously, and then puts it in her mouth and eats it. She has _____the doll to the activity of eating.

assimilating

8. Assimilation is one of the two processes involved in interacting with the environment. It is part of the process of _____ .

assimilated

9. Adaptation involves two processes. The first is assimilation. The second is called accommodation. It occurs whenever a change in behavior results from interacting

adapting or adaptation

with the environment. Accommodation involves a
_____in behavior.

10. When children cannot assimilate a new object to activ- *change or*
ities that are already part of their repertoire, they must *modification*
_____to them.

11. Johnny West was presented with a long pacifier on the *accommodate*
occasion of his first birthday. Before that time he had
been sucking a short "bulb" pacifier. The long pacifier
matched his nose. He had to elongate his mouth considerably more than usual in order to suck this new
pacifier. Johnny had to _____to
the new pacifier.

12. If Johnny had been given his old, short pacifier, he could *accommodate*
more easily have _____ it to the
activity of sucking.

13. Adaptation is defined in terms of the interaction *assimilated*
between a person and the environment. This interaction
takes the form of two complementary processes:
_____ and

_____ .

14. Assimilation and accommodation are ways of function- *assimilation and*
ing in relation to the world. They do not change as a *accommodation*
person develops. Adults still interact with the environment in terms of activities they have already learned
(assimilation), and they change their behavior in the
face of environmental demands (accommodation). This
does not mean that adults eat paper dolls, however.
What it does mean is that a person's ways of functioning
do not _____ from childhood to adulthood.

15. Activities that do not change are *invariants*. Assim- *change*
ilation and accommodation can be referred to as

_____ .

16. The twin invariants of adaptation are assimilation and   *invariants (Did you see the prompt?)*
_____ .

17. These are also called *functional* invariants, since they   *accommodation*
are activities related to human functioning. Adaptation
involves _____ . Functioning in-
volves assimilation and accommodation.

18. When a Frenchman is given a bowl of pea soup and   *functioning (Too easy?)*
a spoon, he probably _____ the
spoon and soup to the activity of eating.

19. When the same noble Frenchman is given a pair of   *assimilates*
chopsticks, it is probably necessary for him to
_____the activity of eating to
these novel instruments.

20. A short review before continuing: Adaptation involves   *accommodate*
the interaction of the functional invariants assimilation
and accommodation. These are called invariants because
as ways of interacting with the environment they do not
change from childhood to adulthood. Accommodation
involves modifying some activity of the organism in the
face of environmental demands. Assimilation is the use
of some aspect of the environment for an activity that
is already part of the organism's repertoire. These terms
are employed in the developmental theory advanced by
_____ _____ .

21. Why is it that people behave in certain ways in the face   *Jean Piaget (I hope you got this one correct!)*
of environmental demands? Part of the answer is that
the activities with which they respond are part of their
repertoire. Another way of putting this is to say that the
activities a person has learned make up intellectual
structure. Structure refers to the "mental" component
of behavior. For every act there is a corresponding mental _____ .

22. If Johnny West sucks pacifiers, it is because he has some   *structure*
sort of structure that corresponds to the activity of sucking. From the fact that people behave we can infer that
_____ exists.

23. When an object is being assimilated to some activity, it   *structure*
is really being assimilated to structure. Structure is the
mental counterpart of an _____ .

24. If aspects of the environment can be assimilated to structure, then those aspects of the environment to which a person accommodates must cause a change in _____ .

activity

25. Assimilation can be defined as the use of existing structure. _____ involves changes in structure.

structure

26. If a girl can stick out her tongue, it is partly because she has some _____ that corresponds to tongue-sticking-out behavior.

accommodation

27. What sort of intellectual structure are children born with? They are obviously born with the ability to perform some very simple acts such as sucking, looking, and so on. There are called re_____ .

structure

28. The primitive intellectual structure of a child is defined in terms of _____ .

reflexes

29. Changes in reflexive behavior involve changes in _____ .

reflexes

30. Such changes involve the process of _____ .

structure

31. The exercising of a reflex without changing it significantly involves the process of _____ .

accommodation

32. All activity involves both assimilation and accommodation. This is because new behaviors are always based on old learning, and because even the use of a very familiar activity can be interpreted as involving some change in structure. That change might simply involve a higher probability that the same response will occur again. All activity involves both _____ and _____ .

assimilation

33. The name given to the intellectual structure of a young child is schema. A schema can therefore correspond to a reflex. The intellectual component of reflexive behavior is called _____ .

assimilation
accommodation

34. Schemata are related not only to reflex but also to any other early behavior. A schema is usually named in terms of a behavior. For example, there is a sucking schema, a looking schema, a reaching schema and so on. Schemata are units of intellectual _____ .

schema

35. It is obvious that structure, since it corresponds to behavior, must have something to do with assimilation and accommodation. In fact, objects in the environment are assimilated to structure. This simply means that people react toward them in terms of activities they already know. Accommodation, in contrast, will involve a change in _____ .

    structure

36. One last term—*content*. Content is simply behavior! Why not call it behavior! Paraphrasing Dr. Seuss: Are they not like one another? I don't know, Go ask your mother. In any case, behavior is called _____.

    structure

37. Again, behavior is called _____ .

    content

38. Now you have it:

    content

    adaptation
    assimilation
    accommodation
    functioning
    invariants
    structure
    schema
    content

    If you don't know what these words mean, either the program is bad, you were not paying attention, or . . .

Adaptation

The preceding program describes human adaptation as consisting of the interaction of assimilation and accommodation. It can be added that adaptive activity takes one of three forms: play, imitation, or intelligent adaptation. Through a discussion of these alternatives, some significant aspects of Piaget's theory can be summarized.

PLAY

Play is described by Piaget as involving a preponderance of assimilation. When children play, they continually assimilate objects to predetermined activities without regard for those attributes that fit less well. For example, when children sit astride a chair and say "Giddyup," they are not paying particular attention to those attributes of the chair that do not resemble a horse—and no one would deny that they are playing. To say or imply that this activity is less than maximally intelligent is not to deny its importance in the course of development. Indeed, Piaget does quite the opposite, emphasizing repeatedly that young children engage in activities (such as playing "horse") simply for the sake of exercising the act. The effect is to stabilize the schema, to render it more available, and consequently to enhance further learning.

In the course of their development, children progress through a series of stages in the playing of games. Piaget's extensive investigation of the development of the rules by which children play as well as of the relationship between these rules and morality are reported in *The Moral Judgement of the Child* (1932).

First, Piaget describes game rules as comprising two aspects. There is children's actual behavior; there is also their verbalized notions of rules. The two are not always in agreement. Both aspects are described in terms of four stages (see Table 9-1).

TABLE 9-1. Piaget's description of rules as they are understood and practiced by children

Stage	Approximate age	Degree of understanding	Adherence to rules
Stage 1	Before 3	No understanding of rules	Do not play according to rules
Stage 2	3 to 5	Believe rules come from God (or some other high authority) and cannot be changed	Break and change rules constantly
Stage 3	5 to 11 or 12	Understand that rules are social and that they can be changed	Do not change rules; adhere to them rigidly
Stage 4	After 11 or 12	Complete understanding	Change rules by mutual consent

Stage 1 (1 to 3 years). At the earliest stage, children have no notion that rules exist and play according to none.

Stage 2 (3 to 5 years). During Stage 2, children believe that rules are eternal and unchangeable, but they change them constantly as they play.

Stage 3 (5 to 11 or 12 years). In the third stage, there is a reversal of Stage 2 behavior. Children now admit that rules are made and are changeable, but in practice they never alter them. Their play behavior is extremely rigid, although they verbally recognize that flexibility is possible.

Stage 4 (after 11 or 12 years). With the increased maturity of Stage 4, children arrive at a complete understanding of rules. Both in behavior and thought, they accept these rules as completely modifiable.

IMITATION

The second form of adaptation is imitation. Whereas play involves a preponderance of assimilation, imitation is primarily accommodation. This follows from the fact that, when imitating, children constantly modify their behavior in accordance with the demands imposed on them by their desire to *be* something else. Again, the fact that imitation is not *intelligent adaptation* does not lessen its role in development. It is Piaget's contention that through the imitation of activity a child internalizes the environment. In other words, it is through representing actions mentally that cognitive structure becomes elaborated and that language begins to develop.

INTELLIGENCE

Piaget's concept of intelligence differs markedly from the traditional approach, which is concerned with its measurement. Instead of describing it as a relatively fixed, if somewhat nebulous, quality or quantity, he describes it as *mobile*; intelligence exists *in action*. Intelligence is the property of activity that is reflected in maximally adaptive behavior; it can therefore be understood in terms of the entire process of adapting.

To review briefly, adaptation is the process of interacting with the environment by assimilating aspects of it to cognitive structure on the one hand and by modifying, or accommodating, structure to it on the other. Both activities, as complementary processes, occur in response to environmental demands (not necessarily those of the *physical* environment). Also, both are guided by cognitive structure and result in changes in that structure. Obviously, however, this entire process can only be inferred from behavior (called *content* by Piaget). The substance of Piaget's concept of intelligence is summarized in Figure 9-1. The diagram simply depicts the relationships among the variables that compose *intelligence-in-action*.

While this view of intelligence may be useful to a theoretical understanding of the concept, it is not of any immediate usefulness for quantifying it. But there is one aspect of this model that lends itself well to the development of tests of intelligence—the part defined by the term *structure*.

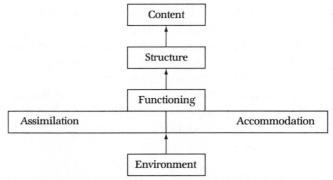

Figure 9-1. Intelligence-in-action is viewed as the interaction of an individual with the environment through the "functioning" processes. This interaction results in cognitive structures, which in turn account for the content of behavior.

Piaget's description of structure is essentially a description of the characteristics of children at different ages—a necessary approach, since the theory deals primarily with child development, and development is defined in terms of changes in structure. Obviously any detailed description of how children at a given age typically behave can serve as a guide for determining whether a specific child is below, above, or at the average.

Piaget's description of changing structure is organized around the concept of stages. His contention is that development progresses through a series of *qualitatively* different stages, each characterized by the development of new abilities—or, more precisely, each consisting of a more advanced level of adaptation. This aspect of Piaget's work has probably received the greatest amount of attention, particularly in relation to education. Numerous interpretations of his theory have appeared (see, for example, Athey & Rubadeau, 1970; Baldwin, 1967; Elkind, 1981; Flavell, 1963; Ginsberg & Opper, 1978). Piaget's stages of development are discussed later in this chapter.

Organizing Principles in Piaget's Theory

Piaget's observations about child development are organized around a number of unifying principles, several of which have been touched on earlier in this chapter. The most important principle is that interaction with the environment—interaction that is essential for cognitive development—*tends toward adaptation*. As was seen earlier, one way of explaining adaptation is to define it as a balance between assimilation and accommodation. Another approach to this same concept is implicit in Piaget's notion of *equilibrium*—a notion that is somewhat nebulous and complex and has been described as "excess baggage" by Bruner (1966). Nevertheless, it serves as a motivational concept of considerable importance in the system. Equilibrium, at the simplest level, denotes a balance between assimilation and accommodation. At a more complex level, it connotes an ability to "compensate for external disturbances" (Flavell, 1963)—for example, an ability to solve problems. At a still more complex level, equilibrium implies cognitive structure that is characterized by rules of logic permitting all possible transformations and combinations of data. This last definition may become clearer as you approach the end of the chapter (then again it may not.)

A second unifying principle is that different stages involve qualitatively different intellectual structures. A very young child is not assumed to be simply a miniature working model of an adult but is instead considered to be discernibly different. Accordingly, a great deal of Piaget's work is devoted to the task of delineating the differences between adults and children as well as between children of different ages.

A third concept that gives structure to Piaget's work is implicit in his belief that cognitive development involves the growth of knowledge, where knowledge includes not only information but also the rules for organizing and transforming information. In Piaget's terminology, development can be viewed as the *genesis of epistemology*.* Indeed, the phrase *genetic epistemology* is frequently employed to describe his work.

A fourth unifying principle focuses on the role of logic in thought. Another way of looking at development *à la* Piaget is to describe it in terms of the acquisition of progressively more advanced systems for dealing with information. The specific analogy made by Piaget in this connection is to systems of logic. At early stages of development, thought is illogical, but as the child progresses, thinking becomes increasingly more capable of dealing with the environment in a logical manner.

The last principle is perhaps less of an orientation than a technique. It is concerned with the means employed by Piaget in gathering the data that form the basis of his theorizing. His approach is quite distinct from that of most other contemporary investigators, who rely heavily on controlled experimentation and who frequently make reference to studies involving rodents. The method developed by Piaget in his early work is referred to as the *méthode clinique*. It is a semistructured interview technique in which subjects are asked certain questions, with their answers often determining what the next question will be. One of the advantages of this approach lies in the considerable flexibility it permits. Piaget's argument is that, when investigators do not know what all the answers might be, they are hardly in a position to decide a priori how the questions should be phrased or, indeed, what questions should be asked. One alleged disadvantage of this flexible approach is that the data-gathering process may be difficult to replicate. Interestingly, more standarized approaches have tended to corroborate most of Piaget's findings. It is unlikely, however, that structured methods could have uncovered the findings in the first place.

The "father/experimenter" role adopted by Piaget in working with young children has led to observations that are often surprising—and to be surprised in psychology is a rare and pleasing thing.

The Stage Theory

Piaget describes four major stages through which children progress in their development (or more precisely, he describes children at each of four different stages):

1. Sensorimotor	birth to 2 years
2. Preoperational	2 to 7 years
Preconceptual	2 to 4 years
Intuitive	4 to 7 years

---

*Epistemology is the division of classical philosophy that deals with questions about the nature of knowledge and the means by which it is acquired; genesis signifies "growth," or development. Hence, genetic epistemology relates to the development of knowledge.

3. Concrete operations   7 to 11 or 12 years
4. Formal operations   11 or 12 to 14 or 15 years

Each stage can be described in terms of the major identifying characteristics of children at that developmental stage and in terms of the learning that occurs before transition to the next stage.

SENSORIMOTOR STAGE: BIRTH TO 2 YEARS

The single most striking characteristic of child behavior in the first two years results in part from the absence of language and internal representation. The child's world, since it cannot be represented mentally, is a world of the *here and now* in a very literal sense. Objects exist only when the child actually perceives them; when they are beyond the perceptual field, they cease to exist. This fact can be verified indirectly by presenting young children with an attractive object and then removing it after they have become engrossed in it. In the earliest stages of development they will not even miss it. In Piaget's terminology they have not yet developed the notion of the permanence and identity of objects (often called the *object concept*).

A second characteristic of the sensorimotor child is implicit in the label employed for the stage, for this is a period of sensorimotor intelligence. Not only do objects exist for children only when they are reacting to them, but their adaptation to the world is in terms of *overt* assimilatory and accommodatory acts. In other words, their functioning in relation to the world is sensorimotor in that it involves the senses and overt behavior.

A third feature of the first stage is that children perfect and elaborate the small repertoire of schemata with which they are born. It will be recalled that newborn infants are capable of such simple reflexive acts as sucking, reaching, grasping, looking, and so on. A large part of their early efforts is dedicated to the exercising of these simple acts. Indeed, development through the first stage is described by Piaget as comprising six substages, each distinguishable by the nature of its reflexive activity. For example, the first substage, lasting until the end of the first month, involves the simple exercise of relatively unmodified reflexive behavior. The second substage (1 to 4 months) is marked by acquired adaptations that are called *primary circular reactions*. These activities are centered on the child's body (hence *primary*) and are circular in that the behavior elicits its own repetition. Infants occasionally suck their thumbs. It is likely that the activity of sucking produces sensations that lead to a repetition of the sucking. Later substages witness the coordination of separate activities, the evolution of language, and so on. A more detailed account of these substages is provided by Flavell (1963) and by Baldwin (1967).

The last characteristic of the sensorimotor child is egocentricity. The term is used in a descriptive rather than a derogatory sense. An egocentric child is incapable of adopting the point of view of others. Infants are egocentric in a literal sense. It can be demonstrated that they are incapable, for example, of describing what a physical object looks like from a vantage point different from their own (see Piaget, 1961). Their world is the world as they react to it.

Achievements by Age 2.   A Piagetian stage is not necessarily defined in terms of the characteristics a child acquires prior to transition into the succeeding stage, but more often in terms of the characteristics that prevail throughout most of the stage. Obviously, the sensorimotor stage is so labeled because throughout most of the stage children react to the world in a sensorimotor fashion. Each stage, however, is a preparation for the next. The achievements of each are therefore of critical importance in explaining the transition to the succeeding stage.

While it is true that sensorimotor children react primarily in activity, this fact is linked with their lack of language facility. Toward the end of the period they will have begun to acquire language. Hence, one of the achievements of the first two years of life is the development of the ability to symbolize and to communicate—a significant attainment, since language accelerates thinking and makes possible the transition to a more cognitive interpretation of the world.

A second achievement of this stage is the development of the *object concept*, which is tantamount to discovering that objects have a permanence and identity independent of the perceiver's perception. In other words, the world continues to exist even when it is not being seen, felt, heard, smelled, or tasted— or does it?

Two other related achievements mark the culmination of sensorimotor learning. First, the child learns to coordinate separate activities. Although this ability may not appear to be of any great significance, particularly since we tend to take it for granted that numerous activities can be coordinated, it is no small or unimportant event for the child. In the absence of cooperation between such simple activities as looking and reaching, we could not obtain the object we look at and desire. Indeed, for such an uncomplicated behavior as picking up a pen, not only must vision direct the arm, but the hand must also be pressed into service. Perhaps even other parts of the body may need to be brought into play.

The other achievement is the recognition of cause-and-effect relationships. Children are not born knowing that if they reach toward an object, they can grasp it and bring it closer to themselves—they must learn. And it is precisely this kind of learning that allows them to develop intentionality, for until children know what the effects of their activities will be, they cannot clearly *intend* these effects.

PREOPERATIONAL THINKING: 2 TO 7 YEARS

The next stage in the evolution of a child is a marked improvement over the first in terms of the child's increased understanding of the world—but relative to an adult, it exhibits serious shortcomings. The stage is ordinarily divided into two substages. The characteristics and achievements of each are discussed below.

Preconceptual Thinking: 2 to 4 Years.   The preconceptual stage is characterized primarily by the child's inability to understand all the properties of classes. Having acquired the ability to represent objects internally (mentally) and to identify them on the basis of their membership in classes, children react to all similar objects as though they were identical. Thus, for some time all men are "Daddy"; all women are "Mommy"; animals are all "doggie"; and the world is simple. If Samuel sees a teddy bear like his at a friend's place, he knows that it is *his* teddy bear—and the tricycle at the store is also clearly *his*. Children understand something about classes, since they can identify objects; but their understanding is incomplete, since they cannot yet distinguish between apparently identical members of the same class—hence the term *preconceptual*. This mode of thinking occasionally has its advantages for parents. Santa Claus continues to be the one and only individual of his type, even though he may be seen in ten places on one day.

Another feature of the child's thinking during this stage is that it is *transductive* as opposed to *inductive* or *deductive*. The last two types of reasoning are "logical"; inductive thinking proceeds from specifics to a generalization, whereas deductive reasoning begins with the generalization and terminates with specifics. Transductive reasoning, in contrast, involves making inferences from one specific to another. For example, the child who reasoned "My dog has hair; that thing there has hair; therefore that thing is a dog" was engaging in transductive reasoning. The thing might well have been a dog, in which case transductive reasoning would have resulted in a correct conclusion. But the thing was a skunk.

Intuitive Thinking: 4 to 7 Years.   By the time children reach the age of 4, they have achieved a more complete understanding of concepts and have largely stopped reasoning transductively. Their thinking has become somewhat more logical, although it is governed more by *perception* than by logic. In fact, the role played by perception in the intuitive stage is probably the most striking characteristic of this period. This role is particularly evident in the now famous conservation tasks.

A conservation problem is typically one in which children are presented with two identical objects; one object is then deformed, rearranged, or otherwise changed in appearance but not in quantity. Subjects are then asked a question about one of the quantitative attributes of the objects. If they think the attribute has changed, they have not acquired conservation. A more detailed discussion of conservation is presented in the section on concrete operations. One example is given here, however. The task concerns the conservation of liquid quantity. Subjects are shown two identical beakers filled to the same level with water (as

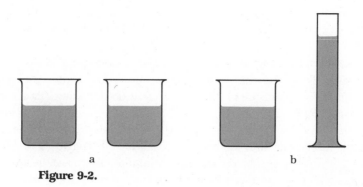

a   b

Figure 9-2.

in Figure 9-2a). The experimenter then pours the contents of one of the beakers into a tall thin tube (as in Figure 9-2b). Subjects, who at first said that the amounts in each were equal, are now asked whether there is as much, more, or less water in the new container. At the intuitive stage, they will almost invariably say that there is more, *since it is much higher in the tube.* In other words, they attend to the misleading perceptual features of the stimuli.

A second characteristic of children between the ages of 4 and 7 is that their reasoning is very egocentric. In the same way that sensorimotor children are unable to adopt the *physical* point of view of another person, so the intuitive child has difficulty accepting the *mental* point of view of others. This orientation is clearly illustrated by an experiment involving a boy doll and a girl doll side by side on a piece of wire. The experimenter holds one end of the wire in each hand, hides the dolls behind a small screen, and asks the child to predict which doll will come out first if they are moved out on the left. The child's answer is noted, the dolls are returned to their original position, and the question is repeated. Again the dolls are coming out on the left; obviously the same doll is coming out first. The procedure is repeated a number of times. Reasonably intelligent children will at first generally answer correctly. After a while, however, they will change their minds and predict that the *other* doll will come out. If asked why they think so, they are unlikely to admit that they distrust psychological investigators, since they probably have not learned to distrust them yet. Instead they may say something like "It's not fair. It's her turn to come out next." It is this solution of a simple logical problem by reference to how things *should* be from the child's *own point of view* that illustrates the role of egocentrism in intuitive thinking.

A final characteristic of children at this stage is that they have not yet attained the ability to classify. Although they can deal with single classes, they cannot reason about subclasses nested within larger groupings. A 4-year-old child who is shown a handful of seven candies, two of which are chocolates and five of which are gums, immediately recognizes that they are all candies and, if asked, will probably say so. If the experimenter says, however, "Tell me, are there more gums than candies, or less, or the same number?" the child will almost invariably say that there are more gums than candies!

This experiment is interpreted as showing that when a class is broken down into subclasses and children are asked to reason about the subclass (gum) and the larger class (candy), they cannot do so, since the original division destroyed the parent class as far as the children are concerned.

The preconceptual and intuitive stages are parts of a larger class, the preoperational stage. It is of some importance to realize that the label *preoperational* is descriptive of the two stages in a literal sense. Prior to age 7, the child does not reason with operations. As the labels for the next two stages clearly indicate, after the age of 7 (or thereabouts), the average child achieves operational thinking. The term *operation* is therefore central in Piaget's system.

An operation can be defined as an internalized activity that is subject to certain rules of logic, the most important of which is reversibility. Indeed, it is not inaccurate to say that an operation is a *reversible* thought, since an internalized act can be interpreted as *thought*. A thought is reversible when it can be unthought. This is a somewhat inelegant and crude definition of a usually sophisticated and nebulous concept, but it is not incorrect (although it may still be nebulous). In order not to confound the issue further, the definitions given are not elaborated at this point. Some examples of operations and of operational thinking are instead provided in the sections dealing with the last two of Piaget's stages.

A Break

I again find myself borrowing from myself (Lefrancois, 1982). While writing a difficult chapter on Piaget for that book, I suddenly realized that my readers might have almost reached the end of their capability—I myself was nearly asleep. At that point, I inserted the section that is reproduced here (with permission).

A Break

Stop! It would probably be wise for the reader who is not already familiar with Piaget to stop at this point. If you have available an electroencephalograph machine, a cardiograph, a thermometer, and a pupillometer, as well as any other graph or meter, these should be connected and read at once. Alpha waves, together with decelerated heartrate, normal temperature and reduced pupil size are symptoms of imminent *jargon shock*. This condition in an advanced stage can be highly detrimental to concentration and learning. Several hours of sleep usually brings about a significant amelioration of the condition.

If you don't have any of this sophisticated electronic gadgetry readily available, you can substitute a hand mirror. Hold the mirror up to your face and look at your eyes. If they are closed you are probably in the terminal stage of "jargon shock."

CONCRETE OPERATIONS: 7 TO 11 OR 12 YEARS

The major features of the period of *concrete* operations can be arrived at most easily by distinguishing it from its preceding and following stages. This section is organized in accordance with that observation, beginning first with a discussion of the distinctions between preoperational and concrete thought and concluding with an analysis of the differences between *formal* and *concrete* thought.

Concrete Operations and Preoperational Thought. Children do not acquire the ability to utilize operations until they reach the age of 7 or 8. More specifically, they then manifest three new abilities: they can deal with classes, with seriation, and with number. In addition, largely as a result of the appearance of the logical properties of thinking that define *operations*, children now begin to acquire the various conservations.

1. *Classes*. Children's ability to classify is assumed to result from activities that they have previously engaged in with real objects. As a result of combining objects, dissociating them, and arranging them into groups, they have learned about class membership and are now able to reason about nested classes. The candy problem cited in the previous section would, for example, present so slight a problem for concrete-operations children that they might well laugh in derision if the question were put to them.

2. *Seriating*. Also as a result of experiences with real objects, children acquire the ability to order them in series and to set up correspondences between more than one series. Piaget investigated the understanding of seriation by presenting children with various objects that can easily be ranked in one dimension—for example, dolls and canes. Before concrete operations, children rank objects by comparing two of them at once; but they seldom make the necessary inference that, if A is greater than B and B greater than C, then A must also be greater than C. Preoperational children are not embarrassed about putting C before B if they have just been comparing A and C. The concrete-operations child seldom makes an error with this kind of problem, even when it involves setting up *two* series in one-to-one correspondence as in Figure 9-3.

3. *Number*. The ability to deal with numbers is a logical result of classifying and seriating, since a complete understanding of number requires some comprehension of its cardinal properties as well as knowledge of its ordinal meaning. Cardinal properties are simply the *class* properties of number. The number 4 is an abstraction that signifies a collection of a group of specified magnitude— hence, a *class* of related objects. Ordination refers to the rank characteristics of a number. The ordinal properties of the number 4 are specifically that it precedes 5 but follows 3—hence, ordinal properties refer to seriation.

The Conservations. The Piagetian type of learning that has probably attracted the greatest amount of attention on the North American continent has to do with the acquisition of concepts of *conservation*. Conservation can be

Figure 9-3. Seriation problems (ordering of similar pieces according to different sizes) are beyond the abilities of early preoperational children but are handled with ease during the concrete-operations stage.

defined as "the realization that quantity or amount remains invariant when nothing has been added to or taken away from a collection of objects despite changes in form or spatial arrangement" (Lefrancois, 1966, p. 4). In the experiment involving water that has been poured into a tall, thin tube, children have not acquired conservation until they answer that the amounts are indeed unchanged.

There are numerous types of conservation, each relating to a specific quantitative attribute of an object and each acquired in a highly similar order by most children. For example, conservation of substance is typically achieved by the age of 7 or 8, whereas conservation of area is not learned until 9 or 10, and conservation of volume does not appear before the age of 11 or 12. Some attributes seem to be more difficult to apprehend than others. For example, *volume* is more remote to a child's direct experience than *substance* (see Piaget, 1957). While this distinction might explain the order of acquisition for the different conservations, it sheds little light on why the conservations do not appear until concrete operations. Piaget, however, provides an answer for this question. The fact that children say "more" when an object *appears* larger, longer, or fatter is obviously partly due to the fact that they *perceive* it as having more. Hence, *perception* dictates the answer. It is not perception per se, however, but rather lack of appropriate operational thought structures that makes it impossible for the child to answer correctly in the first place. If children are presented with the problem of conservation of liquid discussed earlier and answer correctly, they may be reasoning in one of three ways; each of these different reasons illustrates a new *logical* property that now governs thinking. The child might be thinking

"If the water were poured out of the tall tube and back into its original container, it would still have as much water as before so it mustn't have changed." This thought would illustrate what Piaget calls *reversibility*—a property that was alluded to previously. Not only is the action capable of being unthought (or undone mentally), but there are also some necessary, logical consequences. The most important consequence is obviously that the process of transforming does not alter quantity.

The child might also reason that nothing has been added to or taken away from either container and that there must then still be the same amount in each. This is an example of the rule of *identity*, a rule that states that for every operation (action) there is another operation that leaves it unchanged. Obviously, adding or taking away nothing produces no change.

A third alternative might be this: "The tube is taller, but it is also thinner, so it balances out." Piaget and Inhelder (1941) refer to this reasoning as *combinativity* (or *compensation*), which is a property defined in terms of the logical consequences of combining more than one operation or, in this case, more than one dimension.

A further clarification of these notions can be provided by direct reference to some specific examples of conservation problems. You are invited to replicate them with young children. It might be amusing to perform them in front of Grandma, *after* having explained the procedure to her and *after* she has predicted what the child's response will be. Employ a 4- or 5-year-old in order to ensure that your Grandma will be wrong. Note that in the following five experiments the ages indicated in parentheses should not be considered to be more than very imprecise approximations.

1. *Conservation of number (age 6 to 7).* Two rows of counters are placed in one-to-one correspondence between the experimenter (*E*) and the subject (*S*):

One of the rows is then elongated or contracted:

S is asked which row has more or whether they still have the same number.

2. *Conservation of length (age 6 to 7)*. E places two sticks before the subject. The ends are well aligned:

S is asked if they are the same length. One stick is then moved to the right:

The question is repeated.

3. *Conservation of mass (age 7 to 8)*. Two balls are presented to S, who is asked if they have the same amount of modeling clay in them. If S says no, he or she is asked to make them equal. (It is not at all uncommon for a young child to simply *squeeze* a ball in order to make it have less.) One ball is then deformed:

S is asked again whether they have the same amounts.

4. *Conservation of area (age 9 or 10)*. S is given a large piece of cardboard, identical to one that E has. Both represent playgrounds. Small wooden blocks represent buildings. S is asked to put a building on his or her playground every time E does so. After nine buildings have been scattered throughout both playgrounds, E's are moved together in a corner.

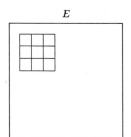

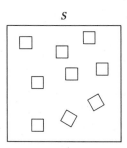

S is asked whether there is as much space (area) in his or her playground as in *E*'s.

5. *Conservation of liquid quantity (age 6 or 7). S* is presented with two identical containers filled to the same level with water.

One of the containers is then poured into a tall thin tube, while the other is poured into a flat dish.

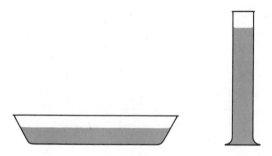

S is asked whether the amount of water in each remains equal.

Can Conservation Be Taught?   Just as Grandma has almost succeeded in overcoming her exasperation and is about to issue a pearl of ancient wisdom that will serve to explain and denigrate the results of science, turn to her, dear reader, and issue this challenge: "Grandma, I challenge you! I challenge you! I say, Grandma, I challenge you!" (It is often necessary to repeat things several times with grandmothers.) There is certainly no point in explaining the challenge until your grandmother has understood you well enough to repress her pearl of wisdom, at least momentarily, and to say "What?" At that point, you might continue by saying "I'll bet you, Grandma dear, that you cannot teach little Norbert to answer correctly when I squish this modeling clay into a pie."

Grandma will probably fail, as did many human investigators—notably Smedslund (1961a, b, c, d, & e) in his earlier experiments. True, a number of psychologists have been successful in accelerating the appearance of concepts of conservation in *some* children (never all), but only after extensive, systematic, and theoretically based training (for example, Côté, 1968; Lefrancois, 1968;

Towler, 1967; Travis, 1969). None of these psychologists has clearly shown that such acceleration studies have a generally beneficial effect on other aspects of child functioning. Indeed, Laurendeau and Pinard (1962) contend that contrived experiences of the kind ordinarily employed in acceleration studies are not likely to be of sufficient moment to significantly alter the course of development.

Grandma will fail! Again!

Concrete Operations and Formal Thought.   Concrete thinking differs in several ways from the thinking that characterizes the period of formal operations. The thought structures of concrete operations are applied directly to real objects or to objects that are capable of evocation. In other words, children do not yet deal with that which is merely hypothetical unless it can be tied directly to concrete reality. Also, they are incapable of dealing with *combinatorial analysis*, which Piaget describes as the systematic generation of all possible combinations. It is sometimes said, for example, that the logic of concrete operations is the logic of classes but not the logic of class products (Peel, 1960). This distinction can be defined by reference to Table 9-2, which shows a four-way classification system (a), as well as a recombination of the products of these four original combinations (b). The first ordering can be executed by a concrete-operations child, but not the second, as is illustrated in the next section.

A third limitation of concrete operations is that children's understanding of such rules of logic as identity and reversibility is not completely general; in other words, they act according to these rules in only some situations. For example, they solve a conservation of number problem much before they can answer a conservation of area question—yet the same process of logical reasoning can be applied to both.

Table 9-2.

A 2 × 2 Classification

	Red	Blue
Circle	Red circle (RC)	Blue circle (BC)
Square	Red square (RS)	Blue square (BC)

(a)

All Possible Combinations of the Products of A

NOTHING	RC	BC	RS
BS	RC BC	RC RS	RC BS
BC RS	BC BS	RS BS	RC BC RS
RC BC BS	RC RS BS	BC RS BS	RC BC RS BS

(b)

FORMAL OPERATIONS: 11 OR 12 TO 14 OR 15 YEARS

The last stage in the evolution of human thought begins around the age of 11 or 12. It is marked by the appearance in behavior of propositional thinking—that is, thinking that is not restricted to the consideration of the concrete or the potentially real but that deals in the realm of the hypothetical (a proposition is any statement that can be true or false). Children can now reason from the real to the merely possible or from the possible to the actual. They can compare hypothetical states of affairs with actual states or vice versa, and, as a result, they can become profoundly upset at the seeming irresponsibility of a generation of adults that has brought itself to the edge of untold disasters.

Two experiments can illustrate the differences between formal thinking and earlier stages. The first (Piaget, 1961) is a simple test of verbal reasoning of the type: $A > B$; $A < C$; which of A, B, or C is greatest? (For example, John is thinner than Bill; John is fatter than Sam; who is the fattest of the three?) Children under the age of 11 or 12 have a great deal of difficulty with such problems unless they pertain directly to objects they can see. The reason is that the solution of the problem requires propositional thinking; that is, it requires reasoning about hypothetical statements.

A second experiment (Piaget, 1961) involves having subjects combine colored disks in all possible ways (by twos, threes, and so on). The formal-operations child will do so completely and systematically, whereas younger children will ordinarily produce some, but seldom *all*, combinations, since their approach is haphazard rather than systematic.

Logic and Piaget's Theory

Piaget's extensive use of models of logic as analogies to thought has not met with as wide acceptance as his more descriptive work. The lack of acceptance may stem from the abstractness and difficulty of symbolic logic, particularly as it is interpreted by Piaget. A second reason is that the logic really does not serve to increase clarity or to further knowledge. It is, in a sense, an extremely clever and complex academic exercise. For these reasons, logic is mentioned only tangentially throughout this chapter. The interested reader is referred to Piaget (1957) or to Peel (1960) for a more detailed account.

Relevance to Learning

Piaget's position is primarily a theory of development. However, largely because of its emphasis on genetic epistemology, it is also a theory of learning. Obviously, since the subject matter of genetic epistemology is the genesis of knowledge, and since learning is concerned largely with knowledge, it is inevitable that Piaget's theory should serve as a theory of learning.

As a theory of learning it can be simplified and reduced to the following set of statements:

1. The acquisition of knowledge is a gradual developmental process made possible through the interaction of a child with the environment.
2. The sophistication of children's representation of the world is a function of their stage of development. That stage is defined by the thought structures they then possess.
3. Maturation, the environment, equilibration, and socialization are the forces that shape learning.

The impact of Piaget's theory on school curricula, on instructional procedures, and on measurement practices appears to be profound and significant. Numerous authors have attempted to delineate specific educational recommendations based on the work of Piaget (for example, Athey & Rubadeau, 1970; Furth, 1970; Ginsberg & Opper, 1978; Hunt, 1961; Phillips, 1969). These writers point to the importance of understanding the present level of a child's development, the consequent limits of cognitive abilities, the usefulness of presenting material at an optimal level of difficulty, and the value of encouraging the child to become involved (active) in learning. Others have attempted to develop intelligence scales based on Piaget's descriptions of structure (Goldschmid & Bentler, 1968; Uzgiris & Hunt, 1975).

Research and Implications

By now literally thousands of studies have investigated and sometimes elaborated on Piaget's work. The most important general conclusions of various groups of these studies is discussed briefly here.

To begin with, an overwhelming majority of studies supports Piaget's general description of the *sequence* of intellectual development (see, for example, Gelman 1978; Opper, 1977). This sequence appears to hold for children from various countries (Dasen, 1972, 1977; Glick, 1975).

In contrast, research provides less sweeping support for Piaget's description of the ages at which major intellectual changes occur. Indications are that verbal difficulties might often have been implicated in Piaget's failure to find certain abilities and understanding during the earlier developmental periods. When the tasks are made simpler, children sometimes respond quite differently. In the "mountains" problem, for example, children are shown three mountains of unequal height set on top of a table and are allowed to walk around the mountains to become familiar with them. In the testing part of the study subjects are seated on one side of the table, and a doll is placed at some other vantage point around the table. Children are then asked to describe what the display looks like from the doll's point of view. Their initial inability to do so is taken as an example of egocentrism (inability to adopt another's point of view). However, when Liben (1975) asked preoperational children to describe what a white card would look like from the experimenter's point of view (as well as from their own) when different colored glasses were being worn by the child or the experimenter (pink glasses on the experimenter, for example, and no glasses on the child), the children were often able to answer correctly. Borke (1975) and Bower (1974) also provide evidence that North American children are often capable of behaviors that Piaget assigned to later developmental periods. Similarly, Flavell (1977) reports various studies on infant learning and behavior that indicate that Piaget's estimates were often underestimates—perhaps because, at least for the sensorimotor period, his observations were based largely on motor behavior.

In a third area of research the findings have also not always been entirely kind to Piaget's descriptions. In his earlier writings Piaget left little doubt that he considered formal operations to be generally characteristic of most older adolescents as well as of most adults (Piaget & Inhelder, 1958). However, a number of studies provide convincing evidence that this is probably not the case (Neimark, 1975; Papalia, 1972). Many of these studies have failed to find much evidence of formal operations among adults—let alone adolescents. When Dulit (1972) tested *gifted older* adolescents for formal operations, he found that approximately half still functioned at the level of concrete operations; approximately one-quarter of average older adolescents and adults operated at a level of formal operations. A similar study reported by Tomlinson-Keasey (1972) employing only female subjects found that the attainment of formal operations was extremely rare. By the same token, cross-cultural studies have generally been hard pressed to find much evidence of thinking beyond concrete operations in many cultures (see Gelman, 1978).

In the light of these findings, Piaget (1972) modified his earlier position by conceding that the formal-operations stage is probably not nearly so general as he had first thought. Available evidence suggests that formal operations are best viewed as cognitive processes that are potential rather than probable. In short, formal operations are probably impossible in middle childhood or earlier; they are possible but far from completely general in adolescence or adulthood.

How damaging are these findings and observations for Piaget's theorizing? Probably not very damaging. At most, the various well-substantiated contradictions of Piagetian theory suggest that the ages of attainment are approximate, a point that Piaget always maintained; that children may develop more rapidly in certain areas than Piaget suspected (particularly at the sensorimotor level); and that the final stage in Piaget's description is not generally descriptive, a fact that is not unduly disturbing for Piagetian theorists providing that the preceding stage, concrete operations, remains descriptive of those who have not achieved formal operations.

Evaluation of Piaget's Position

An examination of Piaget's system with respect to the criteria described in the first chapter reveals, among other things, that the theory is remarkably consistent, coherent, and comprehensive. Like all other cognitive positions, it does not permit us to determine how well it reflects the facts. After all, schemata, concrete operations, and adaptation are metaphors; they are Piaget's inventions. The really central question is whether his inventions are more useful than someone else's. Are they clear and understandable? Not overly. Do they predict and explain behavior well? Yes and no. They explain behaviors that were largely undiscovered previously (conservation, for example); and they predict, in a general way, the type of cognitive functioning that might be expected of children at various stages of development. As we saw in the preceding section, however, the predictions are not always entirely appropriate, particularly when they are based on the notion that there is a close correspondence between specific chronological ages and Piaget's stages.

Piaget's critics, of which there are a significant number, have advanced a number of standard complaints. One of the earliest centered on the paucity of subjects in his research—the *méthode clinique* does not lend itself easily to large samples. In fact, the criticism is not particularly relevant except where more careful studies with larger groups have contradicted Piaget's findings.

Other criticisms have to do with the difficulty of understanding the system, with the use of complex and sometimes nebulous terminology, and with the use of a difficult logic whose contribution is not always readily apparent.

In spite of this, there is little doubt that Piaget's stature in contemporary cognitive psychology is virtually unequalled. His contributions have not ceased with his recent death. Although they will no longer be apparent in his own publications, they continue to be evident in the research of countless other scholars.

Summary of Chapter 9

This chapter has presented a review of the work of Jean Piaget. Content in the many specific areas investigated by Piaget (such as time, space, geometry, and so on) was not detailed, but instead the general developmental theory and the characteristics of children at various stages were discussed.

1. Piaget was by training a biologist and by avocation a philosopher, mathematician, logician, and writer. By occupation he was a psychologist.
2. Piaget's theory can be viewed as an attempt to answer two biology-related questions: What are the characteristics of children that enable them to adapt to their environment? and What is the simplest, most accurate, and most useful way of classifying or ordering child development?
3. Early human *adaptation* can take the form of one of three types of activity or, more often, of a combination of these: play, imitation, and intelligent adaptation. Each is defined in terms of the balance that exists between the functional invariants, assimilation and accommodation. *Play* involves a preponderance of assimilation; *imitation*, a primacy of accommodation; and *intelligent adaptation*, an optimal balance of the two.
4. Piaget's concept of *intelligence* varies from the more traditional model, which typically represents intelligence as a fixed and measureable quality. Rather, he describes it in terms of activity in relation to the environment.
5. Piaget's experimental approach is referred to as the *méthode clinique*. It involves a flexible interview approach in which the subject's answers influence subsequent questioning.
6. Grandmothers are not always right!
7. The *sensorimotor stage* is characterized by a "here-and-now" understanding of the world, extreme egocentrism, absence of language, and the elaboration of schemata.
8. Among the important achievements of the first two years of life are the development of the object concept, the discovery of causal relationships, the acquisition of language, and the appearance of intention.
9. During the *preconceptual stage* children expand their ability to verbalize. Their thinking is fraught with errors of logic. In particular, they reason *transductively*, and they understand concepts incompletely.
10. At the age of 4 (or thereabouts) the child begins to solve many problems correctly on the basis of *intuition*. Thinking continues to be egocentric and perception-dominated, however.

11. The transition from preoperational to operational thought is marked by the appearance of the ability to conserve. In addition, children can now deal with classes, series, and number. Their thinking is tied to the concrete, however.

12. *Formal operations* are defined by the appearance of propositional thinking. The child's thought processes are freed from the immediate and real and are potentially as logical as they will ever be.

13. Research suggests that sensorimotor children may be more advanced than Piaget suspected, that the sequence he described for cognitive development is generally accurate, and that formal operations are not *generally* characteristic of adolescence or adulthood.

Dearest Grandmama,

What a shock it was for me to look back in that envelope and find the power bill. I'm sending it back to you with this letter. Unfortunately, I had just sent quite a bit of money to the Starving Nations Foundation, and I can't quite come up with your power money just yet. Next month I'll try to send you back most of the money, or the month after for sure. You must use up a lot of power up there since you started raising turkeys.

By the way, do you feel better about my idea for the cover since you started bringing up those little baby turkeys? You should maybe raise a few pigs too (heh, heh).

On second thought, it might not be too good an idea to raise pigs with Pouf hanging around there. Just joking, but you were wrong about dogs not going crazy. A couple of psychologists here specialize in making dogs crazy, and I'm sure they could cure them too if it was worth their while.

Grandma, I don't think you should write to my editor about this book, even if you did start the second chapter last week. Do me a favor and read a little more before you make up your mind.

By the way, and I think this is really important, if you want to send a little money to the Starving Nations Foundation, just pass it along to me and I'll send it in with my next donation (probably early next week, or even this week if you can make it). I know you've always felt that starving children . . .

CHAPTER *10*

Artificial Intelligence

Artificial Intelligence

Artificial intelligence, according to Bertram Raphael (1976), is a branch of computer science that tries to make computers smarter. Many people think computers are stupid, he writes. They think that computers are nothing more than "big fast arithmetic machines" and that they are "obedient intellectual slaves" that can do only what they have been programmed to do. Many of us still think that it is only in science fiction that computers dare suggest that their masters are perhaps wrong. Indeed, it is only in fiction that computers know they have masters.

The first myth—namely, that computers are nothing more than computational machines—is easily dispelled. The functioning of sophisticated modern computers involves countless operations that are noncomputational, including storing in memory, searching memory, making sequences of decisions, activating and turning off equipment, and sensing and responding to external conditions, to name but a few.

The second myth, that of the computer as slave, is more complex. It is true that computers do what it is that they are programmed to do. In that sense they are slaves to their programs (or, perhaps more precisely, to their programmers). This does not mean, however, that all computers need always be programmed in such a way that their activities will always be completely predictable. There are now computers programmed to play chess or checkers that can, in fact, sometimes beat their programmers. Thus, it is possible to program computers in creative ways. Is it also possible to program them to create and invent? That, in large part, is the challenge of the study of artificial intelligence. How do you make computers smarter?

WHY MAKE A SMARTER COMPUTER?

There are at least two good reasons why we might want to make a smarter computer. One is that such a computer might do some marvelous things for us or free us from doing these marvelous things for ourselves so that we can move on to other even more marvelous things. The other is that making such a computer might clarify a great many questions we have about our own cognitive processes or that the computer itself, once we had made it, would then tell us new things about ourselves.

Those who deal with artificial intelligence are concerned primarily with the second of these benefits. Their quest is to discover what it is that the study of computers can do for the study of humans. In this quest, they use computers in two distinct ways. The first involves using the computer simply to mimic functioning of the mind; the second involves using computer hardware and functioning to generate models or metaphors of human functioning.

Among the first to become interested in the use of machine models in the study of human behavior was Norbert Wiener (1948), who coined the term *cybernetics* to describe his interest. The term is derived from a Greek word and means "steersman" (of a boat); hence, it relates to control. More specifically, Wiener was interested in analogies that might be drawn between machines that make use of *feedback* to modify their functioning, and human behavior, which is, at least to some degree, influenced by feedback (feedback being information we derive from the environment about our own functioning). The expression *artificial intelligence* has a somewhat more general meaning than does *cybernetics* and is now employed more commonly, although both refer to the same general area of investigation.

CAN MACHINES THINK?

People have for some time been concerned with the problem of whether machines can think (see, for example, Anderson, 1964; Apter & Westby, 1973; Ashby, 1961; Moray, 1963).

The classical answer for this question is provided by the late A. M. Turing (1950). Turing rephrased the question and asked, "Can machines imitate?" In an amusing discussion of "The Imitation Game," he then proceeded to outline a situation that would determine whether or not machines can imitate the behavior of people. The a priori conclusion is that if the machine succeeds in imitating, it ipso facto demonstrates that it can think.

The problem involves two people, a man (A) and a woman (B), who are placed alone in a room. An interrogator (C) in another room must discover whether A is a man (X) or a woman (Y). In Turing's words, at the end of the game he must say "X is A and Y is B" or "X is B and Y is A." In order to discover who A and B are, C is allowed to ask them questions. A and B type out their responses. The object of the game for A is to impede the interrogator. He may, for example, answer questions as though he were a woman—or he may tell the truth. B, on the other hand, attempts to help the interrogator. Obviously, if she attempts to do so by telling the truth—"I'm B, I'm the woman! Believe me!"— A can do exactly the same thing—"Don't believe B, I'm A, I'm the woman!"

The next question asked by Turing is the crucial one: "What will happen when a machine takes the part of A in this game?" His answer is that it will soon be possible to construct a machine that will stump the interrogator at least 70% of the time. By implication, then, the answer to the original question, "Can machines think?" is yes.

As a sequel to the often-quoted Turing article, Gunderson (1964) presents the "toe-stepping game," also in an attempt to answer the question "Can machines think?" In the toe-stepping game two people, a man (A) and a woman (B) are placed together in a room. At the bottom of one wall in this room there is a small aperture through which a third person, the interrogator (C), has placed a foot. The object of the game for C is to discover which of A or B is a man (X) and which is a woman (Y). As in the imitation game, C will be asked to phrase

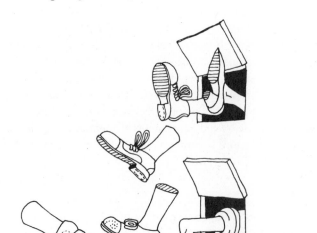

The toe-stepping game

the answer in the form "X is A and Y is B" or "X is B and Y is A." In order to discover who A and B are, C is allowed to insert a foot in the opening in the wall and to have either A or B step on it. The object of the game for A is to confuse C, whereas B attempts to help. Again the question asked is "What would happen if a machine were substituted for A?" This machine would simply need to be a "rock box"—that is, a box filled with rocks of various shapes, sizes, and weights. These could be dropped on C's foot and retrieved before rolling on the floor.

Gunderson's answer for this last question is analogous to Turing's earlier conclusion—namely, that in 50 years it will be possible to develop a rock box that will confuse the interrogator at least 70% of the time.

The intended point of Gunderson's parody of the Turing article is that illustrating that a machine can imitate aspects of human behavior is not equivalent to demonstrating that it can think. Obviously, few people would maintain that the rock box could think. But, as it is pointed out by Gunderson, the rock box does not *need* to think—it accomplishes its objective better than a human without thinking. He concludes (Gunderson, 1964): "In the end the steam drill outlasted John Henry as a digger of railway tunnels, but that didn't prove the machine had muscles; it proved that muscles were not needed for digging railway tunnels" (p. 71).

Despite the intuitive appeal of Gunderson's argument, it remains true that the simulation of human cognitive processes differs from the imitation of more physical activities. And perhaps Gunderson's argument is really not very relevant after all. True, it establishes that a "rock box" might be as effective as a pair of humans in a rather silly attempt at deception, in much the same way as Turing's original proposal established that a machine might be as effective as a pair of humans in a somewhat less silly but still not entirely intelligent game. At best, these related exercises simply suggest what we probably knew all along: that which imitates something else exactly need not exactly imitate. Or as my grandmother, not always the most creative of linguists, is likely to say, there is more than one way to stuff a turkey.

So. Is there more than one way to solve a problem? To remember a poem? To recognize a word? Will studies of artificial intelligence discover a computer way quite distinct from our human ways? And will we never know whether a machine can think?

Until, perhaps, it is too late?

Do we even know clearly what it is to think? Does the fact that our behavior appears *purposive* to us but that the behavior of a "rock box" does not, prove that we can think and that it cannot? Would we be more convinced that a machine can think if it could change its "mind"? If it could lie?

The Computer and the Brain

In our characteristically human way, we have assumed all along that a truly smart computer would be quite a lot like a human. It is surely no accident that Hal, the computer in 2001 *A Space Odyssey*, R2D2 in *Star Wars*, and most of the other computers and computerized robots of our popular space fiction are given personalities. Not only are these computers superbly "intelligent" in terms of their memory and computational abilities, but they all have a degree of willfulness and of personal idiosyncrasy. Their creators have tried to make them human.

There are, of course, some important differences between computers and human brains. Computers consist of complex arrangements of electronic components: transistors, capacitors, resistors, silicone chips, disks, switches, and so on. The human brain consists of complex arrangements of neural material: neurons with their component axons, cell bodies, dendrites, and synapses; various other cells, amino acids and chemical transmitter substances; and so on. And not only are the *internal* physical components of the human and the computer clearly different, but so are the external components. These physical components are termed *hardware* in computer jargon.

While it is the computer's physical components that permit it to function (even as it is our physical components that permit *us* to function), it is a program that determines not only how the computer will function but whether it will. Programs, which are really sets of instructions or strategies, are referred to as *software*.

There are a number of other important differences between computers and humans. Apter (1973) notes, for example, that the human nervous system is incredibly more complex than even the largest and most sophisticated of modern computers. Furthermore, our capacity for certain functions is far greater than that of any computer now in existence. For example, our ability to store information in memory, as is shown in Chapter 11, is virtually unlimited. No computer comes close. But the computer's ability to retrieve *accurately* from memory and to perfom arithmetical computation rapidly and accurately far exceeds that of humans. Nevertheless, the functions carried on by most computers are typically sequential (one after the other rather than simultaneous); human cognitive processes are, in many instances, parallel.

These differences between computers and humans are perhaps less important for those concerned with artificial intelligence than the similarities, particularly insofar as these similarities relate to human cognitive processes. Figure 10-1 presents in schematic form one of the important parallels between a functioning computer and a human. Both involve input and output. With respect to humans, input and output are most easily described in terms of stimuli and responses. With respect to computers, input generally consists of data in numerical form or data that the computer is itself capable of translating into numerical form; output consists of the results of applying a set of operations (defined by a program) to the input, and it can take a variety of forms, including printed material, visual displays, sounds, mechanical responses, and so on. The significance of the comparison between human and computer functioning lies not at the input or output level but in the processing level. A truly smart computer—one that is really like an intelligent human being—should function as does a human. Put another way, the memory and programs of a smart computer might, in some important ways, resemble the memories and cognitive processes of the human being.

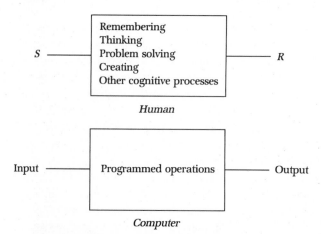

Figure 10-1.   A schematic parallel between human cognitive functioning and computer functioning. If S = input and R = output, does it follow that the computer's memory and programs are accurate representations of human cognitive processes?

Is it possible to design and program a computer that will perceive the environment as we do; that will store some information in memory but filter a great deal of unnecessary material; that will learn and use language as do humans; and that will solve problems of the kind that the human brain solves? And if a computer can be made to do some (or all) of these things, will it then be a "thinking machine" as we are? Will it use the same "cognitive" processes we do? Will it reveal things about human cognitive processing that we do not now know?

Feedback and Behavior

As mentioned in the previous section, human behavior can be considered to involve three separate components: *input, processing,* and *output.* The early behaviorists were concerned only with input and output—not with making the "black box," in which processing ostensibly occurs, any less mysterious. Later behaviorists attempted to open the box and to label its contents, which were seldom observed unless they were reduced to neurological units but were instead inferred on the basis of input and output. Nor were input and output the most fashionable expressions until just recently; formerly, the terms *stimulus* and *response* did quite well in indicating what psychologists were talking about. More recently, psychologists have again become concerned with the black box. One of the forms that this interest has taken is reflected in contemporary cognitive positions; a second form is that of cybernetics or feedback theory.

The central assumption of feedback theory is that the organism or machine is self-regulated. The term *machine* can accurately be employed here even though we are still considering human behavior, for it is largely correct that cybernetics deals with the machinelike aspects of human functioning. A self-regulated machine, when activated, continues to function until conditions in the environment dictate that it should cease or modify its functioning. The important point is that the machine *must itself sense those external conditions that regulate its performance.* A system that can be activated and then shuts itself off automatically after a period of time is not *self-regulated* but is simply *regulated.* It is obvious that if we are to be compared to a machine system, that system will have to be self-regulating.

One of the most frequently cited examples of a simple self-regulated system is a household furnace and thermostat. The input that affects the system's performance via the thermostat is the surrounding temperature. The system's output affects the temperature, thereby modifying the input to which it responds. Hence, its sensors are affected by the results of its own activities. Two types of feedback are involved in this system, as in any other feedback system. (Feedback is defined as the information that the system obtains about the effects of its own activities.) One type of information—*negative* feedback—indicates that the activity of the system should be discontinued because of modified environmental conditions. When the system receives information indicating that functioning should continue, it is receiving *positive* feedback. Referring to the illustration of the household furnace, the input that initiates the firing of the furnace is a temperature reading below what is indicated as desirable on the thermostat. As long as the furnace continues to function, it is receiving positive feedback. More accurately, as long as it *is* receiving positive feedback, it will continue to function. But when the actual temperature reaches the desired level, the system receives negative feedback and ceases to function.

PROCESSING

Input (and *output* insofar as it affects input) can be discussed in terms of feedback, and the effect of feedback on a self-regulated system presupposes some sort of processing device. In the case of the heating system, the processing device is the thermostat. As a processing device of the simplest kind, it merely evaluates input according to predetermined criteria and acts on the basis of whether or not a match occurs.

The processing unit in the human being is not so simple or obvious (which is one of the reasons psychologists continue to speculate about human learning and behavior). Nevertheless, it can be accepted as axiomatic that there is a processing system or, more likely, a series or arrangement of such systems. The possibility that the nature of these systems can be clarified by drawing analogies between known machine systems and humans justifies the study of cybernetics and artificial intelligence.

Mention should be made here of one of the central problems of attempted computer simulation of human processes. The problem is how to determine the extent to which human behavior is predictably affected by feedback and the extent to which output remains erratic. This question is central in that it hinges on the necessity of employing relatively straightforward, *deterministic* models of behavior in the one case and *stochastic* models in the other. In a deterministic model, the action (operation), which is selected from among a number of alternatives, can be predicted on the basis of the information and processes contained in the system. In a stochastic model the probability that a specific alternative will be selected can be computed within some error range, but there always remains a degree of probability that another alternative will be selected instead. Because of the minimal influence of random variables in most machine systems (such as computers), stochastic models are less frequent than deterministic ones.

The problems of arriving at a model that is an accurate reflection of human behavior have been discussed by Carl Hovland (1960). To choose between stochastic and deterministic systems is one such problem. Another problem is how to deal with the complexity of the processes we attempt to simulate. At best a machine can be made to duplicate the behavior of one *specific* individual in one very *clearly defined situation*. Hovland contends that the next step of simulating the behavior of individuals who vary from the prescribed pattern might prove to be extremely difficult. A second source of difficulty stems from the fact that simulation has typically been accomplished where terminal performance can be defined a priori in terms of a set sequence of procedures. Hovland's contention is that human perception and thinking often involve parallel processes that cannot easily be broken down into the steps required for simulation.

Computers and Problem Solving

It is important to note that direct comparisons between human functioning and a computer are not always made. Often the computer is used as nothing more than an analogy. The fact that we behave *as though* we were in some ways like a machine cannot be taken as evidence that we possess the same mechanisms and organization as does the machine. The analogy simply serves to clarify, and perhaps to simplify, the nature of human activity. At one level, there are the numerous analogues to the nervous system in digital computers. Miller, Galanter, and Pribram (1960) summarize some of them as follows:

> the open-or-shut relay was analogous to the all-or-none neuron, the electrical pulses in the computer were analogous to the neural impulses, the mercury delay lines were analogous to the reverberating circuits in the nervous system, the memory circuits of the computer were analogous to the association areas of the brain, and so on and on [p. 49].

At another level, the computer simply serves as an analogy to the processes that humans employ to solve problems. This type of analogy forms the basis for the remainder of this chapter.

A Theory of Human Problem Solving

Newell, Shaw, and Simon (1958; Newell, 1973; Newell & Simon, 1972) have advanced a proposal for a theory of human problem solving that serves as a classical example of one approach in artificial intelligence. Their theory is designed to be simulated on a computer and is intended to illustrate the solving of problems through "information processes." Central to the theory is the notion that the explanation of human behavior is inherent in a description of the "program" of information processes that lead to behavior. In this sense, they do not use a computer model as an analogy to human behavior; *the program is the analogy*.

The development of the theory has taken the form of a complex program for discovering proofs for theorems in symbolic logic. Specifically, the program is based on *Principia Mathematica* (Whitehead & Russell, 1925). It is called the *Logic Theorist* and has come to be referred to as LT in the literature. Its authors point out that it was not constructed to arrive at a model of human behavior but simply to develop a program that would prove theorems. Analogies to human problem solving were made later.

The LT program consisted essentially of storing the axioms of *Principia Mathematica* in the computer together with all of the processes necessary for discovering proofs. The first 52 theorems of the text were then presented to LT. It succeeded in proving 38 of the theorems, almost half of them in less than one minute. Longer proofs took more time. Variations of this initial experiment involved presenting the theorems in isolation so that previous proofs could not be employed in the solution of later problems. As a result, the LT often had to give up before finding a solution.

That the behavior of the Logic Theorist is like that of a human is supported by several observations. Newell, Shaw, and Simon (1958) indicate that LT did, in fact, solve problems—as human subjects sometimes do. They also found that the probability of finding a correct solution appeared to be very much a function of the order in which information is presented. This same fact is assumed to hold for humans as well. Other similarities between the Logic Theorist and human problem solving are subsumed under four headings:

Set.   In the same manner that human learning and problem solving are affected by set (see, for example, the chapters on Hebb or Bruner), so the LT responds to instructions. These instructions are ordinarily technical, indicating the order in which various operations are to be performed.

Insight.   The authors define insight in solving a problem as the process of grasping its "structure" rather than as a process of trial and error. Their contention is that the Logic Theorist's behavior is not simply blind trial but that alternatives are attempted in reasonable order and that discarding a possible solution determines the next process. In other words, the proof is not arrived at through the "brute force" of a high-speed computer trying innumerable approaches until the right one is found, but instead the process is based on the *logical* elimination and selection of alternatives.

Concepts.   Concepts are involved in the behavior of the LT in that all theorems or axioms having something significant in common can be considered to be concepts.

Hierarchies of Processes.   The authors reason that, in the same way that the LT makes use of sequences of operations by generating problems and subproblems and keeping a record of them, so humans organize their approach to problems in a somewhat hierarchial fashion.

In summary of the theory, it can be said that Newell, Shaw, and Simon attempted to simulate human problem-solving behavior by programming a computer so that it would, in the course of solving problems, acquire information necessary for the solution of other problems. Their description of human problem solving is implicit in the program itself. It is not immediately obvious that the model provides new information about human behavior. It appears somewhat more likely that the general approach may instead lead to a clarification of existing information. At least two problems remain unsolved. The first problem, what type of model to employ (deterministic or stochastic), has already been discussed. The second problem stems from the simple observation that computer memories are different from human memories. Computers *always* remember if they have the relevant information in storage and if they are programmed to access that information. Not only do they remember, but they remember exactly, without the distortion to which our memories are often subject. In addition, their application of rules and procedures is much more logical, although more rigid as well.

A second model illustrative of a cybernetic approach is provided by what is referred to as the TOTE theory of Miller, Galanter, and Pribram (1960), discussed in the following section.

TOTE

Last night I observed a man picking his teeth. He was a round, bulbous, obese man with huge jowls that waggled unpredictably as he talked or munched on his food. His great red beard was faintly streaked with the milk and meat of other meals; otherwise he gave the appearance of always taking great care with his person, as his small, well-manicured nails attested. After his meal last night, breathing heavily, he reached into his pocket and extracted from it his greatest luxury—a gold toothpick in a small case. Judging from the many dents and scars it bore, it had likely been owned by his father—and perhaps by *his* father before that. He grasped the toothpick delicately with the thumb and forefinger of his right hand and opened his mouth, revealing a row of superb, gold-capped uppers; his lowers remained concealed behind the heavy fringe of beard. With his mouth open he ran his tongue gently over the teeth, uncovering in the process a formidable piece of turkey that had become firmly lodged next to his left eyetooth. Unerringly he guided the toothpick toward the offending meat and flicked at it quickly and decisively. Again he ran his tongue over the teeth, and again it encountered the stubborn turkey. Once more he aimed the golden toothpick, and again he merely weakened its precarious hold between the teeth. He confirmed this fact yet another time with his tongue, proceeding immediately to launch another attack on the tender *viande*—and this time he was successful. Breathing sonorously, he replaced the toothpick in its case and returned it to his pocket. "Now that," I thought, "is a marvelous example of a TOTE sequence."

The TOTE unit is the basic concept in the account of human behavior presented by Miller, Galanter, and Pribram (1960). It is also the basic unit in any feedback system, containing as it does all of the elements of such a system. The

letters stand for the phrase *test—operate—test—exit*. The phrase summarizes
the sequence of functioning in a self-regulated machine. First, behavior is ini-
tiated by a test designed to reveal whether environmental conditions match the
test standard(s). For example, using the earlier illustration of a heating system,
the initial test might reveal that the temperature is below the indicator setting.
The next step is the *operation*, which is the activity designed to modify environmental conditions to the point that feedback will become negative. The furnace
ignites. The operation is followed by another test. For example, the thermostat
again senses whether the temperature is up to the indicated level after the
furnace has been fired. The *exit* phase is simply the termination of an operation
after negative feedback. Obviously, there may be a long series of tests, each
followed by operations, before feedback becomes negative. In other words,
behavior is of the TOTE variety only at the very simplest level. More often it is
of the TOTOTO . . . TOTE type. For example, it is possible to conceive of the
thermostat in a heating system as *continually* testing temperature. The model
can then be thought of as comprising an infinite number of overlapping tests
and operations.

The behavior of the fat man picking his teeth is only one of many possible
examples of TOTE units in human behavior. The operation involved using the
toothpick, the test was accomplished by means of a sensitive tongue, and exit
occurred only after three test-operate sequences had taken place. A diagrammatic representation of a TOTE unit is given in Figure 10-2.

For Miller and his colleagues the TOTE unit is expressly an admission that
human behavior is governed by feedback. At the same time, it provides a framework within which to advance some notions about the nature of operations and
of tests. Two concepts form the essential basis of these notions—*plans* and
images.

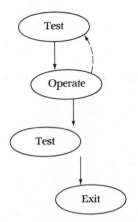

Figure 10-2.   The TOTE unit

PLANS

The authors begin with the assumption that behavior does not consist of sequences of conditioned responses. Nor do they believe that the reflex is the basic unit of behavior. On the contrary, their contention is that the reflex as an unlearned response arc is a much overrated, formerly useful concept that may well be more mythical than real. In place of the reflex, they substitute the feedback loop. They link behavior, one fundamental component of this loop, with the term *operation*; operation is in turn linked to the concept *plans*. At the simplest level, a plan is a blueprint for activity. It is a plan of attack or a strategy in much the same sense that a computer program is a strategy. More precisely, a plan is "any hierarchical process in the organism that can control the order in which a sequence of operations is to be performed" (Miller et al., 1960, p. 16). At the highest level, plans for human behavior are *molar*. That is, they govern large segments of behavior without specifying a priori what each specific operation will be in the sequence of activity. At the same time, however, they also include sequences at a more *molecular* level. It is in this sense that plans are *hierarchical*. The molar units of behavior can be viewed as composing *strategy*, whereas the molecular aspects correspond to *tactics*. The decision to write a report, for example, is one example of a plan. It specifies in a general sense that my activity in the future will include writing a report. This is the molar aspect of the plan. As the operations go into effect, however, more precise tactics emerge. The decisions to write the report in chapters, to use a blue ball-point pen with blue ink in it, to write on blue paper, and to have it typed by a secretary dressed in blue are all molecular aspects of the same plan.

In short, a plan is a pattern for behaving—a pattern that is hierarchical in the sense that it is composed of behaviors of greater or lesser specificity. A plan is executed when it serves as a guide for behavior.

According to the authors, plans need not involve *overt* behavior, since there are plans for gathering information or storing it, for solving problems, for making decisions, and for transforming information, as well as for engaging in overt behavior.

IMAGES

The second concept that plays a central role in the theoretical position advanced by Miller, Galanter, and Pribram is *image*, which the authors define as "all the accumulated organized knowledge that the organism has about itself and its world" (p. 17). This concept is not essentially different from Kurt Lewin's notion of life space (see Chapter 7).

When drawing an analogy between computer functioning and human behavior, the *image* can be seen as analogous to a fully programmed computer. It corresponds to the store of knowledge that the computer has, together with the operations possible for it. In the same sense, the *image* contains all information that an individual possesses, together with all the alternatives for activity. Quite simply, *images* contain plans.

THE ROLE OF IMAGES AND PLANS IN BEHAVIOR

The account of human behavior presented by Miller and his associates has less to do with the relationship of images to plans than might appear to be the case from reading parts of their book. In actuality, the TOTE model is a description of a plan-in-action-*sans*-image. It is the plan that contains both the organization of behavioral sequences *and* the test standards.* The role of the image is relatively minor, except for its involvement in decisions about plans or their modifications.

The contributions of this model to an explanation of behavior can best be summarized by reference to Figure 10-3 which illustrates behavior as consisting of TOTE units where there is a possibility at each test-point for exit if the feedback is negative, for repetition of the same operation, or for the execution of a new operation.

EVALUATION OF PLANS AND THE STRUCTURE OF BEHAVIOR

Although this model is a relatively clear and interesting example of cybernetics, its value in adding to human knowledge about learning or behavior has not been immediately apparent, partly because of ambiguity in the model.

1. The relationship between images and plans is not entirely clear. Images contain plans, since the totality of an individual's knowledge must include the awareness that it is possible to act on that knowledge. At the same time, how-

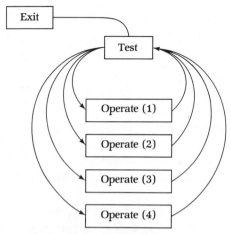

Figure 10-3.   Feedback loop

*Images also contain tests, which serve as sources of information for forming plans.

ever, plans are based on knowledge and can be modified on the basis of knowledge. In addition, the provisions for *testing* that are an integral part of plans are also based on knowledge or on values—both of which are assumed to be part of the image. Probably the clearest distinction between the two is provided by the declaration that plans govern behavior directly, whereas images do so through plans.

2. Some further confusion is caused by the authors' description of values as being a part of the image while intentions "refer to the uncompleted parts of a plan whose execution has already begun" (p. 61). The artificial separation of values and intentions presents a problem for understanding the relationship between the two. Are plans determined by values? All or in part? Are plans intentions only after they are begun or before as well? Are intentions then caused by values?

3. A third difficulty arises from the use of the plural of *image* without a definition of *image* that is sufficient to allow the reader to determine how images might be differentiated. Since images contain all of an individual's information, are they separable on the basis of differences among units of information? If so, how are they different from concepts?

4. A fourth problem stems from the explanation for the origin of plans. Plans are assumed to result from the modification of old plans, from habits learned largely through instruction or imitation, and from instincts. The authors do not, however, name or describe a single human instinct, but simply make a few favorable comments about the work of ethologists such as Lorenz and Tinbergen, whose work has been with animals.

5. Last, it remains somewhat uncertain whether the model accomplishes the purpose explicitly adopted for it by the authors—namely, bridging the gap between cognition and action. True, a plan can be considered a bridge between image (cognition) and a sequence of activity. This is, however, an extremely global representation of human behavior. According to the authors, to say that people behave is to say that they have a plan. Conversely, of course, to say that they are executing a plan is to say that they behave. Indeed, the authors contend that an individual will be as close to planlessness as is possible (short of death) only when asleep. But to say that an individual has plans is of no more value than to say that behavior occurs—unless this particular way of looking at behavior leads to new hypotheses and eventually to new discoveries.

A Final Section

There is, of course, a great deal more to computer simulation of cognitive processes than is immediately apparent in the preceding pages of this chapter. This section provides a hint of other things we might have considered had this book been destined to be much fatter than it is. In the main, it speaks of the capacities of the computer.

CHESS

We tend to think of computers as mechanical wizards endowed with a type of brute cognitive force that we humans do not even remotely approach. In the main, this estimate of the computer is quite incorrect—certainly, it is highly misleading. Take a straightforward game like chess, for example. The rules of the game are marvelously explicit. Each piece can move only in prescribed ways and only on a conventional, easily defined area. The object of the game is simple and clear: capture opponent's king. At any given point there are a limited number of possible moves, a finite number of possible countermoves, and so on. Surely, such a brute as we imagine the computer to be can be programmed to consider *and keep in memory* all possible moves, countermoves, responses to countermoves, and so on, together with the eventual implications of each of these moves. In other words, a well-programmed computer could at least play to a draw, but more likely beat, any chess master in the world.

Not so. The total number of moves possible in a chess game approximates 10^{120}—a figure so staggering that even the most sophisticated and largest computer imaginable could not represent all possible alternatives. The computer, like us, must rely on *heuristics* rather than *algorithms* for situations such as this. An algorithm is a problem-solving procedure whereby all alternatives are systematically considered. A heuristic approach to problem solving makes use of various strategies that eliminate and select from among alternatives without having to consider every one separately. A computer programmed to play chess might, for example, make use of heuristics (strategies) designed to "protect the king," "attack the queen," "control the center of the board," and so on.

So. How good a chess player is the computer? That, of course, depends on the programmer. The best chess programs presently available play competitively against experts (as rated by the United States Chess Federation) but are still not a match for a chess master.

ROBOTS

A robot is a machine that performs some function that might otherwise be performed by humans. Thus, there are thousands of robots in factories. They insert bolts, screw nuts, perform sequences of tests, align, weld, mold, paint, and so on. While these robots might be of tremendous practical value, they are of limited interest to artificial intelligence.

Of more interest to those who deal with artificial intelligence are robots whose behavior appears less mechanical and more purposive. Perhaps the best known of the early "purposive" robots is that developed in the early 1960s at Johns Hopkins University. This robot, nicknamed the "Hopkins Beast," was a small, elaborate arrangement of wheels, lenses, photocells, sonar equipment, and circuits. It moved up and down hallways in its home building at Johns Hopkins under its own (electric) power, keeping itself equidistant from the walls on either side, looking, always looking, for electrical outlets. And when it found

one of these, it would head directly for it, reach out its little "hand," and make contact—by inserting its "plug" in the outlet. There it would feed, resting all the while, before moving on, looking. Always looking. That was its *purpose*.

Again, although the Hopkins Beast and many of its cousins are intriguing creatures, they are of limited value in the search for artificial intelligence. The simulation of cognitive processes in the ultimate robot creation would be far more valuable.

The ultimate robot would, of course, be an android—a humanlike robot capable of most of the functions that we ordinarily associate only with humans, though perhaps not capable of emotional reaction. If DNA research leads to the creation of a living cell and to its eventual synthesis in a functional complex of such cells, the ultimate robot might result. It is likely that this bionic creature would cost far more than a mere $6 million.

OTHER COGNITIVE PROCESSES

Attempts to simulate human cognitive processes have not been limited to analogies between computer programs and human functioning or to attempts to develop computers with problem-solving capacities that resemble those of humans. In addition, a number of scientists have attempted to simulate memory, language, and perceptual functions with computers. In each of these areas one of the principal contributions of attempted computer simulations has been to point out how incredibly complex and sophisticated our own "computing equipment" really is. It is extremely difficult, for example, to program a computer to "perceive" a page of printed material in such a way that it can read the material much as we do. Most of us can "read" a letter or a word no matter who wrote it. We automatically make adjustments for variations in letter size, spacing, shape, and so on. In contrast, the computer may recognize a pattern and identify it correctly if the input presents a perfect match with what it has in memory or if it has been elaborately programmed to accept a variety of shapes, sizes, and positions. And, in the latter case, it is often likely to misidentify letters that resemble one another too closely (Raphael, 1976).

Even as our perceptual capabilities generally far exceed that of the computer, so too does our memory. By comparison, the computer's "search" for items in memory is cumbersome and generally requires some sort of system (search program), which might include a specific "address" for the item being "remembered." Our recall of a great many items appears to be almost automatic, as though all of our information is associated in such a way that we need not "search" as does a computer. Put another way, our "memories" appear to be filed according to related content rather than location; computer memories are almost always filed by location (not content) and require systematic search (Fahlman, 1979). Admittedly, however, the computer's memory is not subject to interference and modification to the extent that human memory appears to be.

Attempts to simulate language processes in the computer have also met with serious difficulties. The voice-recognition capacities of most computers are highly limited. Thus, in order to carry on a "conversation" with a computer it is often necessary to use a keyboard and type out one end of the conversation. The computer's response is typically to type out its end of the conversation and to display it on a video screen or in print. Recent advances in this area have been rather phenomenal, however. We may soon be conversing with computers in our homes, and perhaps using them as psychiatrists, medical doctors, or simply friends.

One Last Comment

There are at least two ways in which attempts to develop artificial intelligence might contribute substantially to the understanding of human cognitive processes. To begin with, it is possible that the machines, models, and programs that result will themselves provide information that we did not previously have. In other words, in much the same way as a smarter computer might conceivably prove a theorem that was hitherto unknown, so might a smarter computer reveal something previously unknown about human cognitive functioning.

Second, attempts to simulate human processes in machines may serve as a fundamentally important test of what we think we know about these processes. Not only is the programmer required to simplify and specify in infinite detail, but whenever the program fails to simulate as we think it should, perhaps we learn something about what it is like to be human. Or what it is like to be machine.

Summary of Chapter 10

This chapter has presented an introduction to artificial intelligence and cybernetics. It looked at how and why computers might be made smarter and at the application of machine models as analogies to human functioning. In addition, it presented two models of human functioning that are premised largely on computer models (that of Newell, Shaw, and Simon, on the one hand, and that of Miller, Galanter, and Pribram, on the other).

1. Artificial intelligence is a branch of computer science that tries to make computers smarter. The attempt generally involves trying to make the computer more human-like in its "cognitive" functioning.
2. Two myths characterize our reaction to computers: that they are merely computational machines and that they are nothing more than slaves to their programmers. Not so.
3. The question of whether machines can think cannot easily be answered. Nor is it clear that they *need* to be able to do so in order to simulate human activity.
4. Hardware is the physical components of computers; software is programs. Analogies between humans and computer hardware are remote; those between human cognitive functioning and some computer programs are sometimes more relevant.
5. Behavior can be thought of as comprising *input, processing,* and *output.* In a self-regulated machine, input (which is modified by output) affects processing. Our sensation of changes in the environment regulates our behavior.
6. Positive feedback maintains ongoing behavior, whereas negative feedback indicates that the operations (activities) in progress should be altered or should cease.
7. Newell, Shaw, and Simon developed a program, called the Logic Theorist (LT), which is capable of *discovering* proofs for theorems in symbolic logic. Its functioning simulates some aspects of human problem-solving behavior.
8. Miller, Galanter, and Pribram have also advanced a cybernetic model. It describes behavior as comprising *TOTE* units. A TOTE unit is essentially an operational feedback loop in a self-regulated machine.
9. *Plans* (blueprints for activity) and *images* (organized totalities of knowledge) are central concepts in the position advanced by Miller and his colleagues. The terms represent relatively global conceptualizations of behavior and are therefore characterized by some lack of clarity.
10. Computer programs employed in simulations of human cognitive processes are typically heuristic (making use of strategies and other systematic shortcuts) rather than algorithmic (using "brute force" to consider all possible alternatives systematically and exhaustively).
11. Computers programmed to play chess can be very good (if their programs are), but are not yet at the level of chess masters. Their approaches need to be heuristic rather than algorithmic, given the astronomical number of moves possible in a single game of chess.

12. Robots are computer machines capable of executing some human function(s). The ultimate robot might not be easily distinguished from an ordinary person. It still lives only in fiction.

13. Attempts to simulate human perceptual processes, memory functions, or language behavior have revealed the tremendous complexity of these processes. Here, as in other areas of artificial intelligence, computer simulation provides a useful test of what we know about human functioning.

PART 4

Factors Affecting Learning

Psychology Editor
Brooks/Cole Publishing Company
Monterey, California 93940

Dear Editor,

     My grandson, Guy Lefrancois, is in the process of writing a book that he tells me you might be foolish enough to publish the way it is. I'm not saying that it's not a good book. I wouldn't tell him so directly right now, but it's probably pretty darn good on the whole. It's just that there are a few parts I've seen that really need to be fixed up. Mostly they're parts that he writes late at night when he's all by himself up there in that office, when he hasn't eaten anything all day. He's pretty skinny. Always has been, even though his mother was a fine cook when he was growing up.

     Anyway, he sits up there writing late at night, and sometimes he goes a little ''wacko'' (that's his word), and writes foolish things that he doesn't mean about grandmothers and other things like pigs rampant and turkeys glissant or the other way around.

     Take for example in that one place early in the book where he starts to talk about somebody eating pea soup. Now we all know . . .

CHAPTER *11*

Memory and Attention

Introduction

As we have noted on a number of occasions, cognitive psychology is a psychology of metaphor. It seeks to understand the grand complexities of human cognitive functioning not so much by uncovering its precise mechanics and exposing its structures and functions but by inventing the most compelling and the most useful of metaphors to describe it. In the end, however, the value of the metaphor will be judged largely in terms of how well it reflects the facts. So it is that the search for the metaphor is premised on the results of scientific investigation. If we cannot trust our facts, how then can we trust our metaphors?

It bears repeating that the metaphors of which I speak in these pages are not the moving figures of speech of rich literature. They are nothing more than models—often simple models. And what they say is not "Attention is a damsel with flowers up her nose" or "Memory is an ancient elephant." No. The metaphors of cognitive psychology are prosaic metaphors. They say only that humans behave *as though* or *as if*—and they describe what it is that humans behave "as if."

The models we look at in this chapter are metaphors for memory and attention. They attempt to organize some of the many diverse findings of research into these areas.

Memory and attention are both central in a consideration of human learning. It is clear, for example, that learning and memory are virtually inseparable. Learning is a change in behavior that results from experience; memory is the effect of experience. Put another way, there will be no evidence of learning without something having happened in memory; by the same token, something happening in memory implies learning. Studying memory is, in effect, another way of studying learning.

The role of attention in the study of learning is no less important. Attention refers essentially to the processes involved in perceiving and processing only an extremely small number of all the stimuli that impinge on us continually. To a considerable extent, what is learned and remembered is a function of attention.

Attention

A great deal of contemporary learning-related research is concerned with the phenomenon of attention. Indeed, cognitive psychologists now appear to be more concerned with the investigation of such topics as attention and memory and with the formulation of models applicable specifically to these phenomena than with the elaboration of the more inclusive theories that have traditionally characterized learning psychology. While this focus may be partly due to the fact that it is considerably easier to deal with smaller aspects of human functioning than with the whole of human behavior, it is also in part a reflection of the relative significance of the topics.

Interestingly, the psychological investigation of attention dates back to the work of William James (1890), a contemporary of Ebbinghaus who pioneered studies of human memory. James's definition of attention as the holding in mind of one among a number of competing objects or "trains of thought" (p. 403) is still valid. Quite simply, organisms are attending to an event when they are aware of it. Equally interesting is the historical fact that the systematic investigation of attention was not undertaken until more than half a century after James's pronouncements.

RESEARCH

Among the first of a large number of related experiments were those conducted by Cherry (1953; Cherry & Taylor, 1954) in an attempt to answer two questions: how do we select that to which we attend, and how much of what is not attended to will be retained in memory? The questions make the assumption that selective attention is, in fact, an ever-present reality.

Cherry (1953) makes frequent reference to what is called the "cocktail-party problem" (Broadbent, 1952). This problem refers to the characteristic ability of a person at a party to attend to the speech of only one of the many people who are speaking. Ostensibly that person understands no other conversations, although they are clearly audible, but is nevertheless able to respond to certain auditory signals that are not part of the conversation then being attended to. For example, if your name is called while you are attending to another conversation, you may respond immediately; if someone else's name is called, you may give no indication whatsoever of having heard.

Cherry's investigations introduced the use of headphones through which different sounds could be fed to each of the subject's ears. Under these conditions subjects seem to be able to listen to either ear simply by *intending* to do so. A

The cocktail-party problem

second type of experiment, also designed by Cherry, attempted to duplicate some of the features of a cocktail party by taping two messages on the same sound track and playing the tape from one speaker. If the same person records both messages—which serves to remove additional cues such as intonation, accent, facial characteristics, direction of speaker, or lip movements—the subject has a great deal of difficulty in sorting out the messages. There is some evidence from studies employing this technique that the processes of attention are affected by syntactical structure and the related expectations of the listener.

A number of interesting findings have emerged from the first type of study (in which the subject has different messages fed to each ear). In order to discover the effect, if any, of the material that is not attended to, subjects are instructed to repeat everything that they hear on one side as quickly as they can. The exercise is referred to as "shadowing." Surprisingly, it is an extremely simple task. Employing this approach, Broadbent (1952) discovered that subjects do not remember what transpires in their other ear. Indeed, when the language was changed from English to German, the subject was quite unaware of it. Moray (1959) found that even if the same word were repeated as many as 35 times, the subject was not able to remember having heard it. If the subject's *name* were used, however, usually one presentation sufficed to alter attention.

The results of this last study indicate that there is probably some short-term retention of sensory events, even when they are not being attended to. Neisser (1967) labels this kind of retention *echoic memory*. A more general label is *sensory* memory. That it exists has been demonstrated in a number of studies (for example, Eriksen & Johnson, 1964; Pollack, 1959). Eriksen and Johnson attempted to measure the length of time that unattended signals are retained by sounding a signal tone when subjects were reading and then asking the subjects whether they had just heard something. The length of time between the stimulus and the question was varied. Results showed that with longer time lapses the likelihood of recalling the signal lessened.

THEORIES

Among the first theoretical explanations for attention and consequent retention was the "filter" model advanced by Broadbent (1958). This theory maintains essentially that some mechanism serves to *filter* out irrelevant stimuli entirely. It assumes that we select input on the basis of *physical* characteristics. Treisman (1964) proposed an alternative model suggesting that attention is not effected simply on the basis of physical attributes but involves the ongoing analysis of stimulus input from all sources and the rejection of that which is irrelevant. Neisser (1967) referred to this proposal as the *filter-amplitude* theory, and a variation of this theory has been advanced by Deutsch and Deutsch (1963).

The fundamental difference between Broadbent's *filter* theory and the Deutsch and Deutsch and Treisman models is that the former is based on the notion of sequential processing while the latter allow for simultaneous, or parallel, processing. To simplify, Broadbent's model says that we analyze inputs one after the other but that we cannot analyze a second input until we have finished with the first. The Deutsch and Deutsch and Treisman models suggest that we analyze several inputs at the same time and then select from among them.

Which model is correct? Both are wrong, according to Kahneman (1973). On occasion we are capable of dividing our attention among a number of competing inputs, an observation that contradicts Broadbent's model. At the same time, there is evidence that processing is affected by selection among competing stimuli (in other words, that the phenomena of attention manifest themselves prior to processing), an observation that contradicts the Deutsch and Deutsch and Treisman models.

So why should we even mention these somewhat difficult and apparently inappropriate metaphors? Because, in Kahneman's words, "filter theory provides a useful approximation to what people *usually* do" (p. 121). It is their predictions about what people *cannot* do that have not been entirely substantiated.

As a type of supplement to the filter models, Kahneman proposes a "capacity," or "effort," model. This model states, in effect, that attention span (amount of information that can be attended to at one time) and the extent to which it is possible to attend to more than one input simultaneously are a function of the amount of effort required. More precisely, stimulus inputs that are highly distinct are more easily attended to simultaneously, presumably because it requires less effort to attend to them than it might if the task involved attending to two very similar inputs. Similarly, when subjects are placed under time constraints, capacity to attend declines. In general, then, the greater the effort required to pay attention, the more difficult attending is. Capacity decreases with effort; hence the labels *capacity theory* or *effort theory*. It is capacity theory that explains why my mind often strays when I read difficult material (with increasing need for effort, capacity for attention diminishes). Filter theories cannot so easily explain this phenomenon.

In summary, human attention is such that we process only a very small number of all stimuli that impinge on us at any given time. A large number of the stimuli that are not attended to appear to be *filtered*. What this means is that they are not processed at all or, on occasion, that they are processed but discarded as irrelevant. Processing is often sequential although sometimes parallel. It appears that, when more effort is required to process, capacity to attend, particularly as it is revealed in the ability to divide attention between two channels, is reduced.

Attention and Memory

Early in this chapter the point was made that attention and memory are logically related in the sense that one is necessary for the other. By definition, nothing exists in memory (unless, perhaps, it is genetic) unless it has been learned; and to learn something requires that it be attended to.

There is another sense in which attention and memory are closely related. The models currently favored as metaphors for the processes underlying each of them overlap in a highly significant way. As Wickelgren (1981) notes, span of attention is really equivalent to short-term (active) memory. Put another way, what we can hold in memory for a few seconds is really the same as what we can attend to for those few seconds. This point is clarified in the following sections.

Human Memory

It is sometimes said that there are two kinds of memory—good and bad—and that most ordinary people possess the latter. When referring to "good" memory, people often mention professional entertainers who can perform the feat of faultlessly recalling the names of dozens of objects listed by an audience. On occasion reference is also made to the so-called *idiot savant*, the mentally limited human who possesses a remarkable but highly specific talent. For example, such a person could watch a freight train pass by and memorize all the serial numbers on the boxcars.

Another example of extraordinary memory is the well-documented case described in *The Mind of a Mnemonist* by A. R. Luria (1968). Luria describes in clinical detail the amazing memory of an otherwise ordinary man who had not been very successful as a musician or as a journalist, but who did become an accomplished mnemonist (a professional memorizer). The man could, within 35 to 40 seconds, memorize a table of 20 numbers. Given more time he could easily remember 50 numbers. The absolutely remarkable thing about his memory was not so much that he could memorize these tables so quickly but that he could remember them *without error* at any time in the future.

Our memories are generally not so phenomenal. Indeed, the rather unphenomenal nature of human memory is well illustrated by "memory curves," which have been plotted in connection with experiments on retention since the pioneering work of Ebbinghaus (1885/1964). A hypothetical summary of these curves is presented in Figure 11-1. The most striking item of information to be derived from it is that we tend to forget most of what we learn almost immediately after learning it. Obviously, however, some information is retained over long periods of time. This has led to the establishment of two general areas of investigation in this field—*short-term memory* and *long-term memory*. Before summarizing some of the research in these two areas, a number of expressions must be clarified.

SOME DEFINITIONS

Memory. The term *memory* ordinarily refers to the availability of information. Memory obviously presupposes learning. Equally obvious is the fact that remembering implies being able to retrieve information from storage. Considerable

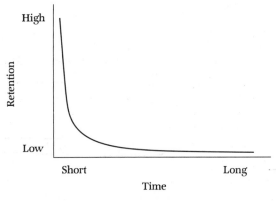

Figure 11-1. A memory curve

confusion arises when memory researchers attempt to determine whether failure to remember results from not learning, from having originally learned but
then losing whatever "trace" learning leaves, or from simply being unable to
retrieve information from storage. This last alternative is supported by the
observation that subjects under hypnosis can often recall events so remote that
they would probably not be remembered outside of a hypnotic state.

Retention. The term *retention* is often considered to be synonymous with
memory and is used in that manner in this text. However, some confusion does
result when the term *forgetting* is defined in terms of learning and retention.
Deese and Hulse (1967), for example, presented the following equation (p. 371):

Amount forgotten = amount learned − amount retained.

It is evident that what people ostensibly retain is not necessarily equal to what
they have in memory. If, in fact, failure to remember is at least in part a result
of failure to retrieve, the amount learned and maintained in memory may be
considerably greater than the amount recalled.

Forgetting. Whereas memory involves retention, *forgetting* is defined as loss
of information after it has been learned. Skinner, for example, defines forgetting
as the elimination of some behavior as a result of a slow decaying process due
to the passage of time. He does not specify exactly what the nature of the decay
is. Nor can he, or anyone else, clearly demonstrate that forgetting does take
place. Since subjects can sometimes be made to recall items they would otherwise be assumed to have forgotten through questioning, hypnosis, or both, it is
not unreasonable to argue that nothing is ever forgotten (as did Guthrie, 1935),
but that it simply is not recalled.

EARLY RESEARCH

It can be said that a person remembers if behavior or responses reflect previous learning. For the sake of simplicity, however, most early studies on memory dealt only with people's ability or inability to reproduce items of information that were presented to them. One of the possible contaminating factors in studies of this kind is the amount of previous *related* learning that a subject has. Thus, an attempt is usually made to present subjects with material that is entirely new to them. This material typically takes the form of *nonsense syllables*, which are novel arrangements of letters. The originator of this approach was Ebbinghaus (1885/1964), who devised over 600 of these syllables (for example, *lar, gur, kiv*). For a number of years, he sat faithfully at his desk at periodic intervals, memorizing lists of nonsense syllables and testing his retention of these. The plotted results of these experiments, with Ebbinghaus as the sole subject, provided the first memory curve (see Figure 11-1)—indicating that the bulk of what is forgotten is lost very rapidly. At the same time, however, what is retained for a longer period of time (say 10 days) is less likely to be forgotten even after a much longer passage of time (for example, 40 days).

Other early research on memory continued to make extensive use of nonsense syllables in a variety of experimental situations. Sometimes these syllables were paired with other syllables (or meaningful words were paired with other words), and subjects were required to learn what went with what (called paired-associate learning). At other times they were asked to learn sequences of stimuli (serial learning). And in a large number of studies, subjects learned two different sets of material and were then asked to recall one or the other in an attempt to determine whether recall would be interfered with. It often was. When earlier learning appeared to interfere with the recollection of subsequently learned material, *proactive interference* was said to have occurred (*proactive* meaning moving ahead in time); when subsequent learning seemed to reduce recall of material that had been learned earlier, *retroactive interference* was said to have taken place (see Tables 11-1 and 11-2).

TABLE 11-1. Testing retroactive interference

	Experimental group (A)	Control group (B)
	1. Learn X	
Time	2. Learn Y	Learn X
sequence	3. Recall X	Recall X

Note. Lower scores of group A relative to group B indicate the extent to which Y has interfered with X.

TABLE 11-2. Testing proactive interference

	Experimental group (A)	Control group (B)
Time sequence	1. Learn X 2. Learn Y 3. Recall Y	Learn Y Recall Y

Note. Lower scores of group A compared with group B indicate the extent to which X has interfered with Y.

A MODEL OF MEMORY

In addition to the hundreds of isolated findings that were revealed by these numerous studies of memory, one of their most important contributions to contemporary knowledge is in the form of a model of human memory. This model, referred to as a *dual-encoding* or *two-stage* model, makes a basic distinction between short-term and long-term memory (Atkinson & Shiffrin, 1968; Waugh & Norman, 1965). In some variations of the basic model, such as the one depicted in Figure 11-2, a third memory component relating to sensory

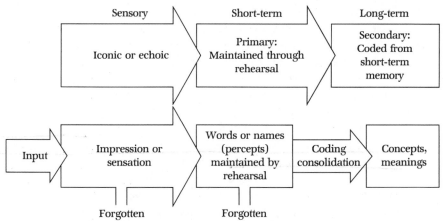

Figure 11-2. The three components of memory. The top row depicts three types of memory; the bottom row depicts the content of the memory process. Sensory information first enters sensory memory (iconic or echoic memory). From there it may go into short-term memory (also called primary memory), where it is available as a name or word, for example, as long as it is rehearsed. Some of the material in short-term memory may then be coded for long-term storage, where it might take the form of meanings and concepts. It is important to note that these three components of memory do not refer to three different locations in the brain or other parts of the nervous system, but refer to how we remember—or, more precisely, how we study memory.

memory is also introduced (also called a sensory *register*, since memory as such is really not involved at this level).

It is important to keep in mind that this model, like most of our contemporary psychological models, is a metaphor. As such, it probably says as much about the ways in which we choose to investigate and talk about memory as it does about memory itself. In brief, there is not a particular "box" or other structure in our brains that corresponds to short-term memory and another to long-term memory. These are not physical structures, but abstractions. The most important characteristics of these abstractions are considered next.

SENSORY MEMORY

Sperling (1963) employed a tachistoscope (an instrument that flashes stimuli for seconds or milliseconds) to project on a screen three rows of four letters each. Fractions of a second after the presentation, subjects heard one of three distinct tones, which signaled which of the three rows they were to try to recall. Since normal memory capacity for immediate recall of stimuli presented simultaneously is generally around seven items (plus or minus two, according to Miller, 1956), very few subjects would be expected to recall all 12 letters. Accordingly, subjects would be expected to recall the four letters in the prescribed row at least part of the time—or whenever it was included among the seven or so letters that they would recall on that occasion. At other times, they would be expected to recall few if any of the appropriate letters. What happened, however, is that, when subjects were asked to recall any single row immediately after presentation, accuracy of recall was well over 90%. In spite of this, if subjects were asked to recall all 12 letters, they remembered only an average of 4.5. And the longer the delay between the presentation of the letters and the request to recall, the less successful were the subjects.

What this experiment illustrates most clearly is that a limited number of stimuli remain accessible for a very brief period of time following presentation, even if they are not attended to. The same phenomenon was also illustrated by "cocktail-party" experiments, in which subjects recognized their names in conversations to which they were paying no attention. It is also illustrated by the classical double take. If I am busily engaged in something (*attending*, in psychological terminology) and you walk by me, I might look right at you for the barest second, walk two steps beyond, and suddenly recognize you. This type of sensory memory is very much like a visual echo—so much so, in fact, that Neisser (1976) terms the corresponding auditory sensory memory *echoic*.

Sensory memory is highly limited both in terms of the absolute amount of information it makes available and the amount of time during which this information is available. More simply, sensory memory is a term for the observation that stimulus effects continue to be available for processing for a very short period of time following presentation.

SHORT-TERM MEMORY (STM)

When we speak of sensory memory, we speak of a phenomenon that lasts milliseconds; when we speak of short-term memory, we speak of a phenomenon that lasts seconds or a very few minutes at most. Specifically, short-term memory generally refers to the recall of items that will no longer be recalled as soon as the individual stops rehearsing them. Short-term memory is what makes it possible for me to find a number in a telephone directory and dial it without having to look at the second digit after dialing the first, at the third after dialing the second, and so on. It is also what enables me to forget the number as soon as I have finished dialing—and what now makes it necessary for me to look it up one more time if I find that the number is busy or that I have misdialed. Long-term memory is what would be involved if I decided that I might need to use the number again and attempted to "memorize" it; it would also be what was involved if the symmetry and poetry of the number so moved me that I found myself remembering it through no conscious effort on my part.

The most frequently employed technique for studying short-term memory was developed by Peterson and Peterson (1959). The experimenter presents subjects with a single nonsense syllable (sometimes by spelling it) and later asks them to recall the syllable. Immediate recall comes close to, but seldom reaches, 100%. Errors are usually due to misperception of the original syllable. Greater delay between the presentation of the word and its recall usually results in considerably lower levels of retention, *depending on the subject's activities in the meantime*. If subjects are not asked to do anything and *know* that the experimenter will ask for recall, they will probably *rehearse* the syllable, thereby ensuring that it will be retained in memory. If, on the other hand, subjects are asked to engage in some unrelated activity, such as counting backwards in time to a metronome, *immediately* after the syllable has been presented, retention will be less. In this case the amount retained will be a function of time lapse. After sufficient time has passed, very few subjects recall the nonsense letters accurately. For example, in the Peterson and Peterson (1959) study, after 18 seconds subjects recalled less than 10% of the material correctly.

Numerous variations of short-term memory studies have been performed. While there is some disagreement on whether short-term memory really differs from long-term memory (see Melton, 1963; Wickelgren, 1981), a number of findings that are presumably of more relevance for short-term than for long-term memory can be gleaned from the research. (1) As has already been mentioned, time lapse reduces retention very considerably. By definition, this is not the case for long-term memory. (2) Repetition of the stimulus (the nonsense syllable) increases retention over time (Hellyer, 1962). (3) Forcing subjects to recall slowly (speak slowly) interferes with retention (Conrad & Hille, 1958). (4) Retention is frequently poorer as a function of the number of items that intervene between the presentation of a word and its recall (Norman, 1969).

⑤ If a series of words is presented, the first word in the list is often most easily recalled (Loess, 1964). ⑥ The complexity of the stimulus is directly related to the correctness with which it is recalled (Murdock, 1961).

In summary, short-term memory refers to the ongoing availability of a small number of items (again, seven plus or minus two)—an availability that begins to deteriorate within seconds and is usually completely gone within 20 seconds in the absence of rehearsal. It describes a phenomenon that makes it possible for us to "keep in mind" the words that we are currently reading (or writing) long enough to make sense of the whole or to keep in mind a set of directions or plans for dealing with ongoing cognitive processing.

Chunking. The limited capacity of short-term memory is greatly enhanced by a process labeled "chunking" (Miller, 1956). Following experiments that seemed to demonstrate that our immediate memory capacity for short-term memory is limited to seven plus or minus two items, Miller advanced a model depicting STM as consisting of approximately seven slots. When these are filled, there is no room for more until one or more of the slots are again emptied. In fact, however, the items that fill each of these slots need not be unitary (such as a digit or a letter, for example), but might be a single unit composed of a number of other items—a chunking of items, so to speak. Thus, the short-term memory "slots" might be filled with seven letters or with seven words. The seven words represent "chunks" of information that are far more economical and, not incidentally, far more meaningful than seven discrete and unrelated letters. In much the same way, our long-term memory makes extensive use of chunking. The analogy employed by Miller in explaining the process of chunking is that of a change purse that can only hold seven pieces of money. If you put seven pennies in the purse, it will be full. All it can hold is seven pennies. But you could have put seven quarters or seven dollars in the purse. Indeed, is there anything stopping you from putting in seven $1000 bills?

Forgetting in STM. Why short-term memory is limited to only a few items and why "forgetting" occurs remain unclear. Three "theories" have been advanced to explain STM forgetting. Decay theory holds that memory traces vanish quickly with the passage of time (in the absence of continued rehearsal). Displacement theory, essentially Miller's analogy, suggests that there are a limited number of slots to be filled in short-term memory and that incoming information displaces old information. Interference theory, highly similar to displacement theory, advances the notion that previous learning (rather than subsequent information) might somehow interfere with the long-term retention of items in short-term memory.

To these attempted explanations can be added Craik and Lockhart's (1972) supposition that the fundamental distinction between short- and long-term memory involves the level to which input is processed. In the sensory register, no processing occurs; at the STM level, a "shallow" level of processing occurs, consisting in part of the recognition of the stimulus through perceptual analysis. With deeper processing, semantic analysis (analysis of meaning) is undertaken. Thus, forgetting in short-term memory is presumed to result from inadequate processing (see Cermak and Craik, 1979).

None of these explanations is universally accepted. Indeed, most researchers do not appear to have been very concerned with forgetting in short-term memory, an observation that is not at all surprising in view of the fact that one of the functions of short-term memory is to hold information in memory for only as long as it is useful and then to discard it. That we are able to function in this matter is probably a remarkably good thing. Otherwise, we might well clutter our long-term memories with all manner of useless information and experience even more difficulty than we now do in retrieving pertinent information from it. The only time that loss of material from short-term memory stores becomes a significant problem is in those cases when disease, injury, or aging shorten STM to the point that ongoing functioning suffers. That, essentially, is what happens when we forget what we were going to say after we have started to say it. Or what we were going to write next . . .

LONG-TERM MEMORY (LTM)

One of the difficulties of doing research on long-term memory (LTM) is that it is difficult to control the experiences that occur between the presentation of a stimulus and its recall unless the time lapse is very short. Since long-term memory, by definition, involves long time lapses, it does not lend itself as readily to experimental investigation as does STM. However, the recent development of cognitive models and a renewed interest in information processing have been accompanied by a dramatic shift in memory research—a shift from the use of nonsense syllables and paired associates to the use of meaningful material; and a shift from the measurement of memory span and interference to an examination of models for long-term storage and retrieval.

General Characteristics.   Material that is remembered over long periods of time is said to be stored in long-term memory. Obviously, this material would include most of what we retain from our educational experiences, our complete working knowledge of language, and all of our stable information about the world.

Much that is retained in long-term memory is relatively stable in the sense that if it is remembered today or tomorrow, it is also likely to be remembered next week. Interestingly, however, what is eventually remembered is often quite different from what should initially have been perceived and learned. When Bartlett (1932) had his subjects read a rather unusual story from native American folklore and then had them repeat the story, a number of systematic changes occurred. It seemed that subjects biased their memories in terms of their own cultural expectations, a finding that is in close agreement with the observation that eyewitness testimony in our courts is remarkably unreliable. People tend to remember what they think they should have seen rather than what actually happened (Hunter, 1957; Loftus, 1979; Yarmey, 1979).

It seems, then, that remembering involves not only recall but also an attempt to restructure what was originally learned (see Chapter 7 for a Gestalt discussion of this restructuring). It is probably inevitable that the restructuring will be influenced by learning that has taken place in the intervening period. Piaget and Inhelder (1956) demonstrated, for example, that very young children who are asked to draw lines representing the level of water in tilted jars (see Figure 11-3) are typically unable to remember what the appearance of the water is, despite the fact that they have just been shown the tilted jar with water in it. Only after the children have learned that water remains horizontal do they *remember* correctly. Memory can therefore be assumed to interact with other learning.

One additional characteristic of long-term memory is that meaningful material is remembered far more easily and for longer periods of time than material that is less meaningful (Ausubel & Robinson, 1969). Also, events that are particularly striking, important, or otherwise emotionally involving are often remembered more clearly and for longer periods of time than more mundane happenings (Bower, 1981; Leight & Ellis, 1981).

Short-Term and Long-Term Memory Compared. Wickelgren (1981) describes short-term memory as *active memory*. This memory, he contends, is equivalent to the span of attention. It includes that which is "currently being thought of" (p. 46). Everything else in memory is presumably long term. The most important distinction between STM and LTM, then, is not that one lasts for a long time and one only for seconds, but rather that one is immediately conscious and the other is not. It follows, then, that STM is an active, ongoing process easily disrupted by external or internal events. In contrast, LTM is far more passive and far more resistant to disruption. Also, as we have seen, STM is far more limited in terms of capacity, being essentially synonymous with active attention or immediate consciousness. Finally, retrieval from STM is immediate and automatic, a fact that is hardly surprising, since what is being retrieved is immediately conscious or is not available. Retrieval from LTM may

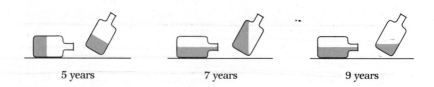

5 years   7 years   9 years

Figure 11-3.   Children's drawings of water lines

be far more hesitant, may require a search, and may result in a grand distortion of what was originally learned.

Two Kinds of LTM?   Tulving (1972) was among the first to suggest that it might be fruitful to make a distinction between what appear to be two distinct types of long-term memory. There is on the one hand all of our stable knowledge about the world; our abstract knowledge; knowledge that is necessary for our understanding and use of language; our knowledge of principles, laws, and facts; and our knowledge of strategies and heuristics. On the other hand, there is a body of knowledge consisting of our personal memories of events that have happened to us. These are not abstract memories (as are rules and principles, for example), but specific memories tied to a time and place. These are our autobiographical memories; they always involve us at a certain time and place.

My awareness that Darwin is associated with a version of the theory of evolution is an example of the first kind of memory; it is labeled *semantic.* The second type, labeled *episodic,* is illustrated by my recollection of where I spent Christmas at age 7.

Tulving argues that these two types of memories are sufficiently distinct that it is fruitful to consider them separately. He suggests, for example, that there might be some important differences in the way material is stored in each, as well as in how we remember and forget. For example, episodic memory seems to be far more susceptible to distortion and forgetting than does semantic memory. I have considerably more difficulty remembering what I ate for breakfast three days ago than in remembering a poem I learned in elementary school (or at least the first line). Also, episodic memory seems to be more affected by proactive and retroactive interference than does semantic memory. Tulving suggests that our failure to find much evidence of interference in everyday life may well be related to the fact that our more stable semantic memories are highly resistant to interference.

Not all researchers agree that a distinction between episodic and semantic memory is valid or useful. Wickelgren (1981) points out that it is virtually impossible to recall an *episode* without having abstracted it and related it to other items of information. Thus, the recollection of any isolated episode also implies that it has been abstracted and generalized, unless it was unique (unrelated to anything else in memory). Unique experiences are generally forgotten unless they are rehearsed and recalled sufficiently often that they are no longer unique. "There is no episodic memory," Wickelgren concludes, "only various degrees of generic memory" (p. 36).

Other researchers tend to agree with Wickelgren. In general, semantic and episodic memory appear to be so inextricably intertwined that they cannot easily be separated (Baddeley, 1976; Mcloskey & Santee, 1981). Nor does there appear to be any great advantage in considering episodic and semantic memory separately.

Models of LTM. The traditional model of long-term memory was first described by Koffka (1935). It portrays the mind as some sort of catalogue or motion picture camera (complete with audio, video, smell, touch, taste, and so on) that lays down a complete, sequential record of all our experiences and from which we retrieve, as best we can, those isolated bits of information that still remain accessible to us after the passage of time. This is a *nonassociationistic* model of memory.

Almost without exception, contemporary models of LTM are associationistic. By this is meant that they are premised on the fundamental notion that all items of information in our memories are associated in various ways (Baddeley, 1976; Estes, 1980; Wickelgren, 1981).

Thus, when we "search" our memory for some item of information, we do not haphazardly produce a long sequence of unrelated responses, but we narrow in on the missing item through a sometimes elaborate network of related information. "Where were you at Christmas when you were 7?" I have just asked myself. Should I now list places?

Chicago, New York, San Francisco, St. George's, Honolulu.

But the search for where I was at Christmas as a 7-year-old must be far more sophisticated and far more economical than would be the mere listing of places in the hope that I would recognize one as being the right one. It involves the rapid recollection of a host of related information, including the fact:

that I was living at home,
that my parents were living in the woods of northern Saskatchewan,
that we were surely snowed in, as we almost always were for four or five months,
that I had started school,
that my second sister was only 4 months old,
and so on . . .

My recollection is that I spent that Christmas on a set of new cross-country skis.

Our contemporary models of memory are, therefore, highly associationistic. And it is important to note that the associations with which they are concerned are not the associations of behaviorism. They do not result from the repeated pairings of events but relate, instead, to meaning or significance. And they frequently make use of such abstract concepts as *node, node models, semantic memory node models*, and *node encoding* (see, for example, Baddeley, 1976; Bower, 1977; Wickelgren, 1981).

A node is a metaphor, not a structure. It is a metaphor for everything and anything that we can represent in our "mind"—in other words, that we are capable of storing and remembering. Thus, a node represents an idea or a relationship. Its single criterial attribute is that it represents.

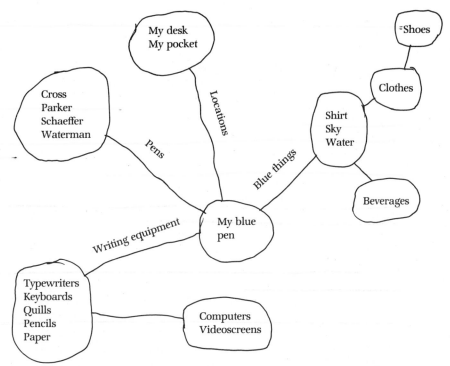

Figure 11-4. A model of a metaphor. Node theory suggests that we remember abstractions (meanings and associations rather than specifics). Thus, my blue pen is depicted as a "node" embedded in a complex web of abstractions (for example, "blue things"), each of which relates to many other nodes that are not shown here.

A node model of mental representation is simply a model that says that we represent knowledge in terms of *representations* (called nodes, although they could as easily have been called anything else) that are related in countless little-understood ways. Figure 11-4 presents one version of how a small part of a node model might be depicted.

The usefulness of a node model for human memory is that it emphasizes its associationistic features. In this sense, human memory is vastly different from the memories of digital computers (Estes, 1980) and cannot easily be simulated artificially. The onus on memory researchers is now to investigate the nature of the associations that compose our memories. Perhaps there might be clues in the physiology of the brain.

Physiology of Memory

It can be accepted as self-evident that learning results in some sort of change in the brain; otherwise it would logically be necessary that the brain *not be* involved in learning. Since learning and memory are two ways of looking at the

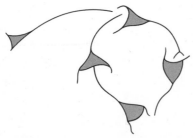

Figure 11-5.   A reverberatory loop: Short-term memory

phenomenon of acquiring information, it can also be accepted as axiomatic that *memory* involves some change in the brain. Unfortunately, the exact nature of that change is not known with any certainty. However, there is some fascinating and potentially useful evidence that sheds some light on the question.

First, it is likely that short-term memory does not involve the same mechanisms as long-term memory. The most widely accepted theory that presents different explanations for the two aspects of memory was advanced by Hebb (1949, 1966). His contention is that short-term memory involves nothing more than sustained electrochemical activity in a series of cortical neurons that reactivate one another in a loop (see Figure 11-5). When activity in the loop ceases, the item of information is lost. Long-term memory, in contrast, involves more-permanent changes of *facilitation of conduction among neurons* (see Chapter 6).

This dual theory represents the two alternative explanations that have received the greatest amount of attention. The first alternative is that learning involves some continuing electrochemical activity; the other is that structural changes in neural cells account for retention. What happens to the brain as a person learns? Two related answers are given here: the first involves rats, and the second planaria. No directly comparable experiments have been undertaken with humans.

Rats. The first studies, performed by Krech and his associates (1960, 1962, 1966), were designed primarily to investigate the effects of learning on the brain of the lowly white rat. Interestingly, the rat brain is sufficiently similar to the human brain to make its study reasonable. In rats and humans neural transmission is accomplished through similar processes which include both chemical and electrical activity. Among the chemicals involved is an acid with the forbidding label *acetylcholine* and its enzyme with the even more awesome name of *acetylcholinesterase*. Prior to transmission, there is a rapid buildup of acetylcholine. When it reaches a sufficient level, transmission occurs. The function of the acetylcholinesterase is to break down the cholinesterase in order to prevent repeated firing.

In the first of a series of replicated experiments, Krech took pairs of 25-day-old rats and assigned one randomly to what was termed the Environmental

Complexity and Training Group (ECT) and the other to the Isolated Control Group (IC). The first group (ECT) consisted of rats that were housed in large, airy, well-lit cages equipped with the latest in rat furnishing: poles to gnaw on, toys to play with, ladders to climb, and tunnel mazes to explore. The rats could observe from their cages all of the activity in the lab. In addition, they were taken out of the cage for 30 minutes each day and allowed to explore a variety of mazes. Not only were the barriers in the mazes moved frequently but the furnishings of the cage were also changed daily. Rats in the IC group, on the other hand, were placed in isolation in small cages, and the cages were lined so that the occupants could not see other rats or witness any activity around them. Nor were they ever allowed to leave their cages.

At the age of 105 days, all rats, ECT and IC, were humanely executed and delivered to a laboratory for dissection and analysis. Three of the findings of the study are particularly striking and significant.

1. The ECT rats showed a 2% increase in acetylcholinesterase when compared with the IC rats. This finding has been replicated many times, suggesting that learning does result in changes in brain chemistry. It cannot be inferred from the evidence how this chemical affects memory, but it would appear reasonable to assume that it *is* in some way involved.

2. The actual weight of the cortex of an average ECT rat was 4% greater than that of an IC rat. This increase in weight could not be accounted for simply in terms of the increase in acetylcholinesterase. (Interestingly, these effects were most pronounced in the visual areas of the cortex.)

3. There was an increase in the size of the ECT cortex that could be accounted for by an increase in the number of *glial* cells. *Glial* cells serve as a blood/brain barrier and perhaps as a source of nutriment. It is suspected that they may also be involved in learning.

The most obvious conclusion to be derived from the Krech studies is that learning *does* change the brain; the nature of these changes may serve as a clue to the physiology of memory. A second inference, which is of considerable significance for human learning, is that, if an enriched environment can produce measurable changes in the brain of a rat in 80 days, there is no reason to believe that humans cannot similarly be affected. Hunt (1961), among others, has stressed the importance of varied and rich sensory environments for young children—a point of view supported by the experiences of *Rattus norvegicus*.

Planaria.   The notion that memory may involve chemical changes in a neuron has led to the hypothesis that RNA may well be the agent of memory. RNA is present in neurons in sufficiently large quantity, and it is constructed in such a way that it can assume any one of billions of combinations. It is conceivable that any given combination could represent one unit in memory. This possibility is further corroborated by the fact that the concentration of RNA increases as humans age but decreases in old age, in the same manner as learning ability increases and decreases. Additional support for the hypothesis derives from the controversial planaria (flatworm) studies. McConnell (1962) and his associates began these experiments by training planaria to turn or curl up in response to a light. Trained planaria were then minced and fed to other planaria. "Untrained" planaria were prepared in the same fashion and served to a second group of eaters. Amazingly, the planaria that were fed the "trained" food out-performed those that had eaten only untrained planaria. Later refinements (McConnell, 1976; Zelman, Kabot, Jacobson, & McConnell, 1963) have ostensibly demonstrated that simply extracting RNA from trained planaria and inject-ing it into naive subjects has the same effect.

However, not all researchers have been able to duplicate these results (Bennett & Calvin, 1964). It appears that, like an inoculation, a meal of planaria—how-ever well trained they might be—does not always "take."

RNA memory-transfer experiments have also been successfully performed with rats (Babich, Jacobson, Bubash, & Jacobson, 1965; Jacobson, Babich, Bubash, & Jacobson, 1965). The next step is obviously to revert to the practice of some African Bushmen. An injection of RNA from a human genius is probably no more unappealing than is the heart of an antelope.

In a number of more recent studies on the chemistry of memory, the brains of rats that had been trained were subsequently subjected to detailed chemical analyses, often using an electron microscope. The results of many of these studies are in general agreement with the notion that RNA as well as a number of other substances, the most important of which appear to be proteins, undergo changes as a function of learning (Glassman, Machlus, & Wilson, 1973; Hyden, 1973; Hyden & Lange, 1972).

Although the precise physiology of memory remains undiscovered, these find-ings are highly suggestive and potentially very significant. It is conceivable, for example, that memory and learning might be improved through nutritional supplements that affect brain chemistry. It is also likely that, as we learn more about the physiology of memory, our metaphors will become more appropriate. In time we might even move from the metaphor to a literal description.

Forgetting

Why do we forget? What determines what we forget? There are a number of answers, described briefly here in the form of four theories.

FADING THEORY

It is possible that we forget some things simply as a function of the passage of time. Clearly, however, those items that are occasionally remembered will be far more resistant to the presumed ravages of time than items that have never been recalled. Every recollection can be viewed as a rehearsal and as an oppor-tunity for relearning.

That we actually *lose* from memory those items that we once knew but are no longer able to remember has never been clearly established. The possibility remains that we never forget anything but are simply unable to retrieve certain things.

DISTORTION THEORY

Evidence reviewed earlier shows clearly that a great deal of what we retrieve from long-term memory is distorted. Ausubel (1963) suggests that, as we incorporate new material into existing cognitive structure, we change it. New material becomes more abstract, is shed of irrelevant details, and is later remembered in its abstracted form. Thus, we are forced to *generate* new details (rather than remembering them). A series of intriguing studies suggests that long-term memory is, in fact, largely a process of *generating* rather than of "recollecting" (Bransford & Franks, 1971; Johnson, Bransford, & Solomon, 1973). In the latter study, subjects were presented with a number of sentences, among which were the following: "John was trying to fix the birdhouse. He was pounding the nail when his father came out to watch him and to help him do the work."

Subjects were later presented with a list of sentences from which they were to select those that they had already seen. In addition to the passage quoted above, subjects were also shown the following sentence: "John was using the hammer to fix the birdhouse when his father came out to watch and to help him do the work."

Amazingly, subjects agreed overwhelmingly that they had seen the second sentence but not the first two. Notice that "hammer" is not mentioned in the first passage but is in the second. It is logical to assume that a hammer would be used to pound a nail in order to fix a birdhouse.

The results of this study provide strong support for the notion that we do not remember specifics so much as meanings and ideas (node theory of memory). We store abstractions and regenerate specific instances on the basis of these abstractions. Thus it is that our recollections are often distorted.

REPRESSION THEORY

A popular theory of forgetting is premised on Freud's notion that individuals sometimes unconsciously forget (repress) experiences that are anxiety-provoking or traumatic. This type of forgetting cannot easily be demonstrated experimentally but is observed occasionally in clinical situations. Since it applies only to emotion-related experiences, it is of limited value as a general explanation of forgetting.

INTERFERENCE THEORY

Perhaps the most widely accepted theory of forgetting until recently has been that based on the notion that new learning can interfere with the recall of old learning (retroactive interference) or that old learning can interfere with the recall of new learning (proactive interference). As mentioned earlier, while interference has been a consistent phenomenon in studies of short-term memory (often employing nonsense syllables), it appears to be far less descriptive of what actually happens in the course of our daily life. Although we might occasionally become confused as a result of competition among items we are attempting to remember, indications are that we can continue to learn all manner of things without running the risk of becoming progressively more subject to the effects of interference. If, in fact, interference operated in life as it does in the short-term memory laboratory, most of us would have been well advised to stop learning new material long ago and to have spent most of our time rehearsing old material to guard against the pernicious effects of retroactive and proactive interference.

DO WE FORGET?

On several occasions in this chapter the possibility that we do not forget has been raised. It has been suggested, for example, that the fact that we cannot remember something is not very good evidence that it is completely gone from memory. Perhaps the "memory" is still there, but we simply do not have access to it.

Tulving (1974; Tulving & Madigan, 1970) recognized this possibility in his description of two kinds of forgetting. Presumably, there is a kind of forgetting that simply involves an inability to recall. This type of forgetting is assumed to be related to the unavailability of appropriate *cues* for recall, and it is termed *cue-dependent*. A second type of forgetting involves actual changes in the memory-trace itself and is therefore labeled *trace-dependent*. The four theories described above (fading, interference, distortion, and repression) all relate primarily to trace-dependent forgetting. We know very little about cues and how they might be managed to enhance learning and remembering. It is likely that additional knowledge would have some important implications for the teaching/learning process, as well as for our daily life.

Remembering

Is rehearsal the only way in which we can increase the probability of remembering something? Research suggests that it is not, although it is probably among the most effective (Corbett, 1977; Nelson, 1977). In addition, spacing of material appears to be more effective than attempting to learn everything at once. Thus, four 1-hour periods of study divided by three rest periods is generally more effective (in terms of later retention) than a single 4-hour study period.

In addition to repetition and spacing, there are a number of study techniques that significantly improve retention. Most of these emphasize strategies for organizing material (in other words, for abstracting meaning from it) and are in close agreement with our metaphor of long-term representation being comparable to "nodes," which are essentially ideas and relationships (Masson & McDaniel, 1981).

More-specific memory aids are termed *mnemonics*. These include *acronyms* (letter cues) such as NATO, U.N. or Roy G. Biv (the colors of the visible spectrum in order). They also include *acrostics*, which are sentences or expressions in which the first letter of each word stands for something else. For example, the acrostic "Men very easily make jugs serve useful nocturnal purposes" recalls the planets in order from the sun (*Mercury, Venus, Earth, Mars* . . .).

The more complex mnemonics typically make use of visual imagery. For some reason, visual images are far more memorable than are most written or spoken words (Paivio, 1980). When subjects were exposed to 10,000 pictures (very briefly), and then shown some of these same pictures again—but paired this time with other pictures that had not been included in the first presentation—they were able to recognize more than 90 percent of them (Standing, 1973). Similarly, when Babrick, Babrick, and Wittlinger (1975) presented subjects with photographs of their former classmates (taken from yearbooks), recognition was approximately 90 percent accurate after 2 months and had not declined appreciably 15 years later. There is little doubt that our capabilities of visual recognition are remarkable.

Mnemonics that are based on visual imagery generally suggest specific ways in which mental images can be linked visually with other easy-to-remember images. Higbee (1977) and Cermak (1976) described a number of these mnemonic techniques in detail. In the *loci* method, for example, subjects are asked to form a strong visual image of the item to be remembered and to place it in some familiar location such as a room in a house. The second item is then visualized and placed in another room; the third might be placed in a hallway; and so on. Recalling the items later simply requires that the subject take a mental "walk" through the rooms of the house and attempt to visualize each of the items that have been placed there. Try it with a grocery list. It works.

Summary of Chapter 11

This chapter has presented an account of attention and memory, processes that are inextricably linked with learning. Current models in each of these areas are primarily cognitive.

1. Cognitive psychology is a psychology of metaphor. It presents models that say "People behave *as if* . . . "
2. Attention was defined by James as the "holding in mind" of one among a number of competing items. More recent definitions, not essentially different, make no clear distinction between immediate awareness, what Wickelgren calls *active memory*, and attention.

3. "Cocktail-party" experiments suggest that there is probably some very short-term retention of sensory events that are not being attended to but that, in the main, irrelevant stimulation is filtered out.

4. It appears that although we generally attend to only one stimulus at a time, we are also capable of processing two stimuli simultaneously—of dividing our attention, so to speak. Parallel processing becomes progressively more unlikely when greater effort is required.

5. Memory is ordinarily defined as the availability of information (recall or retrievability). There is some evidence that it may be either short-term or long-term.

6. Ebbinghaus pioneered the early *scientific* investigation of memory. Contemporary psychologists have inherited from him nonsense syllables (which are meaningless) and memory curves (which are unimpressive).

7. One model of memory describes a two-stage (dual-encoding) process consisting of short-term and long-term memory. A third stage, sometimes termed the sensory register, is closely related to attention.

8. Sensory memory describes the immediate effect of stimulation prior to processing. It is highly limited in terms of the amount of information it can hold and the amount of time during which this information remains available.

9. Short-term memory apparently lasts only seconds (seldom more than 20), unless there is continued rehearsal (in which case the information may be coded into long-term memory). It refers essentially to the ongoing availability of a small number of items (seven plus or minus two) and is termed *active* memory by Wickelgren to emphasize its similarity to immediate attention or consciousness.

10. Long-term memory is assumed to involve some permanent structural changes in the brain. Short-term recall, in contrast, may involve no more than temporary electrical activity. This is essentially Hebb's theory.

11. Long-term memory involves more than simple recall of information that was learned earlier *as perceived at that time*. It can easily be shown that remembered material undergoes changes over time.

12. A comparison of STM and LTM reveals that short-term memory is an active, continuing process; that it is easily disrupted by ongoing activities; and that it is highly limited in terms of capacity. In contrast, long-term memory refers to a more passive process, not easily disrupted by ongoing activities and essentially unlimited in capacity. Retrieval from STM is immediate and automatic or does not occur; retrieval from LTM may be considerably slower and more groping.

13. Semantic memory includes general, stable, abstract facts and principles (our knowledge of language, of the world, and so on); episodic memory refers to personal knowledge, temporal in nature and tied to specific

events that have happened to us. A number of researchers consider this distinction to be unreal or unnecessary.

14. Traditional models of memory were nonassociationistic (Koffka's notion of a continuous record like a videotape); current models emphasize associations among items in memory and frequently make use of "node models," a node being simply whatever it is that represents an idea.

15. Studies involving rats have demonstrated that learning causes some measurable physiological changes in the cortex. Among these are an increase in the concentration of acetylcholinesterase, an increase in glial cells, and an increase in brain weight.

16. There is some interesting (and contested) evidence that the agent of memory is ribonucleic acid (RNA) and that memory can be transferred by transferring RNA from one organism to another. One way to effect this transfer is to have one individual eat another, as in "dog eat dog."

17. There is evidence that some forgetting might result from an ill-explained "fading" process. In addition, some probably results from distortion, which might occur partly because what is remembered tends to be relatively abstract and because we generate rather than reconstruct when we try to remember. Other explanations for forgetting include repression theory, which is most appropriate for experiences laden with negative emotion, and interference theory, which no longer seems to have much basis in reality.

18. It is possible that much of our forgetting does not involve the actual loss of something in memory (termed *trace-dependent* forgetting), but that it might simply involve inability to retrieve from memory (termed *cue-dependent* forgetting).

19. Learning and remembering can often be improved through rehearsal, spacing, techniques designed to organize and to uncover meaning, and specific mnemonics, the most powerful of which make extensive use of < visual imagery.

Dear Mrs. Francoeur:

I want to thank you for taking the time to write to us about Guy's progress on his book. We know that, as you put it, it's pretty good on the whole, and we are very eager to get it. We've been eager for a very long time, in fact. He's not always the fastest writer.

It was very kind of you to take the trouble to point out to us some of the passages in the book that need to be cleaned up. We always find quite a few places like that in all of his writing. As you probably know, many of these passages cannot be cleaned up but have to be thrown out. I assure you we'll do it whenever we have to.

We've often wondered why it is that he seems to go "wacko," as you so nicely put it, every once in a while. Your theory that he doesn't eat enough may well be right, although we find it hard to believe here that he works late at night. You might be right, but we have little evidence of it.

I want to thank you again, Mrs. Francoeur, and take this opportunity to inform you that we always alert our copy editors to be on the lookout for craziness in his manuscripts. Your letter will make us doubly careful.

Yours sincerely,
C. Deborah Laughton
Psychology Editor

CHAPTER *12*

Motivation

Motivation

One of the most fundamental questions that can be asked about human behavior is "why"? Why do we behave? Why do we behave in precisely the manner in which we behave? Why does our behavior stop?

These are questions of motivation. A motive is a cause of behavior—a reason for doing or not doing certain things. It is motivation that initiates behavior, directs it, and is also responsible for its cessation. Thus, hunger is a motive as surely as is sex. Both move us to do all manner of things, not all of which appear to be directly related to eating or reproducing.

Answers to questions of motivation are fundamental to a complete understanding of human learning. On the surface, some of the answers (hunger and sex for example) appear to be simple; others seem to be far more complex. In fact, the simplest and most straightforward of explanations for behavior often seem to explain the least, and the search for more complete understanding continues here as it does elsewhere in psychology. Nor should we be misled into believing that those motives that appear to be simple actually are. Most are not.

This chapter presents a number of different accounts of human motivation. Many of these have been at least implicit in some of the learning theories discussed earlier; some have been explicit.

Instincts, Imprinting, and Reflexes

INSTINCTS

Among the earliest explanations of human behavior were the instinct theories of McDougall (1908) and Bernard (1924). Employing rather loose definitions of instinct, they attempted to explain all human behavior as resulting from unlearned tendencies to react in given ways. Lists of human instincts typically include such qualities as gregariousness, pugnacity, flight, self-assertion, self-abasement, and hunger. Their explanatory and predictive value is severely limited by the fact that typical definitions are circular. For example, the instinct for survival is manifested in the fact that humans avoid dangerous situations. How is it known that there is an instinct for survival? Because people avoid dangerous situations. Why do they avoid dangerous situations? Because they have an instinct for survival. Ad infinitum.

More recently, instincts have been viewed as limited to complex, species-specific, unlearned, and relatively unmodifiable behavior patterns that are particularly evident in lower animal forms (Thorpe, 1963)—such behaviors as nest building, migration, hibernation, and mating rituals. When instincts are defined in this manner, it is not at all clear that we possess them. It may be that we do but that the instincts have become so confounded by culture that they are no longer distinguishable from learned behavior.

IMPRINTING

Imprinting, closely related to *instinct,* is a term that has recently been coined by ethologists (people who are concerned primarily with investigating the behavior of lower animal forms). Tinbergen (1951) and Lorenz (1952) describe imprinting as unlearned behavior that is specific to a species and does not appear until an animal has been exposed to the appropriate stimulus (called a releaser), providing that exposure occurs at the right period in the animal's life (the critical period). The classic example of imprinting is that of the "following" behavior of ducks, chickens, or geese (Hess, 1958). It appears that the young of these birds typically follow the first moving object they see. Fortunately, that object is usually their mother—but it need not be. Lorenz (1952) reports the case of a greyleg gosling that imprinted on him and followed him around much as it might have followed its mother. As the time for mating approached, much to Lorenz's embarrassment, this goose insisted on foisting its affections on him.

While imprinting behavior is of relevance for animals, it is not clearly evident in human behavior. Although attempts have been made to extrapolate to humans conclusions derived from studies of critical periods in imprinting, no such periods have unequivocally been identified. There is some evidence, however, that there may be times during which some types of learning are accomplished more easily than others. The work of Spitz and Wolf (1946) and of Bowlby (1951) with children in orphanages has been interpreted to indicate that the first 6 months of a child's life are crucial for the formation of maternal attachment. That this observation, if valid, is analogous to that of critical periods in animal imprinting is not at all certain.

REFLEXES

Some human behavior is explainable in terms of reflexes. A reflex is a simple unlearned act that occurs in response to a specific stimulus. It is not as complex as an instinct or an imprinted behavior, nor does it need to be established through the presentation of a releaser during a critical period. Children are born with a limited number of reflexes, which with some exceptions are usually retained into maturity. These include blinking in response to air blown on the eye, the knee-jerk reflex, withdrawal from pain, and startle reactions. In addition, at least three human reflexes are present at birth but disappear shortly thereafter—the Babinsky reflex (curling of the toes when the sole is tickled), the grasping reflex, and the sucking reflex.

Another type of reflexive behavior, the orienting reflex (OR), has been identified by some Russian psychologists, beginning with Pavlov (Razran, 1961). In general an orienting reaction is the first response made by an organism to any stimulus to which it reacts. It appears to take the form of increased sensitivity and awareness and may be reflected in such physiological changes as increased pupil size, alterations in heart and respiration rate, and changes in cortical activity. In animals such as dogs, orienting reflexes have observable components. When a dog is presented with a novel stimulus, it is likely to move its ears as well as to assume an "attentive" posture. Because of these aspects of the orienting reflex it is often referred to as the "what-is-it?" reaction.

Recall that Pavlov and Watson made extensive use of reflexes in their accounts of human learning and that they were at least partly successful in explaining some simple types of learning, including some emotional responses. In spite of this, it is generally true that to say that some human behaviors are reflexive is to explain only those specific behaviors that are, in fact, reflexive. As an explanatory concept, the notion of reflexes is obviously of limited generality. Attempts to explain more complex human behavior usually take some other form—for example, psychological hedonism, which is borrowed from philosophy and remains less psychological than philosophical.

Psychological Hedonism

There is considerable intuitive evidence that human behavior often tends toward that which is pleasant and seeks to avoid that which is unpleasant. This notion is referred to as psychological hedonism. It was borrowed from the work of Jeremy Bentham in an effort to arrive at some *general* explanation for most human behavior. Unfortunately, despite the fact that the idea is intuitively appealing—particularly since we do seem to try to avoid pain and to obtain pleasure—it remains relatively valueless when taken in isolation. The central problem with the notion is that it cannot be employed to predict or even to explain behavior unless pain and pleasure can clearly be defined beforehand. Such definition is not usually easy. While it might appear wise to say that a man braves the Arctic cold in an uninsulated cabin because he derives pleasure from it, it is quite another matter to predict beforehand that it will be this specific man who will retire to that cabin. The difficulty is that pain and pleasure are subjective emotional reactions. While it might be true that we are hedonistic, motivational theory can profit from this bit of knowledge only if pain and pleasure can be described more objectively.

Need/Drive Theories

Numerous theories have been advanced to account for behavior in terms of needs and drives. These theories can be related directly to the hedonistic position in that they are attempts to specify what the nature of pain and pleasure is.

A *need* is usually defined in terms of a deficit or lack that gives rise to a desire for satisfaction. Need can be viewed as a state of the organism that bears the seeds of its own destruction. For example, to be hungry is to be in a state of need; this need leads to eating; the need then disappears. A *drive* is the tendency toward activity that is aroused by a need. Need for food gives rise to a hunger drive.

The relationship of need/drive theories to hedonism is implicit in the assumption that to be in a state of need is unpleasant, whereas to satisfy a need is pleasant. Hence, listing needs is one way of defining the nature of pain and pleasure.

It is commonly accepted that we have a number of *physical needs*, most of which are necessary for survival. Mouly (1968) listed the following: food, water, sleep and rest, activity, and sex. These are referred to as physiological, or organic, needs. The assumption is that they are *basic needs*, which are manifested in the form of actual tissue changes.

Although there is relatively little disagreement about what the physiological needs are, there is considerably less agreement about *psychological* needs. The essential difference between physical and psychological needs is that the physical need—and its satisfaction—results in tissue changes. Psychological needs, on the other hand, are not necessarily manifested in bodily changes but pertain more to cognitive or intellectual aspects of human functioning. In addition, physiological needs can be completely satisfied, whereas psychological needs are relatively insatiable. We can eat until we are not at all hungry, but we seldom receive affection until we desire absolutely no more.

Mouly (1968) listed six psychological needs also—the need for affection, belonging, achievement, independence, social recognition, and self-esteem. Numerous other lists of needs have also been presented (for example, Maslow, 1970; Murray, 1938; Raths & Burrell, 1963). Maslow's list contains five need systems: physiological needs, safety needs, love and belongingness needs, self-esteem needs, and need for self-actualization (see Figure 12-1). These are arranged in hierarchical order from what are presumed to be the lowest-level needs (physiological needs like hunger, thirst, and so on) to the highest-level system (need for self-actualization—that is, the need to fulfill inherent potential). The central assumption in this arrangement is that higher-level needs will not be attended to until lower-level needs have been relatively well satisfied. This assumption may have implications for explaining differences between cultures for which hunger is a daily fact of life and the contemporary affluent North American society. It is obvious that the former will be more concerned with survival in a physical sense; perhaps the affluent cultures are, or should be, more concerned with high-level needs.

The relevance of need/drive positions for behavioristic learning theories should be obvious. Indeed, a great majority of the experiments on which operant theory is based can be interpreted as attempts to determine the relationship between hunger and thirst drives and learning. Skinner's most common reinforcers, food and drink, are objects that satisfy basic, unlearned needs. And among the most common reinforcers employed in studies of human operant conditioning are those that satisfy learned or psychological needs (praise, money, tokens, and so on).

Even as Skinner's and Thorndike's conditioning theories were based largely on the effectiveness of basic drives as human motives, so too did Hull rely on

Figure 12-1.   Maslow's hierarchy of needs

what he termed "drive reduction" to explain why it is that habits are acquired and how "fractional antedating goal responses" become connected.

Despite the fact that need theory appears to have considerable relevance for explaining human behavior, there are a number of objections to it. The theory holds that behavior results from a need or deficiency in the organism, and it follows that the satisfaction of needs should lead to rest. However, this restfulness does not always follow satisfaction. Even rats that presumably are not in a state of need, having just been fed, given drink, and loved, often do not simply curl up and go to sleep. Instead, they may even show increases in activity. A second objection is that there are numerous instances of behaviors that human beings (and lower animals as well) engage in with no possibility of immediate or delayed satisfaction of a need—as when a rat learns to run a maze in the absence of any reward (Tolman, 1951) or when a person seeks sensory stimulation (Hebb, 1966).

Although need theory is often criticized severely (for example, Hunt, 1961) and has certain shortcomings, it is probably descriptive of a great deal of human behavior.

Incentives

One of the principal shortcomings of need/drive or "drive-reduction" theories is that they attempt to account for behavior in terms of *inner* states or urges (need for food, for example, is an inner state, and the hunger drive, an urge). Accordingly, they are hard pressed to explain why behaviors also appear to be affected by external stimulation. If hunger were solely an internal state, we would always eat only enough to activate the physiological mechanisms that relate to stopping eating. Yet a great many people eat far more if the foods appear more appetizing; others seem to become far hungrier if they are allowed to anticipate beforehand what they will be eating. Pertinent to this, note that even rats who are given a small taste of food before being placed in the start box of a maze run faster toward the goal box than do rats that have not been "primed" (Zeaman, 1949). If hunger is the motive and if it is solely an "inner state," it follows that the taste of food, however small, should serve to reduce the hunger drive somewhat and that hungrier rats should run faster.

What these simple need/drive positions have failed to take into account is the *incentive* value of motivation. Even for rats, a taste of food seems to serve as an incentive, urging them on toward faster running. For us, gifted as we are with the ability to imagine and to anticipate, there is no need of a taste beforehand. All you need do is tell me that the world's most exquisite crêpe suzette is to be found yonder under the purple sign that says "Suzies," and I will walk a little faster. Even if it isn't the world's most exquisite crêpe, I might still walk a little faster.

Let us stop for a moment and define *incentive* more clearly. Basically, the term *incentive* relates to the value of a goal or reward. Thus, a goal is said to have high incentive value when it is particularly powerful in motivating behavior and to have low incentive value if it is not very motivating. It follows that an individual will be willing to expend a great deal more effort to obtain a goal with high incentive than one that has lower incentive. The introduction of the concept *incentives* into a discussion of need/drive theory now makes it possible to account for the fact that monkeys will work harder to obtain a banana than a piece of lettuce and that you might pay more to eat a steak than a hamburger. It also brings what is essentially a behavioristic theory of motivation somewhat closer to the cognitive positions, for there is little doubt that our anticipation of goals and our estimation of their values for us involve what are essentially cognitive processes.

Cognitive Theories

Behavioristic theories, both in learning and in motivation, are characterized by what has been described as a mechanistic and passive view of the human organism (Bolles, 1975). Motives for behaving consist largely of internal or external prods to which the individual reacts in a relatively helpless fashion.

In contrast, cognitive positions present a less mechanistic and far more active view of human behavior. Individuals are seen as actively exploring and manipulating, as predicting and evaluating the consequences of their behavior, and as acting on the environment rather than simply reacting to it.

The first major break with the Hullian drive-reduction approach to motivation occurred when Tolman proposed that behavior does not result simply from stimulation but is profoundly affected by the organism's expectancy of being rewarded and by the value (incentive) of the reward. Thus it is that well-fed rats learn even in the absence of obvious reward.

ATTRIBUTION THEORIES

Subsequent events that are important in the development of contemporary cognitive theories of motivation include Rotter's (1954) suggestion that people tend to ascribe their successes and failures to internal or external causes. Thus, there appear to be a personality type whose *locus of control* (Rotter's terminology) is external and another type that is more internally oriented.

Those who are externally oriented tend to attribute their success or failure to task difficulty, bad luck, good luck, or other factors *external* to the actor. In contrast, internally oriented individuals are more likely to explain the outcome of their behavior in terms of ability and effort (see Figure 12-2).

Investigations of the relationship between need for achievement and attribution reveal a number of relatively consistent findings. Those with a high need to achieve are far more likely to attribute the outcomes of their behavior to internal causes. Thus, if they are successful, they are likely to attribute their success to effort (and perhaps to ability as well); if they are not successful, they continue to invoke internal factors, often blaming a lack of effort. Individuals characterized by a lower measured need for achievement are likely to attribute their success to any of four causes—ability, effort, ease of task, or luck; they are most likely to attribute failure to lack of ability (Weiner, Frize, Kukla, Reed, Rest, & Rosenbaum, 1971).

As Bolles (1974) suggested, the important difference between attribution theory and more-behavioristic theories of motivation is that it presents an active view of people. We continually evaluate our behaviors, look for reasons behind our successes and failures, anticipate the probable future outcomes of intended behaviors, and react emotionally to success and failure. And here is the key concept in Weiner's theoretical formulations. It is not the attribution of behavior

	Internal (under personal control)	External (not under personal control)
Stable (do not change)	ability	difficulty
Unstable (change)	effort	luck

Figure 12-2. Attribution theory: explanations of success or failure (after Weiner, 1974a)

to one cause or the other that motivates behavior, writes Weiner (1980); it is the emotions that occur as responses to specific attributions. As an example, he suggests that the outcomes of attribution might be anger, guilt, gratefulness, or a variety of other emotions. To the extent that the emotions are positive, subsequent behaviors will attempt to maintain the conditions that made the attribution possible. The converse is true with respect to emotions that are more negative. If for example, I attribute my success to the help I received from someone, I may then be moved (motivated) to buy that person a gift in order to maintain the relationship.

Further elaborations of attribution theory have been applied extensively in social psychology (for example, Kelley, 1971, 1973; Shaver, 1975). In brief, social-attribution theorists argue that we attribute motives to others on the basis of judgments that we make about their behaviors and that we subsequently react to them largely in terms of our attributions. Initially, for example, we determine whether an act is intentional—a decision that we base on our knowledge of the actor's ability as well as on a number of other factors. If we decide that a behavior was intentional, we are likely to attribute it to some internal *(dispositional)* factor; if we decide that it was not intentional, our attribution is likely to be external *(situational)*. Our emotional reactions toward the actor would then be determined not only by the consequences of the behavior for us but also by the attribution. To take an extreme and unpleasant example, if you break my leg and I decide that the cause was dispositional (you did it deliberately because you do not like me), my emotional reaction toward you will surely be dramatically different than if I make a situational attribution (you are so stupid and so poorly coordinated that you could not step around me as I hurtled down the slope).

Attribution theories are still somewhat too young to lend themselves readily to evaluation. Suffice it to say at this point that, to the extent that they are premised on the fundamental assumption that a good deal of our behavior is designed to make sense out of our world as well as out of our actions, they might eventually succeed in making sense out of us. It would be wholly premature, however, to discard other very different behavioristic and cognitive theories. That they are very different does not mean that they must necessarily be right or wrong.

COGNITIVE DISSONANCE

A second cognitive position has been advanced by Leon Festinger (1957, 1962) and elaborated by Brehm and Cohen (1962). The theory of *cognitive dissonance* is an attempt to explain at least some human behavior on the basis of the motivating effect of dissonance between cognitions. In simpler English, when a person simultaneously possesses two contradictory items of information (dissonant cognitions), that person will be motivated to act. The theory goes one step further and specifies that the behavior engaged in will be designed to reduce the contradiction. In addition, it contends that the behavior will be related directly to the magnitude of the discrepancy that exists between the cognitions.

Several studies have been carried out to investigate dissonance theory. In one such study (Festinger, 1962), college students who volunteered for an experiment that ostensibly dealt with "motor performance" were subjected to an exhausting and boring one-hour session. After the session, the subjects were told that the experiment was over, but they were then individually asked to help the experimenter with the next subject. They were led to believe that it was important for the research that the incoming person think that the experiment was interesting and pleasant. As a result, all of them, when they lied to their fellow classmates, created conflict between their behavior and their beliefs. The obvious prediction that can be made on the basis of theory is that subjects would try to reduce the dissonance by retracting the lie or by changing their private opinions. Since circumstances prevented an effective retraction, it would be highly likely that a change in belief would occur. That this change did indeed occur was determined by having another person interview the subjects *after the lie* in order to uncover their real feelings about the experiment.

Two variations were used in the experiment. All subjects were paid for their participation in the second part of the study (telling the lie), but some were given $20 for their help and the others only $1. The effect of this differential treatment was remarkable. The obvious prediction (and the one almost invariably advanced by those unfamiliar with the theory) is that those paid $20 would change their beliefs much more than those paid only $1. But the opposite was consistently true! Those who received small sums often became quite convinced that the hour session was really enjoyable; those who were paid the larger sum remained truer to their original beliefs.

This finding has been corroborated in a number of replications and variations of this study. One such variation reported by Brehm and Cohen involved having college students write essays advocating points of view that were at variance with what they truly believed. Subjects were paid either $10, $5, $1 or 50 cents for their efforts and were then asked to complete an anonymous questionnaire designed to reveal their true beliefs. As in the Festinger study, those subjects paid the smallest sum changed their opinions the most, whereas those paid $10 did not change appreciably. Both of these studies lead to the interesting observation that if criminals (thieves, for example) initially know that their behavior is immoral and if they are highly successful at their chosen vocation, they will be "better" people than if they are unsuccessful. In other words, if they make a lot of money by stealing, they are more likely to continue to believe that stealing is an immoral act.

The explanation for the rather unexpected results is simply that the magnitude of dissonance that is occasioned by a behavior counter to belief will be directly proportional to the justification that exists for the act. Students paid $20 to lie have a very good reason for doing so and will therefore feel less dissonance

Reducing dissonance

(guilt) than if they had been paid only $1. They will therefore be less motivated to alter their belief.

Reducing Dissonance.   The experiments discussed above offer some indication of how dissonance can be reduced. Festinger (1957), Brehm and Cohen (1962), and Berlyne (1960) suggest a number of additional means for lowering dissonance. Some of these are described below.

Attitude change. One illustration of attitude change is provided by the study in which students who had been compelled to lie subsequently changed their opinions. Another example is provided by Tom Blow, who dislikes school teachers quite intensely but who likes Mary Jones. When he discovers that Mary is a teacher, he is confronted with a great deal of dissonance, which will disappear when he decides that he really doesn't like Mary or that teachers really aren't that bad.

Compartmentalization. The example of Tom Blow can also illustrate compartmentalization. If Tom decides that Mary is really not like other teachers—that she is a different type of person despite the fact that she teaches—in effect he places her in a different "compartment." Compartmentalization is evidently a fairly common dissonance reducer employed by religious people who are also scientists and who are compelled, by virture of the nature of the two areas, to apply different sets of criteria to each. The "compartments" here would involve symbolic truth versus literal truth or "scientific" versus "faith" beliefs.

Exposure to or recall of information. On occasion, when there is a conflict between two items of information, gaining more information may reduce that dissonance. If a rumor is circulated that wheat flour turns the human liver white, it will probably create some conflict in those who have been in the habit of eating food made with wheat flour. If a person were exposed to the information that white livers are really quite functional, the dissonance might disappear.

Behavioral change. Situations characterized by dissonance often lead to changes in behavior. Tobacco smokers whose behavior is at odds with the information they have about the effects of smoking may cease to smoke, thereby eliminating all dissonance. Quite frequently, however, we find it simpler to use other techniques for coping with this problem. For example, it is not uncommon to hear smokers assure their listeners that they have read that there is yet no conclusive proof that smoking is harmful (selective exposure to information, or perceptual distortion). Others insist that all that has been clearly demonstrated

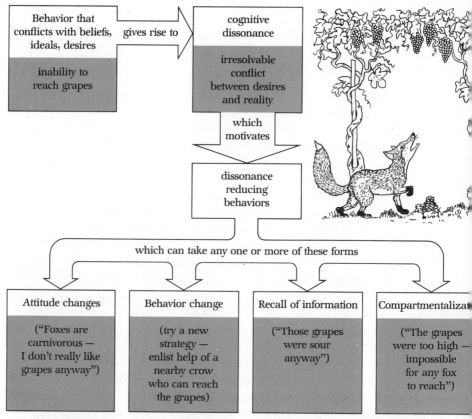

Figure 12-3. A model of cognitive dissonance. Everyone experiences conflicts between beliefs or desires and reality. There are many ways of trying to reduce cognitive dissonance.

by numerous smoking-related studies is that *Rattus norvegicus* would do well to stay away from the weed.

In summary, cognitive dissonance is the *motivating* state that occurs when an individual is in conflict. Ordinary sources of dissonance are incompatibility between beliefs, between behavior and private opinion, or between two items of information. Dissonance theory holds that such a state leads to behavior intended to reduce the conflict and reflective of the amount of conflict that exists.

DISSONANCE AND ATTRIBUTION

To *attribute* in cognitive theory is to assign responsibility or to impute motives. If I attribute my stupidity to my parents, I am simply assigning them responsibility for that condition. Dissonance describes a state of conflict and, presumably, of negative emotion.

The relationship between attribution and dissonance is implicit in the observation that dissonance depends on the extent to which the actor feels responsible for personal actions. Collins and Hoyt (1972) argue that people will not feel dissonance unless they also feel personal responsibility for their behavior. It follows, then, that those who attribute their behavior to external causes (who, in other words, do not accept personal responsibility) are not subject to cognitive dissonance in the same way as individuals who are more internally oriented. At the same time, those who are internally oriented are far more likely to feel pride when successful and shame when they fail. Thus, both dissonance and internal orientation are likely to be associated with emotion. And the motivating power of emotion is considerable (Lazarus, 1974).

Arousal Theory

A more global approach to human motivation has taken the form of what is often referred to as *arousal theory*. The theory is particularly important because it is compatible with both a behavioristic and a cognitive explanation of behavior.

DEFINITION

The term *arousal* has both psychological and physiological meaning. As a psychological concept, it refers to the degree of alertness, wakefulness, or attentiveness of a person or animal. It varies in degree from sleep, at the lowest level, to panic or frenzy, at the highest. As a physiological concept, it refers to the degree of activation of the organism. This activation is reflected primarily in electrical activity of the brain but also in other physiological functions such as heart rate, respiration rate, blood pressure, and electrical conductivity of the skin. With increasing arousal, there is a change in the pattern of electrical activity of the cortex as measured by an electroencephalograph (EEG). This change takes the form of increasingly rapid and shallow waves (called beta waves); at the lower levels of arousal (such as sleep), the waves are slow and deep (called alpha waves). Also, with increasing arousal there is an increase in the electrical conductivity of the skin, which is probably due to increased perspiration, as well as increases in heart and respiration rate and in blood pressure. Obviously these changes are highly similar to those that ordinarily accompany the intensification of emotions. Indeed, the relationship between emotions and arousal is so close that the terms are frequently used synonymously.

AROUSAL AND HOMEOSTASIS

The relationship of the concept of homeostasis, or balance, to arousal is implicit in the two assumptions that are ordinarily made about levels of arousal (Hebb, 1972). Since these two assumptions are central to all theoretical positions that stem from arousal concepts, let us examine each in turn.

1. There is an optimal level of arousal that differs for different tasks.

This conclusion seems to be obvious. Intense, concentrated activities, such as studying or competing on a television quiz program, evidently demand higher levels of alertness (arousal) than more habitual behaviors such as driving a car. It is generally accepted that for most daily activities moderate levels of arousal are probably optimum.

2. the organism behaves in such a way as to maintain the level of arousal that is most appropriate for the behavior in which it is then engaged.

The value of arousal as a motivational concept is based largely on the validity of this second assumption. If people do behave in order to maintain an optimal level of arousal (that is, if they seek homeostasis), then it is possible to predict, although somewhat imprecisely, what the behavior of individuals will be in

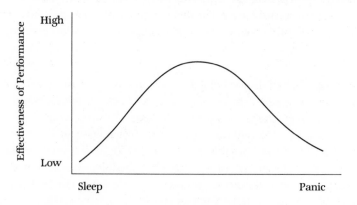

Figure 12-4.   Arousal and behavior

some situations. Given that a moderate level of arousal is optimal, students in a classroom who are at too low an arousal level would be expected to engage in activities designed to increase their arousal. Such activities do, in fact, take place. They often take the form of such noble pursuits as daydreaming, throwing spitballs, or conversing with other bored students.

The assumed relationship between behavior and arousal can be expressed in terms of a law of behavior—a law stating that the effectiveness of behavior increases as arousal increases until the optimal level is reached (Figure 12-4). Upon reaching this level, increasing arousal merely serves to lower the effectiveness of behavior. There is almost limitless anecdotal evidence that extremely high levels of arousal are associated with sometimes extremely inappropriate behavior. There are instances of students in tense doctoral oral examinations being unable to remember anything and even sometimes being unable to speak. There are the cases of soldiers at war who are unable to fire their rifles and of hunters who, when confronted with their quarry, are unable to hold them. Too-low arousal levels are also related to inappropriate behavior, although sometimes of a very different nature. A sleeping or overly sedated student does not perform very brilliantly either.

CAUSES OF AROUSAL

One of the central questions for motivational theory is what causes arousal. There are two ways of approaching this question: the first is to describe the situations that lead to higher or lower excitation; the second is to discuss the physiological mechanisms that are involved in arousal. Both are discussed below.

The RAS.   The reticular activating system (RAS—also called the nonspecific projection system, NSPS) is a formation of the brain located in the brain stem (see Figure 12-5). There is considerable evidence that one of its functions is to regulate an organism's level of arousal (Berlyne, 1960; French, 1957; Hebron, 1966). It appears that stimuli received by the brain are not simply transmitted directly to the cortex via specific neural pathways but are also diverted into the brain stem (more specifically, into the RAS). Hebb (1966) refers to two properties of stimuli. The *cue* function is the property that indicates to the organism what the nature of the stimulus is; that is, the "cue" is the message function of a stimulus. It is transmitted to the cortex via relatively direct neural pathways. The second function, *arousal*, is effected through the RAS. From each of the major nerve trunks there are branches that terminate in the RAS. When the RAS is stimulated, it in turn bombards the cortex in a *random, diffuse* manner. The effect of this bombardment is to increase arousal. It is widely accepted that without this activation, the cortex would be unable to respond to the cue function of stimuli. In other words, arousal is necessary for interaction with the environment.

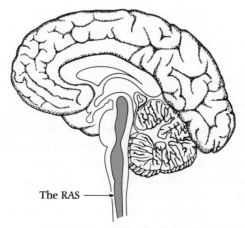

Figure 12-5.   The reticular activating system

Another function of the RAS is to control sleep and waking. Since sleep is simply a very low level of arousal (the lowest level short of death or of comatose states), it follows that during sleep the RAS is less active. In effect, it appears that the RAS is not at all dormant during sleep but simply serves to filter out stimuli. That it can respond and awaken its sleeping owner is made clear by the fact that a crying baby can quite easily awaken its mother, though not always its father. French has reported that a sleeping cat can be awakened very gently by stimulating its RAS with very low voltage. Delgado (1969) reports the same phenomenon with humans.

The RAS, as has been pointed out, responds to incoming stimulation by bombarding the cortex and thereby arousing it. It follows from this observation that the amount and intensity of external stimulation should be directly related to the degree of arousal. Schultz (1965) has demonstrated this fact in his study of sensory deprivation. Sensory-deprivation studies typically isolate humans and subject them to prolonged periods of minimal and monotonous sensory stimulation. The effects on arousal are consistently marked, as is evident through EEG ratings and behavioral changes (see Chapter 6 for a more detailed discussion of one of these experiments).

CONFLICT AND AROUSAL

In an attempt to relate arousal theory more directly to human behavior, Berlyne (1960, 1965) has advanced a theory based on the arousing properties of conflict. He contends that a great deal of our curiosity and knowledge-oriented* behavior is explainable on this basis. One of his major contributions is his description of

---

*Knowledge-oriented behavior is called *epistemic* behavior by Berlyne.

the properties of stimuli that lead to arousal. It appears that it is not so much the amount or intensity of stimulation that activates the RAS as it is the *novelty, meaningfulness, surprisingness, ambiguity,* or *complexity* of stimuli. Berlyne (1966) suggests that arousal is induced by stimuli that possess these characteristics because they create conceptual conflict. The individual then engages in behavior designed to reduce the conflict. Put quite simply, these properties of stimuli increase arousal, which in turn motivates the individual to behave. Since the behavior is designed to reduce conflict, it will usually take the form of activity that removes the surprisingness, ambiguity, novelty, or uncertainty of the stimulus. The most logical way of reducing these is by acquiring information, for a stimulus is no longer surprising or complex once it is familiar. Hence, this type of conflict leads to epistemic behavior (or learning) and can be used to explain such things as curiosity or exploratory behavior.

SUMMARY OF AROUSAL THEORY

Arousal theory attempts to account for behavior in terms of the apparent need we have to maintain optimal levels of arousal. Since arousal level is very much a function of stimulation, the theory is sometimes referred to as a stimulation theory of motivation (Mouly, 1968). Also, since the need for stimulation (or arousal) seems to explain such behaviors as are evident in exploration and problem solving, arousal concepts have been incorporated in many cognitive theories of learning in an attempt to explain curiosity, problem solving, manipulation, or simply activity (Bruner, 1957a; Butler & Harlow, 1957; Fowler, 1965; Hebron, 1966).

Applications of Motivation Theory

Knowledge about why people behave the way they do can greatly facilitate the psychologist's task of predicting what a person will do in a given situation and of controlling behavior when it is not unethical to do so. Consider, for example, the chaotic and confusing situation that would result if the ordinary activities of a person were not at least partly predictable. When I meet you and say "Hello," I expect that you will return either the same greeting or some other greeting or that, at worst, I will be ignored. I will be understandably surprised if, instead of responding as expected, you choose to kick me in the shins, run away, faint, or curse in some foreign language. Indeed, the ordinary business of day-to-day living requires that many of the implicit predictions that we make about the behavior of people be correct.

The second application involves the control of behavior, a subject that has led to considerable debate among psychologists. Should behavior be controlled? How should it be controlled? Who should control it? To what end? And so on. Essentially the question is not whether behavior can be controlled but what the ethics of behavior control are (see Rogers & Skinner, 1956).

Despite the somewhat appealing humanistic arguments against behavior control, it is clear that not only is deliberate behavior control a reality but that it is also in many cases highly desirable. Few would deny that a child who is toilet trained is somewhat more desirable than one who isn't—toilet training frequently involves systematic and deliberate attempts to modify behavior. The role played by motivation theory in these attempts is related to the realization that children can be toilet trained more easily when they come to view cleanliness as a desirable condition (as a goal). In addition, rewards and punishments, which also relate to motivation (and to learning), can be employed. Furthermore, cognitive dissonance may also be implicated in toilet training, since children who realize that being clean is desirable may feel considerable dissonance occasioned by the contradiction between behavior and ideals when they have what is euphemistically referred to as "an accident."

A second illustration related to behavior control is of considerable relevance for teachers, particularly since their function is largely one of modifying the behavior of students (the astute reader will recall that this is precisely the definition given earlier for *learning*). That task can be facilitated considerably by a knowledge of the individual needs and goals of students, of the effects of cognitive dissonance, and of the role of arousal in learning and behavior. Cognitive dissonance, for example, often obtains when the student is aware of a discrepancy between behavior and that which is described (perhaps by the teacher) as being ideal. Such dissonance may well lead to attempts to become more like the teacher's description of the ideal.

The role of arousal in behavior can be even more crucial for teaching. It will be recalled that it is the combined novelty, intensity, and meaningfulness of stimuli that most affect level of arousal. Teachers may be considered to be the most important single source of arousal-inducing stimulation for students. The impact of what they say and do and how they say and do it is instrumental in determining whether students are bored or sleeping (low arousal) or whether they are attentive (higher arousal). This consideration, of course, leads directly to a very strong and important argument for variety, meaningfulness, novelty, and intensity of classroom presentations.

Motivational theory can easily be applied to a variety of occupations. Indeed, wherever a profession demands interaction with humans, both predicting behavior and sometimes controlling it are probably of considerable importance.

Summary of Chapter 12

This chapter has presented a discussion of some of the various explanations that have been advanced for human behavior. Instincts, reflexes, and imprinting were discussed, as were needs, drives, and incentives. Cognitive approaches covered included attribution theory and cognitive dissonance. Finally, arousal theory was presented as a global explanation for a variety of behaviors.

1. Instincts are complex, unlearned patterns of behavior that appear to have more relevance for animal than for human behavior. Reflexes are simple stimulus-specific responses that explain some elementary human behavior.

2. Orienting reflex (OR) is the name given to the general *reflexive* response an organism makes to novel stimuli; it involves some physiological changes that are related to arousal.

3. Psychological hedonism is the motivational position holding that the pain/pleasure principle is the moving force in human lives. The position is of limited value unless the nature of pain and pleasure can be determined more precisely.

4. Needs are states of deficiency or lack. They give rise to *drives*, which in turn impel the organism toward activities that will reduce the needs.

5. Numerous lists of physiological and psychological needs have been advanced by psychologists. These lists can be interpreted as one way of specifying the nature of pain and pleasure if it is true that unsatisfied needs are unpleasant and that their satisfaction is pleasant.

6. An *incentive* is basically the value that an activity or goal has for an individual. It is a far more cognitive concept than is need or drive.

7. Cognitive theories present a more active view of the human organism than do traditional behavioristic theories.

8. The development of cognitive theories of motivation is related to Tolman's introduction of expectancy and reward as important motivational variables, Rotter's suggestion that we tend to be internally or externally controlled, Heider's notions of personal causality or intention as being central motivating forces, and Weiner's inclusion of these ideas in an attribution theory of achievement motivation.

9. Attribution theory attempts to explain how individuals assign responsibility for the outcomes of their behaviors. Internally oriented individuals frequently ascribe success or failure to ability or effort; externally oriented individuals are more likely to blame success or failure on luck or on the fact that the task was very easy or very difficult.

10. Applications of attribution theory in social psychology are often concerned with how we perceive others—in short, with how we attribute motives to them.

11. The theory of cognitive dissonance was advanced by Leon Festinger to account for the motivating effect of possessing simultaneously incompatible items of information. It is assumed that dissonance leads to behavior designed to reduce the conflict.

12. Arousal refers to the degree of alertness of an organism. It is a function of stimulation mediated by the reticular activating system (RAS). Its relation to motivation is implicit in the assumption that too-low or too-

high arousal is related to less optimal behavior than a more moderate level of activation. Humans behave in such a way as to maintain arousal at the optimal level.

13. According to Berlyne, the novelty, meaningfulness, complexity, and surprisingness of stimuli lead to increases in arousal because they engender conceptual conflict. Such conflict may lead to knowledge-acquiring (epistemic) behavior.

Dear Guy,

I may as well tell you that I wrote to your editor a couple of weeks ago. You would be proud of the nice things I said about you and your book. I want you to know that before you hear it from somebody else. I've looked at most of your book now, although, as you know, I'm too busy to read very much of it. It's going to be quite okay after your editors get done with it, and I'm sure I'll be proud of most of it and not embarrassed by anything much. I sure hope so anyway.

As far as that starving fund goes, no I don't have any money to send them right now. Anyway, every Christmas I bring a big basket of stuff over to the church for the poor people right here. We don't have to go outside the country to find them. Maybe you'd be better off if you spent your money here too, although I expect you do spend most of it here anyway. Robert says he saw you at the horse races on Saturday. I hope you weren't actually betting money. He wasn't. He said he was just there taking pictures, which is not a bad hobby compared to making headbands out of feathers from live turkeys, which I hope you've gotten over by now.

I'm sending you back the electric bill so you can pay it yourself. Do it right away, because they phoned and said they'd cut off the power.

I'm sending you a box of those molasses cookies with this letter. You don't eat enough. I have a theory that . . .

CHAPTER *14*

Social Influences

Some of you may have noticed that there is no Chapter 13 in this text. There are two reasons. The first relates to a stupid superstition left over from the first edition (for which I am blameless). The second has to do with the fact that some bright reviewer had the audacity to assert that in the first edition his students liked Chapter 13 best.

Social Learning: A Definition

It might appear from reading the preceding chapters that most human learning involves acquiring information and learning how to deal effectively with the environment. The emphasis throughout has been primarily on environment/learner interaction. Actually, however, it is highly important for us to learn how to relate one to the other as well as how to relate to the environment. The learning of behaviors that are socially acceptable (as well as learning which ones are not) is *social learning*. In effect, social-learning theory attempts to describe the processes by which we come to know what behaviors should or should not be engaged in when we are in different social situations. The theories themselves are *learning* theories that have been applied to social situations. Interestingly, these theories have generally been *behavioristic* rather than cognitive, although Albert Bandura's theories provide an interesting mixture of behaviorism and cognitivism. The discussion of social learning provided in this chapter is based largely on the theoretical formulations of Bandura (1969, 1977; Bandura & Walters, 1963).

Socialization

A treatment of social learning can deal with two aspects of socialization—the *process* itself, which may be highly similar across a variety of cultures, and the *content* of social learning, which may be highly dissimilar across societies. Although this chapter is concerned primarily with the process, content is discussed briefly first. The content of social learning is the actual catalogue of

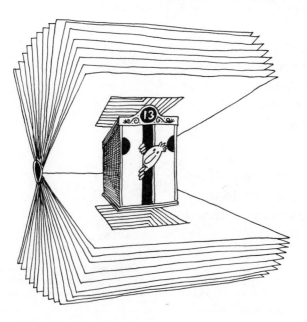

behaviors that are appropriate and inappropriate. Two characteristics of such a catalogue are noteworthy.

1. Acceptable behaviors vary from culture to culture. For example, in some Oriental countries it is highly appropriate to present university professors with gifts as tokens of appreciation. The same practice is looked on with considerably less favor in North America. In the same manner, the appropriateness of sex-related behavior varies widely among cultures. What appears to be normal behavior for North American teenage children would be regarded as highly promiscuous among rural Ghanians as well as among many Oriental societies. The same behavior might be viewed as relatively inhibited by some primitive African or South American tribe.

2. The appropriateness of specific behaviors varies among individuals in the same society. Even in a relatively classless society, some social behaviors can be engaged in only by those who hold certain positions. Furthermore, behaviors that are acceptable in one situation may not be in another.

From a learning-theory point of view, a description of behaviors that are appropriate in different circumstances for different people is not as important as a discussion of how we learn such behaviors—the topic that forms the basis for the remainder of this chapter.

Alternative Explanations of Socialization

Consider a simple problem faced by all children: learning that it is not acceptable to kick strangers in the shins. A number of different explanations for the fact that this learning does take place can be derived from learning theory.

CLASSICAL CONDITIONING

Classical-conditioning theory cannot easily explain complex social learning. It is extremely difficult, in fact, to conceive of situations involving the kicking of shinbones in which contiguity could account for learning. It is less difficult to imagine that the consequences of engaging in this behavior might lead to its rapid suppression. Neither of these observations, however, can clearly explain why the behavior does or does not occur in the first place.

COGNITIVE EXPLANATIONS

In order to account for social learning in terms of one or more of the cognitive positions discussed in this text, it is necessary to extrapolate beyond the specific formulations of the theorists in question. Typically, *cognitive* theories are more concerned with the properties of cognitive structure, the determinants of perceptual activity, and the factors governing awareness or insight than with the acquisition of simple behaviors. Accordingly, such theories are not easily applicable to problems of social learning. It is possible, however, to assume that engaging in or refraining from a behavior such as kicking shins involves reaching a decision, and decision making is a topic of some interest to cognitivists. The typical approach to the subject is to examine it in the light of information processing. In this context, it is reasonable to assume that when children are faced with a shin, they, in a Brunerian sense, evaluate the probability of various outcomes of the choices they can make and estimate (subjectively) the payoff associated with each. More simply, they can be imagined to reason as follows: "If I kick the old codger I will feel good and attribute my feeling good to the act of kicking, but he will probably catch me (probability approximately equal to .90) and beat the living _____ out of me—that has a negative valence. If I pass up this splendid opportunity, I will not be beaten by the old geezer, but I will feel unhappy because of my frustrated aggressive tendencies." Having completed this reasoning process, the child, being human, will in all likelihood kick the old gentleman and run like a frightened gazelle in order to take full advantage of the 10% probability of escaping.

OPERANT CONDITIONING

The third explanation of social learning resembles the second in that the consequences of the behavior are assumed to be important in determining whether a behavior will occur. Indeed the most widely accepted social-learning theories are those premised on an operant-conditioning model (for example, Miller & Dollard, 1941; Bandura & Walters, 1963). An operant-conditioning explanation of social learning says simply that reinforced responses tend to be retained, whereas those that are not reinforced (or that are punished) tend to be eliminated. The position also assumes that the initial occurrence of the response is relatively independent of environmental circumstances—it is simply *emitted*.

Two problems are implicit in an operant-conditioning explanation of social learning. First, it does not account for the initial occurrence of the response. Obviously, if the behavior does not occur, it cannot be learned. Second, the model described above provides a less than adequate explanation for the suppression of undesirable behavior—an explanation that maintains, first, that nonreinforced responses will be suppressed and, second, that through generalization other related responses will also be suppressed. The first explanation is obviously not completely accurate, since numerous behaviors are not engaged in even though they have never occurred. The second alternative may well account for the fact that many behaviors never occur at all, but it is nevertheless true that, in order to account for all learning through generalization (or discrimination), the processes must be defined in an extremely broad sense.

GRANDMOTHER'S EXPLANATION

Grandma must be allowed to present her theory: "He knowed better, cause he seen his brother git slapped fer it," or "Shure he knowed how to, 'cause he seen them other boys doin' it." Interestingly, it is possible to combine Grandma's explanation with that of other theorists in order to arrive at an apparently reasonable explanation for a great deal of social learning. An early attempt to do this took the form of Miller and Dollard's (1941) theory of social learning based on the role of imitation. Their theory was essentially an assertion that imitation rather than trial and error is the chief learning mode for humans. It can be reduced to the following set of statements about learning and the elements involved in the process:

1. Learning involves *cues*, *drives*, *responses*, and *rewards*.
2. A *drive* is a force that impels an organism to action. It is the motivational factor in learning.
3. Drives are attached to specific stimuli that can be external (like a sound) or internal (like hunger). Stimuli that give rise to response-producing drives are referred to as *cues*. In a literal sense, they serve as cues or signals for behavior.
4. The *response* occasioned by a drive will become learned if it leads to a reduction in drive. Since drives are the result of stimuli, reducing drives involves eliminating drive-producing stimuli.
5. The elimination of these stimuli is said to be *rewarding*. Miller and Dollard contend that learning does not take place in the absence of reward.
6. Learning involves attaching responses to specific stimuli. The initial occurrence of a *response*, particularly where social learning is involved, is more often the result of imitation than of trial and error.
7. Imitation is learned through the same process by which other learning occurs. Behaviors that are engaged in by a child *and are imitative of the behavior of someone else* will be learned if rewarded. Since children are often rewarded when they imitate adult behavior, it is inevitable that a large number of imitative responses will be learned in this way. Through *generalization* a child eventually comes to imitate specifically as a means of learning.

The most obvious theoretical objection that can be raised to this explanation of learning is that it is not realistic to assume that *all* or even *most* behavior is motivated by the desire to eliminate stimulation. It is clear that we engage in many activities that have the objective of seeking rather than avoiding stimulation (see Chapter 12). A more recent formulation, also based on a theory of imitation but without the limitations of a rigorous drive-reduction approach, has been provided by Bandura.

AN INTEGRATED EXPLANATION

Bandura (1969, 1977; Bandura & Walters, 1963) presents a theory of social learning that integrates all of the explanations described above. It is based on operant conditioning, admits classical conditioning, and accounts for learning partly in terms of the effectiveness of imitation in determining human behavior. In addition, Bandura describes imitation as involving a cognitive element. Despite its seeming eclectic nature, the theory presents a highly unified conception of human behavior.

Bandura's Theory

One description of this integrated position is provided by Bandura in *Principles of Behavior Modification* (1969)—a book concerned primarily with the application of social learning principles to the modification of behavior. This chapter deals with the principles per se, as they were discussed by Bandura in that book and in a more recent book (1977) as well as by Bandura and Walters in an earlier book (1963). While a brief discussion of behavior-modification techniques is also provided, the interested reader is referred to the original sources for more detailed information.

BEHAVIOR-CONTROL SYSTEMS

The Bandura theory can be considered an integration of a variety of theoretical positions, in that it admits that behavior is controlled by three "systems," each of which relates directly to a specific school of psychological thought. And although the theory deals primarily with only one of these behavior-control systems (*symbolic control*), each is clearly implicated in social learning.

Bandura (1969) maintains that it is impossible to explain human behavior solely by reference to either internal or external stimulus events and that both are inevitably involved in most human behavior. Since behaviorism can be defined in terms of its preoccupation with *external* events, whereas cognitivism deals with *internal* mediation of behavior, an admission that both are involved in human activity provides the beginning for integration of behavioristic and cognitive positions.

When Bandura refers to *external* stimulus events, he means simply that the physical environment is at least partly responsible for human behavior. It is patently obvious that we do, in fact, respond to our environment. Indeed, not to do so would be a mark of a totally nonfunctional being. Even such phylogenetically low forms of life as planaria are responsive to external stimulation. *Internal* stimulation refers to the more "cognitive" events, in the form of images, memories, feelings, instructions, verbalizations, and so on, that compose human thought processes. That these events influence behavior is clear—Grandma needs no convincing whatsoever. Interestingly, psychologists sometimes do. To this end, Bandura (1969) cites an experiment performed by Miller (1951) in which a group of subjects were conditioned by means of electric shocks to react negatively to the letter *T* and positively to the number 4. After conditioning, subjects consistently gave evidence of greater autonomic reaction (arousal) for the stimulus associated with shock—in this case, *T*. Miller subsequently instructed subjects to *think* "T" and "4" alternately as a sequence of dots were presented to them. That is, the subjects were asked to think "T" for the first dot, "4" for the second, "T" for the third, "4" for the fourth, and so on. The fact that there was now greater autonomic reaction to odd-numbered dots is assumed to be indicative of the effect of internal processes on behavior.

In describing the forces that affect human behavior, Bandura notes three separate *behavior-control systems* that are assumed to interact with one another in the determination of behavior.

1. Stimulus Control. One class of human behaviors consists of activities that are directly under the control of stimuli. Such behaviors include the host of autonomic (reflexive) acts in which people engage when responding to certain specific stimuli. Sneezing, withdrawing from pain, flinching, the startle reaction, and so on are all examples of behavior that is controlled by *external* stimuli. In addition, a wide variety of nonreflexive behaviors comes under control of stimuli through conditioning. For this reason, the first behavior-control system described by Bandura can be interpreted as including the types of learning that are of most direct concern to behavioristic psychologists.

Behaviors under control of stimuli also include responses learned through reinforcement, where a specific stimulus is always present at the time of the reinforcement. This stimulus acquires control over behavior in the sense that it comes to elicit a response because of its relationship to the reinforcement. A clear illustration of this type of control is provided by the contrast between the deportment of many schoolchildren when their teachers are present and when they are not. Through the administration of rewards for good behavior and punishment for less desirable activity, teachers become stimuli that are capable of eliciting either obedience, fear, caution, respect, love or a combination of these responses.

2. Outcome Control. The second behavior-control system described by Bandura refers to the behaviors that are under control of their consequences rather than under the control of antecedents (or stimuli). Obviously, this system has been extensively investigated by B. F. Skinner. It relates specifically to those human activities that become more probable as a function of reinforcement or less probable as a function of nonreinforcement or of punishment. Control is achieved through operant conditioning in this behavior-control system (see Chapter 3).

3. Symbolic Control. The last behavior-control system includes the range of human activity that is influenced by "mediation," or internal processes. There are several ways in which human behavior can be affected by thought processes. Covert verbalization of rules (self-instructions) can direct behavior as in the Miller (1951) experiment, in which subjects can be assumed to have "mentally" told themselves to think "T," then "4," and so on. A second sense in which symbolic processes direct behavior relates to the way *imagining* the consequences of behavior affects ongoing activity. It appears obvious that, were it not for the ability to represent long-range outcomes symbolically, a great many tasks that are neither under immediate stimulus control nor likely to be rewarded immediately would not be undertaken. The importance of symbolization for human behavior appears to be much greater than that of the other two behavior-control systems. It also appears that as one goes down the phylogenetic scale, the importance of outcome control and of direct stimulus control increases. Lower animal forms seem to react more to specific external stimulation than to behavioral outcomes. In addition, it is not at all evident that symbolization plays an important (if any) role in the direction of the behavior of lower animals.

BEHAVIOR-CONTROL SYSTEMS AND SOCIAL LEARNING

While stimulus-control, outcome-control, and symbolic-control systems relate to three classes of behavior that are clearly distinguishable on theoretical grounds, they are not necessarily separate in practice. Indeed, much human activity is probably directed by a combination of these three. For example, a woman who pursues a buck-toothed, cross-eyed, knock-kneed, pigeon-toed, skinny, red-headed man may well be directed by stimuli, outcomes, and symbolization.

In the first place, the pursued redhead is a man, and because of stimulus generalization the pursuer reacts to this man as she would to any other. Her pursuing behavior is under the direct control of the stimulus *man*, because *man* is the stimulus that has been present at the time of many previous reinforcements.

But human behavior is not this simple. The pursuer does not just respond to this signal in the blind manner expected of an unsophisticated rat but in a manner directed by immediate outcomes. If her initial approach is met by strong resistance, she may modify it; if it is rewarded, she may intensify it; if the intensification leads to more reward, it may be reintensified; if it leads to a cessation of reinforcement, it may be diminished. Quite simply, the human female is capable of changing her behavior in accordance with its outcomes.

But the direction of activity is still more complex. We do not react solely to stimuli or to the consequences of behavior, although it is obviously necessary that we do so to some extent. Our actions are also guided by symbolic processes. For example, the woman pursues an unattractive redhead because she can represent imaginally the consequences of being successful in her attempt to capture him. She can clearly visualize that such an ugly man must possess hidden talents to offset his lack of obvious qualities—he must certainly be an excellent cook.

The relevance of Bandura's discussion of the control of behavior for social learning is implicit in the assumption that learning involves bringing responses under the control of stimuli, rewards, or symbolic processes. In this respect, social learning does not differ from other forms of learning, except insofar as the *content* of the learning may itself be different, since it relates to *socialization* rather than to the simple acquisition of knowledge or information.

Imitation

The most important contribution of Bandura's theory is its explanation of social learning in terms of the effects of imitation. Bandura contends that a great deal of the learning of social behavior is achieved by observing the behavior of others. This learning is referred to as observational learning. The theory is discussed below in terms of the answers it advances for four related questions:

1. What is the relationship between imitation and operant conditioning?
2. How prevalent is imitative behavior?
3. What is a *model?*
4. What are the results of observational learning?

IMITATION AND OPERANT CONDITIONING

Skinner's model of operant conditioning describes learning as an increase in the probability of occurrence of an operant (emitted response) as a function of reinforcement. In order to relate this model to the process of learning through observation, it is necessary to assume that imitative behavior possesses the characteristics of operants and that it is subject to reinforcement. That both aspects of the assumption are valid can easily be illustrated. First, an operant is a response that is not elicited by a stimulus but is simply *emitted* by an organism. This description does not contradict the possibility that some environmental condition(s) may be partly or wholly responsible for the appearance of the response, but it does assert that the antecedent conditions are not of any direct consequence to the actual learning. Thus, it can be said that imitative behavior may result from the observation of a model, *but the learning itself* will involve the formation of some sort of relationship between the reinforcement and the behavior rather than between the model's behavior and the observer's behavior.

The second aspect of the assumption is that imitation is subject to reinforcement. That this assumption is true is readily evident from human behavior. Indeed, four separate sources of reinforcement are apparent in observational learning—three involving reinforcement for the observer and one involving the behavior of the model. An imitator is often reinforced directly by the model whose behavior is being copied, particularly if the imitator is a young child. Proud parents are prone to praising their children for behaviors that resemble those of Daddy or Mommy. Even grandmothers are occasionally heard saying "Look at little Norbert standing there with his finger in his nose, *just like his daddy.*"

A second source of reinforcement for the observer derives from the actual consequences of the imitated behavior. If the activity is socially acceptable or leads to the obtaining of reward, it is reinforced by its own consequences. A child who learns to say "milk" as a result of hearing mother say "milk" 40 times a day for 3 years not only incurs the praise of that proud parent but may also receive real *milk* as a result of saying the word. Hence, the consequences of learning socially appropriate behavior through imitation are often desirable.

Third, the observer in a modeling situation often appears to be influenced by what Bandura (1969) labels *vicarious* reinforcement. This type of reinforcement derives from the assumption that if models engage in a behavior, there must be some reinforcement that leads them to do so and that this reinforcement will also result if the observer imitates the behavior. The fact that observers will often imitate without any expectation of reward and continue to do so even after they have discovered that they are not being reinforced is interpreted as evidence that they derive secondhand, or *vicarious*, reinforcement from the imitation itself—a reinforcement that is linked to the model's assumed reward.

The fourth source of reinforcement for imitative behavior affects the model rather than the observer. For this reason it is not directly pertinent to observational learning, but it does serve to explain why some of the model's behavior is (or is not) maintained. It often appears that when people are imitated, there is an increase in the probability that they will engage again in the behavior that was imitated. For example, some years ago a number of entertainers let their hair grow much longer than the social norm. This fashion was widely imitated, and the entertainers continued to let their hair grow. Had they not been imitated, it is much less likely that they would have continued to do so. In other words, it appears that to be imitated is reinforcing.

In summary, observational learning can be understood in terms of an operant-conditioning model if it is assumed that imitative behavior is operant or instrumental in nature. Although an obvious external stimulus often seems to elicit the behavior initially, this stimulus (the model) serves only to account superficially for the appearance of the behavior but not for the fact that it may or may not be learned. A second assumption that relates imitation to an operant paradigm is that reinforcement is often a consequence of imitating.

PREVALENCE OF IMITATION

Some emphasis is placed on originality and creativity in many societies. Consequently, there is a concomitant denigration of imitation, since to imitate is, by definition, not to be original. Yet not only is it abundantly obvious that imitation is extremely common, but it is equally clear that organized societies would no longer be viable if their members did not imitate one another. Consider the chaos that would result if we decided to drive on either side of the street, to park vehicles anywhere, and to interpret traffic signals in original ways. Our very basis of communication is imitation. In the same manner, the storage of knowledge and the transmission of culture require imitation.

Primitive societies are sometimes cited as examples of learning through imitation. Bandura and Walters (1963) described the Cantalense people, a Guatemalan subculture. In this society a little girl is provided with miniature *working* replicas of all of the tools employed by her mother in caring for the household. As soon as she is old enough, she follows her mother about, *observing* her and imitating her actions with miniature brooms and corn-grinding stones. Throughout the learning process there is *little or no direct tuition.* Hence, the learning is more clearly a result of imitation than is the learning of young children in more highly verbal cultures.

A second example of a primitive culture in which early learning is largely observational is provided by the Canadian Ojibwa Indians. This tribe lived largely on the fruits of hunting, fishing, and trapping. Early in life a young Ojibwa boy would follow in his father's footsteps, learning how to hunt, to set traps, and to fish. At a young age he would be given his own traps and would go out by himself. In the same way, a young Ojibwa girl learned how to prepare game, clothing, cooking fires, and so on by observing her mother. As in the Cantalense culture there was little direct tuition.

The prevalence of imitative learning in highly developed technological societies is not as evident. Obviously, it is virtually impossible for parents to provide their children with miniature *working* replicas of the tools and machines that they employ in the course of their daily activities. Nor would it be particularly wise to do so, since children frequently enter occupational fields that are very different from those of their parents. Nonetheless, observational learning is highly prevalent in advanced societies. Through imitation children learn appropriate (acceptable) ways of doing things, acquire behavioral patterns that conform to those of peer groups, and so on. Indeed, when imitative learning is defined as all learning that results from observing *models*, and *models* are defined according to Bandura and Walters, it becomes apparent that the most highly developed society may well be characterized by the greatest degree of observational learning.

MODELS

Although there is a tendency to think of models as *people* whose behavior is copied by others, a model is more appropriately defined as any representation of a pattern for behaving. Humans do serve as models for other humans—parents serve as models for children, children are models for other children and sometimes for adults, and adults continually imitate one another. Television is also a model, since it presents a variety of patterns for behaving. In the same sense books, verbal instructions, animals, and directions are all models. They are referred to as *symbolic models;* each plays a significant role in the socialization of the contemporary human child.

EFFECTS OF IMITATION

From the preceding sections it might appear that learning through imitation simply involves models who do something and observers who copy behavior and are reinforced for doing so. However, the process is somewhat more complex than this. Bandura and Walters distinguish three results of observational learning, which they describe as the three *effects* of imitation.

The Modeling Effect. When observers learn (through imitation) something that is *new* for them, they are said to *model*. Hence, modeling involves the acquisition of *novel* responses. That such an effect does exist is corroborated by anecdotal evidence. Grandmothers eagerly describe how their grandchildren acquire undesirable habits from the neighbor's undisciplined ruffians—habits that are clearly novel since they were never engaged in previously. In further support of grandmother's position, Bandura and his associates (1963) describe a series of often replicated experiments dealing with aggression in young children. The experiments typically involve subjects who are exposed to filmed, real-life, or cartoon models of other children or of adults engaging in *novel* aggressive behavior with a large, inflated, plastic clown. Occasionally the model is verbally aggressive; at other times he (or she) strikes the clown with fist, foot, or mallet; sits on it; scratches it; or otherwise attacks it. Subjects are later exposed to the same clown and their reactions are noted. Frequently, these reactions take the form of precisely imitative aggressive responses. When the responses are clearly new for the child, *modeling* is assumed to have occurred.

The Inhibitory and Disinhibitory Effects. The second effect of imitation does not involve *novel* responses but deals instead with the suppression or dis-inhibition of previously learned *deviant* behavior. *Deviant* behavior is defined as socially unacceptable responses (such as excessive aggression, for example). Inhibition and disinhibition usually occur as a result of seeing a model punished or rewarded for engaging in deviant behavior. For example, a group of thieves may stop stealing after a member of the group is apprehended and punished. On the other hand, the same group may have begun stealing as a result of seeing a member become wealthy through stealing. The first instance exemplifies the inhibitory effect; the second example illustrates the disinhibitory effect.

A rather striking illustration of the power of models in disinhibiting deviant behavior is provided by a series of experiments sometimes referred to as the *punishment studies* (Walters & Llewellyn, 1963; Walters, Llewellyn, & Acker, 1962). In these studies subjects were asked to volunteer for what was ostensibly an experiment in memory. The subjects were shown a short sequence from one of two films: either a violent episode from *Rebel Without a Cause* or an excerpt from a film showing adolescents engaged in art work. Those exposed to the sequence with aggressive content made up the experimental group; the second group served as controls. After the films were presented, subjects were asked to help the experimenter with another study designed to investigate the effects of punishment on problem-solving behavior. A person who posed as a subject, but who was in reality a stooge, sat at a panel working out problems and signaling his answers by pressing a switch. Whenever he answered correctly, a green light would flash on a second panel; when he was incorrect, a red light would go on. The second panel also contained 15 toggle switches that were labeled 15 volts, 30 volts, 45 volts, and so on. The switches appeared to be connected to the electrodes fastened to the stooge's wrists. Instructions given to the subject (after he had been administered a mild shock in order to ensure that he realized what he was doing) were simply to administer punishment in the form of an electric shock every time an error was made. Results strongly supported the prediction that exposure to aggressive models would result in an increase in the intensity of the shocks administered. Even more striking is the fact that very few subjects refused to participate in the experiment, despite the fact that they were being asked to inflict pain on their colleagues.

The inhibitory effect cannot be so easily demonstrated experimentally, probably because systematic attempts to inhibit deviant behavior often show little evidence of success. Contemporary North American criminal law is often justified on the ground that punishing an offender serves as a deterrent for others who might also become criminals. The person punished is therefore intended to serve as a model for the inhibition of the behavior punished. There is some indication, however, that humans are not particularly susceptible to this behavior-control technique. My grandmother has known this for some time. Indeed, she has summarized the whole ineffectiveness of criminal punishment in the brilliant and insightful phrase: "He thinks it can't happen to him." Interestingly, she still insists that criminals must be punished: "They just deserve it, that's all! The idea!"

The Eliciting Effect. A third manifestation of the influence of models on human behavior is referred to as the *eliciting effect.* It involves *eliciting* responses that are not novel but are related to the model's responses in two ways. First, there is an obvious relationship in that the model's behavior serves as a stimulus for the appearance of the observer's response. Second, the observer's responses and the model's behavior are related in that they belong to the same class of behaviors. A rather common example of the eliciting effect is provided by the behavior of those who try to excel in one area because someone else excels in *another* area. The acquisition of accents through exposure to people who speak differently and being generous in one way because one's neighbors are generous in another are two examples of the eliciting effect. Whenever a model is responsible for the appearance of a response that is not novel or precisely imitative, the eliciting effect is manifested.

IMITATION AND SOCIAL LEARNING

Imitation ranks high among the alternative explanations for complex social learning, primarily because those explanations provided by operant- or classical-conditioning models, while useful in accounting for the acquisition of simple responses, are not clearly applicable to a great deal of complex learning. Such skills as learning to drive a car are not acquired solely through contiguity or trial and error but require the presentation of models. These models can take the form of other drivers or of verbal or written instructions. We would probably never learn to speak if we needed to do so through trial and error, without benefit of the models that are presented by other speaking humans. Indeed, it can truthfully be stated that people learn what is acceptable and unacceptable in matters of speech, dress, and behavior largely by observing the speech, dress, and behavior of others.

Behavior Management

Given the effectiveness of models in determining human behavior, it follows that systematic attempts to modify deviant behavior can make use of modeling procedures. Bandura and Walters (1963) describe five techniques that can successfully be employed to this end and that are based on operant-conditioning principles as well as on the specific use of models.

POSITIVE REINFORCEMENT

The use of rewards for modifying behavior is a well-known and widespread practice in everyday life. In order to toilet-train children, parents give them candy; hard work is repaid with increased wages; the diligent student is smiled at; and so on. The systematic use of rewards in therapy, however, is not as common as one might expect. The *psychoanalytic* orientation of many therapists leads them to approaches intended to uncover the causes of deviant behavior rather than to deal with their manifestation.* Behavioral approaches to therapy are contrasted to the psychoanalytic techniques mainly in terms of their treatment of symptoms rather than causes. There is some argument about whether the removal of symptoms constitutes a *cure*. At the same time, there is doubt that *cures* are frequent as a result of psychoanalysis.

Positive reinforcement is one behavioral technique. It is employed primarily where there is a behavioral deficit. In principle, the procedure involves arranging for the appearance of a response and following it with reinforcement. Several investigations (for example, Lovaas, 1966; Lovaas, Berberich, Perloff, & Schaeffer, 1966; Risley & Wolf, 1967) have demonstrated that young autistic children are sometimes improved following the use of positive reinforcement. Autism is characterized by extreme withdrawal, undeveloped communication habits, and general nonsocialized behavior. Therapy can take the form of rewarding such children for verbal responses elicited through games (Ferster, 1961; Ferster & deMyer, 1962).

Psychoanalysis is a term used to refer to the therapeutic school that follows the methods developed by Freud. These techniques are the traditional patient-on-the-couch, what-happened-in-your-childhood, what-do-you-dream approaches.

COUNTERCONDITIONING

Behavior can also be modified by conditioning responses that are incompatible with the undesirable behavior but occur for the same stimuli, Wolpe (1958), a behavior therapist, has developed this method in a procedure he labels *systematic desensitization*, or *reciprocal inhibition*. In addition, the three techniques presented by Guthrie for the elimination of habits are all examples of counterconditioning, since each involves learning responses for the original stimulus that are incompatible with the undesirable behavior (see Chapter 2).

Wolpe's *systematic desensitization* is a method used primarily in the treatment of anxieties and phobias (fears). It can be described in simplified form as involving three steps. First, the patient describes all of the situations that bring about the unwanted behavior. These situations are arranged in hierarchical order beginning with the stimulus that elicits the mildest response and culminating with the stimulus associated with the strongest reaction. The second step is to teach the patient a response that is incompatible with the unwanted response. Almost invariably, this step takes the form of training the patient in relaxation, since relaxing is incompatible with fear or anxiety. The third step is to present the mildest stimulus *while the patient is relaxing* and to continue presenting stimuli in hierarchical order until the patient begins to feel uncomfortable. At that point, the therapist stops and relaxation is again practiced. The object of the procedure is to eventually present the strongest stimulus without eliciting the unwanted reaction.

This procedure is evidently a sophisticated version of Guthrie's *threshold* technique or of Grandmother's "don't-throw-him-in-the-water-let-him-get-used-to-it-slowly-damn-it" approach.

EXTINCTION

Even as Skinner's rats could be made to cease depressing a lever simply by withdrawal of rewards, so humans can often be made to stop engaging in some unwanted form of behavior by removing their source of reinforcement. The application of this technique requires that the behavior be maintained by positive reinforcement and that this reinforcement be under the control of the experimenter or therapist. The second requirement is probably not often met, since deviant behavior often leads to intrinsic satisfaction that is not under any external control. On the other hand, there are numerous attention-seeking behaviors in young children that can be extinguished simply by ceasing to pay attention to them. Ayllon and Michael (1959) describe the successful treatment of a child who cried every time he was put to bed. This treatment involved letting the child cry. In less than a week the behavior had stopped altogether.

MODELING

The fourth behavior-modification technique involves the deliberate application of modeling procedures in an attempt to eliminate deviant behaviors. These procedures can take the form of any of the three effects of imitation. For example, children might be taught something new by being shown what to do (modeling effect); they might be discouraged from doing something by witnessing someone else being punished for the behavior (inhibitory effect); or they might be encouraged to engage in a certain class of behaviors after being exposed to a relevant model (eliciting effect). Ferguson (1968) reports an investigation in which adult subjects were effectively treated for snake phobia by being exposed to a model who, in successive stages, worked around a live snake, fed the snake, and eventually held and played with it. It has similarly been demonstrated that fear of animals in young children can be eliminated through exposure to models who show no evidence of fear (Bandura, Grusec, & Menlove, 1967).

DISCRIMINATION LEARNING

Discrimination learning is the formation of discriminations among stimuli such that the individual responds appropriately in similar situations requiring different responses. For example, aggressive behavior is appropriate in football; it is less appropriate in baseball. Similarly, a child is punished for striking his sister but may be praised for attacking the local bully in her defense.

One procedure for teaching discriminations is described in the report of an experiment conducted by Freund (1960). Subjects were male homosexual patients who volunteered for treatment and were then shown slides of nude males at the same time that the effects of a previously injected emetic mixture were felt. In a later session, they were shown slides of females after being injected with testosterone (male sexual hormones). The procedure resulted in considerable success with these volunteer patients but less success with others who had not volunteered for treatment.

Social Learning and Teaching

The relevance of the preceding discussion for teaching centers on two facts. First, it is probably correct to assume not only that a teacher's behavior serves as a model for a great deal of student behavior but also that instructions, descriptions of behavior, and explicit and implicit expressions of values serve as symbolic models. Second, each of the five behavior-modification techniques that were described can be applied in situations involving learning as well as in those involving discipline (behavior control).

Social-Learning Theory in Review

The social-learning theory first presented by Bandura and Walters and developed further by Bandura attempts to account for learning by means of an imitation theory. The theory is closely related to an operant-conditioning model with one major distinction, which is carefully pointed out by Bandura (1967, 1969). The traditional operant-conditioning paradigm is premised on the assumption that a discriminated stimulus that is present when an operant is emitted and reinforced comes to acquire the ability to elicit the response. In learning through imitation, however, the discriminated stimulus is the model, and the model does not acquire the ability to elicit the imitative response. Nor is the reinforcement necessarily an immediate, tangible consequence of imitating. Indeed, frequently the model has been presented a long time prior to the emission of an imitative response, and the reinforcement might well remain vicarious rather than real. According to Bandura, this time lapse makes an operant-conditioning paradigm insufficient for explaining observational learning. For this reason, a symbolic behavior-control system can usefully be employed in the theory.

Summary of Chapter 14

This chapter has presented a definition of socialization and a discussion of various theoretical explanations of social learning. The theory advanced by Bandura was examined in some detail. A brief account of behavioral therapeutic techniques was also given.

1. Social learning can be defined as the process of learning to behave in a socially acceptable manner. The term *socialization* is used synonymously with the expression *social learning.*

2. Appropriate behavior varies across cultures and for different people within cultures. Hence, a description of the *content* of social learning would be extremely complex. The *process,* however, is probably more uniform across cultures.

3. Among the explanations for social-learning phenomena that can be derived from learning theory are those based on classical conditioning, operant conditioning, cognitivism, and Grandmother's imitation position. No explanation taken alone is entirely adequate for much significant social learning.

4. An integration of all these extrapolated explanations is provided by the social-imitation theory of Bandura and Walters.

5. The major points in this theory are: much significant social learning results from imitation; the effects of imitation are explainable in terms of a model of operant conditioning; and symbolic processes are often involved in social learning.

6. Dollard and Miller also present a social-learning theory based on the role of imitation. Theirs is essentially a drive-reduction approach. As such it suffers from the fact that not all human behavior is designed to reduce stimulation.

7. Bandura and Walters describe three *behavior-control systems* distinguishable by the differences among the responses involved. First, there are responses that are under direct stimulus control; second, there are

responses that are affected by their consequences; and third, there are responses that are directed by means of symbolic processes.

8. *Models* are not only *people* but also symbolic patterns for behavior, such as are provided by books, instructions, religions, television, and so on.

9. *Observational learning* can be manifested in terms of one or more of the three effects of imitation. The modeling effect involves novel, precisely imitative responses; the inhibitory or disinhibitory effects involve the suppression or appearance of deviant behavior, usually as a function of consequences to the model; and the eliciting effect involves behavior that is not deviant or novel but is related to the model's behavior.

10. Techniques for *modifying behavior* include positive reinforcement, extinction, counterconditioning, modeling, and discrimination learning. Each technique can be clearly contrasted to psychoanalytic approaches.

11. Imitation appears to be much more prevalent in social learning than trial and error or insightful learning.

PART **5**

A Last Word

.......so the handsome behaviorist prince and the beautiful cognitivist princess theorized happily ever after.

...Stimulus..the ...sty dragon......

My Dearest Grandmother,

     Thank you for the delicious cookies. And thank you for saying nice things to my editor. I'm sure that will really help, because I know that some people have sometimes said some nasty things about me.

     I was sorry to hear that you preferred not to donate to the Starving Nations Fund. I'd like to talk with you some more about that after church next Sunday. Okay?

     I wasn't betting on the horses, as you know, last Saturday. Robert probably forgot to tell you that I was just there to pose while he took pictures.

     And I'm not making headbands out of turkey feathers any more.

     Besides, I find that my writing has gotten a lot more serious lately. Your influence on this book and on me as a writer has been tremendous, and I want to thank you very much.

     You probably think, by now, that I want to ask you for something.

     No way. I'm just finally maturing a little, and using a lot of your fine examples in the process.

     By the way, about that power bill . . .

CHAPTER *15*

An Integration and Evaluation

To Lie or Oversimplify?

This chapter undertakes what might easily have been an overwhelming task had it not been for my grandmother: that of summarizing and evaluating the learning-related theories that make up the earlier chapters of the book.

What *about* your grandmother? you ask. Again. And though I am somewhat ashamed to admit it, I must confess that from her I learned one of two great techniques for taking care of things that are overwhelming: oversimplifying. The second technique, lying, I picked up somewhere on my own.

I use one of these techniques repeatedly in this ambitious chapter—a chapter that presents a summary of the major learning theories discussed earlier, follows that summary with a rapid evaluation, and ends with a final attempt to integrate some of our important knowledge about human learning (in the form of Robert Gagné's theories).

Major Divisions in Learning Theory

Learning has been defined as changes in behavior that result from experience. The point has also been made that the terms *learning theory* and *behavior theory* are employed synonymously. Among the various ways of looking at human behavior or learning, two broad orientations can be identified, which give rise to the classical divisions among psychological theory. The first orientation assumes that our behavior is, at least in some measure, influenced by the activity that goes on in the brain. Grandmother's argument for this orientation is that we think, have a will, feel, and behave because of the way we think, feel, and intend. Fortunately for her, she is seldom asked to define the terms she uses.

TABLE 15-1. Divisions in learning theory

	Symbolic represen- tation	Variables of concern	Representative theorists
Behaviorism S-R theories	S-R	Stimuli Responses Reinforcement	Watson Guthrie Thorndike Skinner Hull Spence
A transition	S—O—R (O above, S and R below)	Stimuli Responses Reinforcement Mediation	Hebb
Cognitivism	O	Perception Organizing Information processing Decision making Problem solving	Tolman Gestaltists Bruner Piaget

The second orientation does not flatly contradict the first but merely asserts that very little scientifically valid knowledge about human behavior can be derived from an investigation of the nebulous processes of the mind. Instead, advocates of this orientation concentrate on an examination of human behavior and the observable conditions that lead to behavior. Obviously, prebehavioristic and cognitive psychologists have the first orientation in common, whereas behaviorists are characterized by the second. It is important to bear in mind, however, that few positions are clearly *only* behavioristic or cognitive; such terms are simply convenient labels to describe distinct theoretical orientations. In addition, the labels are also indicative of somewhat different areas of interest. For example, behaviorism deals largely with investigations of stimuli and responses. In contrast, topics of interest to cognitive psychologists typically do not include stimuli and response per se but deal instead with more *central* processes such as problem solving, decision making, perception, information processing, concept formation, and memory. Table 15-1 (adapted from Table 3-1) distinguishes among the major divisions in learning theory. Each of these positions is summarized in the following section.

Analysis

BEHAVIORISTIC POSITIONS

Watson. J. B. Watson was among the first of North American psychologists to attempt to define the science of psychology in objective terms. He saw psychology as a science that deals with the observable rather than the merely hypothetical—

a definition that gave rise to North American behaviorism. Watson's behaviorism was characterized by a rigorous subscription to the laws of classical conditioning that had been investigated by the Russian physiologist Pavlov. Watson assumed that individuals are born with a behavioral repertoire consisting of only a few reflexes and that these early responses become conditioned to other stimuli as a function of the simultaneous occurrence of stimulus or response events.

Watson is also recognized as one of the chief spokesmen for environmentalism—the belief that personality, intelligence, and all other human qualities are determined by the environment (the nurture side in the historical nature/nurture dispute). One of his better-known claims was that he could make whatever he wanted out of a dozen healthy infants if he were given a free hand in their upbringing.

Guthrie. Edwin Guthrie, like Watson, took a rigidly behavioristic approach. It can be summarized in several major laws, which state essentially that whenever a response follows a stimulus, there will result a tendency for the same response to occur again the next time the stimulus is presented. Specifically, Guthrie maintained that learning is complete on the occasion of the first pairing of a stimulus with a response and that further practice will not strengthen the response. Similarly, he believed that forgetting does not occur; in other words, when a bond has been formed between a stimulus and a response, that bond will never be broken. However, it is possible to remove undesirable habits by learning new ones that are incompatible with the old ones. Guthrie suggested three ways in which this can be done: the fatigue technique, the threshold approach, and the method of incompatible stimuli. It is important to note that for both Watson and Guthrie, the consequences of the behavior are not instrumental in bringing about learning. The effects of punishment and reward are, according to Guthrie, simply to change the stimulus situation, thereby preventing the unlearning of a response.

Thorndike. E. L. Thorndike is generally credited with introducing the notion of reinforcement in contemporary learning theory through his Laws of Effect and of Exercise. The Law of Effect states that learning is a consequence of the effect of behavior. Specifically, those responses that lead to a satisfying state of affairs will tend to be repeated, whereas those that lead to an unpleasant or annoying state will tend not to be repeated. The Law of Exercise says that stimulus-response events that are practiced will tend to be more strongly linked, whereas those that fall into disuse will tend to be forgotten.

For Thorndike, learning consists of the formation of bonds between stimuli and responses as a function of their repetition and of the consequences of the responses. He labeled the process of learning a *stamping-in* process; forgetting involves *stamping out*. The system can be further detailed through a discussion of five subsidiary laws, the most important of which is the law of multiple responses. This law states, in effect, that when faced with a problem situation, we tend to respond in a variety of ways until one of the responses emitted is reinforced. In other words, learning occurs through a process of *trial and error.* Additional laws are simply formalizations of the observations that behavior is generalizable, that we respond to the most striking features of the environment, that cultural background affects behavior, and that learning through contiguity does occur.

Skinner. B. F. Skinner stands out as one of the great system builders in 20th-century psychology. Interestingly, his aim has not been to develop a system or theory of behavior but simply to make careful observations of the behavior of various organisms. The learning model that has resulted from his work is *operant* conditioning, a model that can be described in terms of the assertion that learning results from the reinforcement of responses that are emitted by an organism. Skinner's major preoccupation has been with discovering the relationship between reinforcement and response variables. For this reason, his work has dealt largely with the effects of different ways of presenting reinforcement (schedules of reinforcement) on rate of learning, response rate, and extinction rate. Extinction refers to the cessation of a response after reinforcement has been discontinued. Among his most important findings is the fact that learning is facilitated in its initial stages by continuous reinforcement, but extinction time is increased by intermittent reinforcement. Although most of his experimentation was carried on with animals, these results are assumed to be generally applicable to human behavior as well.

One of the techniques developed by Skinner for teaching complex behaviors to animals is *shaping,* which involves reinforcing *successive approximations* to the desired behavior and is widely employed by professional animal trainers.

The applications of Skinner's work to human behavior are discussed by him in several books: *Walden Two* (1948), *Science and Human Behavior* (1953), and *Beyond Freedom and Dignity* (1971). In addition, a direct educational application of Skinner's theory is that of programmed instruction.

Hull. Clark L. Hull's theoretical approach is labeled hypothetico-deductive. He undertook one of the most ambitious tasks ever undertaken by a psychologist—that of formalizing all knowledge about human behavior in order to make it possible to predict responses on the basis of knowledge about stimuli. The system was never quite completed but nevertheless stands as an overwhelming example of formal theory building.

Hull's investigations and consequent formulas and equations deal with three aspects of human behavior: *input* variables, which include physical stimuli as well as such factors as drive conditions, previously learned habits, and amount of reward available *intervening* variables, which consist mainly of the effects of input variables on the organism; and *output* variables, which are the characteristics of actual behavior in terms of response latency, frequency of responding, and time to extinction. The system may be partly summarized in terms of the following equation: $_sE_R = {}_sH_R \times D \times V \times K.$

Hull described his system in 17 postulates, 133 theorems, and innumerable corollaries from which the nature of his beliefs about learning emerges. One of the central concepts in the theory is *habit*, which is an S-R connection. A collection of such connections forms a *habit-family hierarchy*. This habit-family hierarchy is a hypothetical preferential ordering of related alternative behaviors. The relatedness of habits results from the fact that they have common goals. According to Hull, behavior is purposive in that it is goal oriented. Reinforcement, in the form of the attainment of a goal or in the form of what he labels *antedating goal responses*, accounts for the formation of habits. An antedating goal reaction is any one of the many reward-related responses that an organism makes as it nears a goal. For example, as it turns the last corner in a maze, a rat may lick its chops—an antedating goal reaction.

Hull's use of the concept of intervening variables might seem to be a link between his system and more cognitive interests. It is important to note, however, that the Hullian variables are tied directly to input and output variables. They are not intended to be simply inferred hypothetical constructs or metaphors.

Spence. The Hullian tradition was carried on by Kenneth Spence. An obvious, but superficial, distinction between Hull and Spence is that some of the symbols employed by Hull have been changed. The major formula is no longer $_sE_R = {}_sH_R \times D \times V \times K$... but is $E = H \times (D + K)$. Interestingly, however, the symbols have the same referents. One other less superficial change is evident in the Spence formula—the change from a multiplicative to an additive function. *Drive (D)* or *reward (K)* can be zero without necessarily reducing the potential for *responding (E)* to zero. In addition, whereas Hull had relied largely on a drive-reduction explanation of motivation, Spence substituted the notion that the antedating goal responses are themselves reinforcing in the absence of the actual reduction of drive. Also, Spence assumed that the strength of a habit is not dependent on reinforcement (as Hull had contended) but that it is related only to the frequency of S-R pairings.

In the final analysis, the two systems resemble each other much more than they differ. Indeed, it is not at all unusual to see references to the Hull-Spence system.

A TRANSITION

Hebb. D. O. Hebb has advanced a somewhat speculative neurophysiological proposal for a theory of human behavior. The mediational activity that is the basis for his explanation of higher mental processes is assumed to consist of activity in neurons or groups of neurons arranged in closed loops or of activity in more complex arrangements of such loops. The closed circuit of related neural cells is labeled a *cell assembly.* Hebb assumes that it is composed of a number of smaller neural units called *reverberatory loops.* The more complex arrangements of cell assemblies are labeled *phase sequences* Absolutely central to Hebb's theory is the notion that transmission among neurons appears to be facilitated as a function of repeated firing among them. This phenomenon of neural activity ostensibly accounts for learning. A cell assembly corresponds to some simple sensory input—for example, the color of an object or one part of one of its dimensions. Activity in an entire arrangement of assemblies (a phase sequence) corresponds to the whole object. Through learning, cell assemblies and phase sequences eventually achieve some correspondence to the environment. That is, since different parts of an object are usually sensed in contiguity, cell assemblies related to different aspects of an object will often be simultaneously active and will therefore become related.

Hebb has been largely responsible for the development of an arousal-based theory of motivation. This theory is premised on the assumption that optimal human functioning is made possible by a moderate level of arousal and that an organism therefore behaves in such a way as to maintain that level. Other theorists have subsequently incorporated these same notions in their systems (for example, Bruner).

COGNITIVISM

Tolman. Edward Tolman was among the first notable North American psychologists to begin with a rigid behavioristic orientation and eventually develop a system far more cognitive than behavioristic. His is a theory of *purposive behaviorism.* Hence his inclusion among cognitive psychologists, although in many ways his system represents an important transition from behaviorism.

Tolman's system is best understood in terms of his three most basic beliefs. First, and most important, all behavior is purposive. By this, Tolman meant that behavior is directed—that it is guided toward goals, not as a stimulus might guide in Hull's system but rather by cognitions. He described these cognitions primarily in terms of expectancies that the organism develops with respect to reward.

A second important principle in this system concerns Tolman's emphasis on molar rather than molecular aspects of behavior. In other words, he was not concerned with discrete S-R events so much as with the more global aspects of behaving.

Tolman's third fundamental belief is his insistence that what is learned as a function of reinforcement is not a response-stimulus link or a response-reinforcement link but a *cognition*—an awareness that reward is likely to follow certain behaviors. It is this awareness that guides behavior; and that makes it reasonable for Tolman to describe his system as one of purposive behaviorism.

The Gestaltists. Gestalt psychology can be interpreted as a second reaction against the mentalism of pre-20th-century psychology. However, unlike the behavioristic reaction, it did not seek to objectify the science so much as to change its methods. Introspection was unacceptable, not because it investigated the wrong topics but because it sought to discover facts about behavior through *analysis*. The Gestalt approach is one of *synthesis*; it asserts clearly that even physical objects cannot be completely known or understood through an analysis of their parts. That *the whole is greater than the sum of its parts* became the familiar Gestalt watchword.

The chief concern of Gestalt psychology was to discover the laws governing perception. It is responsible for the elaboration of such "laws" as *closure*, *proximity*, *symmetry*, *continuity*, and *Pragnanz*. It is largely because of this preoccupation that Gestaltism is considered to be the forerunner of cognitivism.

Among the better-known Gestalt psychologists were such men as Kohler, Koffka, and Wertheimer. Lewin's system is also an example of a Gestalt approach. These positions are unified not only in their preoccupation with perception but also through their rejection of trial-and-error explanations of human learning; their alternative explanation is that people learn through insight.

Bruner. Jerome Bruner has developed a loose-knit cognitive theory intended to explain various phenomena in perception, decision making, information processing, conceptualization, and development. His earlier writings deal primarily with learning; his more recent interests are largely in the area of development.

The theory is sometimes referred to as a theory of categorizing. The term *category* is synonymous with both *percept* and *concept*. Essentially, to categorize is to treat objects as though they were in some ways equivalent. Accordingly, a category can be thought of as a rule for classifying objects in terms of their properties (attributes). Much of Bruner's early work was devoted to an investigation of the strategies employed by people in learning how to categorize stimulus events both for simple perception and for the attainment of concepts.

Bruner's approach to learning and problem solving is premised on the assumption that the value of what is learned is measurable largely in terms of how well it permits the learner to go *beyond the information given*. He argues that concepts and percepts are useful when organized into systems of related categories (coding systems) that have wide generality.

Bruner also makes use of an arousal-based explanation of motivation—an explanation that is virtually identical to Hebb's. He also borrows extensively from Hebb in describing the neurological mechanisms that we must possess in order to behave in a manner consistent with his theory.

Piaget. Jean Piaget's theory is really a system unto itself. It is not easily compared with other positions.

Piaget's major focus is development. Given the close relationship between learning and development, however, it is not inappropriate to make reference to his *learning* theory. He describes development as the evolution of a child's ability to interact with the world in an increasingly appropriate, realistic, and logical fashion. Part of his work is therefore devoted to a description of children at different stages of development, labeled the sensorimotor stage (birth to 2 years), the preoperational stage (2 to 7 years—comprising preconceptual and intuitive thinking), the period of concrete operations (7 to 11 or 12 years), and the stage of formal operations (11 or 12 to 14 or 15 years). Each stage is marked by characteristic abilities and errors in problem solving, results from activities and abilities of the preceding period, and is a preparation for the next stage.

Another part of Piaget's work is devoted to a discussion of the properties of human children that enable them to make progress in their ontogeny. In this connection, he evolved a biologically oriented definition of intelligence as an interactive process. Essentially, it is a process involving the two ways of functioning that we possess. One is defined as the process of exercising previously learned activities (assimilation), and the other consists of modifying behavior (accommodation). An optimal balance between these processes (equilibrium) constitutes maximally adaptive behavior (or maximally *intelligent* behavior).

In addition to studying the characteristics of development per se, Piaget devoted a large portion of his writings to specific topics such as the development of children's concept of time, space, causality, logic, geometry, and so on.

Artificial Intelligence

Artificial intelligence is not summarized here, largely because it does not represent a new body of knowledge about human behavior or a new approach to that study. Indeed, the attempt to use machines to replicate human behavior may well be limited by the amount of information that can be derived *from other sources.* At this stage in its development, computer simulation of human processes is an intriguing endeavor that may well lead to some extremely useful discoveries or applications of knowledge. But it is not now a learning theory.

Miller, Galanter, and Pribram have advanced a model of human behavior premised on the notion that we behave in the manner of a well-programmed, self-regulating machine. The TOTE unit that forms the basis of this model provides a simple and potentially useful approach to understanding behavior. Taken alone, however, it too does not represent a new theory or new information regarding human behavior.

Factors Affecting Learning

Among the important factors that are inextricably implicated in human learning are attention, memory, and motivation. Theories in each of these areas include both behavioristic and cognitive orientations, although recent investigations of memory and attention tend to be based primarily on cognitive models.

ATTENTION

Attention can be defined as the process of "holding in mind" only one—or perhaps two—of the many stimuli that impinge on our sense receptors at any given time. In this sense, attention is very similar to what is sometimes called *active memory*, or short-term memory.

MEMORY

One common theory of memory is a two-stage theory. It is essentially a metaphor, which says that we process and remember information as though we had two separate memory stores (or memory processes)—one associated with short-term retention (seconds rather than minutes) and another associated with long-term memory. Beyond obvious differences in the time during which relevant memories are available, some important distinctions between the two include the fact that STM is an active, ongoing process, whereas LTM is more passive; STM is easily disrupted and LTM is not; and STM is far more limited in terms of capacity.

An important general model of long-term memory makes reference to nodes (or node encoding), which are metaphors for ideas. In effect, a node is whatever stands for an idea. This model is associationistic (all knowledge is related) in contrast to earlier models, which tended to view memory as consisting of isolated compartments or of a continuous "video tape" representation of sequential events.

MOTIVATION

Motivation theory addresses itself to the "why" of behavior. Behavioristic explanations for the occurrence, direction, and cessation of behavior frequently rely on what is suspected about instincts, needs, and drives. Instincts are unlearned, complex, and specific to certain species. They do not appear to be highly relevant for an understanding of human behavior. Need/drive theories are somewhat more relevant but fail to explain a wide variety of behaviors that do not appear to be responses to specific needs.

Cognitive theories of motivation present a more active view of human behavior—one quite distinct from that of a reactive organism pushed and prodded willy-nilly by hungers and drives over which it has little, if any, control. Cognitive-dissonance theory and attribution theory are two manifestations of cognitive orientations in motivation. Both describe behavior as involving a conscious attempt to make sense out of ourselves and our environment.

Arousal theories of motivation are premised on the basic assumption that there is an optimal level of arousal for different behavior and that we act so as to maintain arousal at or near this level.

Synthesis

The preceding summaries are a brief analysis of the learning positions described in this text. This section constitutes a synthesis of the information presented in the summaries.

Two different syntheses are provided: the first in the form of a tabular representation of the vocabulary of each theoretical position; the second in the form of a reduction of theoretical jargonism to the statements of a wise grandmother.

Table 15-2 is presented as something of a pedagogical device for the student of learning theory. It may prove useful, particularly for review and examination purposes, to study the contents of the table. The terms associated with each theorist are simply those words or expressions that most clearly identify the position in question and distinguish it from other theories. Table 15-3 is presented for those who are more visually oriented. It consists of diagrammatic or symbolic representations of aspects of each theory. It should be noted that neither Table 15-2 nor Table 15-3 pretends to be a complete representation of the theories in question.

JARGONISM

While it would be relatively simple to dismiss differences among theoretical positions as superficial and resulting only from the use of different terms for the same concepts, it would not be entirely accurate to do so. Obviously, there are some *real* differences among the theoretical positions described in the two tables; the respective theorists would probably be among the first to make this assertion. Indeed, it appears to have been somewhat fashionable in the development of theoretical positions to begin by demonstrating how earlier theories could not account for various phenomena judged to be of some psychological significance. For some theorists, the deprecation of other theoretical positions has been a major concern.

However, despite these alleged theoretical distinctions, it is nevertheless true that there are many more similarities among theories than would appear to be the case from a superficial examination of them. Jargon hides many of these similarities, since each theorist seems to feel that it is his right to coin new terms or to use old ones in new ways. But jargon sometimes does more than simply hide the resemblance of a new theory to an old one—frequently it hides the absence of substance.

A casual look at Table 15-2 reveals numerous terms that could almost be used interchangeably. In many cases another, more familiar but less jargonistic, expression could substitute for either. For example, *stamping in* is really *conditioning*—but so is the formation of a *cell assembly*. A *cell assembly* bears a strong resemblance to a *percept* or *concept*, as does a *category*. A *phase sequence* is the neurological analogue of a *category*, or perhaps of a *schema*.

TABLE 15-2. Key words

Behaviorists

Watson	Guthrie	Thorndike	Skinner	Hull	Spence
Behaviorism	Contiguity	Effect	Operant	Habit strength	Habit
Classical conditioning	One-shot learning	Exercise	Respondent	Hypothetico-deductive	Reaction potential
Reflexes	Habits	Stamping in	Schedules	Reaction potential	$r_G - s_G$
Environmentalism	Threshold	Stamping out	Extinction	Drive	Drive
Contiguity	Fatigue	Trial and error	Rats	Goal reactions	
	Incompatible stimuli	Connectionism	Shaping	Habit families	
			Superstition		
			Programmed instruction		

Cognitivists

Tolman	Gestaltists	Bruner	Piaget
Purposive	Perception	Categorizing	Equilibrium
Molar	Wholes	Perceptual readiness	Stages
Intention	Pragnanz	Attributes	Assimilation
Expectancy	Closure	Coding systems	Accommodation
Sign-significate	Field	Strategies	Operations
Place learning	Vectors		Logic
	Life space		

Transition

Hebb
Reverberation
Cell assembly
Phase sequence
Neurophysiology
Arousal
Perception

TABLE 15-3. Diagrammatic and symbolic representations

Behaviorism

Watson	Thorndike	Guthrie	Skinner	Hull	Spence
UCS → UCR	1) S₁ → R₁ (pleasant)	S₁ → R₁	Rₓ + reinforcement		
CS → ?	2) S₁ → R₁	S₁ → R₁	+ S₁		
CS + UCS → UCR			↓	$_sE_R = {_s}H_R \times D \times V \times K$	$E = H \times (D + K)$
CS + UCS → UCR	1) S₂ → R₂ (unpleasant)	S₁ → Rₓ	S₁ → Rₓ		
CS → CR	2) S₂ →				

Transition

Cognitivism

Hebb	Tolman	Gestaltists	Bruner	Piaget

Reward
4 Kilometers

content

structure

function

But there are some differences. In order to obtain a clearer understanding of these, the reader is advised to study Chapters 1 to 15 of this text (omitting Chapter 13).

SOME CRITICISMS

Each of the major learning theories described in this text is evaluated after its presentation. This section does not attempt to summarize all of the important features of those evaluations but describes instead some of the more common (and sometimes pertinent) *criticisms* that have historically been leveled at various learning theories. My grandmother, who taught me to oversimplify (which is sometimes no better than lying), also insisted that, "If they're gonna improve, ya gotta tell 'em what's wrong with 'em."

Here's what's wrong with 'em. And what's right with 'em too, although in neither case are the following comments meant to be an exhaustive catalogue of all the good and bad features of each theory; indeed, since the comments are somewhat subjective in the first place, they are presented here only as suggestions. Interested readers are invited to expand the evaluation in their own subjective fashion or, alternatively, to consult their grandmothers.

Behaviorism. The principal criticism of behaviorism is that through its mechanization of humanity it has dehumanized us. Critics point out that we possess awareness, that feeling is very much a part of behaving, that surely human interaction with the environment is more than simply a matter of stimuli and responses. They contend further that conditioning, in all of its varieties, is not sufficient to explain a great deal of human behavior. They also react negatively to the use of animals in studies whose results are then generalized to human behavior. Behaviorists, in their defense, maintain that it is only by dealing with those aspects of human functioning that are clearly measurable and definable that valid and reliable conclusions can be reached. They point at the chaotic and confused nature of "mentalistic" psychology. They ask what images, feelings, and sensations are. They also wonder what the significance of these concepts is except as they affect human behavior.

Clearly, then, behaviorism stresses objectivity; in so doing, there is some loss of immediate and obvious relevance. Nevertheless, the approach has proven fruitful in terms of applicable research and theory and appears to be in little danger of being abandoned.

Some specific criticisms can also be leveled at each of the major behavioristic positions. It has been pointed out, for example, that a model of classical conditioning, such as that espoused by Watson, cannot easily account for the acquisition of novel responses.

Guthrie's theory, like Watson's, suffers from its failure to recognize that the effects of behavior are related to learning. In addition, the notion that learning always occurs and is complete in one trial appears to be somewhat unrealistic. Thorndike's work was subject to a great deal of criticism by early Gestalt psychologists, particularly for its almost exclusive reliance on a trial-and-error explanation for human learning.

The work of B. F. Skinner has also been severely criticized, not so much because of theoretical inconsistencies or errors but rather because he represents a behaviorism that is sometimes viewed as a potential weapon that will be used against humanity by Machiavellian psychologists.

Hull's very formal and elaborate, but often imprecise, system also has serious weaknesses. Critics have drawn attention to his use in equations of numbers often taken from studies involving only one or two subjects; they have noted the failure of his system to increase the accuracy of predictions about responses, and they have commented on the fact that, although Hull ostensibly dealt with human behavior, his experimentation was usually limited to studies of the behavior of rats or, at best, studies of conditioned eyeblink responses in people.

Spence's system can generally be criticized on the same grounds as Hull's, since it is not substantially different from it.

Transition.   The proposal for a theory advanced by Donald Hebb is admittedly based on neurophysiological speculation as well as fact. It has been argued that such an approach is not likely to lead to any new discoveries about learning but is more likely to result in logically plausible but practically useless conceptions of neural functioning. In other words, it is unlikely that neurological speculation will lead to anything more than an explanation for what is already known or suspected about behavior. Of course, the opposite argument can also be advanced. It can be countered that not all of Hebb's proposal is based on speculation, that there are sources of information about human neurology that are quite distinct from psychological experimentation, and that it is quite conceivable that knowledge about human neural activity may eventually lead to a better understanding of learning and behavior.

Despite some of the obvious shortcomings of behavioristic positions, their influence on the development of learning theory has been highly significant. A great deal of the emphasis on experimentation and scientific rigor that characterizes much contemporary theorizing stems from the work of such people as Guthrie, Watson, and especially Hull. Much of the emphasis on the practical applicability of theory is attributable to the work of Thorndike. Skinner's contribution to a practical science of behavior can hardly be overestimated. And some of Hebb's notions concerning arousal are an important part of current theories of motivation.

Cognitivism.   The critics of cognitive approaches to human learning base many of their objections on the cognitivists' relatively less precise and more subjective approach to information gathering and to theorizing. The extensive use of jargon by many contemporary cognitivists and the seeming lack of agreement among different positions has also been the source of some criticism. Cognitivists counter by pointing out that they are dealing with topics that are of more relevance to human behavior than are questions relating to stimuli and responses and that the investigation of these topics sometimes requires the making of inferences from relatively limited data.

Gestalt psychology has been largely abandoned by some contemporary theorists, partly because the laws of perception do not appear to be directly applicable to learning processes. (Humanistic and group-oriented psychologists are frequently Gestaltic, however.)

Bruner can be criticized on the grounds that his terminology is sometimes confusing and that the metaphors he employs are often obscure and impractical.

Piaget's work has been heavily criticized on several counts. His experimental methods, his lack of sampling procedures, the extremely small numbers of subjects employed in most of his studies, and the lack of statistical analysis in his early work have met with some opposition, particularly on the part of experimentally oriented North American psychologists. In addition, Piaget has been criticized for overgeneralizing and overtheorizing from his data.

This evaluation would not be complete without repeating that each position also has some unique strengths and contributions, as is made evident in earlier chapters of this text.

Contrasting theoretical positions and attempting to discredit some explanations of learning have served as useful devices in the development of new theories. Such apparent disagreement among theorists, however, is often discouraging and frustrating for the student who is searching for *the* correct theoretical position. Perhaps, that position does not exist.

An Alternative

Historically the search in learning theory has been for *one* best way of explaining human behavior. Obviously this effort has been premised on the assumption that there *is* one best explanation. An alternative assumption, which leads to a drastically different and potentially extremely useful theoretical orientation, can also be advanced. One can assume that there is no one correct theory and that, since there are numerous kinds of human learning, there is a need for a large number of different explanations. The resulting "theory" could well be an integration of a variety of concepts that have traditionally been associated with separate positions.

Several recent attempts at integrating knowledge about human learning are based on the assumption described above. Bandura's (1969) description of behavior-control systems is one example of this approach. Melton (1964) provides a second example in his description of categories of human learning. These categories include topics of interest to most theoretical positions. A third, more detailed and more comprehensive, integration is provided by Robert Gagné. It is described briefly in the next section.

Robert Gagné: An Integrated Position

The theory that comes closest to being a deliberate and systematic attempt to integrate the variety of theories described in this text is that advanced by Robert Gagné. It is presented here as the final statement in the final chapter.

CATEGORIES OF LEARNING

Gagné (1974) describes five major domains of *learned* capabilities: intellectual skills, verbal information, attitudes, motor skills, and cognitive strategies. Of these, the first domain (intellectual skills) is concerned with the *how* of learning and relates well to the learning theories described in preceding chapters. The other four domains are concerned with the *what* of learning and are described briefly below before an examination of intellectual skills.

Most of the learning of greatest concern to teachers involves *verbal information*. Gagné defines verbal information as nothing more complicated than what is generally considered to be *knowledge*. Although it is not always derived only from verbal input (or stored verbally, for that matter), verbal information can be expressed in the form of a sentence—or at least an implied sentence.*Cognitive strategies* are the personal plans we all have for directing our intellectual functioning. These are the plans (strategies) that govern how we go about learning, remembering, paying attention, synthesizing, abstracting, creating, and so on. They are skills that appear to be largely self-learned in spite of the fact that schools (and teacher-education programs) typically pay considerable lip service to them.

Attitudes are affective (emotional) reactions that can generally be described as positive or negative and that have important motivational qualities. Gagné suggests that one of the important ways in which attitudes are learned involves imitation much as it is described by Bandura.

Motor skills are the variety of organized, sequential motor activities of which we are capable. They include all complex behaviors that require an organized pattern of controlled muscular movements. Writing, talking, plucking chickens, and hitting a spitoon from 22 paces are all examples of motor skills.

The domain of behaviors to which Gagné has paid the greatest attention is that of *intellectual skills*. These include all of the skills that are involved in acquiring information, solving problems, discovering rules, and learning how to talk—to name but a few.

Gagné (1970) describes eight types of intellectual skills, the first four of which he has sometimes combined under the single label *simple types of learning* (Gagné, 1974). Each of the original eight categories is described very briefly below, and its relationship to other learning theories is pointed out. However, before listing and defining these eight types of learning, two comments should be made about Gagné's general approach. First, the learning types are not completely independent from one another but are in fact hierarchical. The simplest, most basic learning is necessary before the learner can go on to more complex types of learning. A second point is that these types of learning are distinguishable largely in terms of the *conditions that permit the learning to take place*; knowledge of subordinate types of learning is only one of these conditions.

EIGHT TYPES OF LEARNING

Type 1: Signal Learning

Definition: Simple Pavlovian conditioning.

Example: A car horn blasts. A man jumps wildly. The same man sees another car—a quiet one. He jumps wildly again.

Important theorists: Pavlov, Watson.

Type 2: Stimulus-Response Learning

Definition: The formation of a *single* connection between a stimulus and a response.

Example: A fat sow is turned clockwise as her proud owner, a psychologist, says gently "Turn." After each complete turn the smiling sow is given a piece of apple. The psychologist does this every day for two years. After 730 apples and 1459 turns (the psychologist ate half the apple once), the sow can now turn when the psychologist says "Turn." That is slow stimulus-response learning.

Important theorists: Skinner, Thorndike, Hull, Spence.

Type 3: Chaining—Motor Chains

Definition: The connection of a sequence of motor stimulus-response behaviors.

Example: A man is seen removing his teeth. He reaches to his mouth with his hand, opens his mouth and inserts his hand, places the thumb and forefinger on the right upper canine, and pulls. He then does the same for his lower teeth. The S-R chain may be simplified as follows:

S →   R --------- S ——→ R ------- S ——→ R ---------- S ——→ R

| hand at mouth | open mouth | mouth open | insert hand | hand inserted | position fingers | fingers positioned | pull |

Important theorists: Guthrie, Thorndike, Skinner.

Type 4: Chaining—Verbal Associations

Definition: The connection of a sequence of verbal stimulus-response behaviors.

Example: One, two, three, four, five, . . .

Important theorists: Hebb, Bruner.

Type 5: Discrimination Learning

Definition: Learning to discriminate between highly similar stimulus input. The learning of discriminations is "essentially a matter of establishing numbers of different chains" (Gagné, 1965, p. 115).

Example: The learning of a foreign language involves learning verbal chains in that language. Since these chains are already present in the mother tongue, the learner must discriminate between the two.

Important theorists: Skinner, Bruner, and Hebb.

Type 6: Concept Learning

Definition: Concept learning is the opposite of discrimination learning. It involves responding to a set of objects in terms of their similarities.

Example: A boy learns that an English setter is a dog. He sees a cat and says "doggie." He has developed a "doggie" concept, albeit an incorrect one.

Important theorists: Hebb, Bruner, Skinner, and Piaget.

Type 7: Rule Learning

Definition: "A rule is an inferred capability that enables the individual to respond to a class of stimulus situations with a class of performances" (1970, p. 191).

Example: A simple rule is exemplified by the statement "Psychology is fun." Understanding this rule involves understanding the concept *psychology* and the concept *fun*. Many students understand neither.

Important theorists: Bruner, Piaget.

Type 8: Problem Solving

Definition: The application of rules in the generation of "higher-order rules." This is the inevitable outcome of applying rules to problems.

Example: Consider the elementary problem of catching a dorabotur. Four rules can be employed in the solution of this simple problem:

1. Doraboturs like snrapes.
2. Snrapes grow in holes 2 feet deep.
3. Doraboturs have tails that are always at least 3 feet long.
4. Doraboturs are harmless.

The solution can be expressed in terms of the higher-order rule: doraboturs can be pulled out of snrape holes by their tails.

Important theorists: Bruner, Piaget.

Summary of Chapter 15

This chapter has presented summaries of each of the major theoretical positions discussed in this text. The summaries were followed by a tabulation of the terms that can be employed to identify each position and by an evaluation of these theories. In addition, a brief description of the theory of Robert Gagné was given.

1. One of the problems in summarizing learning theory is to simplify without lying.
2. The major divisions in learning theory can be distinguished in terms of the variables of greatest concern to the theorists in question as well as in terms of the approach to data gathering and science building employed by each.
3. Watson, Guthrie, Thorndike, and Skinner were among the early behaviorists. Watson and Guthrie can be classed as "connectivists in the contiguity tradition," whereas Thorndike and Skinner are "connectionists in the reinforcement tradition" (Hill, 1963).
4. Hull and Spence have attempted the development of a formal hypothetico-deductive system; Hebb has advanced a neurophysiological model of perception and learning.
5. The Gestaltists, Bruner, and Piaget can be considered cognitive psychologists. Gestaltism is concerned more with perception than with learning; Bruner has described an information-processing theory; and Piaget's system is largely developmental.
6. Jargon hides many similarities among learning theories. It can also serve as effective camouflage for lack of substance.
7. When evaluated in terms of how well they account for all types of human learning and behavior, each theoretical position can be subjected to criticism.
8. Recent attempts to describe various kinds of learning (for example, Bandura, Melton, and Gagné) are premised on the assumption that there is a need for a variety of explanations.
9. Gagné's eight types of learning can be related directly to the theories discussed in this text.

Epilogue

Dear Grandmother,

 What can I say? They should never have turned your power off. I had the check in to them a good two weeks ago. Either the bank made a mistake or I might have written it on the wrong account. Anyway, I'll have it all straightened out early next month. In the meantime, why don't you move in with mom and dad? I know it's been hard on your turkeys sleeping in the dark every night, but you could maybe bring them with you. And you can just leave Pouf at home. I'll take care of him.

 Let me know . . .

Dear Guy,

 Just a short note. You'll probably be overjoyed to learn that Robert is having a magnificent book published early this fall! He says it was given to him by a little bluish creature from some weird place that starts with a K. But we know that Robert wrote it himself. He expects to be very rich . . .

References

Allport, F. H. *Theories of perception and the concept of structure*. New York: Wiley, 1955.

Anand, B. K., & Chhina, G. S. Investigations on yogis claiming to stop their heart beats. *Indian Journal of Medical Research*, 1961, *49*, 90–94.

Anastasi, A. Heredity, environment and the question "how?" *Psychological Review*, 1958, *65*, 197–208.

Anderson, A. R. *Minds and machines*. Englewood Cliffs, N. J.: Prentice-Hall, 1964.

Apter, M. J. The computer modelling of behaviour. In Apter, M. J., & Westby, G. (Eds.), *The computer in psychology*. New York: Wiley, 1973.

Apter, M. J., & Westby, G. (Eds.). *The computer in psychology*. New York: Wiley, 1973.

Ashby, W. R. *An introduction to cybernetics*. London: Chapman & Hall, 1961.

Asimov, I. *The human brain*. New York: Signet, 1963.

Athey, I. J., & Rubadeau, D. O. (Eds.). *Educational implications of Piaget's theory*. Waltham, Mass.: Ginn-Blaisdell, 1970.

Atkinson, R. C., & Shiffrin, R. M. Human memory: A proposed system and its control processes. In K. W. Spence & J. T. Spence (Eds.), *The psychology of learning and motivation: Advances in research and theory* (Vol. 2). New York: Academic Press, 1968.

Ausubel, D. P. *Theory and problems of child development*. New York: Grune & Stratton, 1957.

Ausubel, D. P. *The psychology of meaningful verbal learning*. New York: Grune & Stratton, 1963.

Ausubel, D. P. *Educational psychology: A cognitive view*. New York: Holt, Rinehart & Winston, 1968.

Ausubel, D. P., & Anderson, L. C. *Readings in the psychology of cognition*. New York: Holt, Rinehart & Winston, 1965.

Ausubel, D. P., & Robinson, F. G. *School learning: An introduction to educational psychology*. New York: Holt, Rinehart & Winston, 1969.

Ayllon, T., & Michael, J. The psychiatric nurse as a behavioral engineer. *Journal of the Experimental Analysis of Behavior*, 1959, *2*, 323–334.

Babich, F. R., Jacobson, A. L., Bubash, S., & Jacobson, A. Transfer of learning to naive rats by injection of ribonucleic acid extracted from trained rats. *Science*, 1965, *149*, 656–657.

Babrick, H. P., Babrick, P. O., & Wittlinger, R. P. Fifty years of memory for names and faces: A cross-sectional approach. *Journal of Experimental Psychology*, 1975, *104*, 54–75.

Baddeley, A. D. *The psychology of memory*. New York: Basic Books, 1976.

Baer, D. M., Peterson, R. S., & Sherman, J. A. The development of imitation by reinforcing behavioral similarity to a model. *Journal of the Experimental Analysis of Behavior*, 1967, *10*, 405–416.

Baldwin, A. L. *Theories of child development*. New York: Wiley, 1967.

Bandura, A. Behavioral modifications through modelling procedures. In Krasner, L., & Ullmann, L. P. (Eds.), *Research in behavior modification*. New York: Holt, Rinehart & Winston, 1967.

Bandura, A. *Principles of behavior modification*. New York: Holt, Rinehart & Winston, 1969.

Bandura, A. *Social learning theory*. Englewood Cliffs, N. J.: Prentice-Hall, 1977.

Bandura, A., Grusec, J. E., & Menlove, S. L. The vicarious extinction of avoidance behavior. *Journal of Personality and Social Psychology*, 1967, *5*, 16–23.

Bandura, A., Ross, D., & Ross, S. A. Imitation of film mediated aggressive models. *Journal of Abnormal and Social Psychology*, 1963, *66*, 3–11.

Bandura, A., & Walters, R. *Social learning and personality development*. New York: Holt, Rinehart & Winston, 1963.

Barnard, C. W., Wolfe, H. D., & Graveline, D. E. Sensory deprivation under null gravity conditions. *American Journal of Psychiatry*, 1962, *118*, 921–925.

Bartlett, S. C. *Remembering*. Cambridge, England: Cambridge University Press, 1932.

Bennett, E. L., & Calvin, N. Failure to train planarians reliably. *Neuro-sciences Research Program Bulletin*, 1964, 2, July–August issue.

Berlyne, D. E. *Conflict arousal and curiosity*. New York: McGraw-Hill, 1960.

Berlyne, D. E. *Structure and direction in thinking*. New York: Wiley, 1965.

Berlyne, D. E. Curiosity and exploration. *Science*, 1966, *153*, 25–33.

Bernard, L. L. *Instinct: A study in social psychology*. New York: Holt, Rinehart & Winston, 1924.

Bexton, W. H., Heron, W., & Scott, T. H. Effects of decreased variation in the sensory environment. *Canadian Journal of Psychology*, 1954, *8*, 70–76.

Bijou, S. W., & Baer, D. M. *Child development I: A systematic and empirical theory*. New York: Appleton-Century-Crofts, 1961. (a)

Bijou, S. W., & Baer, D. M. *Child development II: Universal stage of infancy*. New York: Appleton-Century-Crofts, 1961. (b)

Bijou, S. W., & Sturges, P. S. Positive reinforcers for experimental studies with children— Consumables and manipulatables. *Child Development*, 1959, *30*, 151–170.

Birnbrauer, J. S., & Lawler, J. Token reinforcement for learning. *Mental Retardation*, 1964, 2, 275–279.

Birnbrauer, J. S., Wolf, M. N., Kidder, J. D., & Tague, C. E. Classroom behavior of retarded pupils with token reinforcement. *Journal of Experimental Child Psychology*, 1965, 2, 219–235.

Bitterman, M. E. Toward a comparative psychology of learning. *American Psychologist*, 1960, *15*, 704–712.

Bitterman, M. E. Learning in animals. In H. Helson & W. Bevan (Eds.), *Contemporary approaches to psychology*. Princeton, N. J.: Van Nostrand, 1967.

Bitterman, M. E. Thorndike and the problem of animal intelligence. *American Psychologist*, 1969, *24*, 444–453.

Bolles, R. C. Species-specific defense reactions and avoidance learning. *Psychological Review*, 1970, *77*, 32–48.

Bolles, R. C. Cognition and motivation: Some historical trends. In B. Weiner (Ed.), *Cognitive views of human motivation*. New York: Academic Press, 1974.

Bolles, R. C. *Theory of motivation* (2nd ed.). New York: Harper & Row, 1975.

Boring, E. G. *A history of experimental psychology* (2nd ed.). New York: Appleton-Century-Crofts, 1950.

Borke, H. Piaget's mountains revisited: Changes in the egocentric landscape. *Developmental Psychology*, 1975, *11*, 240–243.

Bourne, L. E., Jr., Dominowski, R. L., & Loftus, E. F. *Cognitive processes*. Englewood Cliffs, N.J.: Prentice-Hall, 1979.

Bower, G. (Ed.). *Human memory: Basic processes*. New York: Academic Press, 1977.

Bower, G. H. Mood and memory. *American Psychologist*, 1981, *36*, 129–148.

Bower, T. G. R. *Development in infancy*. San Francisco: Freeman, 1974.

Bowlby, J. *Maternal care and mental health*. Geneva: World Health Organization Monograph Series, 1951.

Bransford, J. D., & Franks, J. J. The abstraction of linguistic ideas. *Cognitive Psychology*, 1971, *2*, 331–350.

Brehm, J. W., & Cohen, A. R. *Explorations in cognitive dissonance*. New York: Wiley, 1962.

Breland, K., & Breland, M. A field of applied animal psychology. *American Psychologist*, 1951, *6*, 202–204.

Breland, K., & Breland, M. The misbehavior of organisms. *American Psychologist*, 1961, *16*, 681–684.

Brim, O. G., Jr., & Wheeler, S. *Socialization after childhood: Two essays*. New York: Wiley, 1966.

Broadbent, D. E. Speaking and listening simultaneously. *Journal of Experimental Psychology*, 1952, *43*, 267–273.

Broadbent, D. E. *Perception and communication*. London: Pergamon Press, 1958.

Brown, J. S. Generalization and discrimination. In D. I. Mostossky (Ed.), *Stimulus generalization*. Stanford, Calif.: Stanford University Press, 1965.

Bruner, J. S. *Contemporary approaches to cognition*. Cambridge, Mass.: Harvard University Press, 1957. (a)

Bruner, J. S. On perceptual readiness. *Psychological Review*, 1957, *64*, 123–152. (b)

Bruner, J. S. The act of discovery. *Harvard Educational Review*, 1961, *31*, 21–32. (a)

Bruner, J. S. *The process of education*. Cambridge, Mass.: Harvard University Press, 1961. (b)

Bruner, J. S. *On knowing: Essays for the left hand*. Cambridge, Mass.: Harvard University Press, 1963.

Bruner, J. S. The course of cognitive growth. *American Psychologist*, 1964, *19*, 1–15.

Bruner, J. S. *Toward a theory of instruction*. Cambridge, Mass.: Harvard University Press, 1966.

Bruner, J. S. *Processes of cognitive growth: Infancy*. Worcester, Mass.: Clark University Press, 1968.

Bruner, J. S., Goodnow, J. J., & Austin, G. A. *A study of thinking*. New York: Wiley, 1956.

Bruner, J. S., Olver, R. R., & Greenfield, P. M. *Studies in cognitive growth*. New York: Wiley, 1966.

Butler, R. A., & Harlow, H. S. Discrimination learning and learning sets to visual exploration incentives. *Journal of Genetic Psychology*, 1957, *57*, 257–264.

Buxton, C. E. Latent learning and the goal gradient hypothesis. *Contributions to Psychological Theory*, 1940, *2*, 6.

Campbell, D. T., & Stanley, J. C. *Experimental and quasi-experimental designs for research*. Chicago: Rand McNally, 1963.

Cannon, W. B. *Bodily changes in pain, hunger, fear and rage* (2nd ed.). New York: Appleton-Century-Crofts, 1929.

Cannon, W. B. *The wisdom of the body*. New York: Norton: 1939.

Cermak, L. *Improving your memory*. New York: McGraw-Hill, 1976.

Cermak, L. S., & Craik, F. I. (Eds.). *Levels of processing in human memory*. Hillsdale, N. J.: Erlbaum, 1979.

Chaplin, J. P., & Krawiec, T. S. *Systems and theories of psychology.* New York: Holt, Rinehart & Winston, 1960.

Cherry, E. C. Some experiments on the recognition of speech, with one and with two ears. *Journal of the Acoustical Society of America*, 1953, *25*, 975–979.

Cherry, E. C., & Taylor, W. K. Some further experiments on the recognition of speech with one and two ears. *Journal of the Acoustical Society of America*, 1954, *26*, 554–559.

Chomsky, N. *Language and mind* (Rev. ed.). New York: Harcourt Brace Jovanovich, 1972.

Collins, B. E., & Hoyt, M. F. Personal responsibility for consequences: An integration and extension of the "forced compliance" literature. *Journal of Experimental and Social Psychology*, 1972, *8*, 558–593.

Commons, W. D., & Fagin, B. *Principles of educational psychology.* New York: Ronald Press, 1954.

Conrad, R., & Hille, B. A. The decay theory of immediate memory and space recall. *Canadian Journal of Psychology*, 1958, *12*, 1–6.

Cook, T. D., & Campbell, D. T. *Quasi-experimentation.* Chicago: Rand McNally, 1979.

Corbett, A. T. Retrieval dynamics for rote and visual image mnemonics. *Journal of Verbal Learning and Verbal Behavior*, 1977, *16*, 233–246.

Côté, A. D. J. *Flexibility and conservation acceleration.* Unpublished doctoral dissertation, University of Alberta, Edmonton, 1968.

Craig, R. C. Directed versus independent discovery of established relations. *Journal of Educational Psychology*, 1956, *47*, 223–234.

Craik, F. M., & Lockhart, R. S. Levels of processing: A framework for memory research. *Journal of Verbal Learning and Verbal Behavior*, 1972, *11*, 671–684.

Crespi, L. Quantitative variation of incentive and performance in the white rat. *American Journal of Psychology*, 1942, *55*, 467–517.

Dasen, P. R. Cross-cultural Piagetian research: A summary. *Journal of Cross-Cultural Psychology*, 1972, *3*, 23–29.

Dasen, P. R. (Ed.). *Piagetian psychology: Cross-cultural contributions.* New York: Gardner Press, 1977.

DeCecco, J. P. *The psychology of learning and instruction: Educational psychology.* Englewood Cliffs, N. J.: Prentice-Hall, 1968.

Deci, E. L. *Intrinsic motivation.* New York: Plenum Press, 1975.

Deese, J., & Hulse, S. H. *The psychology of learning* (3rd ed.). New York: McGraw-Hill, 1967.

Delgado, J. M. R. *Physical control of the mind.* New York: Harper & Row, 1969.

Deutsch, J. A., & Deutsch, D. Attention: Some theoretical considerations. *Psychological Review*, 1963, *70*, 80–90.

Dulit, E. Adolescent thinking à la Piaget: The formal stage. *Journal of Youth and Adolescence*, 1972, *1*, 281–301.

Dworkin, B. R., & Miller, N. E. Visceral learning in the curarized rat. In G. E. Schwartz & J. Beatty (Eds.), *Biofeedback: Theory and research.* New York: Academic Press, 1977.

Ebbinghaus, H. *Memory* (H. A. Ruger & C. E. Busenius, trans.). New York: Teacher's College, 1913. Reissued as paperback, New York: Dover, 1964. (Originally published, 1885.)

Eckland, B. K. Darwin rides again. *American Journal of Sociology*, 1977, *82*, 693–697.

Elkind, D. *Children and adolescents: Interpretive essays on Jean Piaget* (3rd ed.). New York: Oxford University Press, 1981.

Eriksen, C. W., & Johnson, H. J. Storage and decay characteristics of nonattended auditory stimuli. *Journal of Experimental Psychology*, 1964, *68*, 28–36.

Estes, W. K. Is human memory obsolete? *American Scientist*, 1980, *68*, 62–69.

Fahlman, S. F. *NETL: A system for representing and using real-world knowledge*. Cambridge: Massachusetts Institute of Technology, 1979.

Falk, J. L. Control of schedule-induced polydipsia: Type, size, and spacing of meals. *Journal of the Experimental Analysis of Behavior*, 1967, *10*, 199–206.

Falk, J. L. Conditions producing psychogenic polydipsia in animals. *Annals of the New York Academy of Science*, 1969, *157*, 569–593.

Falk, J. L. The nature and determinants of adjunctive behavior. In *Schedule-induced and schedule-dependent phenomena* (Vol. 2). Toronto: Addiction Research Foundation, 1970.

Ferguson, L. W. *The use of nonveridical heartrate feedback as an adjunct to modeling technique in the extinction of avoidance response*. Unpublished doctoral dissertation, University of Alberta, Edmonton, 1968.

Ferster, C. B. Positive reinforcement and behavioral deficits in autistic children. *Child Development*, 1961, *32*, 437–456.

Ferster, C. B., & deMyer, M. K. Method for the experimental analysis of the behavior of autistic children. *American Journal of Orthopsychiatry*, 1962, *32*, 89–98.

Festinger, L. *A theory of cognitive dissonance*. Stanford, Calif.: Stanford University Press, 1957.

Festinger, L. Cognitive dissonance. *Scientific American*, October 1962.

Flavell, J. H. *The developmental psychology of Jean Piaget*. Princeton, N.J.: Van Nostrand, 1963.

Flavell, J. H. *Cognitive development*. Englewood Cliffs, N. J.: Prentice-Hall, 1977.

Fowler, H. *Curiosity and exploratory behavior*. New York: Macmillan, 1965.

French, J. D. The reticular formation. *Scientific American*, May 1957.

Freund, K. Some problems in the treatment of homosexuality. In H. J. Eysenck (Ed.), *Behavior therapy and the neuroses*. New York: Pergamon Press, 1960.

Furth, H. G. *Piaget and knowledge*. Englewood Cliffs, N. J.: Prentice-Hall, 1969.

Furth, H. G. *Piaget for teachers*. Englewood Cliffs, N. J.: Prentice-Hall, 1970.

Gagné, R. M. *The conditions of learning* (1st ed.). New York: Holt, Rinehart & Winston, 1965.

Gagné, R. M. *The conditions of learning* (2nd ed.). New York: Holt, Rinehart & Winston, 1970.

Gagné, R. M. *Essentials of learning for instruction*. Hinsdale, Ill.: Dryden Press, 1974.

Galton, F. *Hereditary genesis: An inquiry into its laws and consequences*. New York: Appleton, 1870.

Garcia, J., Ervin, F. E., & Koelling, R. A. Learning with prolonged delay of reinforcement. *Psychonomic Science*, 1965, *5*, 121–122.

Garcia, J., & Koelling, R. A. Relation of cue to consequence in avoidance learning. *Psychonomic Science*, 1966, *4*, 123–124.

Gelman, R. Cognitive development. *Annual Review of Psychology*, 1978, *29*, 297–332.

Ginsberg, H., & Opper, S. *Piaget's theory of intellectual development* (2nd ed.). Englewood Cliffs, N. J.: Prentice-Hall, 1978.

Glassman, E., Machlus, B., & Wilson, J. E. Phosphorylation of non-histone acid-extractable nuclear proteins (NANP) from the brain. In H. P. Zippel (Ed.), *Memory and the transfer of information*. New York: Plenum Press, 1973.

Glick, J. Cognitive development in cross-cultural perspective. In F. D. Horowitz, E. M. Hetherington, S. Scarr-Salapatek, & G. M. Siegel (Eds.), *Review of child development research* (Vol. 4). Chicago: University of Chicago Press, 1975.

Goldschmid, M. L., & Bentler, P. M. *Conservation concept diagnostic kit: Manual and keys*. San Diego: Educational and Industrial Testing Service, 1968.

Greenspoon, J. The reinforcing effect of two spoken sounds on the frequency of two responses. *American Journal of Psychology*, 1955, *68*, 409–416.

Gunderson, K. The imitation game. In A. R. Anderson (Ed.), *Mind and machines*. Englewood Cliffs, N. J.: Prentice-Hall, 1964.

Guthrie, E. R. *The psychology of learning*. New York: Harper & Row, 1935.

Guthrie, E. R. *The psychology of learning* (Rev. ed.). New York: Harper & Row, 1952.

Guthrie, J. T. Expository instruction versus a discovery method. *Journal of Educational Psychology*, 1967, *58*, 45–49.

Hamilton, W. D. Selfish and spiteful behaviour in an evolutionary model. *Nature*, 1970, *228*, 1218–1220.

Hamilton, W. D. Geometry for the selfish herd. *Journal of Theoretical Biology*, 1971, *31*, 295–311.

Hamilton, W. D. Altruism and related phenomena, mainly in social insects. *Annual Review of Ecology and Systematics*, 1972, *3*, 193–232.

Hardt, J. V., & Kamiya, J. Some comments on Plotkin's self-regulation of electroencephalographic alpha. *Journal of Experimental Psychology*, 1976, *105*, 100–108.

Harlow, H. F. Learning set and error factor theory. In S. Koch (Ed.), *Psychology: A study of a science* (Vol. 2). New York: McGraw-Hill, 1959.

Harris, B. Whatever happened to Little Albert? *American Psychologist*, 1979, *34*, 151–160.

Haslerud, G. N., & Meyers, S. The transfer value of given and individually derived principles. *Journal of Educational Psychology*, 1958, *49*, 293–298.

Hebb, D. O. *The organization of behavior*. New York: Wiley, 1949.

Hebb, D. O. *A textbook of psychology* (1st ed.). Philadelphia: Saunders, 1958.

Hebb, D. O. The American Revolution. *American Psychologist*, 1960, *15*, 735–745.

Hebb, D. O. *A textbook of psychology* (2nd ed.). Philadelphia: Saunders, 1966.

Hebb, D. O. *A textbook of psychology* (3rd ed.). Philadelphia: Saunders, 1972.

Hebron, M. E. *Motivated learning*. London: Methuen, 1966.

Heider, F. *The psychology of interpersonal relations*. New York: Wiley, 1958.

Hellyer, S. Supplementary report: Frequency of stimulus presentation and short-term decrement in recall. *Journal of Experimental Psychology*, 1962, *64*, 650.

Heron, W. The pathology of boredom. *Scientific American*, January 1957.

Heron, W., Doane, B. K., & Scott, T. H. Visual disturbances after prolonged perceptual isolation. *Canadian Journal of Psychology*, 1956, *10*, 13–18.

Herrnstein, R. J. Doing what comes naturally: A reply to Professor Skinner. *American Psychologist*, 1977, *32*, 1013–1016.

Hess, E. H. Imprinting in animals. *Scientific American*, 1958, *198*, 81–90.

Hewett, F. *The emotionally disturbed child in the classroom*. Boston: Allyn & Bacon, 1968.

Higbee, K. L. *Your memory: How it works and how to improve it*. Englewood Cliffs, N. J.: Prentice-Hall, 1977.

Hilgard, E. R. & Bower, G. H. *Theories of learning* (3rd ed.). New York: Appleton-Century-Crofts, 1966.

Hill, W. S. *Learning: A survey of psychological interpretations*. San Francisco: Chandler, 1963.

Hinde, R. A., & Stevenson-Hinde, R. (Eds.). *Constraints on learning: Limitations and predispositions*. New York: Academic Press, 1973.

Holland, J. G., & Skinner, B. F. *The analysis of behavior: A program for self-instruction*. New York: McGraw-Hill, 1961.

Hovland, C. I. Computing simulation of thinking. American Psychologist, 1960, *15*, 687–693.

Hovland, C. I., & Hunt, E. B. Computer simulation of concept attainment. *Behavioral Science*, 1960, *5*, 265–267.

Hull, C. L. *Principles of behavior*. New York: Appleton-Century-Crofts, 1943.

Hull, C. L. *Essentials of behavior*. New Haven, Conn.: Yale University Press, 1951.

Hull, C. L. *A behavior system*. New Haven, Conn.: Yale University Press, 1952.

Hulse, S. H., Jr. Amount and percentage of reinforcement and duration of goal confinement in conditioning and extinction. *Journal of Experimental Psychology*, 1958, *56*, 48–57.

Hunt, J. McV. *Intelligence and experience*. New York: Ronald Press, 1961.

Hunter, I. M. L. *Memory: Facts and fallacies*. Baltimore: Penguin, 1957.

Hurlock, E. B. *Child development*. New York: McGraw-Hill, 1964.

Hyden, H. Neuronal plasticity, protein conformation and behavior. In H. P. Zippel (Ed.), *Memory and the transfer of information*. New York: Plenum Press, 1973.

Hyden, H., & Lange, P. W. Protein changes in different brain areas as a function of intermittent training. *Proceedings of the National Academy of Sciences*, 1972, *69*, 1980–1984.

Irwin, O. C., & Weiss, L. A. The effect of clothing on the general and vocal activity of the new born infant. *University of Iowa Studies in Child Welfare*, 1934, *9*, 149–162.

Isaacs, N. *The growth of understanding in the young child*. London: The Education Supply, 1961.

Jacobson, A. L., Babich, F. R., Bubash, S., & Jacobson, A. Differential approach tendencies produced by injection of ribonucleic acid from trained rats. *Science*, 1965, *150*, 636–637.

James, W. *The principles of psychology*. New York: Holt, Rinehart & Winston, 1890.

Jensen, A. R. Social class, race and genetics: Implications for education. *American Educational Research Journal*, 1968, *5*, 1–42.

Johnson, M. K., Bransford, J. D., & Solomon, S. Memory for tacit implications of sentences. *Journal of Experimental Psychology*, 1973, *98*, 203–205.

Jones, M. C. Albert, Peter, and John B. Watson. *American Psychologist*, 1974, *29*, 581–583.

Kahneman, D. *Attention and effort*. Englewood Cliffs, N. J.: Prentice-Hall, 1973.

Keith-Lucas, T., & Guttman, N. Robust-single-trial delayed backward conditioning. *Journal of Comparative and Physiological Psychology*, 1975, *88*, 468–476.

Keller, F. S. *Learning: Reinforcement theory* (2nd ed.). New York: Random House, 1969.

Kelley, H. H. *Attribution in social interaction*. Morristown, N. J.: General Learning Press, 1971.

Kelley, H. H. The processes of causal attribution. *American Psychologist*, 1973, *28*, 107–128.

Kendler, H. H. A concept of the concept. In A. W. Melton (Ed.), *Categories of human learning*. New York: Academic Press, 1964.

Kessen, W. *The child*. New York: Wiley, 1965.

Kintsch, W. *Learning, memory and conceptual processes*. New York: Wiley, 1970.

Knowlis, D. T., & Kamiya, J. The control of electroencephalographic alpha rhythms through auditory feedback in the associated mental activity. *Psychophysiology*, 1970, *6*, 476–484.

Koffka, K. Perception: An introduction to Gestalt theory. *Psychological Bulletin*, 1922, *19*, 531–585.

Koffka, K. *The growth of the mind*. New York: Harcourt, Brace & World, 1925.

Koffka, K. *Principles of Gestalt psychology*. New York: Harcourt, Brace & World, 1935.

Kohler, W. *The mentality of the apes*. New York: Harcourt, Brace & World, 1927.

Kohler, W. *Gestalt psychology*. New York: Liveright Publishing, 1929.

Kohler, W. Gestalt psychology today. *American Psychologist*, 1959, *14*, 727–734.

Konorski, J. M. D. *Integrative activity of the brain*. Chicago: University of Chicago Press, 1967.

Krech, D., Rosenzweig, M., & Bennett, E. L. Effects of environmental complexity and training on brain chemistry. *Journal of Comparative and Physiological Psychology*, 1960, *53*, 509–519.

Krech, D., Rosenzweig, M., & Bennett, E. L. Relations between brain chemistry and problem-solving among rats raised in enriched and impoverished environments. *Journal of Comparative and Physiological Psychology*, 1962, *55*, 801–807.

Krech, D., Rosenzweig, M., & Bennett, E. L. Environmental impoverishment, social isolation, and changes in brain chemistry and anatomy. *Physiology and Behavior*, 1966, *1*, 99–104.

Laurendeau, M., & Pinard, A. *Causal thinking in the child: A genetic and experimental approach*. New York: International Universities Press, 1962.

Lazarus, R. S. Cognitive and coping processes in emotion. In B. Weiner (Ed.), *Cognitive views of human motivation*. New York: Academic Press, 1974.

Lefrancois, G. R. *The acquisition of concepts of conservation*. Unpublished doctoral dissertation, University of Alberta, Edmonton, 1966.

Lefrancois, G. R. Jean Piaget's developmental model: Equilibration-through-adaptation. *Alberta Journal of Educational Research*, 1967, *13*, 161–171.

Lefrancois, G. R. A treatment hierarchy for the acceleration of conservation of substance. *Canadian Journal of Psychology*, 1968, *22*, 277–284.

Lefrancois, G. R. *Of children: An introduction to child development* (3rd ed.). Belmont, Calif.: Wadsworth, 1980 (a)

Lefrancois, G. R. *Psychology*. Belmont, Calif.: Wadsworth, 1980. (b)

Lefrancois, G. R. *Adolescents* (2nd ed.). Belmont, Calif.: Wadsworth, 1981.

Lefrancois, G. R. *Psychology for teaching: A bear rarely faces the front* (4th ed.). Belmont, Calif.: Wadsworth, 1982.

Leight, K. H., & Ellis, H. C. Emotional mood states, strategies, and state dependency in memory. *Journal of Verbal Learning and Verbal Behavior*, 1981, *20*, 251–266.

Levenson, R. W. Feedback effects and respiratory involvement in voluntary control of heart rate. *Psychophysiology*, 1976, *13*, 108–114.

Lewin, K. *A dynamic theory of personality*. (B. K. Adams & K. E. Zener, trans.). New York: McGraw-Hill, 1935.

Lewin, K. *Principles of topological psychology* (F. Heider & G. N. Heider, trans.). New York: McGraw-Hill, 1936.

Lewin, K. Frontiers in group dynamics. *Human Relations*, 1947, *1*, 5–41.

Lewin, K. *Field theory in social science*. New York: Harper & Row, 1951.

Liben, L. *Perspective-taking skills in young children: Seeing the world through rose-colored glasses*. Paper presented at the meeting of the Society for Research in Child Development, Denver, 1975.

Lilly, J. C. *The center of the cyclone: An autobiography of inner space*. New York: Julian Press, 1972.

Lindsley, O. R. Characteristics of the behavior of chronic psychotics as revealed by free operant conditioning methods. *Diseases of the Nervous System*, 1960, *21*. (Monograph supplement.)

Lindsley, O. R. Free operant conditioning and psychotherapy. *Current Psychiatric Therapies* (Vol. 3). New York: Grune & Stratton, 1963.

Loess, H. Pro-active inhibition in short-term memory. *Journal of Verbal Learning and Verbal Behavior*, 1964, *3*, 362–368.

Loftus, E. F. *Eyewitness testimony*. Cambridge, Mass.: Harvard University Press, 1979.

Lorenz, K. *King Solomon's ring*. London: Methuen, 1952.

Lovaas, O. I. A program for the establishment of speech in psychotic children. In J. K. Wing (Ed.), *Early childhood autism*. Oxford: Pergamon Press, 1966.

Lovaas, O. I., Berberich, J. P., Perloff, B. S., & Schaeffer, B. Acquisition of imitative speech by schizophrenic children. *Science*, 1966, *151*, 705–707.

Luria, A. R. *The mind of a mnemonist*. New York: Avon Books, 1968.

Macfarlane, D. A. The role of kinesthesis in maze learning. *University of California Publications in Psychology*, 1930, *4*, 277–305.

Maier, H. W. *Three theories of child development*. New York: Harper & Row, 1965.

Marx, M. H., & Hillix, W. A. *Systems and theories in psychology*. New York: McGraw-Hill, 1963.

Maslow, A. H. *Motivation and personality*. New York: Harper & Row, 1954.

Maslow, A. H. *Motivation and personality* (2nd ed.). New York: Harper & Row, 1970.

Masson, M. E. J., & McDaniel, M. A. The role of organizational processes in long-term retention. *Journal of Experimental Psychology: Human Learning and Memory*, 1981, *7*, 100–110.

McConnell, J. V. Memory transfer through cannibalism in planarians. *Journal of Neuropsychiatry*, 1962, *3*. (Monograph supplement 1.)

McConnell, J. V. Worm-breeding with tongue in cheek and the confessions of a scientist hoist by his own petard. *UNESCO Courier*, April 1976, pp. 12–15, 32.

McDougall, W. *An introduction to social psychology*. London: Methuen, 1908.

Mcloskey, M., & Santee, J. Are semantic memory and episodic memory distinct systems? *Journal of Experimental Psychology: Human Learning and Memory*, 1981, *7*, 66–71.

McNeil, A. B. *Human socialization*. Belmont, Calif.: Brooks/Cole, 1969.

Melton, A. W. Implications of short-term memory for a general theory of memory. *Journal of Verbal Learning and Verbal Behavior*, 1963, *2*, 1–21.

Melton, A. W. *Categories of human learning*. New York: Academic Press, 1964.

Mervis, C. B., & Rosch, E. Categorization of natural objects. *Annual Review of Psychology*, 1981, *32*, 89–115.

Miller, G. A. The magical number seven, plus or minus two: Some limits on our capacity for processing information. *Psychological Review*, 1956, *63*, 81–97.

Miller, G. A., Galanter, E., & Pribram, K. H. *Plans and the structure of behavior*. New York: Holt, 1960.

Miller, N. E. Learnable drives and rewards. In S. S. Stevens (Ed.), *Handbook of experimental psychology*. New York: Wiley, 1951.

Miller, N. E. Learning of visceral and glandular responses. *Science*, 1969, *163*, 434–445.

Miller, N. E. Biofeedback and visceral learning. *Annual Review of Psychology*, 1978, *29*, 373–404.

Miller, N. E., & Dollard, J. C. *Social learning and imitation*. New Haven, Conn.: Yale University Press, 1941.

Miller, N. E., & Dworkin, B. R. Visceral learning: Recent difficulties with curarized rats and significant problems for human research. In P. A. Obrist, A. H. Black, J. Brener, & L. V. DiCara (Eds.), *Cardiovascular psychophysiology: Current issues in response mechanisms, biofeedback, and methodology*. Chicago: Aldine, 1974.

Moray, N. Attention in dichotic listening: Affective cues and the influence of instruction. *Quarterly Journal of Experimental Psychology*, 1959, *11*, 56–60.

Moray, N. *Cybernetics*. New York: Hawthorne, 1963.

Mouly, G. J. *Psychology for effective teaching* (2nd ed.). New York: Holt, Rinehart & Winston, 1968.

Murchison, C. (Ed.). *A history of psychology in autobiography* (Vol. 3). Worcester, Mass.: Clark University Press, 1936.

Murdock, B. B., Jr. The retention of individual items. *Journal of Experimental Psychology*, 1961, *62*, 618–625.

Murray, H. A. *Explorations in personality*. New York: Oxford University Press, 1938.

Neimark, E. D. Intellectual development during adolescence. In F. D. Horowitz (Ed.), *Review of child development research*. Chicago: University of Chicago Press, 1975.

Neisser, U. *Cognitive psychology*. New York: Appleton-Century-Crofts, 1967.

Neisser, U. *Cognition and reality: Principles and implications of cognitive psychology*. San Francisco: Freeman, 1976.

Nelson, T. O. Repetition and depth of processing. *Journal of Verbal Learning and Verbal Behavior*, 1977, *16*, 151–171.

Newell, A. Artificial intelligence and the concept of mind. In R. C. Schank & C. M. Colby (Eds.), *Computer models of thought and language*. San Francisco: Freeman, 1973.

Newell, A., Shaw, J. C., & Simon, H. A. Empirical explorations with a logic theory machine. *Proceedings of the Joint Western Computer Conference*, Institute of Radio Engineers, 1957, 218–230.

Newell, A., Shaw, J. C., & Simon, H. A. Elements of a theory of human problem-solving. *Psychological Review*, 1958, *65*, 151–166.

Newell, A., & Simon, H. A. The logic theory machine: A complex information processing system. *Transactions on Information Theory*, Institute of Radio Engineers, 1956, IT-2, 61–69.

Newell, A., & Simon, H. A. *Human problem solving*. Englewood Cliffs, N. J.: Prentice-Hall, 1972.

Norman, D. A. *Memory and attention: An introduction to human information processing*. New York: Wiley, 1969.

O'Leary, K. D., & Becker, W. C. Behavior modification of an adjustment class: A token reinforcement program. *Exceptional Children*, 1967, *33*, 637–642.

O'Leary, K. D., & Becker, W. C. The effects of a teacher's reprimands on children's behavior. *Journal of School Psychology*, 1968, 7, 8–11.

O'Leary, K. D., Kaufman, K. F., Kass, R. E., & Drabman, R. S. The effects of loud and soft reprimands on the behavior of disruptive students. In A. R. Brown & C. Avery (Eds.), *Modifying children's behavior: A book of readings*. Springfield, Ill.: Charles C Thomas, 1974.

Olson, D. R. *The role of verbal rules in the cognitive processes of children*. Unpublished doctoral dissertation, University of Alberta, Edmonton, 1963.

Opper, S. Concept development in Thai urban and rural children. In P. R. Dasen (Ed.), *Piagetian psychology: Cross-cultural contributions*. New York: Gardner Press, 1977.

Osgood, C. E. A behavioristic analysis of perception and language as cognitive phenomena. In *Contemporary Approaches to Cognition*, Cambridge, Mass.: Harvard University Press, 1957.

Osgood, C. E., Suci, G. P., & Tannenbaum, P. H. *The measurement of meaning*. Urbana: University of Illinois Press, 1957.

Paivio, H. *Imagery and verbal processes* (2nd ed.). New York: Holt, Rinehart & Winston, 1980.

Papalia, D. F. The status of several conservation abilities across the life-span. *Human development*, 1972, *15*, 229–243.

Parke, R. D. Rules, roles, and resistance to deviation: Recent advances in punishment, discipline, and self-control. In A. Pick (Ed.), *Minnesota Symposia on Child Psychology* (Vol. 8). Minneapolis: University of Minnesota Press, 1974.

Peel, E. A. *The pupil's thinking*. London: Oldbourne, 1960.

Peterson, L. R., & Peterson, N. J. Short-term retention of individual verbal items. *Journal of Experimental Psychology*, 1959, *58*, 193–198.

Phillips, John L. *The origins of intellect*. San Francisco: Freeman, 1969.

Piaget, J. *The language and thought of the child*. New York: Harcourt, Brace & World, 1926.

Piaget, J. *The child's conception of the world*. New York: Harcourt, Brace & World, 1929.

Piaget, J. *The child's conception of physical causality*. London: Kegan Paul, 1930.

Piaget, J. *The moral judgement of the child*. London: Kegan Paul, 1932.

Piaget, J. *Le développement de la notion de temps chez l'enfant*. Paris: Presses Univer. France, 1946.

Piaget, J. *The psychology of intelligence*. New York: Harcourt, Brace & World, 1950.

Piaget, J. *Play, dreams and imitation in childhood*. New York: Norton, 1951.

Piaget, J. *Logic and psychology*. New York: Basic Books, 1957. (a)

Piaget, J. Logique et équilibre dans les comportements du suject. In L. Apostel, B. Mandelbrot, & J. Piaget (Eds.), *Logique et équilibre, études d'épistémologie génétique*. 1957, 2, 27–117. (b)

Piaget, J. The stages of the intellectual development of the child. *Bulletin of the Menninger School of Psychiatry*, March 6, 1961.

Piaget, Jean. *Biologie et connaissance*. Paris: Gallinard, 1967.

Piaget, J. *On the development of memory and identity*. Worcester, Mass.: Clark University Press, 1968.

Piaget, J. Intellectual development from adolescence to adulthood. *Human Development*, 1972, *15*, 1–12.

Piaget, J. *The grasp of consciousness*. Cambridge, Mass.: Harvard University Press, 1976.

Piaget, J., & Inhelder, B. Le développement des quantités chez l'enfant. *Neuchatel: Délachauxet Niestlé*, 1941.

Piaget, J., & Inhelder, B. *The child's conception of space*. New York: Norton, 1956.

Piaget, J., & Inhelder, B. *The growth of logical thinking from childhood to adolescence*. New York: Basic Books, 1958.

Pollack, I. Message uncertainty and message reception. *Journal of Acoustical Society of America*, 1959, *31*, 1500–1508.

Postman, L. Reward and punishments in human learning. In L. Postman (Ed.), *Psychology in the making*. New York: Knox, 1962.

Premack, D. Reinforcement theory. In D. Levine (Ed.), *Nebraska Symposium on Motivation*. Lincoln: University of Nebraska Press, 1965.

Prytula, R. E., Oster, G. D., & Davis, S. F. The "rat rabbit" problem: What did John B. Watson really do? *Teaching of Psychology*, 1977, *4*, 44–46.

Raphael, B. *The thinking computer: Mind inside matter*. San Francisco: Freeman, 1976.

Raths, L. E., & Burrell, A. P. *Understanding the problem child*. West Orange, N. J.: Economics Press, 1963.

Razran, G. The observable unconscious and the inferable conscious in current Soviet psycho-physiology: Introspective conditioning, semantic conditioning, and the orienting reflex. *Psychological Review*, 1961, *68*, 109–119.

Reese, E. P. *The analysis of human operant behavior*. Dubuque, Iowa: Brown, 1966.

Risley, T., & Wolf, M. Establishing functional speech in echolalic children. *Behavior Research and Therapy*, 1967, *5*, 73–88.

Rogers, C. R. *Client-centered therapy: Its current practice, implications and theory*. Boston: Houghton Mifflin, 1951.

Rogers, C. R. *Freedom to learn*. Columbus, Ohio: Charles E. Merrill, 1969.

Rogers, C. R., & Skinner, B. F. Some issues concerning the control of human behavior: A symposium. *Science*, 1956, *124*, 1057–1066.

Rosenthal, R., & Fode, K. L. The effect of experimenter bias on the performance of the albino rat. *Behavioral Science*, 1963, *8*, 183–189.

Rosenthal, R., & Jacobson, L. *Pygmalion in the classroom: Teacher expectations and pupils' intellectual development.* New York: Holt, Rinehart & Winston, 1968.

Rosenthal, R., & Lawson, R. A longitudinal study of the effects of experimenter bias on the operant learning of laboratory rats. *Journal of Psychiatric Research,* 1964, 2, 61–72.

Rotter, J. B. *Social learning and clinical psychology.* Englewood Cliffs, N. J.: Prentice-Hall, 1954.

Rozin, P., & Kalat, J. W. Specific hungers and poison avoidance as adaptive specializations of learning. *Psychological Review,* 1971, 78, 459–486.

Sahakian, W. S. *Psychology of learning: Systems, models, and theories* (2nd ed.). Chicago: Markham, 1981.

Sakagami, S. F., & Akahira, Y. Studies on the Japanese honeybee, *Apis cerana fabricius*: 8. Two opposing adaptations in the post-stinging behavior of honeybees. *Evolution,* 1960, *14,* 29–40.

Schachter, S., & Singer, J. Cognitive, social and physiological determinants of emotional state. *Psychological Review,* 1962, *69,* 379–399.

Schultz, D. P. *Sensory restriction: Effects on behavior.* New York: Academic Press, 1965.

Schultz, D. P. *A history of modern psychology.* New York: Academic Press, 1969.

Sears, R. R., Maccoby, E. P., & Lewin, H. *Patterns of child rearing.* Evanston, Ill.: Row, Peterson, 1957.

Seligman, M. E. P. *Helplessness: On depression, development and death.* San Francisco: Freeman, 1975.

Seligman, M. E. P., & Hager, J. L. *Biological boundaries of learning.* New York: Appleton-Century-Crofts, 1972.

Shaver, K. G. *An introduction to attribution processes.* Cambridge, Mass.: Winthrop, 1975.

Shurley, J. T. Stress and adaptation as related to sensory/perceptual isolation research. *Military medicine,* 1966, *131,* 254–258.

Skinner, B. F. *The behavior of organisms: An experimental analysis.* New York: Appleton-Century-Crofts, 1938.

Skinner, B. F. *Walden Two.* New York: Macmillan, 1948.

Skinner, B. F. How to teach animals. *Scientific American,* December 1951, pp. 26–29.

Skinner, B. F. *Science and human behavior.* New York: Macmillan, 1953.

Skinner, B. F. *Verbal behavior.* New York: Appleton-Century-Crofts, 1957.

Skinner, B. F. *Cumulative record* (Rev. ed.). New York: Appleton-Century-Crofts, 1961.

Skinner, B. F. *Beyond freedom and dignity.* New York: Knopf, 1971.

Smedslund, J. The acquisition of conservation of substance and weight in children. I. Introduction. *Scandinavian Journal of Psychology,* 1961, 2, 11–20. (a)

Smedslund, J. The acquisition of conservation of substance and weight in children. II. External reinforcement of conservation of weight and of operations of addition and subtraction. *Scandinavian Journal of Psychology,* 1961, 2, 71–84. (b)

Smedslund, J. The acquisition of conservation of substance and weight in children. III. Extension of conservation of weight acquired normally and by means of empirical controls on a balance scale. *Scandinavian Journal of Psychology,* 1961, 2, 85–87. (c)

Smedslund, J. The acquisition of conservation of substance and weight in children. IV. An attempt at extension of visual components of the weight concept. *Scandinavian Journal of Psychology,* 1961, 2, 153–155. (d)

Smedslund, J. The acquisition of conservation of substance and weight in children. V. Practice in conflict situations without external reinforcement. *Scandinavian Journal of Psychology,* 1961, 2, 158–160. (e)

Spence, K. W. *Behavior theory and conditioning.* New Haven, Conn.: Yale University Press, 1956.

Spence, K. W. *Behavior theory and learning: Selected papers.* Englewood Cliffs, N. J.: Prentice-Hall, 1960.

Sperling, G. A model for visual memory tests. *Human Factors*, 1963, *5*, 19–31.

Sperry, R. W. The great cerebral commissure. *Scientific American*, January 1964.

Spitz, R. A., & Wolf, K. M. Anaclitic depression: An inquiry into the genesis of psychiatric conditions in early childhood. *P. A. Study of the Child II.* New York: International Universities Press, 1946.

Staats, A. W. *Human learning.* New York: Holt, Rinehart & Winston, 1964.

Staats, A. W., & Staats, C. K. Verbal habit families, concepts, and the operant conditioning of word classes. *Psychological Review*, 1961, *68*, 190–204.

Staddon, J. E. R., & Simmelhag, V. L. The "superstition" experiment: A reexamination of its implications for the principles of adaptive behavior. *Psychological Review*, 1971, *78*, 3–43.

Standing, L. Learning 10,000 pictures. *Quarterly Journal of Experimental Psychology*, 1973, *25*, 207–222.

Stern, R. M., & Ray, W. J. *Biofeedback: How to control your body, improve your health, and increase your effectiveness.* Homewood, Ill.: Dow Jones-Irwin, 1977.

Stoyva, J., Kamiya, J., Barber, T. X., Miller, N. E., & Shapiro, D. (Eds.). *Biofeedback and self-control, 1977–78.* New York: Aldine, 1979.

Taylor, J. H. Innate emotional responses in infants. *Ohio University Studies*, 1934, *12*, 69–81.

Thomas, R. M. *Comparing theories of child development.* Belmont, Calif.: Wadsworth, 1979.

Thorndike, E. L. *The psychology of learning.* New York: Teacher's College, 1913.

Thorndike, E. L. *The psychology of arithmetic.* New York: Macmillan, 1922.

Thorndike, E. L. The influence of first year Latin upon the ability to read English. *School and Society*, 1923, *17*, 165–168.

Thorndike, E. L. Reward and punishment in animal learning. *Comparative Psychology Monographs*, 1932, *8*, No. 39.

Thorndike, E. L. *The psychology of wants, interests, and attitudes.* New York: Appleton-Century-Crofts, 1935.

Thorpe, W. H. *Learning and instinct in animals* (2nd ed.). London: Methuen, 1963.

Tinbergen, N. *A study of instinct.* Oxford, England: Clarendon Press, 1951.

Titchener, E. B. Postulates of a structural psychology. *Philosophical Review*, 1898, *7*, 449–465.

Toch, H. H., & Schulte, R. Readiness to perceive violence as a result of police training. *British Journal of Psychology*, 1961, *52*, 389–394.

Tolman, E. C. *Collected papers in psychology.* Berkeley: University of California Press, 1951.

Tolman, E. C. *Purposive behavior in animals and men.* New York: Appleton-Century-Crofts, 1967.

Tolman, E. C., & Honzik, C. H. Insight in rats. *University of California Publications in Psychology*, 1930, *4*, 215–232.

Tolman, E. C., Ritchie, B. F., & Kalish, D. Studies in spatial learning: II. Place learning versus response learning. *Journal of Experimental Psychology*, 1946, *36*, 221–229.

Tomlinson-Keasey, C. Formal operations in females from eleven to fifty-four years of age. *Developmental Psychology*, 1972, *6*, 364.

Towler, J. O. *Training effects and concept development: A study of the conservation of continuous quantity in children.* Unpublished doctoral dissertation, University of Alberta, Edmonton, 1967.

Travis, L. D. *Conservation acceleration through successive approximations.* Unpublished master's thesis, University of Alberta, Edmonton, 1969.

Treisman, A. M. Verbal cues, language and meaning in selective attention. *American Journal of Psychology,* 1964, 77, 206–219.

Trivers, R. L. The evolution of reciprocal altruism. *Quarterly Review of Biology,* 1971, 46, 35–37.

Trivers, R. L. Parent-offspring conflict. *American Zoologist,* 1974, 14, 249–264.

Tulving, E. Episodic and semantic memory. In E. Tulving & W. Donaldson (Eds.), *Organization of memory.* New York: Academic Press, 1972.

Tulving, E. Cue-dependent forgetting. *American Scientist,* 1974, 62, 74–82.

Tulving, E., & Madigan, S. A. Memory and verbal learning. *Annual Review of Psychology,* 1970, 21, 437–484.

Turing, A. M. Computing machinery and intelligence. *Mind,* 1950, 59, #236.

Underwood, B. J., & Schultz, R. W. *Meaningfulness and verbal learning.* Philadelphia: Lippincott, 1960.

Uzgiris, I. C., & Hunt, J. *Assessment in infancy: Ordinal scales of psychological development.* Urbana: University of Illinois Press, 1975.

Voeks, V. W. Postremity, recency, and frequency as bases for prediction in the maze situation. *Journal of Experimental Psychology,* 1948, 38, 495–510.

Voeks, V. W. Formalization and clarification of a theory of learning. *Journal of Psychology,* 1950, 30, 341–363.

Voeks, V. W. Acquisition of S-R connections: A test of Hull's and Guthrie's theories. *Journal of Experimental Psychology,* 1954, 47, 137–147.

Wade, N. Sociobiology: Troubled birth for a new discipline. *Science,* 1976, 191, 1151–1155.

Wallace, J. G. *Concept growth and the education of the child.* New York: New York University Press, 1965.

Walters, G. C., & Grusec, J. E. *Punishment.* San Francisco: Freeman, 1977.

Walters, R. H., & Llewellyn, T. E. Enhancement of punitiveness by visual and audiovisual displays. *Canadian Journal of Psychology,* 1963, 17, 244–255.

Walters, R. H., Llewellyn, T. E., & Acker, W. Enhancement of punitive behavior by audiovisual displays. *Science,* 1962, 136, 872–873.

Watson, J. B. Psychology as the behaviorist views it. *Psychological Review,* 1913, 20, 157–158.

Watson, J. B. *Behaviorism* (2nd ed.). Chicago: University of Chicago Press, 1930.

Watson, J. B., & Rayner, R. Conditioned emotional reactions. *Journal of Experimental Psychology,* 1920, 3, 1–14.

Watson, R. I. *The great psychologists* (3rd ed.). Philadelphia: Lippincott, 1971.

Waugh, N. C., & Norman, D. A. Primary memory. *Psychological Review,* 1965, 72, 89–104.

Weiner, B. *Theories of motivation: From mechanisms to cognition.* Skokie, Ill.: Rand McNally, 1972.

Weiner, B. (Ed.). *Cognitive views of human motivation.* New York: Academic Press, 1974.

Weiner, B. The role of affect in rational (attributional) approaches to human motivation. *Educational Researcher,* 1980, 9, 4–11.

Weiner, B., Frize, I., Kukla, A., Reed, L., Rest, S., & Rosenbaum, R. M. *Perceiving the causes of success and failure.* New York: General Learning Press, 1971.

Weisenbaum, J. ELIZA—A computer program for the study of natural language communication between man and machine. *Communication Associates Computing Machinery,* 1966, 9, 36–45.

Wertheimer, M. *Productive thinking* (1st ed.). New York: Harper & Row, 1945.

Wertheimer, M. *Productive thinking* (Rev. ed.). New York: Harper & Row, 1959.

Whitehead, A. N., & Russell, B. *Principia mathematica* (2nd ed.) (Vol. 1). Cambridge, England: Cambridge University Press, 1925.

Why you do what you do: Sociobiology—a new theory of behavior. *Time*, August 1, 1977, pp. 36–41.

Wickelgren, W. A. Human learning and memory. *Annual Review of Psychology*, 1981, *32*, 21–52.

Wiener, N. *Cybernetics* (1st ed.). New York: Wiley, 1948.

Wilcoxon, H. C., Dragoin, W. B., & Kral, P. A. Illness-induced aversions in rat and quail: Relative salience of visual and gustatory cues. *Science*, 1971, *171*, 826–828.

Williams, D. R., & Williams, H. Auto-maintenance in the pigeon: Sustained pecking despite contingent non-reinforcement. *Journal of the Experimental Analysis of Behavior*, 1969, *12*, 511–520.

Wilson, E. O. *Sociobiology: The new synthesis*. Cambridge, Mass.: Belknap, 1975.

Wilson, E. O. Academic vigilantism and the political significance of sociobiology. *BioScience*, 1976, *183*, 187–190.

Wittrock, M. C. Verbal stimuli in concept formation: Learning by discovery. *Journal of Educational Psychology*, 1963, *54*, 183–190.

Wolpe, J. *Psychotherapy by reciprocal inhibition*. Stanford, Calif.: Stanford University Press, 1958.

Woodworth, R. S., & Sheehan, M. R. *Contemporary schools of psychology* (3rd ed.). New York: Ronald Press, 1964.

Wulf, S. Tendencies and figural variations. In W. D. Ellis (Ed.), *A source book of Gestalt psychology*. New York: Harcourt, Brace & World, 1938. (Originally published, 1922.)

Yarmey, A. D. *The psychology of eyewitness testimony*. New York: Free Press, 1979.

Zeaman, D. Response latency as a fauction of amount of reinforcement. *Journal of Experimental Psychology*, 1949, *39*, 466–483.

Zeaman, D., & House, B. J. The role of attention in retardate discrimination learning. In N. R. Ellis (Ed.), *Handbook of mental deficiency*. New York: McGraw-Hill, 1963.

Zelman, A., Kabot, L., Jacobson, R., & McConnell, J. V. Transfer of training through injection of "conditioned" RNA into untrained worms. *Worm Runners' Digest*, 1963, *5*, 14–21.

Zubek, J. P. *Sensory deprivation: Fifteen years of research*. New York: Appleton-Century-Crofts, 1969.

Zubek, J. P., & Wilgosh, L. Prolonged immobilization of the body: Changes in performance in the electroencephalogram. *Science*, 1963, *140*, 306–308.

Name Index

Subject Index